Presentation Book A

Level 3

**Siegfried Engelmann
Susan Hanner**

A Division of The McGraw·Hill Companies

Columbus, Ohio

Table of Contents

Lesson 1 2	Lesson 26 143
Lesson 2 8	Lesson 27 148
Lesson 3 14	Lesson 28 152
Lesson 4 22	Lesson 29 157
Lesson 5 28	Lesson 30 163
Lesson 6 35	Lesson 31 167
Lesson 7 41	Lesson 32 172
Lesson 8 46	Lesson 33 177
Lesson 9 52	Lesson 34 183
Lesson 10 58	Lesson 35 187
Lesson 11 61	Lesson 36 194
Lesson 12 66	Lesson 37 198
Lesson 13 71	Lesson 38 203
Lesson 14 76	Lesson 39 208
Lesson 15 81	Lesson 40 213
Lesson 16 88	Lesson 41 216
Lesson 17 93	Lesson 42 222
Lesson 18 99	Lesson 43 227
Lesson 19 104	Lesson 44 232
Lesson 20 110	Lesson 45 237
Lesson 21 113	Lesson 46 244
Lesson 22 119	Lesson 47 249
Lesson 23 125	Lesson 48 254
Lesson 24 131	Lesson 49 260
Lesson 25 136	Lesson 50 264

www.sra4kids.com

SRA/McGraw-Hill

A Division of The McGraw-Hill Companies

Copyright © 2002 by SRA/McGraw-Hill.

All rights reserved. Except as permitted under the United States Copyright Act, no part of this publication may be reproduced or distributed in any form or by any means, or stored in a database or retrieval system, without the prior written permission of the publisher, unless otherwise indicated.

Send all inquiries to:
SRA/McGraw-Hill
8787 Orion Place
Columbus, OH 43240-4027

Printed in the United States of America.

ISBN 0-07-569117-5

3 4 5 6 7 8 9 BCM 08 07 06 05 04

Lessons 1–5 • Planning Page
Looking Ahead

	Lesson 1	Lesson 2	Lesson 3	Lesson 4	Lesson 5
Lesson Events	Reading Words Comprehension Passage Written Items Story Reading Written Items Independent Work Workcheck Writing-Spelling Activity	Reading Words Comprehension Passage Written Items Story Reading Written Items Independent Work Workcheck Writing-Spelling Activity	Reading Words Comprehension Passage Written Items Story Reading Written Items Independent Work Workcheck Writing-Spelling	**Vocabulary Sentence** Reading Words Vocabulary Review Comprehension Passage Written Items Story Reading Written Items Independent Work Workcheck Writing-Spelling	Vocabulary Review Reading Words Comprehension Passage Written Items Story Reading Written Items Independent Work Workcheck Writing-Spelling Activity
Vocabulary Sentence				#1: You <u>measure</u> your <u>weight</u> in <u>pounds</u>.	#1: You <u>measure</u> your <u>weight</u> in <u>pounds</u>.
Reading Words: Word Types	modeled words –s words mixed words	modeled words mixed words	modeled words multi-syllable words –ed words mixed words	modeled words –ing words multi-part words mixed words	modeled words 2-syllable words words with endings mixed words
New Vocabulary	rule striped	whole moop make-believe facts wise strange	great danger destroy grove during	seasons million bark	hooves
Comprehension Passages	*Living Things*	*Make-Believe Animals*	*Trees*	*Apple Trees*	*Forest Fires*
Story	*The Tiger and the Frog*	*Bob and Don Find Moops*	*Don Washes the White Spot*	*The Little Apple Tree*	*Campers Come into the Forest*
Skill Items	Deductions	Deductions	Deductions	Deductions	Deductions
Special Materials	Drawing materials for activity	Drawing materials for activity			Drawing materials for activity
Special Projects/ Activities	Activity after lesson 1	Activity after lesson 2			Activity after lesson 5

Lesson 1

Materials: For lessons 1–145, each student will need a pencil, a colored pen or pencil for marking, a textbook, worksheets and lined paper.

EXERCISE 1

READING WORDS

Column 1

a. You're starting a new reading program today. For most lessons, you'll need a textbook, a worksheet, a pencil, and lined paper.
 • **Find lesson 1 in your textbook.** ✓
 • **Touch column 1.** ✓
 • (Teacher reference:)

1. rule	4. tiger
2. page	5. striped
3. people	6. straight

b. **Word 1 is rule. What word?** (Signal.) *Rule.*
 • **Spell rule. Get ready.** (Tap for each letter.) *R-U-L-E.*
 • **A rule tells you what to do. Here's a rule about streets: Don't stand in the middle of streets. Tell me a rule about brushing your teeth.**
  (Call on different children. Ideas: *Brush your teeth after you eat; brush your teeth before you go to bed*; etc.)
c. **Word 2 is page. What word?** (Signal.) *Page.*
 • **Spell page. Get ready.** (Tap for each letter.) *P-A-G-E.*
d. **Word 3 is people. What word?** (Signal.) *People.*
 • **Spell people. Get ready.** (Tap for each letter.) *P-E-O-P-L-E.*
e. **Word 4 is tiger. What word?** (Signal.) *Tiger.*
 • **Spell tiger. Get ready.** (Tap for each letter.) *T-I-G-E-R.*
f. **Word 5 is striped. What word?** (Signal.) *Striped.*
 • **If something is striped, it has stripes. The American flag is striped.**
g. **Word 6 is straight. What word?** (Signal.) *Straight.*

h. **Let's read those words again, the fast way.**
 • **Word 1. What word?** (Signal.) *Rule.*
 • **Word 2. What word?** (Signal.) *Page.*
 • **Word 3. What word?** (Signal.) *People.*
 • **Word 4. What word?** (Signal.) *Tiger.*
 • **Word 5. What word?** (Signal.) *Striped.*
 • **Word 6. What word?** (Signal.) *Straight.*
i. (Repeat step h until firm.)

Column 2

j. **Find column 2.** ✓
 • (Teacher reference:)

1. babies	3. kittens
2. flies	4. spiders

 • **All these words end with the letter S.**
k. **Word 1. What word?** (Signal.) *Babies.*
 • **Word 2. What word?** (Signal.) *Flies.*
 • **Word 3. What word?** (Signal.) *Kittens.*
 • **Word 4. What word?** (Signal.) *Spiders.*
l. (Repeat step k until firm.)

Column 3

m. **Find column 3.** ✓
 • (Teacher reference:)

1. water	3. through
2. living	4. sugar

n. **Word 1. What word?** (Signal.) *Water.*
 • **Word 2. What word?** (Signal.) *Living.*
 • **Word 3. What word?** (Signal.) *Through.*
 • **Word 4. What word?** (Signal.) *Sugar.*
o. (Repeat step n until firm.)

Individual Turns

(For columns 1–3: Call on individual students, each to read one to three words per turn.)

EXERCISE 2

COMPREHENSION PASSAGE

a. **Find part B in your textbook.** ✓
 • **You're going to read a story about a boy named Tom. First you'll read the information passage. It gives some facts about living things. I'll call on different students to read. Everybody else follow along, and point to the words that are being read. If you don't have your place when I call on you to read, you lose your turn.**

b. Everybody, touch the title. ✓
- (Call on a student to read the title.) *[Living Things.]*
- Everybody, what's the title? (Signal.) *Living Things.*
- So this selection tells about living things.

c. (Call on individual students to read the passage, each student reading two or three sentences at a time. Ask the specified questions as the students read.)

Living Things

(Student reads:)

> Here is a rule about all living things: **All living things grow, and all living things need water.**

(You read:)

- Everybody, keep your finger on the word **water** while I ask questions.
- Listen to the rule again: All living things grow, and all living things need water.
- Everybody, say the rule about all living things. Get ready. (Signal.) *All living things grow, and all living things need water.*
- (Repeat until firm.)
- The rule tells two facts about all living things. What's the first fact? (Signal.) *All living things grow.*
- What's the second fact? (Signal.) *All living things need water.*

> Are trees living things? Yes. So you know that trees grow and trees need water.
> Dogs are living things. So do dogs grow?

- Everybody, keep your finger on the word **grow** while I ask a question.
- Do dogs grow? (Signal.) *Yes.*

> **Do dogs need water?**

- Everybody, what's the answer? (Signal.) *Yes.*

> People are living things. Do people grow?

- Everybody, what's the answer? (Signal.) *Yes.*

> **Do people need water?**

- Everybody, what's the answer? (Signal.) *Yes.*

> Here is another rule about all living things: **All living things make babies.**

- Listen to that rule again: All living things make babies.
- Everybody, say that rule about all living things. Get ready. (Signal.) *All living things make babies.*
- (Repeat until firm.)

> Trees are living things. So trees make baby trees.
> Are fish living things?

- Everybody, what's the answer? (Signal.) *Yes.*

> **So what do fish make?**

- What's the answer? (Call on a student. Accept *babies* or *baby fish*.)

> Are spiders living things?

- Everybody, what's the answer? (Signal.) *Yes.*

> **So what do spiders make?**

- Everybody, what's the answer? (Call on a student. Accept *babies* or *baby spiders*.)
- Yes, trees, fish and spiders all make babies.

> Remember the rule: All living things make babies.

- You learned two rules about all living things. All living things grow, and all living things need water. That's one rule. Everybody, what's the other rule about all living things? (Signal.) *All living things make babies.*
- Remember the rules about all living things.

EXERCISE 3
WRITTEN ITEMS

Note: Students will need lined paper, regular pencils, and marking pens or pencils of a different color.

a. You're going to write answers to items about what you just read. You'll write your answers on lined paper.
b. **Take out a piece of lined paper.** ✓
- Write your name at the top of the paper. ✓
- Number your paper from 1 through 13. Skip every other line. That means, leave a line between each line you number. Pencils down when you're finished.
(Observe students and give feedback.)
c. Find part C in your textbook. ✓
- The questions in part C are about living things. I'll read each question and call on someone to answer it. Follow along. Don't write anything until I tell you to write.
d. (For each item: Read the item. Call on a student to answer it.)
- Item 1: What do all living things need? *[Water.]*
- Item 2: What do all living things make? *[Babies.]*
- Item 3: Do all living things grow? *[Yes.]*
- Item 4: Are flies living things? *[Yes.]*
- Item 5: Write the letters of **3** things you know about flies. Tell me the 3 things you know. *[Flies need water. Flies grow. Flies make babies.]*
- Item 6: Are dogs living things? *[Yes.]*
- Item 7: So you know that dogs need <u>blank</u>. What's the answer? *[Water.]*
- Item 8: And you know that dogs make <u>blank</u>. What's the answer? *[Babies.]*
- Item 9: Are chairs living things? *No.*
- Item 10: Do chairs need water? *No.*
e. Now you're going to write the answers for part C without looking at the passage. Read item 1 to yourself, and write the answer next to the number **1** on your paper. Raise your hand when you've done that much.
(Observe students and give feedback.)
f. Now read item 2 to yourself and write the answer next to the number **2** on your paper. Raise your hand when you've done that much.
(Observe students and give feedback.)
g. Now read the rest of the items to yourself and answer them. Raise your hand when you've finished part C.
(Observe students and give feedback.)
h. We're going to check your answers for part C. Here are the rules: Use your marking pencil to make an **X** next to any item that is wrong. If the answer is right, don't make any mark. If it's wrong, make an **X** next to it. Don't change any answers, and don't mark over any answers.
i. (For each item: Read the item. Call on a student to answer it. If an answer is wrong, say the correct answer.)
- Item 1: What do all living things need? *[Water.]*
- Everybody, write **X** next to item 1 if you got it wrong. ✓
- Item 2: What do all living things make? *[Babies.]*
- Item 3: Do all living things grow? *[Yes.]*
- Item 4: Are flies living things? *[Yes.]*
- Item 5: Write the letters of **3** things you know about flies. What letters did you write? *[A, C, E.]*
- Item 6: Are dogs living things? *[Yes.]*
- Item 7: So you know that dogs need <u>blank</u>. What's the answer? *[Water.]*
- Item 8: And you know that dogs make <u>blank</u>. What's the answer? *[Babies.]*
- Item 9: Are chairs living things? *[No.]*
- Item 10: Do chairs need water? *[No.]*
j. Now use your marking pencil to fix up any items you got wrong. Do not erase anything you wrote. Write the correct answer close to the answer that is wrong.
(Observe students and give feedback.)
k. You'll do items 11 through 13 later.

EXERCISE 4
STORY READING

a. Find part D in your textbook. ✓
- We're going to read this story two times. First you'll read it out loud and make no more than 4 errors. Then I'll read it and ask questions. Remember to follow along when someone else is reading.
b. Everybody, touch the title. ✓
- (Call on a student to read the title.) *[The Tiger and the Frog.]*
- Everybody, what's the title? (Signal.) *The Tiger and the Frog.*

- So what is this story about? (Call on a student. Idea: *A tiger and a frog.*)

First Reading

c. (Call on individual students to read the story, each student reading two or three sentences at a time. Do not ask questions during this reading.)

- (Correct errors: Tell the word. Direct the student to reread the sentence.)
- (If the group makes more than 4 errors, direct the students to reread the story.)

D   The Tiger and the Frog

Tom's brother had two pets. One pet was a frog. The other pet was a big mean tiger. Tom's brother kept his pets in boxes. One day Tom said, "I want to play with your pet frog."

Tom's brother said, "Here is the rule about where I keep that frog. **I keep the frog in the box that is striped.**" Then Tom's brother said, "Don't get mixed up, because I keep my pet tiger in one of the other boxes."

Tom said the rule to himself. Then he went into the room with the boxes.

Here is what Tom saw.

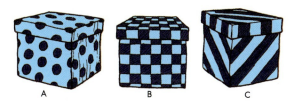

A   B   C

Tom looked at box A. He tried to think of the rule his brother had told him.
　Is box A striped?
　So is the frog inside box A?
Tom looked at box B.
　Is box B striped?
　So is the frog inside box B?
Tom looked at box C. After looking at all the boxes, Tom opened box B.
　Did a frog hop out of box B?
Turn to the next page and you will see what happened.

Second Reading

d. (After the group has read the selection making no more than 4 errors:)
Now I'll read the story and ask questions. Follow along:

> **The Tiger and the Frog**
>
> **Tom's brother had two pets. One pet was a frog. The other pet was a big mean tiger.**

- Everybody, keep your finger on the word **tiger** while I ask questions. Name the two pets that Tom's brother had. (Call on a student. Idea: *A tiger and a frog.*)
- Everybody, which pet would be safe to play with? (Signal.) *A frog.*
- Why wouldn't it be safe to try to play with that tiger? (Call on a student. Idea: *Because it was mean.*)

> **Tom's brother kept his pets in boxes. One day Tom said, "I want to play with your pet frog."**
>
> **Tom's brother said, "Here is the rule about where I keep that frog. I keep the frog in the box that is striped."**

- Everybody, keep your finger on the word **striped** while I ask questions. Read the rule with me. Get ready. *I keep the frog in the box that is striped.*
- Say the rule without looking. Get ready. (Signal.) *I keep the frog in the box that is striped.*
- (Repeat until firm.)

> **Then Tom's brother said, "Don't get mixed up, because I keep my pet tiger in one of the other boxes."**
>
> **Tom said the rule to himself. Then he went into the room with the boxes.**
>
> **Here is what Tom saw.**
>
>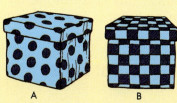
>
> A   B   C

- Everybody, how many boxes are in the room? (Signal.) *Three.*
- Is the frog in box A, box B, or box C? (Signal.) *Box C.*
- How do you know the frog is in box C? (Call on a student. Idea: *Because it's striped.*)

> **Tom looked at box A. He tried to think of the rule his brother had told him.**

- Everybody, get ready to say the last part of that rule. I keep the frog (signal) *in the box that is striped.*
- (Repeat until firm.)

Lesson 1   5

> **Is box A striped?**

- Everybody, what's the answer? (Signal.) *No.*

> **So is the frog inside box A?**

- Everybody, what's the answer? (Signal.) *No.*

> **Tom looked at box B.
> Is box B striped?**

- Everybody, what's the answer? (Signal.) *No.*

> **So is the frog inside box B?**

- Everybody, what's the answer? (Signal.) *No.*

> **Tom looked at box C.**

- Everybody, is that box striped? (Signal.) *Yes.*
- So is the frog inside box C? (Signal.) *Yes.*

> **After looking at all the boxes, Tom opened box B.**

- Everybody, did Tom open the right box? (Signal.) *No.*
- How do you know box B is not the right box? (Call on a student. Idea: *Because box B isn't striped.*)

> **Did a frog hop out of box B?**

- Everybody, what's the answer? (Signal.) *No.*

> **Turn to the next page and you will see what happened.**

- Everybody, do it. ✓
- What happened when Tom opened box B? (Call on a student. Idea: *The tiger jumped out of the box.*)
- What is that peeking out of box C? (Call on a student.) [*The frog.*]

EXERCISE 5
WRITTEN ITEMS
Story Items

a. Find part E in your textbook. ✓
- These questions are about today's story. Today's story told about a tiger and a frog. I'll read each item and call on someone to answer it. Follow along. Don't write anything until I tell you to write.

b. (For each item: Read the item. Call on a student to answer it.)
- Item 11: What's the title of today's story? The choices are **The Tiger and the Dog, The Tiger and the Frog,** and **The Dog and the Frog.** You'll write one of those choices. Which choice? [*The Tiger and the Frog.*]
- Item 12: Name **2** pets that Tom's brother had. [*Tiger, frog.*]
- Item 13: Did Tom open the right box? [*No.*]

Skill Items

> *Note:* Make sure each student has worksheet lesson 1, side 1 and side 2. Students are to write their name on their worksheet.

c. The rest of the items for today's lesson are on your lesson 1 worksheet. **Find item 1 on your worksheet.** ✓
- (Teacher reference:)

1. **Finish the rule** that Tom's brother told Tom. "I keep the frog in the box that is _____."
2. Is this box striped? _____
3. So is the frog in this box? _____
4. Is this box striped? _____
5. So is the frog in this box? _____
6. Use the rule and **underline** the box that has a frog in it.

- Item 1: Finish the rule that Tom's brother told Tom. "I keep the frog in the box that is <u>blank</u>." What's the answer? [*Striped.*]

6 Lesson 1

- Item 2: Is this box striped? *[Yes.]*
- Item 3: So is the frog in this box? *[Yes.]*
- Item 4: Is this box striped? *[No.]*
- Item 5: So is the frog in this box? *[No.]*
- Item 6: Use the rule and underline the box that has a frog in it. Tell me the letter of the box with the frog. *[C.]*

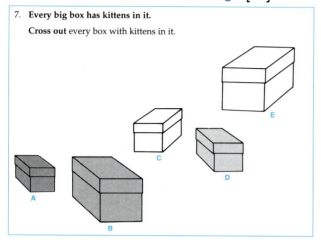

7. Every big box has kittens in it.
   Cross out every box with kittens in it.

- (Teacher reference:)
- Item 7: Every big box has kittens in it. Everybody, say the rule. Get ready. (Signal.) *Every big box has kittens in it.*
- You're going to cross out every box with kittens in it.

End-of-Lesson Activities

INDEPENDENT WORK

Now you're going to complete the written work without looking at the story. Start with your worksheet. Then finish the items in your textbook, beginning with item 11. Read the items to yourself and answer them. Raise your hand when you've finished. (Observe students and give feedback.)

WORKCHECK

Note: Students will need marking pens or pencils of a different color. You will need the Answer Key book.

a. We're going to check the rest of the answers on your lined paper and the answers on your worksheet. Here are the rules: Use your marking pencil to make an **X** next to any item that is wrong. If the answer is right, don't make any mark. If it's wrong, make an **X** next to it. Don't change any answers and don't mark over any answers.

b. Let's start with your worksheet. (For each item: Read the item. Call on a student to answer it. If the answer is wrong, say the correct answer.)
- Item 1: Finish the rule that Tom's brother told Tom. "I keep the frog in the box that is blank." What's the answer? *[Striped.]*
- Everybody, write **X** next to item 1 if you got it wrong. You should have written the word **striped** in the blank.
- Item 2: Is this box striped? *[Yes.]*
- Item 3: So is the frog in this box? *[Yes.]*
- Item 4: Is this box striped? *[No.]*
- Item 5: So is the frog in this box? *[No.]*
- Item 6: Use the rule and underline the box that has a frog in it. Tell me the letter of the box with the frog. *[C.]*
- Everybody, you should have underlined box C.
- Item 7: Every big box has kittens in it. Cross out every box with kittens in it. Which boxes have kittens? *[B, E.]*
- Everybody, you should have crossed out boxes B and E.

c. Now let's check the rest of the items on your lined paper.
- Item 11: What's the title of today's story? *[The Tiger and the Frog.]*
- Item 12: Name 2 pets that Tom's brother had. *[Tiger, frog.]*
- Item 13: Did Tom open the right box? *[No.]*

d. Now use your marking pencil to fix up any items you got wrong. Do not erase anything you wrote. Write the correct answer close to the answer that is wrong. Before you hand in your independent work, all the items you missed must be fixed up. (Observe students and give feedback.)

e. (At the end of the workcheck have students record the total number of errors they made at the top of their lined paper.)

WRITING-SPELLING

(Present Writing-Spelling lesson 1 after completing Reading lesson 1. See Writing-Spelling Guide.)

ACTIVITY

(Present Activity 1 after completing Reading lesson 1. See Activities Across the Curriculum.)

Lesson 2

EXERCISE 1

READING WORDS

Column 1

a. **Find lesson 2 in your textbook.** ✓
- Touch column 1. ✓
- (Teacher reference:)

1. whole	4. covered
2. moop	5. make-believe
3. carry	6. facts

b. Word 1 is **whole.** What word? (Signal.) *Whole.*
- Spell **whole.** Get ready. (Tap for each letter.) *W-H-O-L-E.*
- The word **whole** that is spelled like this means all of it—the whole thing. Here's another way of saying **all of a banana: a whole banana.**
- Everybody, what's another way of saying **all of a vacation?** (Signal.) *A whole vacation.*

c. Word 2 is **moop.** (Rhymes with **hoop.**) What word? (Signal.) *Moop.*
- Spell **moop.** Get ready. (Tap for each letter.) *M-O-O-P.*
- A **moop** is a make-believe animal you're going to read about.

d. Word 3 is **carry.** What word? (Signal.) *Carry.*
- Spell **carry.** Get ready. (Tap for each letter.) *C-A-R-R-Y.*

e. Word 4 is **covered.** What word? (Signal.) *Covered.*
- Spell **covered.** Get ready. (Tap for each letter.) *C-O-V-E-R-E-D.*

f. Word 5 is **make-believe.** What word? (Signal.) *Make-believe.*
- **Make-believe** is another word for **pretend.** Here's another way of saying **It was a pretend story: It was a make-believe story.**
- Everybody, what's another way of saying **They told about a pretend animal?** (Signal.) *They told about a make-believe animal.*

g. Word 6 is **facts.** What word? (Signal.) *Facts.*
- Sentences that give you information are facts. Here's a fact about trees: Trees have roots. Tell me another fact about trees. (Call on a student. Ideas: *Trees are living things; trees have leaves; trees need water*, etc.)

h. Let's read those words again, the fast way.
- Word 1. What word? (Signal.) *Whole.*
- Word 2. What word? (Signal.) *Moop.*
- Word 3. What word? (Signal.) *Carry.*
- Word 4. What word? (Signal.) *Covered.*
- Word 5. What word? (Signal.) *Make-believe.*
- Word 6. What word? (Signal.) *Facts.*

i. (Repeat step h until firm.)

Column 2

j. Find column 2. ✓
- (Teacher reference:)

1. through	4. field
2. straight	5. page
3. forest	

k. Word 1. What word? (Signal.) *Through.*
- Word 2. What word? (Signal.) *Straight.*
- Word 3. What word? (Signal.) *Forest.*
- Word 4. What word? (Signal.) *Field.*
- Word 5. What word? (Signal.) *Page.*

l. (Repeat step k until firm.)

Column 3

m. Find column 3. ✓
- (Teacher reference:)

1. striped	3. wise
2. pointed	4. strange

n. Word 1. What word? (Signal.) *Striped.*
- Word 2. What word? (Signal.) *Pointed.*

o. Word 3. What word? (Signal.) *Wise.*
- Someone who is **wise** is very smart. Another way of saying **a very smart woman** is **a wise woman.**

p. Word 4. What word? (Signal.) *Strange.*
- If something looks strange, it does not look like you think it should look. A strange cow does not look like other cows. A strange tree does not look like other trees.

- Your turn. What do you know about a **strange cow?** (Signal.) *It doesn't look like other cows.*
- What do you know about a **strange house?** (Signal.) *It doesn't look like other houses.*

q. Let's read those words again.
- Word 1. What word? (Signal.) *Striped.*
- Word 2. What word? (Signal.) *Pointed.*
- Word 3. What word? (Signal.) *Wise.*
- Word 4. What word? (Signal.) *Strange.*

r. (Repeat step q until firm.)

Individual Turns

(For columns 1–3: Call on individual students, each to read one to three words per turn.)

EXERCISE 2
COMPREHENSION PASSAGE

a. Find part B in your textbook. ✓
- You're going to read a story about finding moops. First you'll read the information passage. It gives some facts about make-believe animals.
- I'll call on different students to read. Everybody else follow along, and point to the words that are being read. If you don't have your place when I call on you to read, you lose your turn.

b. Everybody, touch the title. ✓
- (Call on a student to read the title.) *[Make-Believe Animals.]*
- Everybody, what's the title? (Signal.) *Make-Believe Animals.*

c. (Call on individual students to read the passage, each student reading two or three sentences at a time. Ask the specified questions as the students read.)

Make-Believe Animals

Here's a real animal.

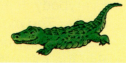

- Everybody, keep your finger on the word **animal** while I ask a question.
- Raise your hand if you know what kind of animal that is. What kind of animal is that? (Call on a student. Ideas: *An alligator; a crocodile.*)

Here's a make-believe animal.
What parts of the animal are make-believe?

- Everybody, keep your finger on the word **make-believe** while I ask a question.
- Everybody, what parts of the animal are make-believe? (Signal.) *The wheels.*

The story you'll read today tells about animals called moops. Moops are make-believe animals. That means there are not really any moops.

- Everybody, are there really any moops? (Signal.) *No.*

EXERCISE 3
WRITTEN ITEMS

Note: Students will need lined paper, regular pencils, and marking pens or pencils of a different color.

a. You're going to write the answers to an item about what you just read. You'll write your answers on lined paper.
- **Take out a piece of lined paper.** ✓
- Write your name at the top of the paper. ✓
- Number your paper from 1 through 9. Skip every other line. Pencils down when you're finished.
(Observe students and give feedback.)

b. Find part C in your textbook. ✓
- The item in part C is about make-believe animals. I'll read the item and call on someone to answer it. Follow along. Don't write anything until I tell you to write.
- (Teacher reference:)

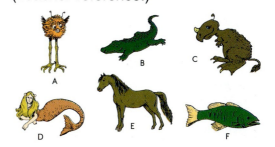

c. Item 1: Write the letter of each make-believe animal. Which animals are make-believe? (Call on a student.) *[A, C, D.]*

d. Now you're going to write the answer for part C without looking at the passage. Read the item to yourself and write the answer next to the number **1** on your paper. Raise your hand when you've finished item 1.
(Observe students and give feedback.)
e. We're going to check your answer for part C. Here are the rules: Use your marking pencil to make an **X** next to the item if it's wrong. If the answer is right, don't make any mark. If it's wrong, make an **X** next to it. Don't change your answer, and don't mark over your answer.
f. Item 1: Write the letter of each make-believe animal. Which letters did you write? (Call on a student.) *[A, C, D.]*
- Everybody, write **X** next to item 1 if you got it wrong. ✓
g. Now use your marking pencil to fix up the item if you got it wrong. Do not erase anything you wrote. Write the correct answer close to the answer that is wrong.
(Observe students and give feedback.)

EXERCISE 4

STORY READING

a. Find part D in your textbook. ✓
- We're going to read this story two times. First you'll read it out loud and make no more than 5 errors. Then I'll read it and ask questions. Remember to follow along when someone else is reading.
b. Everybody, touch the title. ✓
- (Call on a student to read the title.) *[Bob and Don Find Moops.]*
- What's going to happen in this story? (Call on a student. Idea: *Bob and Don find moops.*)
- Everybody, are moops real animals or make-believe animals? (Signal.) *Make-believe animals.*

First Reading

c. (Call on individual students to read the story, each student reading two or three sentences at a time.)

- (Correct errors: Tell the word. Direct the student to reread the sentence.)
- (If the group makes more than 5 errors, direct the students to reread the story.)

Second Reading

d. (After the group has read the selection making no more than 5 errors:)
Now I'll read the story and ask questions. Follow along.

Bob and Don Find Moops

Don and Bob lived near a strange forest.

- Everybody, keep your finger on the word **forest** while I ask a question. What is a forest? (Call on a student. Idea: *A place where lots of tall trees grow close together.*)

There were many strange animals in the forest. One strange animal was a moop. Moops were little animals with long hair. They made very good pets.

- Everybody, keep your finger on the word **pets** while I ask questions. Do you think moops are mean? (Call on a student.) *[No.]*
- Why not? (Call on a student. Idea: *Because they make good pets.*)

One day Don and Bob went out to get pet moops.

- Where did they go to get them? (Call on a student. Idea: *To the strange forest.*)

On the path through the forest they met a wise old man. The wise old man said, "A moop makes a good pet. But do not cut a moop's hair. Here's the rule about a moop: <u>The more you cut its hair, the faster its hair grows.</u>"

- Everybody, read that rule with me. Get ready. *The more you cut its hair, the faster its hair grows.*
- Say the rule without looking. Get ready. (Signal.) *The more you cut its hair, the faster its hair grows.*
- (Repeat until firm.)

Don listened to the old man. But Bob did not listen.
Don found a pet moop, and Bob found a pet moop. Don took his pet moop home and put it in a box.

Idea: *Took his moop home and put it in a box.*)

> **Bob took his pet moop home and looked at it. Bob said, "The hair on this moop is too long. So I will cut it."**

- Everybody, what's the rule about cutting the moop's hair? (Signal.) *The more you cut its hair, the faster its hair grows.*
- So what's going to happen to Bob's moop? (Call on a student. Idea: *The hair will grow faster.*)

> **Bob started to cut the moop's hair, but the hair started to grow back. So Bob cut more hair. But the more he cut the hair, the faster the hair grew.**
>
> **Soon the moop's hair was so long that it filled the room. Soon the hair was so long that Bob could not find his moop.**

- Why couldn't Bob find his moop? (Call on a student. Idea: *Because the hair was so long.*)

> **Don kept his moop for years. Don had a lot of fun with his moop. But Bob did not have fun with his moop. He never found his moop. All he could see was a room full of hair.**
> **THE END**

- Why didn't Bob have fun with his moop? (Call on a student. Idea: *Because he couldn't find his moop.*)

EXERCISE 5

WRITTEN ITEMS

Story Items

a. Find part E in your textbook. ✓
- These questions are about today's story. Today's story told about Bob and Don finding moops. I'll read each item and call on someone to answer it. Follow along. Don't write anything until I tell you to write.

b. (For each item: Read the item. Call on a student to answer it.)
- Item 2: What is the title of today's story? The choices are **Moops Find Bob and Don, Bob and Don Find Moops,** and **Bob and Don Find Mops.** You'll write one of those choices. Which choice? *[Bob and Don Find Moops.]*
- Item 3: Write the 2 missing words. The wise old man said, "The more you cut its blank, the blank its hair grows." Say the sentence with the words that go in each blank. [*The wise old man said, "The more you cut its hair, the faster its hair grows.]*
- Item 4: Who did not listen to the wise old man? *[Bob.]*
- Item 5: What happened to the moop's hair when Bob cut it? *[Idea: Hair started to grow back.]*
- Item 6: Did Bob have fun with his moop? *[No.]*
- Item 7: Are moops **real** or **make-believe?** *[Make-believe.]*
- (Teacher reference:)
- Item 8: One of the pictures shows Don's

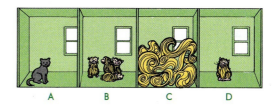

moop in a room. What's the letter of that picture? *[D.]*
- Item 9: One of the pictures shows Bob's moop in a room. What's the letter of that picture? *[C.]*

Skill Items

> *Note:* Make sure each student has worksheet lesson 2, side 1 and side 2. Students are to write their name on their worksheet.

c. The rest of the items for today's lesson are on your lesson 2 worksheet. **Find item 1 on your worksheet.** ✓
- Item 1: Find out who has a moop that eats glass. Here's the rule: **All mean moops eat glass.** Everybody, say the rule. Get ready. (Signal.) *All mean moops eat glass.*
- Jean's moop is mean. Everybody, so does Jean's moop eat glass? (Signal.) *Yes.*
- Meg's moop is mean. Everybody, so does Meg's moop eat glass? (Signal.) *Yes.*
- Fran's moop is not mean. So we don't

- Fran's moop is not mean. So we don't know if Fran's moop eats glass.
- Jack's moop is not mean. So we don't know if Jack's moop eats glass.
- Tom's moop is not mean. So we don't know if Tom's moop eats glass.
- Who has a moop that eats glass? Figure out everybody who has a moop that eats glass. Write the names on your paper. Raise your hand when you're finished.
(Observe students and give feedback.)

d. Find the rule above item 2. ✓
- I'll read the rule and call on someone to answer each item. Here's a rule: Tim's frogs are spotted. Everybody, say the rule. Get ready. (Signal.) *Tim's frogs are spotted.*
- Item 2: Is frog A spotted? *[No.]*
- Item 3: So is frog A one of Tim's frogs? *[No.]*
- Item 4: Is frog B spotted? *[Yes.]*
- Item 5: So is frog B one of Tim's frogs? *[Yes.]*
- Item 6: Use the rule and underline Tim's frogs. Tell me the letters of Tim's frogs. *[D, G.]*

Review Items

e. The rest of the items are review items. These are items from the last lesson.
- Item 7: What do all living things need? *[Water.]*
- Item 8: What do all living things make? *[Babies.]*
- Item 9: Do all living things grow? *[Yes.]*
- Item 10: Are ants living things? *[Yes.]*
- Item 11: Underline 3 things you know about ants. Tell me the 3 things you know. *[Ants make babies; Ants grow; Ants need water.]*

End-of-Lesson Activities

INDEPENDENT WORK

Now you're going to complete the written work without looking at the story. Start with your worksheet. Then finish the items in your textbook, beginning with item 2. Read the items to yourself and answer them. Raise your hand when you're finished.
(Observe students and give feedback.)

Note: Students will need marking pens or pencils of a different color.

WORKCHECK

a. We're going to check the rest of the answers on your lined paper and the answers on your worksheet. Here are the rules: Use your marking pencil to make an **X** next to any item that is wrong. If the answer is right, don't make any mark. If it's wrong, make an **X** next to it. Don't change any answers and don't mark over any answers.

b. Let's start with your worksheet. (For each item: Read the item. Call on a student to answer it. If the answer is wrong, say the correct answer.)
- Item 1: Find out who has a moop that eats glass. Here's the rule: All mean moops eat glass.

- Jean's moop is mean.   • Jack's moop is not mean.
- Meg's moop is mean.   • Tom's moop is not mean.
  • Fran's moop is not mean.

- Who has a moop that eats glass? *[Jean, Meg.]*
- Everybody, write **X** next to item 1 if you got it wrong. You should have written the names **Jean** and **Meg.**
- Item 2: Is frog A spotted? *[No.]*
- Item 3: So is frog A one of Tim's frogs? *[No.]*
- Item 4: Is frog B spotted? *[Yes.]*
- Item 5: So is frog B one of Tim's frogs? *[Yes.]*
- Item 6: Use the rule and underline Tim's frogs. Tell me the letters of the frogs you underlined. *[D, G.]*
- Item 7: What do all living things need? *[Water.]*
- Item 8: What do all living things make? *[Babies.]*
- Item 9: Do all living things grow? *[Yes.]*
- Item 10: Are ants living things? *[Yes.]*
- Item 11: Underline 3 things you know about ants. What did you underline? *[Ants make babies; Ants grow; Ants need water.]*

c. Now let's check the rest of the items on your lined paper.
Item 2: What is the title of today's story? *[Bob and Don Find Moops.]*
- Item 3: Write the 2 missing words. The wise old man said, "The more you cut its *[hair]*, the *[faster]* its hair grows."
- Item 4: Who did not listen to the wise old man? *[Bob.]*

- Item 5: What happened to the moop's hair when Bob cut it? [Idea: *Hair started to grow back.*]
  - Item 6: Did Bob have fun with his moop? [*No.*]
  - Item 7: Are moops real or make-believe? [*Make-believe.*]
  - Item 8: One of the pictures shows Don's moop in a room. What's the letter of that picture? [*D.*]
  - Item 9: One of the pictures shows Bob's moop in a room. What's the letter of that picture? [*C.*]
d. Now use your marking pencil to fix up any items you got wrong. Do not erase anything you wrote. Write the correct answer close to the answer that is wrong. Remember, before you hand in your independent work, all the items you missed must be fixed up.
(Observe students and give feedback.)

e. (At the end of the workcheck have students record the total number of errors they made at the top of their lined paper.)

Note:
Preview Literature lesson 1, secure materials, and reproduce blackline masters. (See the Literature Guide.)

WRITING-SPELLING

(Present Writing-Spelling lesson 2 after completing Reading lesson 2. See Writing-Spelling Guide.)

ACTIVITY

(Present Activity 2 after completing Reading lesson 2. See Activities Across the Curriculum.)

Lesson 3

EXERCISE 1

READING WORDS

Column 1

a. **Find lesson 3 in your textbook.** ✓
  - **Touch column 1.** ✓
  - (Teacher reference:)

1. great	4. grove
2. danger	5. measure
3. destroy	6. weight

b. **Word 1 is great. What word?** (Signal.) *Great.*
  - **Spell great. Get ready.** (Tap for each letter.) *G-R-E-A-T.*
  - **Great is another word for wonderful.**
  - **Everybody, what's another way of saying They had a wonderful time?** (Signal.) *They had a great time.*
c. **Word 2 is danger. What word?** (Signal.) *Danger.*
  - **Spell danger. Get ready.** (Tap for each letter.) *D-A-N-G-E-R.*
  - **When you're in a place where you could get hurt, you're in danger of getting hurt. Everybody, what do you know about a place where you could get robbed?** (Signal.) *You're in danger of getting robbed.*
d. **Word 3 is destroy. What word?** (Signal.) *Destroy.*
  - **Spell destroy. Get ready.** (Tap for each letter.) *D-E-S-T-R-O-Y.*
  - **If you ruin something so it can't be fixed, you destroy that thing. Everybody, what's another way of saying She ruined the sand castle?** (Signal.) *She destroyed the sand castle.*
  - **What's another way of saying The storm ruined the city?** (Signal.) *The storm destroyed the city.*
e. **Word 4 is grove. What word?** (Signal.) *Grove.*
  - **Spell grove. Get ready.** (Tap for each letter.) *G-R-O-V-E.*
  - **A grove of trees is a small group of trees. What do we call a small group of trees?** (Signal.) *Grove.*

f. **Word 5 is measure. What word?** (Signal.) *Measure.*
g. **Word 6 is weight. What word?** (Signal.) *Weight.*
h. **Let's read those words again, the fast way.**
  - **Word 1. What word?** (Signal.) *Great.*
  - **Word 2. What word?** (Signal.) *Danger.*
  - **Word 3. What word?** (Signal.) *Destroy.*
  - **Word 4. What word?** (Signal.) *Grove.*
  - **Word 5. What word?** (Signal.) *Measure.*
  - **Word 6. What word?** (Signal.) *Weight.*
i. (Repeat step h until firm.)

Column 2

j. **Find column 2.** ✓
  - (Teacher reference:)

1. <u>make</u>-believe	4. <u>howl</u>ed
2. <u>to</u>gether	5. <u>branch</u>es
3. <u>dur</u>ing	

  - **Part of each word is underlined. You'll read that part. Then you'll read the whole word.**
k. **Word 1. What's the underlined part?** (Signal.) *make.*
  - **What's the whole word?** (Signal.) *Make-believe.*
  - **Word 2. What's the underlined part?** (Signal.) *to.*
  - **What's the whole word?** (Signal.) *Together.*
  - **Word 3. What's the underlined part?** (Signal.) *dur.*
  - **What's the whole word?** (Signal.) *During.*
  - **Word 4. What's the underlined part?** (Signal.) *howl.*
  - **What's the whole word?** (Signal.) *Howled.*
  - **Word 5. What's the underlined part?** (Signal.) *branch.*
  - **What's the whole word?** (Signal.) *Branches.*

l. Let's read those words again the fast way.
- Word 1. What word? (Signal.) *Make-believe.*
- Word 2. What word? (Signal.) *Together.*
- Word 3. What word? (Signal.) *During.*
- Word 4. What word? (Signal.) *Howled.*
- Word 5. What word? (Signal.) *Branches.*

m. (Repeat step l until firm.)

Column 3

n. Find column 3. ✓
- (Teacher reference:)

1. covered	4. crashed
2. washed	5. cracked
3. pointed	

- All these words end with the letters **E-D**. The ending makes different sounds in the words.

o. Word 1. What word? (Signal.) *Covered.*
- Word 2. What word? (Signal.) *Washed.*
- Word 3. What word? (Signal.) *Pointed.*
- Word 4. What word? (Signal.) *Crashed.*
- Word 5. What word? (Signal.) *Cracked.*

p. (Repeat step o until firm.)

Column 4

q. Find column 4. ✓
- (Teacher reference:)

1. twig	4. ground
2. during	5. facts
3. carry	6. bark

r. Word 1. What word? (Signal.) *Twig.*
- A twig is a tiny branch.

s. Word 2. What word? (Signal.) *During.*
- If something happens during the night, it happens while the night is going on.
- Everybody, what's another way of saying **It happened while the movie was going on?** (Signal.) *It happened during the movie.*

t. Word 3. What word? (Signal.) *Carry.*
- Word 4. What word? (Signal.) *Ground.*
- Word 5. What word? (Signal.) *Facts.*
- Word 6. What word? (Signal.) *Bark.*

u. Let's do those words again.
- Word 1. What word? (Signal.) *Twig.*
- Word 2. What word? (Signal.) *During.*
- Word 3. What word? (Signal.) *Carry.*
- Word 4. What word? (Signal.) *Ground.*
- Word 5. What word? (Signal.) *Facts.*
- Word 6. What word? (Signal.) *Bark.*

v. (Repeat step u until firm.)

Column 5

w. Find column 5. ✓
- (Teacher reference:)

1. roots	4. ripe
2. trunk	5. flowers
3. whole	

x. Word 1. What word? (Signal.) *Roots.*
- Word 2. What word? (Signal.) *Trunk.*
- The trunk of a tree is the main part that comes out of the ground.
- Everybody, what do we call the main part of the tree that comes out of the ground? (Signal.) *Trunk.*

y. Word 3. What word? (Signal.) *Whole.*
- Word 4. What word? (Signal.) *Ripe.*
- Fruit that is ready to eat is ripe. Everybody, what do we call an apple that is ready to eat? (Signal.) *A ripe apple.*
- Word 5. What word? (Signal.) *Flowers.*

z. Let's do those words again the fast way.
- Word 1. What word? (Signal.) *Roots.*
- Word 2. What word? (Signal.) *Trunk.*
- Word 3. What word? (Signal.) *Whole.*
- Word 4. What word? (Signal.) *Ripe.*
- Word 5. What word? (Signal.) *Flowers.*

a. (Repeat step z until firm.)

Individual Turns

(For columns 1–5: Call on individual students, each to read one to three words per turn.)

EXERCISE 2

COMPREHENSION PASSAGE

a. Find part B in your textbook. ✓
- You're going to read a story about Don. First you'll read the information passage. It gives some facts about trees. I'll call on different students to read. Everybody else follow along, and point to the words that are being read. If you don't have your place when I call on you to read, you lose your turn.

b. Everybody, touch the title. ✓
- (Call on a student to read the title.) *[Trees].*
- Everybody, what's the title? (Signal.) *Trees.*

c. (Call on individual students to read the passage, each student reading two or three sentences at a time. Ask the specified questions as the students read.)

Trees

Trees have roots. The roots are under the ground.

- Everybody, keep your finger on the word **ground** while I ask questions.
- Look at picture 1. It shows what a tree would look like if you could see through the ground. Touch the top of the ground. ✓
- Touch the roots. ✓

The roots do two things. The roots hold the tree up to keep it from falling over. The roots also carry water from the ground to all parts of the tree.

- Listen to those two things again: The roots keep the tree from falling over . . . And the roots carry water from the ground to all parts of the tree.
- What's the first thing the roots do? (Call on a student. Idea: *Keep the tree from falling over.*)
- What's the other thing the roots do? (Call on a student. Idea: *Carry water.*)

Trees could not live if they did not have roots.
   Here's another fact about trees. Trees do not grow in the winter because the ground is cold. In the spring, trees start to grow.

- Everybody, when don't trees grow? (Signal.) *In the winter.*
- Why don't trees grow in the winter? (Call on a student. Idea: *Because the ground is cold.*)
- Everybody, when do trees start to grow? (Signal.) *In the spring.*

The sun makes the ground warmer in the spring. First the top of the ground gets warm. Then the deeper parts of the ground get warm.

- Where does the ground get warm first? (Call on a student. Idea: *At the top.*)
- Everybody, look at picture 2. It shows layers in the ground. Each layer has a letter. Tell me the letter of the layer that gets warm **first** in the spring. (Signal.) *A.*
- Tell me the letter of the layer that gets warm **last** in the spring. (Signal.) *D.*

Small trees begin to grow before big trees grow.

- Everybody, which trees start to grow first in the spring, small ones or big ones? (Signal.) *Small ones.*

Small trees grow first because their roots are not very deep in the ground. Their roots are in warmer ground. So their roots warm up before the roots of big trees warm up.

- Everybody, touch the roots of the smallest tree. ✓
- Almost all the roots of that tree are in layer A. In the spring, those roots are in the layer that gets warm first.
- Now touch the roots of the biggest tree. ✓
- The bottom of those roots are in layer D. That's the layer that warms up last in the spring.
- Remember, the roots do two things. Who can name both things the roots do? (Call on a student. Idea: *Hold the tree up and carry the water.*)
- Everybody, in the spring, which trees start growing first, big ones or small ones? (Signal.) *Small ones.*
- Why do small trees start growing first in the spring? (Call on a student. Idea: *Because their roots are not very deep.*)

EXERCISE 3

WRITTEN ITEMS

Note: Students will need lined paper, regular pencils, and marking pens or pencils of a different color.

a. You're going to the write answers to items about what you just read.
- **Take out a piece of lined paper.** ✓
- Write your name at the top of the paper. ✓

- Number your paper from 1 through 17. Remember to skip every other line. Pencils down when you're finished.
  (Observe students and give feedback.)
b. Find part C in your textbook. ✓
- The questions in part C are about trees. I'll read each question and call on someone to answer it. Follow along. Don't write anything until I tell you to write.
c. (For each item: Read the item. Call on a student to answer it.)
- Item 1: What part of a tree is under the ground? *[Roots.]*
- Item 2: Roots keep the tree from <u>blank</u>. (Idea: *Falling over.*)
- Item 3: Roots carry <u>blank</u> to all parts of the tree. *[Water.]*
- Item 4: Could trees live if they didn't have roots? *[No.]*
- Item 5: When do trees begin to grow? *[In the spring.]*
- Item 6: Trees begin to grow when their roots get <u>blank</u>. *[Idea: Warm.]*
- (Teacher reference:)

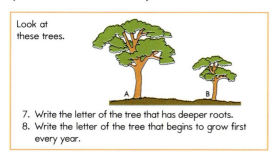

- Item 7: Write the letter of the tree that has deeper roots. Which tree has deeper roots? *[A.]*
- Item 8: Write the letter of the tree that begins to grow first every year. Which tree begins to grow first? *[B.]*
- (Teacher reference:)

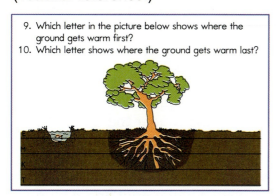

- Item 9: Which letter in the picture below shows where the ground gets warm first? *[E.]*
- Item 10: Which letter shows where the ground gets warm last? *[T.]*
d. Now you're going to write the answers for part C without looking at the passage. Read item 1 to yourself and write the answer next to the number **1** on your paper. Raise your hand when you've done that much.
  (Observe students and give feedback.)
e. Read the rest of the items in part C to yourself and answer them. Raise your hand when you've finished part C.
  (Observe students and give feedback.)
f. We're going to check your answers for part C. Here are the rules: Use your marking pencil to make an **X** next to any item that's wrong. If the answer is right, don't make any mark. If it's wrong, make an **X** next to it. Don't change any answers, and don't mark over any answers.
g. (For each item: Read the item. Call on a student to answer it. If an answer is wrong, say the correct answer.)
- Item 1: What part of a tree is under the ground? *[Roots.]*
- Everybody, write **X** next to item 1 if you got it wrong. ✓
- Item 2: Roots keep the tree from <u>blank</u>. (Idea: *Falling over.*)
- Item 3: Roots carry <u>blank</u> to all parts of the tree. *[Water.]*
- Item 4: Could trees live if they didn't have roots? *[No.]*
- Item 5: When do trees begin to grow? *[In the spring.]*
- Item 6: Trees begin to grow when their roots get <u>blank</u>. (Idea: *Warm.*)
- Item 7: Write the letter of the tree that has deeper roots. Which letter did you write? *[A.]*
- Item 8: Write the letter of the tree that begins to grow first every year. Which letter did you write? *[B.]*
- Item 9: Which letter in the picture below shows where the ground gets warm first? *[E.]*
- Item 10: Which letter shows where the ground gets warm last? *[T.]*
h. Now use your marking pencil to fix up any items you got wrong. Do not erase anything you wrote. Write the correct answer close to the answer that is wrong.
  (Observe students and give feedback.)

Lesson 3 17

EXERCISE 4
STORY READING

a. Find part D in your textbook. ✓
- We're going to read this story two times. First you'll read it out loud and make no more than 5 errors. Then I'll read it and ask questions. Remember to follow along when someone else is reading.

b. Everybody, touch the title. ✓
- (Call on a student to read the title.) [*Don Washes the White Spot.*]
- Everybody, what's the title? (Signal.) *Don Washes the White Spot.*
- So what's the story about? (Call on a student. Idea: *Don washing a white spot.*)

First Reading

c. (Call on individual students to read the story, each student reading two or three sentences at a time.)

- (Correct errors: Tell the word. Direct the student to reread the sentence.)
- (If the group makes more than 5 errors, direct the students to reread the story.)

Second Reading

d. (After the group has read the selection making no more than 5 errors:)
Now I'll read the story and ask questions. Follow along.

> **Don Washes the White Spot**
>
> Don had a pretty white coat. But he didn't like white coats. He wanted a blue coat.

- Everybody, keep your finger on the word **coat** while I ask questions. What color coats didn't he like? (Signal.) *White.*
- What color did he like? (Signal.) *Blue.*

> Don said, "I'll buy a blue coat." So he started to walk to town. He had to walk through the strange forest to get to town. Don met the wise old man on the path through the forest. Don told the wise old man, "I'm on my way to get a blue coat."
> The wise old man said, "I will give you a blue coat." The wise old man held up a pretty blue coat.

> The coat had one little white spot on it. The old man pointed to the spot and said, "Do not try to wash this spot away. Here's the rule: <u>The more you wash this spot, the bigger it will get.</u>"

- Everybody, who had a blue coat? (Signal.) *The wise old man.*
- What color was the spot on that coat? (Signal.) *White.*
- Listen to the rule about that spot: The more you wash this spot, the bigger it will get.
- Everybody, say the rule with me. Get ready. *The more you wash this spot, the bigger it will get.*
- Say the rule without looking. Get ready. (Signal.) *The more you wash this spot, the bigger it will get.*
- (Repeat until firm.)
- What happens to the spot if you wash it a little bit? (Call on a student. Idea: *It gets a little bigger.*)
- What happens to the spot if you wash it a lot? (Call on a student. Idea: *It gets a lot bigger.*)

> Don did not listen to the old man. Don took the pretty blue coat home. Then he said to himself, "I don't like that little spot on the coat. I will wash it away."

- Everybody, what will happen to the spot when Don washes it? (Signal.) *It will get bigger.*

> So Don got some soap and water. Then he started to wash the spot. He washed a little bit and the spot got a little bigger. Don washed some more. And the white spot got bigger. Don washed and washed and washed. And the spot got bigger and bigger and bigger. The more Don washed, the bigger the spot got.
> Soon the white spot was so big that it covered the whole coat. The whole coat was white. Now Don did not have a white coat and a blue coat. He had two white coats. Don said, "I hate white coats."

18 Lesson 3

- What color was the coat when Don started out? (Signal.) *Blue.*
- Why did it turn white? (Call on a student. Idea: *Because Don kept washing the spot.*)

EXERCISE 5
WRITTEN ITEMS
Story Items

a. Find part E in your textbook. ✓
- These questions are about today's story. Today's story told about Don and the white spot. I'll read each item and call on someone to answer it. Follow along. Don't write anything until I tell you to write.

b. (For each item: Read the item. Call on a student to answer it.)
- Item 11: What's the title of today's story? The choices are **Don Washes the Moop, Don Washes the White Spot,** and **Don Spots the White Moop.** You'll write one of those choices. Which choice? *[Don Washes the White Spot.]*
- Item 12: Did Don like white coats? *[No.]*
- Item 13: The old man said, "The more you wash this spot, the blank it will get." *[Bigger.]*
- Item 14: What color was the coat that the old man gave Don? *[Blue.]*
- Item 15: What happened to the spot when Don washed it? (Idea: *It got bigger.*)
- Item 16: What color was the coat after Don washed it? *[White.]*
- (Teacher reference:)

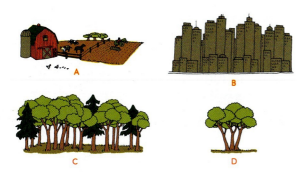

- Item 17: Write the letter of the picture that shows a forest. What letter shows a forest? *[C.]*

Skill Items

Note: Make sure each student has worksheet lesson 3, side 1 and side 2.

c. The rest of the items for today's lesson are on your lesson 3 worksheet. **Find the instructions at the top of your worksheet.** ✓
- I'll read: Use the rules and see which frogs are Mike's and which frogs are Jean's. Here are the rules: Jean's frogs are spotted. Mike's frogs are not spotted.
- (Teacher reference:)

Use the rules and see which frogs are Mike's and which frogs are Jean's. Here are the rules:
- Jean's frogs are spotted. • Mike's frogs are not spotted.

1. Is this frog spotted? _____
2. So who does this frog belong to? _____
3. How do you know this frog doesn't belong to Jean? _____

4. Is this frog spotted? _____
5. So who does this frog belong to? _____
6. How do you know this frog doesn't belong to Mike? _____

7. **Make a box around** Jean's frogs.
8. **Underline** Mike's frogs.

- Item 1: Is this frog spotted? *[No.]*
- Item 2: So who does this frog belong to? *[Mike.]*
- Item 3: How do you know this frog doesn't belong to Jean? *[Idea: Doesn't have spots.]*
- Item 4: Is this frog spotted? *[Yes.]*
- Item 5: So who does this frog belong to? *[Jean.]*
- Item 6: How do you know this frog doesn't belong to Mike? *[Idea: It has spots.]*
- Item 7: Make a box around Jean's frogs. Which frogs will you make a box around? *[E, G, H.]*
- Item 8: Underline Mike's frogs. Which frogs will you underline? *[C, D, F.]*
- (Teacher reference:)

9. Find out who is smart.
   Rule: **The people with hats are smart.**
   - Kim has a hat.
   - Pete has a hat.
   - Tom does not have a hat.
   - Jane has a hat.
   - Ron does not have a hat.

   Who is smart? _____   _____   _____

Lesson 3   19

- Item 9: Find out who is smart. Here's the rule: The people with hats are smart. Everybody, say the rule. Get ready. (Signal.) *The people with hats are smart.*
- Kim has a hat. Everybody, so is Kim smart? (Signal.) *Yes.*
- Pete has a hat. So is Pete smart? (Signal.) *Yes.*
- Tom does not have a hat. So we don't know if Tom is smart.
- Jane has a hat. Everybody, so is Jane smart? (Signal.) *Yes.*
- Ron does not have a hat. So we don't know if Ron is smart.
- Who is smart? Figure out everybody who is smart. Write the names for item 9. Raise your hand when you've done that much.
  (Observe students and give feedback.)

Review Items

d. The rest of the items are review items. These are items from the last two lessons.
- Item 10: Are snakes living things? [*Yes.*]
- Item 11: Underline 3 things you know about snakes. What 3 things will you underline? [*Snakes grow; Snakes need water; Snakes make babies.*]
- (Teacher reference:)

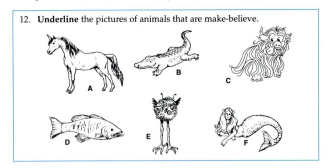

- Item 12: Underline the pictures of animals that are make-believe. Tell me the letters of the pictures you will underline. [*A, C, E, F.*]

End-of-Lesson Activities

INDEPENDENT WORK

Now you're going to complete the written work without looking at the story. Start with your worksheet. Then finish the items in your textbook, beginning with item 11. Read the items to yourself and answer them. Raise your hand when you're finished. (Observe students and give feedback.)

WORKCHECK

Note: Students will need marking pens or pencils of a different color.

a. We're going to check the rest of the answers on your lined paper and the answers on your worksheet. Here are the rules: Use your marking pencil to make an **X** next to any item that is wrong. If the answer is right, don't make any mark. If it's wrong, make an **X** next to it. Don't change any answers and don't mark over any answers.

b. Let's start with your worksheet. (For each item: Read the item. Call on a student to answer it. If the answer is wrong, say the correct answer.)
- I'll read: Use the rules and see which frogs are Mike's and which frogs are Jean's. Here are the rules: Jean's frogs are spotted. Mike's frogs are not spotted.
- Item 1: Is this frog spotted? [*No.*]
- Everybody, write **X** next to item 1 if you got it wrong.
- Item 2: So who does this frog belong to? [*Mike.*]
- Item 3: How do you know this frog doesn't belong to Jean? [*Idea: It doesn't have spots.*]
- Item 4: Is this frog spotted? [*Yes.*]
- Item 5: So who does this frog belong to? [*Jean.*]
- Item 6: How do you know this frog doesn't belong to Mike? [*Idea: It has spots.*]
- Item 7: Make a box around Jean's frogs. Which frogs did you box? [*E, G, H.*]
- Item 8: Underline Mike's frogs. Which frogs did you underline? [*C, D, F.*]
- Item 9: Find out who is smart. Rule: **The people with hats are smart.** Kim has a hat. Pete has a hat. Tom does not have a hat. Jane has a hat. Ron does not have a hat. Who is smart? [*Kim, Pete, Jane.*]
- Item 10: Are snakes living things? [*Yes.*]
- Item 11: Underline 3 things you know about snakes. What 3 things did you underline? [*Snakes grow; Snakes need water; Snakes make babies.*]

- Item 12: Underline the pictures of animals that are make-believe. Which animals did you underline? *[A, C, E, F.]*
c. Now let's check the rest of the items on your lined paper.
- Item 11: What's the title of today's story? *[Don Washes the White Spot.]*
- Item 12: Did Don like white coats? *[No.]*
- Item 13: The old man said, "The more you wash this spot, the <u>blank</u> it will get." *[Bigger.]*
- Item 14: What color was the coat that the old man gave Don? *[Blue.]*
- Item 15: What happened to the spot when Don washed it? *[Idea: It got bigger.]*
- Item 16: What color was the coat after Don washed it? *[White.]*
- Item 17: Write the letter of the picture that shows a forest. Which letter did you write? *[C.]*

d. Now use your marking pencil to fix up any items you got wrong. Do not erase anything you wrote. Write the correct answer close to the answer that is wrong. Remember, before you hand in your independent work, all the items you missed must be fixed up.
(Observe students and give feedback.)
e. (At the end of the workcheck have students record the total number of errors they made at the top of their lined paper.)

WRITING-SPELLING

(Present Writing-Spelling lesson 3 after completing Reading lesson 3. See Writing-Spelling Guide.)

Lesson 4

EXERCISE 1
VOCABULARY

a. Find page 338 in your textbook. ✓
- These are sentences that you'll be working with during the year. They contain vocabulary words that you'll learn.
- Touch sentence 1. ✓
- It says: You measure your weight in pounds. Everybody, read that sentence. Get ready. (Signal.) *You measure your weight in pounds.*
- Close your eyes and say the sentence. Get ready. (Signal.) *You measure your weight in pounds.*
- (Repeat until firm.)

b. Listen: You **measure** your weight in pounds. When you **measure** something, you find out how long it is or how hot it is or how heavy it is or how tall it is.

c. The sentence tells about measuring **weight.** The **weight** of an object is how heavy that object is. Who knows how much they weigh? (Call on a student.)

d. The sentence says: You measure your weight in **pounds. Pounds** are the unit you use to measure weight. If the scale says 49, it means you weigh 49 pounds.

e. Listen to the sentence again: You measure your weight in pounds. Everybody, say that sentence. Get ready. (Signal.) *You measure your weight in pounds.*
- Remember, to find out how heavy or long something is, you **measure.**

f. Everybody, what word tells **what you do** to find out how heavy or how long something is? (Signal.) *Measure.*
- What **unit** do you use to measure weight? (Signal.) *Pounds.*
- What word tells how many pounds something is? (Signal.) *Weight.*
- (Repeat step f until firm.)

EXERCISE 2
READING WORDS

Column 1

a. Find lesson 4 in your textbook. ✓
- Touch column 1. ✓

- (Teacher reference:)

1. alive	4. millions
2. seasons	5. measure
3. terrible	6. weight

b. Word 1 is **alive.** What word? (Signal.) *Alive.*
- Spell **alive.** Get ready. (Tap for each letter.) *A-L-I-V-E.*

c. Word 2 is **seasons.** What word? (Signal.) *Seasons.*
- Spell **seasons.** Get ready. (Tap for each letter.) *S-E-A-S-O-N-S.*
- Each year has four seasons: spring, summer, fall, winter. Everybody, what do we call spring, summer, fall and winter? (Signal.) *Seasons.*

d. Word 3 is **terrible.** What word? (Signal.) *Terrible.*
- Spell **terrible.** Get ready. (Tap for each letter.) *T-E-R-R-I-B-L-E.*

e. Word 4 is **millions.** What word? (Signal.) *Millions.*
- Spell **millions.** Get ready. (Tap for each letter.) *M-I-L-L-I-O-N-S.*
- A **million** is a very, very large number. If you had a **million** dollars, you'd be very rich.

f. Word 5. What word? (Signal.) *Measure.*
- (Repeat for word 6.)

g. Let's read those words again, the fast way.
- Word 1. What word? (Signal.) *Alive.*
- (Repeat for words 2–6.)

h. (Repeat step g until firm.)

Column 2

i. Find column 2. ✓
- (Teacher reference:)

1. during	4. glowing
2. blowing	5. growing
3. cheering	

- All these words end with the letters **I-N-G.**

j. Word 1. What word? (Signal.) *During.*
- (Repeat for words 2–5.)

k. (Repeat step j until firm.)

Column 3

22 Lesson 4

Column 3

l. Find column 3. ✓
- (Teacher reference:)

1.	<u>app</u>le	4.	<u>mean</u>er
2.	<u>love</u>d	5.	<u>crack</u>ed
3.	<u>great</u>est	6.	<u>crash</u>ed

- These words have more than one part. The first part of each word is underlined.

m. Word 1. What's the underlined part? (Signal.) *app.*
- What's the whole word? (Signal.) *Apple.*
- Word 2. What's the first part? (Signal.) *love.*
- What's the whole word? (Signal.) *Loved.*
- Word 3. What's the first part? (Signal.) *great.*
- What's the whole word? (Signal.) *Greatest.*
- Word 4. What's the first part? (Signal.) *mean.*
- What's the whole word? (Signal.) *Meaner.*
- Word 5. What's the first part? (Signal.) *crack.*
- What's the whole word? (Signal.) *Cracked.*
- Word 6. What's the first part? (Signal.) *crash.*
- What's the whole word? (Signal.) *Crashed.*

n. Let's read those words again, the fast way.
- Word 1. What word? (Signal.) *Apple.*
- (Repeat for words 2–6.)

o. (Repeat step n until firm.)

Column 4

p. Find column 4. ✓
- (Teacher reference:)

1.	grove	4.	howled
2.	bark	5.	branches
3.	trunk	6.	care

q. Word 1. What word? (Signal.) *Grove.*
- Word 2. What word? (Signal.) *Bark.*
- The bark of a tree is the covering of the tree trunk and branches. It's like the skin. Some trees have very thick bark. Everybody, what do we call the covering of the tree trunk? (Signal.) *Bark.*
- Word 3. What word? (Signal.) *Trunk.*
- (Repeat for words 4–6.)

r. Let's read those words again.
- Word 1. What word? (Signal.) *Grove.*
- (Repeat for words 2–6.)

s. (Repeat step r until firm.)

Column 5

t. Find column 5. ✓
- (Teacher reference:)

1.	pretty	4.	flowers
2.	twig	5.	Tina
3.	ripe	6.	destroy

u. Word 1. What word? (Signal.) *Pretty.*
- (Repeat for words 2–6.)

v. (Repeat step u until firm.)

Individual Turns

(For columns 1–5: Call on individual students, each to read one to three words per turn.)

EXERCISE 3

VOCABULARY REVIEW

a. Here's the new vocabulary sentence: You measure your weight in pounds.
- Everybody, say the sentence. Get ready. (Signal.) *You measure your weight in pounds.*
- (Repeat until firm.)

b. Remember, the word **measure** tells **what you do** to find out how long or how heavy something is. Everybody, what word tells what you do to find out how long or how heavy something is? (Signal.) *Measure.*
- The word **weight** tells how many pounds something is. Everybody, what word tells how many pounds something is? (Signal.) *Weight.*
- And the unit of weight named in the sentence is **pounds**. Everybody, what's the unit of weight? (Signal.) *Pounds.* Yes, you measure your weight in pounds.

c. Say the sentence again. Get ready. (Signal.) *You measure your weight in pounds.*
- (Repeat until firm.)

d. What word tells **what you do** to find out how heavy or how long something is? (Signal.) *Measure.*
- What word tells how many pounds something is? (Signal.) *Weight.*
- What unit do you use to measure weight? (Signal.) *Pounds.*

Lesson 4 23

- Raise your hand if you know how many pounds you weigh. (Call on different students to tell their weight.)

EXERCISE 4
COMPREHENSION PASSAGE

a. Find part B in your textbook. ✓
- You're going to read a story about an apple tree. First you'll read the information passage. It gives some facts about apple trees. Remember to follow along.
b. Everybody, touch the title. ✓
- (Call on a student to read the title.) [Apple Trees.]
- Everybody, what's the title? (Signal.) *Apple Trees.*
c. (Call on individual students to read the passage, each student reading two or three sentences at a time. Ask the specified questions as the students read.)

> **Apple Trees**
>
> Apple trees are different from forest trees. Forest trees are tall and straight. Apple trees are short and not so straight. Forest trees have very small branches. Apple trees have large branches.
>
> Here is a forest tree. Here is an apple tree.

- Everybody, which tree is tall and straight? (Signal.) *Forest tree.*
- Which tree is short and not so straight? (Signal.) *Apple tree.*
- Which tree has small branches? (Signal.) *Forest tree.*
- Which tree has larger branches? (Signal.) *Apple tree.*

> Apple trees have white flowers in the spring. Later, in the summer, a little apple starts growing from each place where there was a flower.

- Everybody, keep your finger on the word **flower** while I ask questions. When do apple trees have flowers? (Signal.) *Spring.*
- An apple grows where something was. Everybody, what **was** in each place where an apple grows? (Signal.) *A flower.*

> By the fall, the apples are big and ripe. They will fall off if they are not picked. The leaves also fall off in the fall. During the winter, the apple tree does not grow. It is in a kind of sleep. It will start growing again in the spring.

- Everybody, when do the apples fall off the tree? (Signal.) *Fall.*
- What else falls off the tree in the fall? (Signal.) *Leaves.*
- Does the apple tree grow during the winter? (Signal.) *No.*
- When does it start growing again? (Signal.) *In the spring.*

> The pictures below show a twig of an apple tree in the spring, the summer, the fall, and the winter.

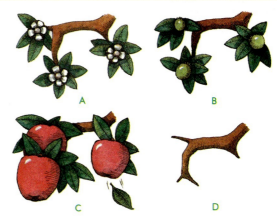

- Everybody, what season is in picture A? (Signal.) *Spring.*
- You can see the twig with the white flowers.
- What season is in picture B? (Signal.) *Summer.*
- What is growing in each place where a white flower was? (Signal.) *An apple.*
- How big are those apples? (Call on a student. Idea: *Tiny.*)
- Everybody, what season is in picture C? (Signal.) *Fall.*
- How has that apple changed since summer? (Call on a student. Ideas: *It got bigger. It turned red.*)
- And you can see a leaf falling off the tree.
- Everybody, what season is in picture D? (Signal.) *Winter.*

- What happened to the leaves and the apples? (Call on a student. Idea: *They fell off the tree.*)

EXERCISE 5
WRITTEN ITEMS

a. Everybody, take out a piece of lined paper. ✓
- Write your name at the top of the paper. ✓
- Number your paper from 1 through 17. Remember to skip every other line. Pencils down when you're finished. (Observe students and give feedback.)

b. Find part C in your textbook. ✓
- The questions in part C are about forest trees and apple trees. I'll read each question and call on someone to answer it. Follow along. Don't write anything until I tell you to write.

c. (For each item: Read the item. Call on a student to answer it.)
- Item 1: What color are the flowers that apple trees make? *[White.]*
- Item 2: When do those flowers come out? *[Spring.]*
- Item 3: What grows in each place where there was a flower? *[Idea: Little apple.]*
- Item 4: Which has a tall straight trunk, a forest tree or an apple tree? *[Forest tree.]*
- Item 5: Which has larger branches, a forest tree or an apple tree? *[Apple tree.]*

d. Read the items in part C to yourself and answer them. Remember, don't look at the passage. Raise your hand when you've finished part C.
(Observe students and give feedback.)

EXERCISE 6
STORY READING

a. Find part D in your textbook. ✓
- This is the first part of a story. You'll read this part today. You'll read other parts in the next lessons.
- We're going to read this story two times. First you'll read it out loud and make no more than 6 errors. Then I'll read it and ask questions. Remember to follow along when someone else is reading.

b. Everybody, touch the title. ✓
- (Call on a student to read the title.) *[The Little Apple Tree.]*
- Everybody, what's the title? (Signal.) *The Little Apple Tree.*

c. (Call on individual students to read the story, each student reading two or three sentences at a time.)

- (Correct errors: Tell the word. Direct the student to reread the sentence.)
- (If the group makes more than 6 errors, direct the students to reread the story.)

d. (After the group has read the selection making no more than 6 errors:) Now I'll read the story and ask questions. Follow along.

The Little Apple Tree

Tina was an apple tree. She loved to hold her leaves out to the sun. She loved to make green leaves and pretty white flowers in the spring. She loved to make big red apples in the fall. And she loved to have a great big sleep every winter.

- Everybody, keep your finger on the word **winter** while I ask questions.
- What did Tina love to make in the spring? (Call on a student. Idea: *Leaves and flowers.*)
- What did she love to make in the fall? (Call on a student. Idea: *Big red apples.*)
- What did she love to **do** in the winter? (Call on a student. Idea: *Sleep.*)

But Tina didn't get to do all the things she loved to do. She didn't live in a nice grove of apple trees. She lived in a forest with big mean trees that didn't care about her. Those big trees took all of the sunshine they could reach. And they didn't leave much for Tina. They dropped leaves and bark and seeds and branches all over little Tina.

- Everybody, did Tina live in a nice grove of apple trees? (Signal.) *No.*
- Where did she live? (Signal.) *In a forest.*
- What kind of trees did she live with? (Call on a student. Idea: *Big mean trees.*)
- They took something and didn't leave much of it for Tina. Everybody, what did they take? (Signal.) *Sunshine.*

Lesson 4 25

- The picture shows big trees taking the sunlight. Poor Tina is mostly in the shadows.
- Those trees are dropping things on her. The story says they dropped leaves, bark, seeds, and branches. Everybody, touch a branch they're dropping on her. ✓
- They seem to be having fun, but Tina doesn't look very happy.

> When the wind started blowing, the big trees would swing and howl and have lots of fun. They didn't let the wind reach Tina.
> And those big trees didn't care what Tina said.
> One spring day, she said, "Please stop dropping things on me. I am trying to make white flowers."

- Everybody, what was she trying to do? (Signal.) *Make white flowers.*
- What were the forest trees doing? (Call on a student. Ideas: *Dropping things on her; having fun; keeping the wind from her.*)

> One of the big trees said, "She doesn't want us to do <u>this</u>." That tree dropped a small branch right on Tina.
> Another big tree said, "Ho, ho. She doesn't want us to do <u>this</u>." That tree dropped a bigger branch on Tina.
> The biggest tree said, "Ho, ho. She really doesn't want us to do <u>this</u>." That tree dropped the biggest branch it had. That branch crashed down on top of Tina. It cracked two of Tina's branches.

- Everybody, which tree dropped the biggest branch it had? (Signal.) *The biggest tree.*
- What did that branch do to Tina? (Call on a student. Idea: *Cracked two of her branches.*)

> The big trees howled and said, "That was good. We really dropped some big ones on that apple tree. Ho, ho."
> **MORE NEXT TIME**

- Those trees are really being mean. How do you think that makes Tina feel? (Call on individual students. Accept reasonable responses.)
- We'll read more about those trees.
- Find the story picture on page 23. You can see that Tina's been hurt.

EXERCISE 7
WRITTEN ITEMS
Story Items

a. Find part E in your textbook. ✓
- These questions are about today's story. Today's story told about Tina. I'll read each item and call on someone to answer it. Follow along. Don't write anything until I tell you to write.

b. (For each item: Read the item. Call on a student to answer it.)
- Item 6: What's the title of today's story? *[The Little Apple Tree.]*
- Item 7: How many apple trees were near Tina? *[None.]*
- Item 8: Who kept the wind and the sunlight away from Tina? *[The tall trees.]*

c. For items 9 through 12, you'll read each thing that Tina did. Then you'll write the season that tells when she did it.
- Item 9: Made big red apples. Was that in winter, spring, summer, or fall? *[Fall.]*
- Item 10: Made leaves and white flowers. What season? *[Spring.]*
- Item 11: Made little apples where each flower was. What season? *[Summer.]*
- Item 12: Went to sleep. What season? *[Winter.]*
- Item 13: Write 3 things the big trees dropped on Tina. Which 3 things did the big trees drop on Tina? *[Bark, branches, leaves.]*

d. (Teacher reference:)

The pictures show the same twig in 4 seasons. **Write the name of the season for each twig.**

| 14. | 15. | 16. | 17. |

- Items 14 through 17: The pictures show the same twig in 4 seasons. You'll write the name of the season for each twig.
- Item 14: What season does that twig show? *[Fall.]*
- Item 15: What season? *[Winter.]*
- Item 16: What season? *[Summer.]*
- Item 17: What season? *[Spring.]*

Skill Items

Note: Make sure each student has worksheet lesson 4, side 1 and side 2.

e. **Find item 1 on your worksheet.** ✓
- (Teacher reference:)

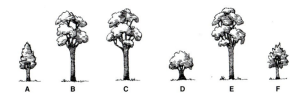

- Item 1: The bigger the forest tree is, the meaner it is. Everybody, say the rule. (Signal.) *The bigger the forest tree is, the meaner it is.*
- 3 of the trees in the picture are very mean. Make a box around those trees. Raise your hand when you've completed item 1.
  (Observe students and give feedback.)

f. Item 2: Find out which dogs just ate a cake. Here's the rule: Every sitting dog just ate a cake. Everybody, say the rule. (Signal.) *Every sitting dog just ate a cake.*
- A black dog is sitting. Everybody, so did the black dog just eat a cake? (Signal.) *Yes.*
- A spotted dog is running. So we don't know if the spotted dog just ate a cake.
- A brown dog is lying down. So we don't know if the brown dog just ate a cake.
- A gray dog is sitting. Everybody, so did the gray dog just eat a cake? (Signal.) *Yes.*
- A white dog is standing. So we don't know if the white dog just ate a cake.
- Which dogs just ate a cake? Everybody, figure out every dog that just ate a cake. Write the dogs on your paper. Raise your hand when you've completed item 2. (Observe students and give feedback.)

Review Items

g. The rest of the items are review items. I'll read the items. Don't say the answers.
- Item 3: Roots keep a tree from <u>blank</u>.
- Item 4: Roots carry <u>blank</u> to all parts of the tree.
- Item 5: When do trees begin to grow? The choices are **in the winter** and **in the spring.** You'll **underline** one of those choices.
- Item 6: Trees begin to grow when their roots get <u>blank</u>.
- Item 7: Which letter shows where the ground gets warm last?
- Item 8: Which letter shows where the ground gets warm first?

End-of-Lesson Activities

INDEPENDENT WORK

Now finish the written work for lesson 4. Remember, don't look at the story. Start with your worksheet. Then finish the items in your textbook, beginning with item 6. Raise your hand when you're finished. (Observe students and give feedback.)

WORKCHECK

a. (Open Answer Key book to lesson 4 and direct students to take out their marking pencils.)
- We're going to check your independent work. Let's start with your worksheet. Remember, if you got an item wrong, make an **X** next to the item. Don't change any answers.
b. (For each worksheet item: Read the item. Call on a student to answer it. If the answer is wrong, say the correct answer. Refer to the Answer Key for the correct answers.)
c. Now let's check your textbook items.
- (Repeat step b for all textbook items.)
d. Now use your marking pencil to fix up any items you got wrong. Remember, all mistakes must be fixed up before you hand in your independent work.

WRITING-SPELLING

(Present Writing-Spelling lesson 4 after completing Reading lesson 4. See Writing-Spelling Guide.)

Lesson 5

EXERCISE 1
VOCABULARY REVIEW

a. Here's the new vocabulary sentence: You measure your weight in pounds.
- Everybody, say the sentence. Get ready. (Signal.) *You measure your weight in pounds.*
- (Repeat until firm.)

b. What word tells **what you do** to find out how heavy or how long something is? (Signal.) *Measure.*
- What word tells how many pounds something is? (Signal.) *Weight.*
- What **unit** do you use to measure weight? (Signal.) *Pounds.*
- Raise your hand if you know how many pounds you weigh. (Call on different students to tell their weight.)

EXERCISE 2
READING WORDS

Column 1

a. **Find lesson 5 in your textbook.** ✓
- Touch column 1. ✓
- (Teacher reference:)

1. hoof	4. sure
2. hooves	5. fence
3. true	6. agree

b. Word 1 is **hoof.** What word? (Signal.) *Hoof.*
- Spell **hoof.** Get ready. (Tap for each letter.) *H-O-O-F.*

c. Word 2 is **hooves.** What word? (Signal.) *Hooves.*
- Spell **hooves.** Get ready. (Tap for each letter.) *H-O-O-V-E-S.*
- **Hooves** are the kind of feet that deer and horses and cows have. **Hoof** tells about one foot. **Hooves** tells about more than one foot. Who can name another animal that has hooves? (Call on a student. Idea: *Goat, sheep,* etc.)

d. Word 3 is **true.** What word? (Signal.) *True.*
- Spell **true.** Get ready. (Tap for each letter.) *T-R-U-E.*

e. Word 4 is **sure.** What word? (Signal.) *Sure.*
- Spell **sure.** Get ready. (Tap for each letter.) *S-U-R-E.*
- That word has a funny spelling.

f. Word 5 is **fence.** What word? (Signal.) *Fence.*

g. Word 6 is **agree.** What word? (Signal.) *Agree.*

h. Let's read those words again, the fast way.
- Word 1. What word? (Signal.) *Hoof.*
- (Repeat for words 2–6.)

i. (Repeat step h until firm.)

Column 2

j. Find column 2. ✓
- (Teacher reference:)

1. <u>sea</u>sons	4. <u>glow</u>ing
2. <u>camp</u>er	5. <u>grow</u>ing
3. <u>matt</u>er	

- Part of each word is underlined. You'll read that part. Then you'll read the whole word.

k. Word 1. What's the underlined part? (Signal.) *sea.*
- What's the whole word? (Signal.) *Seasons.*
- Word 2. What's the underlined part? (Signal.) *camp.*
- What's the whole word? (Signal.) *Camper.*
- Word 3. What's the underlined part? (Signal.) *matt.*
- What's the whole word? (Signal.) *Matter.*
- Word 4. What's the underlined part? (Signal.) *glow.*
- What's the whole word? (Signal.) *Glowing.*
- Word 5. What's the underlined part? (Signal.) *grow.*
- What's the whole word? (Signal.) *Growing.*

l. Let's read those words again, the fast way.
- Word 1. What word? (Signal.) *Seasons.*
- (Repeat for words 2–5.)

m. (Repeat step l until firm.)

Column 3

n. Find column 3. ✓
- (Teacher reference:)

1. millions	4. knocked
2. greatest	5. meaner
3. blowing	

- All these words have an ending.

o. Word 1. What word? (Signal.) *Millions.*
- (Repeat for words 2–5.)

p. (Repeat step o until firm.)

Column 4

q. Find column 4. ✓
- (Teacher reference:)

1. terrible	4. campfire
2. cheering	5. alive
3. curly	

r. Word 1. What word? (Signal.) *Terrible.*
- (Repeat for words 2–5.)

s. (Repeat step r until firm.)

Column 5

t. Find column 5. ✓
- (Teacher reference:)

1. animals	3. another
2. destroy	4. danger

u. Word 1. What word? (Signal.) *Animals.*
- (Repeat for words 2–4.)

v. (Repeat step u until firm.)

Individual Turns

(For columns 1–5: Call on individual students, each to read one to three words per turn.)

EXERCISE 3
COMPREHENSION PASSAGE

a. Find part B in your textbook. ✓
- In today's story, the trees are afraid of a forest fire. First you'll read the information passage. It gives some facts about forest fires. Remember to follow along.

b. Everybody, touch the title. ✓
- (Call on a student to read the title.) [Forest Fires.]
- Everybody, what's the title? (Signal.) *Forest Fires.*

c. (Call on individual students to read the passage, each student reading two or three sentences at a time. Ask the specified questions as the students read.)

Forest Fires

A forest is a place with lots of tall trees that are close together. The inside of a forest is very dark.

Sometimes, a forest burns. That's called a forest fire.

- Everybody, keep your finger on the word **fire** while I ask questions. What do we call a place where there are lots of tall trees close together? (Signal.) *A forest.*
- Sometimes, something bad happens to forests. Everybody, what's that? (Signal.) *A forest fire.*

Here are facts about forest fires. The danger of a forest fire is greatest in the fall.

- Listen: If the danger is greatest in the fall, in which season would there be the most forest fires? (Signal.) *Fall.*

The danger of a forest fire is not very great in the winter or spring. In these seasons things are wet and trees do not have dry leaves.

The danger of a forest fire is not very great in the summer because the leaves on the trees are alive. So they are not dry.

- Everybody, in the winter is the ground usually wet or dry? (Signal.) *Wet.*
- So are there lots of **dry** leaves on the ground? (Signal.) *No.*
- In the summer are the leaves on the trees alive or dead? (Signal.) *Alive.*

In the fall, the leaves die and become dry. Many dry leaves are on the ground in the fall. So if a small fire starts, it may grow larger as it moves through the dry leaves on the ground. Soon, that fire may leap up into the trees and become a terrible forest fire.

- Everybody, in the summer, are the leaves dead or alive? (Signal.) *Alive.*

- Are they wet or dry? (Signal.) *Wet.*
- In the fall, are the leaves dead or alive? (Signal.) *Dead.*
- Are they wet or dry? (Signal.) *Dry.*
- There are also dry twigs and branches on the ground that burn easily.

> **Forest fires kill wild animals and trees. Large forest fires may burn for weeks. They may destroy millions of trees. And it may take more than 200 years for the forest to grow back.**

- Forest fires kill trees. Everybody, what else do they kill? (Signal.) *Animals.*
- Yes, sometimes animals can't escape from the forest in time and they die in the fire.
- Everybody, about how long could it take for a forest to grow back? (Signal.) *200 years.*
- That's a long time.

EXERCISE 4
WRITTEN ITEMS

a. Everybody, take out a piece of lined paper. ✓
- Write your name at the top of the paper. ✓
- Number your paper from 1 through 15. Remember to skip every other line. Pencils down when you're finished. (Observe students and give feedback.)

b. Find part C in your textbook. ✓
- The questions in part C are about forest fires. I'll read each question and call on someone to answer it. Follow along. Don't write anything until I tell you to write.

c. (For each item: Read the item. Call on a student to answer it.)
- Item 1: In which season is the danger of forest fires greatest? *[Fall.]*
- Item 2: In the fall, are the leaves on trees dead or alive? *[Dead.]*
- Item 3: Are dead leaves wet or dry? *[Dry.]*
- Item 4: In summer, are the leaves on trees dead or alive? *[Alive.]*
- Item 5: Are those leaves wet or dry? *[Wet.]*
- Item 6: A forest fire may burn for blank. What's the answer? *[Weeks.]*
- Item 7: A forest fire kills both blank and blank. What words go in the blanks? *[Plants, animals.]*
- Item 8: About how many years could it take for the forest to grow back? *[200 years.]*

d. Remember, don't look at the passage. Read the items to yourself and answer them. Raise your hand when you've finished part C. (Observe students and give feedback.)

EXERCISE 5
STORY READING

a. Find part D in your textbook. ✓
- This is the second part of the story about Tina, the apple tree. We're going to read this story two times. First you'll read it out loud and make no more than 6 errors. Then I'll read it and ask questions. Remember to follow along when someone else is reading.

b. Everybody, touch the title. ✓
- (Call on a student to read the title.) *[Campers Come into the Forest.]*
- Everybody, who's going to come into the forest in this part of the story? (Signal.) *Campers.*

c. (Call on individual students to read the story, each student reading two or three sentences at a time.)

> - (Correct errors: Tell the word. Direct the student to reread the sentence.)
> - (If the group makes more than 6 errors, direct the students to reread the story.)

d. (After the group has read the selection making no more than 6 errors:) Now I'll read the story and ask questions. Follow along.

> **Campers Come into the Forest**
>
> **Tina was very sad all summer and all fall.**

- Everybody, keep your finger on the word **fall.** Why was she sad during these seasons? (Call on a student. Ideas: *Because the big trees were mean to her; the big trees blocked the sun; the big trees dropped things on her.*)

> **The only thing the big trees let Tina do was sleep when winter came. They went to sleep too. But in the spring when Tina woke up and tried to make little green leaves, the big trees started dropping things and making jokes.**

- Everybody, what was the only season that the big trees didn't bother Tina? (Signal.) *Winter.*
- Why didn't they bother her during the winter? (Call on a student. Idea: *They were sleeping.*)

> "That apple tree doesn't like it when we do <u>this</u>," they would say and then drop something on her.
> Things were bad all spring and all summer.
> On one fall day, the trees were meaner than ever. Tina had made lots of big red apples. The big trees were trying to drop branches on her and knock off her apples.

- The big trees bothered her in the spring and summer. What mean things did they do? (Call on a student. Ideas: *Dropped things on her; blocked her sunlight.*)
- Everybody, what time of year was it when they tried to drop branches to knock off her apples? (Signal.) *Fall.*
- What a mean game.

> They would say, "She doesn't like it when we do <u>this</u>," and they would drop a branch. If the branch knocked off an apple, the big trees would cheer. This game went on until the big trees had no more branches they could let go of. Poor Tina had only three apples left.

- How did the big trees knock off the apples? (Call on a student. Idea: *Dropped branches.*)
- Everybody, every time the big trees knocked off an apple, what would they do? (Signal.) *Cheer.*
- How many apples did Tina end up with? (Signal.) *Three.*
- Why didn't the big trees keep on playing this game until Tina had no apples at all? (Call on a student. Idea: *They had no more branches they could let go of.*)

> Just then three campers came into the forest. They made a fire. The big trees got scared.
> One big tree said, "What is the matter with those campers? Don't they know they should not make fires in the fall?"
> Another big tree said, "Yes, things are dry. And we hate forest fires."
> After a while, the campers put dirt on the fire and started to leave. They didn't see that part of the fire was still glowing.

- Everybody, who made the fire? (Signal.) *Campers.*
- When they left, was the fire out? (Signal.) *No.*
- What was the fire doing? (Call on a student. Ideas: *Glowing; still burning.*)
- What was the danger if that fire started up? (Call on a student. Idea: *It would start a forest fire.*)
- One tree said that things were dry in the forest. That means the forest would burn easily.

> "Oh, no," one of the trees said, as the campers were leaving. "That fire will start up as soon as the wind blows."
> Another tree said, "And it will make a forest fire. And we will burn up."
> **MORE NEXT TIME**

- Everybody, what could make the fire start up? (Signal.) *Wind.*
- What would the fire turn into? (Signal.) *Forest fire.*
- What would happen to all the forest trees? (Call on a student. Idea: *They would burn up.*)
- Look at the picture. ✓

- The trees are talking. What is the first tree saying? (Call on a student.) *["That fire is glowing."]*

- What's the other tree saying? (Call on a student.) *["It will make a forest fire."]*
- You can see Tina. There is a lot of stuff on the ground around her. Why are there so many branches on the ground? (Call on a student. Idea: *Because the big trees were dropping them on Tina.*)
- Everybody, how many apples does she still have? (Signal.) *Three.*

EXERCISE 6
WRITTEN ITEMS
Story Items
a. Find part E in your textbook. ✓
- These questions are about today's story. I'll read each item and call on someone to answer it. Follow along. Don't write anything until I tell you to write.

b. (For each item: Read the item. Call on a student to answer it.)
- Item 9: Did Tina feel happy or sad? *[Sad.]*
- Item 10: What did the big trees do to knock off her apples? *[Dropped branches.]*
- Item 11: How many apples did she have left at the end of the game? *[Three.]*
- Item 12: The big trees didn't knock off the rest of her apples because they didn't have any more <u>blank</u>. What's the answer? *[Things to drop.]*
- Item 13: Who came to the forest at the end of the game? *[Campers.]*
- Item 14: What did the campers make? *[A fire.]*
- Item 15: The big trees saw something the campers did not see. What was that? *[A glowing fire.]*

Skill Items
c. **Find item 1 on your worksheet.** ✓
- To work item 1, you have to use the information the item gives you. Follow along: The bigger the wind, the faster it moves the forest fire. Everybody, say the rule. Get ready. (Signal.) *The bigger the wind, the faster it moves the forest fire.*
- Each picture shows a wind. Circle the 3 pictures that will make fires that move fastest. Raise your hand when you're finished.

(Observe students and give feedback.)

Review Items
d. The rest of the items are review items. I'll read the items. Don't say the answers.
- Item 2: What color are the flowers that apple trees make?
- Item 3: When do those flowers come out?
- Item 4: What grows in each place where there was a flower?
- Item 5: Which has larger branches, an apple tree or a forest tree? You'll underline one of those choices.
- Item 6: Which has a tall straight trunk, an apple tree or a forest tree? You'll underline one of those choices.
- The pictures show the same twig in 4 seasons. For items 7 through 10, you'll write the name of the season below each twig.

End-of-Lesson Activities

INDEPENDENT WORK
Now finish the written work for lesson 5. Remember, don't look at the story. If an item has choices, you underline the right choice. Start with your worksheet. Then finish the items in your textbook, beginning with item 9. Raise your hand when you're finished.

(Observe students and give feedback.)

WORKCHECK
a. (Direct students to take out their marking pencils.)
- We're going to check your worksheet and textbook items. Let's start with your worksheet. Remember, if you got an item wrong, make an **X** next to the item. Don't change any answers.

b. (For each worksheet item: Read the item. Call on a student to answer it. If the answer is wrong, say the correct answer. Refer to the Answer Key for the correct answers.)

c. Now let's check your textbook items.
- (Repeat step b for textbook items.)

d. Now use your marking pencil to fix up any items you got wrong. Remember, all mistakes must be fixed up before you hand in your independent work.

WRITING-SPELLING

(Present Writing-Spelling lesson 5 after completing Reading lesson 5. See Writing-Spelling Guide.)

ACTIVITY

(Present Activity 3 after completing Reading lesson 5. See Activities Across the Curriculum.)

Lessons 6–10 • Planning Page

Looking Ahead

	Lesson 6	Lesson 7	Lesson 8	Lesson 9	Lesson 10
Lesson Events	Vocabulary Review Reading Words Comprehension Passage Story Reading Paired Practice Written Items Independent Work Workcheck Writing-Spelling	**Vocabulary Sentence** Reading Words Vocabulary Review Comprehension Passage Story Reading Paired Practice Written Items Independent Work Workcheck Writing-Spelling	Vocabulary Review Reading Words Comprehension Passage Story Reading Paired Practice Written Items Independent Work Workcheck Writing-Spelling	Vocabulary Review Reading Words Comprehension Passage Story Reading Paired Practice Written Items Independent Work Workcheck Writing-Spelling	Reading Checkouts Test Marking the Test Test Remedies Literature Lesson
Vocabulary Sentence	#1: You <u>measure</u> your <u>weight</u> in <u>pounds</u>.	#2: They <u>waded</u> into the <u>stream</u> to <u>remove</u> <u>tadpoles</u>.	#2: They <u>waded</u> into the <u>stream</u> to <u>remove</u> <u>tadpoles</u>.	#2: They <u>waded</u> into the <u>stream</u> to <u>remove</u> <u>tadpoles</u>.	
Reading Words: Word Types	modeled words compound words mixed words	o-u words c-e words multi-syllable words mixed words	modeled words words with endings c-e words mixed words	modeled words c-e words mixed words	
New Vocabulary	thousand half centimeter garden			ruler thought	
Comprehension Passages	*Camels and Pigs*	*More Facts About Camels*	*Facts About Centimeters*	*Felt-Tipped Pens*	
Story	*Tina is Happy*	*The Camel and the Pig*	*The Camel and the Pig Trade Parts*	*Joe Williams Wants a New Job*	
Skill Items	Deductions Vocabulary sentence	Deductions	Deductions Quotations	Deductions Quotations Vocabulary sentence	Test: Deductions; Vocabulary sentences #1, 2
Special Materials					Thermometer charts, *materials for literature project.
Special Projects/ Activities					

Lesson 6

EXERCISE 1
VOCABULARY REVIEW

a. Here's the new vocabulary sentence: **You measure your weight in pounds.**
  • Everybody, say the sentence. Get ready. (Signal.) *You measure your weight in pounds.*
  • (Repeat until firm.)
b. What word tells how many pounds something is? (Signal.) *Weight.*
  • What word tells **what you do** to find out how heavy or how long something is? (Signal.) *Measure.*
  • What **unit** do you use to measure weight? (Signal.) *Pounds.*
  • Raise your hand if you know how many pounds you weigh. (Call on different students to tell their weight.)

EXERCISE 2
READING WORDS

Column 1
a. **Find lesson 6 in your textbook.** ✓
  • Touch column 1. ✓
  • (Teacher reference:)

  1. thousand   4. half
  2. should   5. centimeter
  3. touch   6. remove

b. Word 1 is **thousand.** What word? (Signal.) *Thousand.*
  • Spell **thousand.** Get ready. (Tap for each letter.) *T-H-O-U-S-A-N-D.*
  • A thousand is equal to ten hundreds. Everybody, what's another way of saying **ten hundred cars?** (Signal.) *A thousand cars.*
  • What's another way of saying **ten hundred dogs?** (Signal.) *A thousand dogs.*
c. Word 2 is **should.** What word? (Signal.) *Should.*
  • Spell **should.** Get ready. (Tap for each letter.) *S-H-O-U-L-D.*
d. Word 3 is **touch.** What word? (Signal.) *Touch.*
  • Spell **touch.** Get ready. (Tap for each letter.) *T-O-U-C-H.*

e. Word 4 is **half.** What word? (Signal.) *Half.*
  • Spell **half.** Get ready. (Tap for each letter.) *H-A-L-F.*
  • If you cut something in half, you get two pieces that are the same size. Each piece is half. Everybody, if you cut something into two pieces that are the same size, what do we call each piece? (Signal.) *Half.*
f. Word 5 is **centimeter.** What word? (Signal.) *Centimeter.*
  • Centimeters are used to tell how long things are. You'll read more about centimeters.
g. Word 6 is **remove.** What word? (Signal.) *Remove.*
h. Let's read those words again, the fast way.
  • Word 1. What word? (Signal.) *Thousand.*
  • (Repeat for words 2–6.)
i. (Repeat step h until firm.)

Column 2
j. Find column 2. ✓
  • (Teacher reference:)

  1. <u>camp</u>fire   4. <u>sun</u>shine
  2. <u>some</u>thing   5. <u>with</u>out
  3. <u>any</u>thing

  • Each of these words is a compound word. A compound word is actually two words stuck together. The first part of each word is underlined.
k. Word 1. What's the underlined part? (Signal.) *camp.*
  • What's the whole word? (Signal.) *Campfire.*
l. Word 2. What's the underlined part? (Signal.) *some.*
  • What's the whole word? (Signal.) *Something.*
m. Word 3. What's the underlined part? (Signal.) *any.*
  • What's the whole word? (Signal.) *Anything.*
n. Word 4. What's the underlined part? (Signal.) *sun.*

- What's the whole word? (Signal.) *Sunshine.*
o. Word 5. What's the underlined part? (Signal.) *with.*
- What's the whole word? (Signal.) *Without.*
p. Let's read those words again.
- Word 1. What word? (Signal.) *Campfire.*
- (Repeat for: **2. something, 3. anything, 4. sunshine, 5. without.**)
q. (Repeat step p until firm.)

Column 3

r. Find column 3. ✓
- (Teacher reference:)

1. garden	4. shame
2. shout	5. flames
3. proud	6. waded

s. Word 1. What word? (Signal.) *Garden.*
- A garden is a place where you grow flowers or vegetables. Everybody, what do we call a place where you grow flowers or vegetables? (Signal.) *Garden.*
- Word 2. What word? (Signal.) *Shout.*
- (Repeat for words 3–6.)
t. Let's read those words again.
- Word 1. What word? (Signal.) *Garden.*
- (Repeat for words 2–6.)
u. (Repeat step t until firm.)

Column 4

v. Find column 4. ✓
- (Teacher reference:)

1. agree	4. bonk
2. true	5. hoof
3. camel	6. stream

w. Word 1. What word? (Signal.) *Agree.*
- Word 2. What word? (Signal.) *True.*
- Word 3. What word? (Signal.) *Camel.*
- You'll learn about camels in today's lesson.
- Word 4. What word? (Signal.) *Bonk.*
- Word 5. What word? (Signal.) *Hoof.*
- Word 6. What word? (Signal.) *Stream.*
x. Let's read those words again.
- Word 1. What word? (Signal.) *Agree.*
- (Repeat for words 2–6.)
y. (Repeat step x until firm.)

Column 5

z. Find column 5. ✓
- (Teacher reference:)

1. hump	4. fence
2. hooves	5. sure
3. curly	6. tadpole

a. Word 1. What word? (Signal.) *Hump.*
- (Repeat for words 2–6.)
b. (Repeat step a until firm.)

Individual Turns

(For columns 1–5: Call on individual students, each to read one to three words per turn.)

EXERCISE 3

COMPREHENSION PASSAGE

a. Find part B in your textbook. ✓
- You're going to read an information passage about camels and pigs. Remember to follow along. ✓
b. Everybody, touch the title. ✓
- (Call on a student to read the title.) [*Camels and Pigs.*]
- Everybody, what's the title? (Signal.) *Camels and Pigs.*
c. (Call on individual students to read the passage, each student reading two or three sentences at a time. Ask the specified questions as the students read.)

Camels and Pigs

In the next lesson, you'll read about a camel and a pig. Camels and pigs are the same in some ways and different in some ways. Both camels and pigs have hooves.

Here's a pig's hoof.   Here's a camel's hoof.

- How are the camel's feet and the pig's feet the same? (Call on a student. Idea: *They are both hooves.*)
- Everybody, do dogs and cats have hooves? (Signal.) *No.*
- What other animals have hooves? (Call on individual students. Ideas: *Goats, cows, horses, moose, deer*, etc.)

36 Lesson 6

The pig's nose and the camel's nose are different.
Which animal has this nose?

• Everybody, which animal does the first nose belong to? (Signal.) *Camel.*

Which animal has this nose?

• Everybody, what's the answer? (Signal.) *Pig.*

The back of each animal is different. One of the animals has a large hump on its back.

• Everybody, which animal does the first back belong to? (Signal.) *Pig.*
• Which animal has the hump? (Signal.) *Camel.*
• Some camels have two humps, but all camels have humps.

A camel's tail and a pig's tail are different. One animal has a long tail. The other animal has a short curly tail.

• Everybody, who has the long tail? (Signal.) *Camel.*
• And the pig has a short curly tail.

One of the animals is very big and the other animal is much, much smaller. Here they are, side by side.

• Everybody, which animal is a lot bigger? (Signal.) *Camel.*
• You'll read more about the differences in the next lesson.

EXERCISE 4
STORY READING
a. Find part C in your textbook. ✓
• This is the last part of the story about Tina, the apple tree. We're going to read this story two times. First you'll read it out loud and make no more than 6 errors. Then I'll read it and ask questions. Remember to follow along when someone else is reading.
b. Everybody, touch the title. ✓
• (Call on a student to read the title.) [*Tina Is Happy.*]
• Everybody, how will Tina feel in this story? (Signal.) *Happy.*
c. (Call on individual students to read the story, each student reading two or three sentences at a time.)

• (Correct errors: Tell the word. Direct the student to reread the sentence.)
• (If the group makes more than 6 errors, direct the students to reread the story.)

d. (After the group has read the selection making no more than 6 errors:)
Now I'll read the story and ask questions. Follow along.

Tina Is Happy

The trees were afraid of a forest fire. A campfire was glowing, and it would make flames as soon as the wind started blowing. The campers who made the fire were leaving. As they walked away, the big trees shouted at each other, "Drop something on those campers. Make them stop and go back."

• The trees wanted to drop something on the campers so they would stop and look around. Everybody, what did the trees hope the campers would see if they looked around? (Signal.) *The fire.*
• And if they saw it, they would put it out.

But the trees didn't have anything to drop. They had dropped all their old branches and leaves on Tina. The campers were now walking under Tina's branches.
The big trees called, "Tina, save us. Save us. Drop something on those campers."

Lesson 6 37

> "Yes," a big tree said, "if you save us we'll be good to you for 100 years."

- What did they want Tina to do? (Call on a student. Idea: *Drop something on the campers.*)
- Everybody, how long did they say they would be good to her if she helped them out? (Signal.) *100 years.*
- That's not even a whole lifetime for some trees, but it's a pretty long time.

> Tina hated to drop her only three apples, but she did. They landed on the campers: bonk, bonk, bonk. The campers stopped and bent over to pick up the apples.

- Listen to that part again:
   Tina hated to drop her only three apples, but she did. They landed on the campers: bonk, bonk, bonk. The campers stopped and bent over to pick up the apples.
- What was that bonk, bonk, bonk sound? (Call on a student. Idea: *Apples hitting campers.*)
- What did the campers do after the apples landed on them? (Call on a student. Idea: *Stopped and bent over to pick up the apples.*)

> One of the campers looked back at the fire and said, "We didn't put out that fire. Shame on us."
> They went back and made sure that the fire was out before they left.

- How do you think Tina and the other trees felt when the campers put out that fire? (Call on a student. Idea: *Relieved.*)

> So now, Tina is happy. The big trees don't drop things on her. In the spring those trees bend far to the side so the sun can reach Tina. Tina can make green leaves and pretty white flowers. If one of the big trees holds a branch out and keeps the sun from reaching her, the other big trees say, "Hey, move your branch. You're taking Tina's sunshine."

- Everybody, how does Tina feel now? (Signal.) *Happy.*
- Did the big trees keep their promise about being nice to her? (Signal.) *Yes.*
- What would they do in the spring to make sure she had plenty of sunshine? (Call on a student. Idea: *Bend far to the side.*)
- And if one of the trees forgot, what would the other trees tell that tree? (Call on a student. Ideas: *Move your branches; you're taking Tina's sunshine.*)

> And in the fall, those trees are very proud when Tina makes apples—lots and lots of big red apples. "Look at all those apples," they say. "And we helped her make them. Good for us."
> Those big trees agree about how much Tina did for them. They say, "Tina gave up her only three apples to save us, so we love that little apple tree."
> THE END

- Everybody, find the story picture on page 35.
- Does this picture show the way things were **earlier** or the way they are **now?** (Signal.) *Now.*
- One of the big trees is saying something to another tree. What's it saying? (Call on a student.) *["Hey, stop taking Tina's sunshine."]*
- Everybody, what season is shown in this picture? (Signal.) *Spring.*
- How do you know it's spring? (Call on a student. Idea: *Tina has white flowers.*)
- Everybody looks pretty happy.

EXERCISE 5

PAIRED PRACTICE

a. As part of most lessons, you're going to work in pairs.

- (Assign an **A** member and a **B** member in each pair.)
- (After assigning all students:)
- All **A** members raise your hand. ✓
- All **B** members raise your hand. ✓
- (Repeat until firm.)

b. You're going to read aloud to your partner. Today, the **A** member of each pair will read first. Then the **B** member will read.
- The **A** members will read from the beginning of the title to the star in the story. Everybody, touch that star. ✓
- The **B** members will start at the star and read to the moon. Everybody, touch the moon. ✓

c. Here are the rules: The student who is not reading follows along. If there is a mistake, that student points out the error and tells the correct word. If there is a problem, raise your hand, and I'll help you out.
- **A** members, start reading. Raise your hand when you've read to the star. (Observe students and give feedback.)
- (Direct **B** members to read from the star to the moon. Praise teams that follow the rules.)

EXERCISE 6
WRITTEN ITEMS

Comprehension Passage Items

a. Find part D in your textbook. ✓
- The questions in part D are about camels and pigs. I'll call on different students to read the items and say the answers. Follow along. Don't write anything until I tell you to write.

b. (For each item: Call on a student to read and answer the item.)

c. (Teacher reference:)

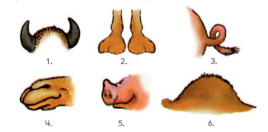

- Read what it says above item 1. *[Some of these parts belong to a cow. Some of them belong to a camel. And some belong to a pig. Write the name of the animal that has the part shown in each picture.]*

- Item 1. What animal? *[Cow.]*
- Item 2. What animal? *[Camel.]*
- Item 3. What animal? *[Pig.]*
- Item 4. What animal? *[Camel.]*
- Item 5. What animal? *[Pig.]*
- Item 6. What animal? *[Camel.]*
- Item 7. *[Which is bigger, a camel or a pig? Camel.]*
- Item 8. *[Which has a longer tail, a camel or a pig? Camel.]*

Story Items

a. Find part E in your textbook. ✓
- The questions in part E are about today's story. Follow along. Don't write anything until I tell you to write.

b. (For each item: Call on a student to read and answer the item.)
- Item 9. *[The big trees didn't drop something on the campers because they didn't have any more things to drop.]*
- Item 10. *[The big trees wanted someone to help them. Who was that? Tina.]*
- Item 11. *[The big trees told Tina that they would be good to her for 100 years.]*
- Item 12. *[How many apples did Tina have before she dropped some? Three.]*
- Item 13. *[How many apples did she drop? Three.]*
- Item 14. *[What did one camper see when he was picking up an apple? The campfire.]*
- Item 15. *[Did the campers put out the fire? Yes.]*
- Item 16. *[Do the big trees still do mean things to Tina? No.]*
- Item 17. *[Write the letters for the 2 things the big trees do to make sure that Tina gets lots of sunshine. A, D.]*

Skill Items

c. **Find item 1 on your worksheet.** ✓
- (Teacher reference:)

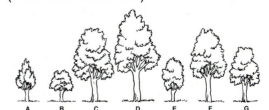

Lesson 6 39

- To work items 1 and 2, you have to use the information above item 1. Follow along: The more sunlight the tree gets, the faster the tree grows. Everybody, say the rule. Get ready. (Signal.) *The more sunlight the tree gets, the faster the tree grows.*
- The trees in the picture are the same age. Item 1: Circle the one tree that got the most sunlight. Do it now. Mark just one tree. Pencils down when you're finished.
  (Observe students and give feedback.)
- Item 2: Cross out the one tree that got the least sunlight. Do it now. Mark just one tree. Pencils down when you're finished.
  (Observe students and give feedback.)

d. The sentence above item 3 says: You measure your weight in pounds. Items 3 through 5 refer to that sentence.
- Item 3: What one word tells what you do to find out how heavy or long something is? Everybody, what word?
  (Signal.) *Measure.*
- Item 4: What one word tells how many pounds something is? Everybody, what word? (Signal.) *Weight.*
- Item 5: What one word names the unit you use to measure weight? Everybody, what word? (Signal.) *Pounds.*

Review Items

e. The rest of the items are review items from other lessons.

End-of-Lesson Activities

INDEPENDENT WORK

Now finish the independent work for lesson 6. Do the worksheet first. For the textbook items, you'll write your answers on your lined paper. Raise your hand when you've finished the worksheet and textbook for lesson 6.
(Observe students and give feedback.)

WORKCHECK

a. (Direct students to take out their marking pencils.)
- We're going to check your worksheet and textbook items. Let's start with your worksheet. Remember, if you got an item wrong, make an **X** next to the item. Don't change any answers.
b. (For each worksheet item: Read the item. Call on a student to answer it. If the answer is wrong, say the correct answer. Refer to the Answer Key for the correct answers.)
c. Now let's check your textbook items.
- (Repeat step b for textbook items.)
d. Now use your marking pencil to fix up any items you got wrong. Remember, all mistakes must be fixed up before you hand in your independent work.

WRITING-SPELLING

(Present Writing-Spelling lesson 6 after completing Reading lesson 6. See Writing-Spelling Guide.)

Lesson 7

EXERCISE 1

VOCABULARY

a. **Find page 338 in your textbook.** ✓
   - Touch sentence 2. ✓
   - This is a new vocabulary sentence. It says: They waded into the stream to remove tadpoles. Everybody, read that sentence. Get ready. (Signal.) *They waded into the stream to remove tadpoles.*
   - Close your eyes and say the sentence. Get ready. (Signal.) *They waded into the stream to remove tadpoles.*
   - (Repeat until firm.)
b. Listen: They waded into the stream to remove tadpoles. When you **wade,** you walk in water that is not very deep.
c. The sentence says they removed something. What did they remove? (Signal.) *Tadpoles.*
d. When you **remove** something, you get rid of it or take it away. What did they get rid of or take away? (Signal.) *Tadpoles.*
e. Tadpoles are **baby toads or frogs.** What are tadpoles? (Signal.) *Baby toads or frogs.*
f. Listen to the sentence again: They waded into the stream to remove tadpoles. Everybody, say the sentence. Get ready. (Signal.) *They waded into the stream to remove tadpoles.*
g. What word tells that they walked through water that was not very deep? (Signal.) *Waded.*
   - What word tells that they got rid of something? (Signal.) *Remove.*
   - What's the name of baby toads or frogs? (Signal.) *Tadpoles.*
   - (Repeat step g until firm.)

EXERCISE 2

Note: Pronounce **ce** as in **ice; ou** as in **out; ir** as in **sir.**

READING WORDS

Column 1

a. Find lesson 7 in your textbook. ✓
   - Touch column 1. ✓
   - (Teacher reference:)

| 1. ce | 2. ou | 3. ir |

   - Each of these letter combinations usually makes a particular sound in words.
   - Combination 1 is **C-E.** It usually says **sss.**
b. Your turn. Tell me the sound for each combination.
   - Combination 1. What sound? (Signal.) *sss.*
   - Combination 2. What sound? (Signal.) *ow.*
   - Combination 3. What sound? (Signal.) *er.*
   - (Repeat step b until firm.)

Column 2

c. Find column 2. ✓
   - (Teacher reference:)

1. ground	4. race
2. pound	5. place
3. around	6. fence

   - The letters **O-U** make the sound **ow** in the first words.
d. Spell word 1. Get ready. (Tap for each letter.) *G-R-O-U-N-D.*
   - What word? (Signal.) *Ground.*
e. The next words rhyme with **ground.**
   - Word 2. What word? (Signal.) *Pound.*
   - Word 3. What word? (Signal.) *Around.*
f. The rest of the words have the letters **C-E.** Those letters usually make the sound **sss.**
g. Word 4. What word? (Signal.) *Race.*
   - (Repeat for words 5 and 6.)
h. Let's read those words again.
   - Word 1. What word? (Signal.) *Ground.*
   - (Repeat for words 2–6.)
i. (Repeat step h until firm.)

Lesson 7   41

Column 3

j. Find column 3. ✓
- (Teacher reference:)

> 1. <u>in</u>side   3. <u>ugli</u>est
> 2. <u>with</u>out   4. <u>touch</u>ing

- Part of each word is underlined. You'll read that part. Then you'll read the whole word.

k. Word 1. What's the underlined part? (Signal.) *in.*
- What's the whole word? (Signal.) *Inside.*

l. Word 2. What's the underlined part? (Signal.) *with.*
- What's the whole word? (Signal.) *Without.*

m. Word 3. What's the underlined part? (Signal.) *ugli.*
- What's the whole word? (Signal.) *Ugliest.*

n. Word 4. What's the underlined part? (Signal.) *touch.*
- What's the whole word? (Signal.) *Touching.*

o. Let's read those words again, the fast way.
- Word 1. What word? (Signal.) *Inside.*
- (Repeat for words 2–4.)

p. (Repeat step o until firm.)

Column 4

q. Find column 4. ✓
- (Teacher reference:)

> 1. sure   4. right
> 2. easy   5. half
> 3. should

r. Word 1. What word? (Signal.) *Sure.*
- (Repeat for words 2–5.)

s. (Repeat step r until firm.)

Column 5

t. Find column 5. ✓
- (Teacher reference:)

> 1. thousand   4. garden
> 2. promise   5. people
> 3. centimeter

u. Word 1. What word? (Signal.) *Thousand.*
- (Repeat for words 2–5.)

v. (Repeat step u until firm.)

Individual Turns

(For columns 1–5: Call on individual students, each to read one to three words per turn.)

EXERCISE 3
VOCABULARY REVIEW

a. Here's the new vocabulary sentence: They waded into the stream to remove tadpoles.
- Everybody, say the sentence. Get ready. (Signal.) *They waded into the stream to remove tadpoles.*
- (Repeat until firm.)

b. What word tells that they got rid of something? (Signal.) *Remove.*
- What word tells that they walked through water that was not very deep? (Signal.) *Waded.*
- What's the name of baby toads or frogs? (Signal.) *Tadpoles.*

EXERCISE 4
COMPREHENSION PASSAGE

a. Find part B in your textbook. ✓
- You're going to read a story about a camel and a pig. First you'll read the information passage. It gives some more facts about camels. Remember to follow along.

b. Everybody, touch the title. ✓
- (Call on a student to read the title.) [*More Facts About Camels.*]
- Everybody, what will you learn more about in this selection? (Signal.) *Camels.*

c. (Call on individual students to read the passage, each student reading two or three sentences at a time. Ask the specified questions as students read.)

> **More Facts About Camels**
>
> In today's lesson, you'll read about camels and pigs. Here are some facts about camels.
> Most camels live in places that are very dry. Sometimes there is no rain for years in these places.
> The camels work like trucks that carry things.

- You can see a picture of a camel carrying a big load and going across a sandy desert. Remember, it may not rain in a place like this for years.

> **Camels do a good job because they can go for ten days without drinking water.**

- Everybody, how long can a camel go without drinking water? (Signal.) *Ten days.*
- Humans can't live on the desert for more than a few hours without drinking water.

> **That's because they can drink a lot of water at one time and store that water in their body. A camel that is 1 thousand pounds can drink as much as 250 pounds of water at one time.**

- Camels can drink an amazing amount of water at one time. Everybody, how much water could a 1000-pound camel drink at one time? (Signal.) *250 pounds.*
- That would be like a 100-pound human drinking 50 glasses of water at one time.

> **The hooves of camels are very wide and flat, so these hooves don't sink in the sand.**

- Why don't camels' hooves sink into the sand? (Call on a student. Idea: *They're very wide and flat.*)

> **Some people ride camels the way we ride horses, and people even have camel races.**

- You can see a picture of a camel race. Camels can run quite fast, nearly as fast as race horses.

EXERCISE 5

STORY READING

a. Find part C in your textbook. ✓
- This is the first part of a new story. You'll read this part today. You'll read the other part in the next lesson.
- We're going to read this story two times. First you'll read it out loud and make no more than 6 errors. Then I'll read it and ask questions. Remember to follow along when someone else is reading.

b. Everybody, touch the title. ✓
- (Call on a student to read the title.) [*The Camel and the Pig.*]
- Everybody, what's the title? (Signal.) *The Camel and the Pig.*
- Everybody, what animals will be in this story? (Signal.) *Camel and Pig.*

c. (Call on individual students to read the story, each student reading two or three sentences at a time.)

- (Correct errors: Tell the word. Direct the student to reread the sentence.)
- (If the group makes more than 6 errors, direct the students to reread the story.)

d. (After the group has read the selection making no more than 6 errors:) Now I'll read the story and ask questions. Follow along.

> **The Camel and the Pig**
>
> Is it better to be tall or better to be short? A pig and a camel did not agree. The camel said, "It is easy to see that it is better to be tall."
>
> "No, that is not true," the pig said. "It is far better to be short than to be tall."
>
> Soon, the camel and the pig were yelling at each other. "It's better to be tall," the camel shouted.
>
> "No way," the pig shouted. "Short is better, better, better."

- Everybody, which two animals were arguing? (Signal.) *Camel and pig.*
- Which animal was short? (Signal.) *Pig.*
- Did the pig argue that it was better to be **tall** or better to be **short?** (Signal.) *Short.*

> **At last a cow became tired of all this shouting and yelling. She said to the camel, "If tall is better, you should be able to show us why it is better." Then she said to the pig, "If short is better, you should be able to show us why it is better." Then the cow said, "If you do not win, you must give something to the one who wins."**

- Everybody, who tried to settle the argument between the pig and the camel? (Signal.) *Cow.*
- The cow said that if short is better, the pig should be able to show that short is better. And if the pig shows that short is better, who would win? (Signal.) *Pig.*

Lesson 7 43

- And what would the camel have to do if the pig wins? (Call on a student. Idea: *Give something to the pig.*)

> The camel said, "I am so sure that I am right, I will give the pig my hump if I do not win."
> The pig said, "And I am so sure I am right, I will give up my nose and my tail."

- Everybody, what was the camel willing to give up? (Signal.) *Hump.*
- What was the pig willing to give up? (Signal.) *Nose and tail.*

> So the camel and the pig went out to see who was right. They came to a garden with a fence around it. Inside were good things to eat.
> The camel said, "I am tall. So it is easy for me to reach over the top and eat all I want." And she ate and ate and ate.
> The pig did not eat because she could not reach over the fence.
> **MORE NEXT TIME**

- Somebody showed that she was right. Everybody, who was that? (Signal.) *Camel.*
- The pig agreed to give up something if she was wrong. Everybody, what was that? (Signal.) *Nose and tail.*
- We'll see what happens next time.

EXERCISE 6
PAIRED PRACTICE

a. You're going to work in pairs.
- All **A** members raise your hand. ✓
- All **B** members raise your hand. ✓
- (Repeat until firm.)

b. Today, the **B** member of each pair will read first. The **B** member will read from the beginning of the title to the star in the middle of the story. Everybody, touch that star. ✓
- The **A** members will read from the star to the end of the story.

c. Remember the rules: The student who is not reading follows along. If there is a mistake, that student points out the error and tells the correct word. If there is a problem, raise your hand, and I'll help you out.

- **B** members, start reading. Raise your hand when you've read to the star. (Observe students and give feedback.)
- (As **B** members complete their reading, direct **A** members to read from the star to the end of the story. Praise teams that follow the rules.)

EXERCISE 7
WRITTEN ITEMS

Comprehension Passage Items

a. Find part D in your textbook. ✓
- The questions in part D are about camels. I'll call on different students to read the items and say the answers. Follow along. Don't write anything until I tell you to write.

b. (For each item: Call on a student to read and answer the item.)
- Item 1. [*Camel hooves keep camels from sinking in sand. How are camel hooves different from pig hooves? They are wider and flatter.*]
- Item 2. [*Are camels used more in wet places or dry places? Dry places.*]
- Item 3. [*Camels can go for <u>ten</u> days without drinking water.*]
- Item 4. [*How many pounds of water can a 1 thousand-pound camel drink at one time? <u>250</u> pounds.*]

Story Items

c. The questions in part E are about today's story.
- Item 5. [*What's the title of this story? The Camel and the Pig.*]
- Item 6. [*Which animal believed that tall was better? Camel.*]
- Item 7. [*Which animal believed that short was better? Pig.*]
- Item 8. [*Which animal got tired of the yelling and shouting? Cow.*]
- Item 9. [*What did the camel agree to give up if she was not right? Hump.*]
- Item 10. [*What did the pig agree to give up if she was not right? Nose, tail.*]
- Item 11. [*Which animal was able to eat at the garden? Camel.*]
- Item 12. [*Why was she able to eat from the garden? She could reach over the fence.*]

Skill Items

d. **Find item 1 on your worksheet.** ✓
- (Teacher reference:)

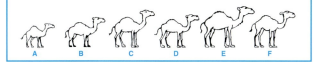

- To work items 1 and 2, you have to use the information the item gives you. Follow along: The bigger the camel, the more water it can drink. Everybody, say the rule. Get ready. (Signal.) *The bigger the camel, the more water it can drink.*
- The pictures show different camels. Item 1: Circle the one camel that can drink the most water. Do it now. Mark just one camel. Pencils down when you're finished.
(Observe students and give feedback.)
- Item 2: Cross out the one camel that can drink the least water. Mark just one camel. Pencils down when you're finished.
(Observe students and give feedback.)

Review Items

e. The rest of the items are review items from other lessons.

End-of-Lesson Activities

INDEPENDENT WORK

Now finish the independent work for lesson 7. Do the worksheet first. If an item has choices, you **underline** the right choice. For the textbook items, you'll write your answers on your lined paper. Raise your hand when you've finished the worksheet and textbook for lesson 7.
(Observe students and give feedback.)

WORKCHECK

a. (Direct students to take out their marking pencils.)
- We're going to check your worksheet and textbook items. Let's start with your worksheet. Remember, if you got an item wrong, make an **X** next to the item. Don't change any answers.
b. (For each worksheet item: Read the item. Call on a student to answer it. If the answer is wrong, say the correct answer. Refer to the Answer Key for the correct answers.)
c. Now let's check your textbook items.
- (Repeat step b for textbook items.)
d. Now use your marking pencil to fix up any items you got wrong. Remember, all mistakes must be fixed up before you hand in your independent work.

WRITING-SPELLING

(Present Writing-Spelling lesson 7 after completing Reading lesson 7. See Writing-Spelling Guide.)

Lesson 8

EXERCISE 1
VOCABULARY REVIEW

a. Here's the new vocabulary sentence: They waded into the stream to remove tadpoles.
- Everybody, say the sentence. Get ready. (Signal.) *They waded into the stream to remove tadpoles.*
- (Repeat until firm.)

b. What's the name of baby toads or frogs? (Signal.) *Tadpoles.*
- What word tells that they walked through water that was not very deep? (Signal.) *Waded.*
- What word tells that they got rid of something? (Signal.) *Remove.*

EXERCISE 2
READING WORDS

Column 1

a. Find lesson 8 in your textbook. ✓
- Touch column 1. ✓
- (Teacher reference:)

1. writing	3. apartment
2. William	4. construction

b. Word 1 is **writing.** What word? (Signal.) *Writing.*
c. Word 2 is a name: **William.** What name? (Signal.) *William.*
d. Word 3 is **apartment.** What word? (Signal.) *Apartment.*
e. Word 4 is **construction.** What word? (Signal.) *Construction.*
f. Let's read those words again, the fast way.
- Word 1. What word? (Signal.) *Writing.*
- (Repeat for words 2–4.)
g. (Repeat step f until firm.)

Column 2

h. Find column 2. ✓
- (Teacher reference:)

1. ugliest	4. without
2. pencils	5. centimeters
3. touching	6. tadpoles

- All these words have an ending.
i. Word 1. What word? (Signal.) *Ugliest.*
- (Repeat for words 2–6.)
j. (Repeat step i until firm.)

Column 3

k. Find column 3. ✓
- (Teacher reference:)

1. cent	4. races
2. chances	5. dances
3. faces	

- These are words that have the letters **C-E.** What sound do those letters usually make? (Signal.) *sss.*
- You'll spell each word and tell me the word.
l. Spell word 1. Get ready. (Tap for each letter.) *C-E-N-T.*
- What word did you spell? (Signal.) *Cent.*
m. Spell word 2. Get ready. (Tap for each letter.) *C-H-A-N-C-E-S.*
- What word did you spell? (Signal.) *Chances.*
n. Spell word 3. Get ready. (Tap for each letter.) *F-A-C-E-S.*
- What word did you spell? (Signal.) *Faces.*
o. Spell word 4. Get ready. (Tap for each letter.) *R-A-C-E-S.*
- What word did you spell? (Signal.) *Races.*
p. Spell word 5. Get ready. (Tap for each letter.) *D-A-N-C-E-S.*
- What word did you spell? (Signal.) *Dances.*
q. Let's read those words again.
- Word 1. What word? (Signal.) *Cent.*
- (Repeat for words 2–5.)
r. (Repeat step q until firm.)

Column 4
s. Find column 4. ✓
- (Teacher reference:)

1. half	4. peeking
2. eaten	5. promise
3. both	6. remove

t. Word 1. What word? (Signal.) *Half.*
- (Repeat for words 2–6.)

u. (Repeat step t until firm.)

Column 5
v. Find column 5. ✓
- (Teacher reference:)

1. erase	4. shaft
2. eraser	5. tipped
3. ink	6. cloth

w. Word 1. What word? (Signal.) *Erase.*
- (Repeat for words 2–6.)

x. (Repeat step w until firm.)

Individual Turns
(For columns 1–5: Call on individual students, each to read one to three words per turn.)

EXERCISE 3
COMPREHENSION PASSAGE

a. Find part B in your textbook. ✓
- The information passage in today's lesson gives some facts about centimeters.

b. Everybody, touch the title. ✓
- (Call on a student to read the title.) [Facts About Centimeters.]
- Everybody, what's the title? (Signal.) *Facts About Centimeters.*

c. (Call on individual students to read the passage, each student reading two or three sentences at a time. Ask the specified questions as students read.)

> **Facts About Centimeters**
>
> The story you're going to read tells about centimeters. Here are facts about centimeters:
> Centimeters are used to tell how long things are.
> Inches also tell how long things are. An inch is longer than a centimeter.

- Which is longer, an inch or a centimeter? (Signal.) *Inch.*

> **Here's an inch:** ─────────
> **Here's a centimeter:** ───
> **Hold up your fingers and show your teacher how long an inch is.**

- Everybody, do it. Put your fingers around the inch and hold up your fingers to show me a space that is one inch long. (Demonstrate by putting a finger at each end of the inch line. Observe students and give feedback.)

> **Now show your teacher how long a centimeter is.**

- Everybody, do it. Show me a centimeter. (Demonstrate by putting a finger at each end of the centimeter line. Observe students and give feedback.)
- Once more: Show me an inch. (Observe students and give feedback.)
- Show me a centimeter. (Observe students and give feedback.)
- Remember an inch is longer than a centimeter.

EXERCISE 4
STORY READING

a. Find part C in your textbook. ✓
- This is the last part of the story about the camel and the pig.
- We're going to read this story two times. First you'll read it out loud and make no more than 8 errors. Then I'll read it and ask questions. Remember to follow along when someone else is reading.

b. Everybody, touch the title. ✓
- (Call on a student to read the title.) [The Camel and the Pig Trade Parts.]
- Everybody, what are the pig and the camel going to do in this story? (Signal.) *Trade parts.*

c. (Call on individual students to read the story, each student reading one or two sentences at a time.)

- (Correct errors: Tell the word. Direct the student to reread the sentence.)
- (If the group makes more than 8 errors, direct the students to reread the story.)

d. (After the group has read the selection making no more than 8 errors:)

Now I'll read the story and ask questions. Follow along:

The Camel and the Pig Trade Parts

The camel had just eaten from a garden. The cow said, "The camel showed that tall is better."

"No," the pig said. "There is another garden down the road. We must go there and I will show you that short is better."

So the camel and the pig and the cow went to the next garden. It had a very high wall, with a hole near the ground. The pig went in the hole and ate good things that were in the garden. The camel didn't eat because the wall was too high.

When the pig came back from the garden, the cow said, "Well, the pig showed that short is better."

- Everybody, at the first garden, which animal won? (Signal.) *Camel.*
- At the next garden, which animal won? (Signal.) *Pig.*
- How did the pig get into that garden? (Call on a student. Idea: *Through a hole near the ground.*)
- Why didn't the camel go through that hole? (Call on a student. Ideas: *The hole was near the ground; the camel was too tall to get through the hole.*)
- Why didn't the camel reach over the wall? (Call on a student. Idea: *The wall was too high.*)

"I win," the pig said.

"No, I win," the camel said.

The cow said to the camel, "The pig showed you that short is better. You agreed to give up your hump. So give it up."

Then the cow said to the pig, "The camel showed you that tall is better. You agreed to give up your nose and your tail. So give them to the camel."

The camel and the pig were very sad, but they did what they promised they would do.

- Both of the animals lost. Everybody, what did the pig have to give up? (Signal.) *Nose and tail.*
- What did the camel have to give up? (Signal.) *Hump.*
- Did the animals do what they promised they would do? (Signal.) *Yes.*

The pig got a great big hump. The camel got a pig's nose and a pig's tail.

The pig looked at the camel and said, "You look bad. That nose and tail don't fit you at all. And you look silly without a hump."

The camel said to the pig, "You don't even have a nose or a tail, and you've got a hump that is bigger than the rest of you."

The cow said, "I will let both of you take back the things you gave up, but you must promise not to yell and fight anymore."

- The cow told the animals that they could take back their parts if they agreed to do something. What's that? (Call on a student. Idea: *Promise not to yell and fight any more.*)

The camel and the pig agreed.

So the camel took back her hump and the pig took back her nose and tail. Then the cow said, "You both look a lot better. And I'm glad that we will not have to hear any more talk about tall and short."

The pig said, "I agree that it is better to be tall some times, but most of the time short is way better than tall."

The camel said, "Not true. Most of the time it's better to be tall than short."

"Oh, no," the cow said and walked away.

THE END

- Everybody, did the camel and the pig keep their promise about not arguing? (Signal.) *No.*
- The pig agreed that tall is better some times, but what did the pig think was better most of the time? (Signal.) *Short.*
- And what did the camel think was better most of the time? (Signal.) *Tall.*
- Find the story picture on page 47. ✓

- The picture shows the camel and the pig with the wrong parts. Who do you think looks funnier?
  (Call on individual students.)

EXERCISE 5
PAIRED PRACTICE

a. You're going to work in pairs.
- All **A** members raise your hand. ✓
- All **B** members raise your hand. ✓
- (Repeat until firm.)

b. Today, the **A** member of each pair will read first. The **A** member will read from the beginning of the title to the star in the middle of the story. Everybody, touch that star. ✓
- The **B** members will read from the star to the end of the story.

c. Remember the rules: The student who is not reading follows along. If there is a mistake, that student points out the error and tells the correct word. If there is a problem, raise your hand, and I'll help you out.
- **A** members, start reading. Raise your hand when you've read to the star.
  (Observe students and give feedback.)
- (As **A** members complete their reading, direct **B** members to read from the star to the end of the story. Praise teams that follow the rules.)

EXERCISE 6
WRITTEN ITEMS
Comprehension Passage Items

a. Find part D in your textbook. ✓
- The questions in part D are about centimeters. I'll call on different students to read the items and say the answers. Follow along. Don't write anything until I tell you to write.

b. (For each item: Call on a student to read and answer the item.)

- Item 1. [Which is longer, an inch or a centimeter? An inch.]
c. (Teacher reference:)

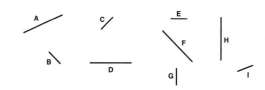

- Item 2. [Some of the lines in the box are one inch long. Some of the lines are one centimeter long. Write the letter of every line that is one inch long.] Which letters? [A, D, F, H.]
- Item 3. [Write the letter of every line that is one centimeter long.] Which letters? [B, C, E, G, I.]

Story Items

d. Find part E in your textbook. ✓
  The questions in part E are about today's story.
- Item 4. [What did the camel agree to give up if she was not right? Hump.]
- Item 5. [What did the pig agree to give up if she was not right? Tail, nose.]
- Item 6. [Who ate at the first garden? Camel.]
- Item 7. [Who ate at the next garden? Pig.]
- Item 8. [How did the pig get food from this garden? Went through a hole.]
- Item 9. [Which parts did the pig give to the camel? Nose, tail.]
- Item 10. [Which part did the camel give to the pig? Hump.]
- Item 11. [Which animals promised not to argue about tall and short? Pig, camel.]
- Item 12. [Did they keep their promise? No.]

Skill Items

e. Find item 1 on your worksheet. ✓
- (Teacher reference:)

- To work items 1 and 2, you have to use the information the item gives you. Follow along: The bigger the pig, the more it sleeps. Everybody, say the rule. Get ready. (Signal.) *The bigger the pig, the more it sleeps.*
- The pictures show different pigs.
  Item 1: Circle the one pig that sleeps the most. Do it now. Mark just one pig. Pencils down when you've done that much.
  (Observe students and give feedback.)
- Now do item 2: Make a box around the one pig that sleeps the least. Mark just one pig. Pencils down when you've done that much.
  (Observe students and give feedback.)

f. Find item 3. ✓
- (Teacher reference:)

Underline everything the cow said in each item.

Sample: "<u>You both look better</u>," the cow said, "<u>and I'm glad you're not fighting</u>."

3. "Well," the cow said, "the pig showed that short is better."
4. "You agreed to give up your hump," the cow said, "so give it up."
5. The cow said, "The camel showed that tall is better."
6. "Take back the things you gave up," the cow said, "but don't yell and fight."

- I'll read the sample item above item 3: "<u>You both look better</u>," the cow said, "<u>and I'm glad you're not fighting</u>." This sentence has two parts that the cow said. Each part is underlined. Here are the two things the cow said: You both look better, and I'm glad you're not fighting.
- Everybody, say the two things the cow said. Get ready. (Signal.) *You both look better, and I'm glad you're not fighting.*
- You can find the parts that somebody said by looking for the quote marks. There are quote marks at the beginning and the end of everything somebody says.
- In items 3 through 6, the cow says something. But the parts she says are not underlined. All the words between the quote marks tell what she said.
- Item 3: "Well," the cow said, "the pig showed that short is better." The cow said two things in that sentence. Everybody, what's the first thing she said? (Signal.) *Well.*
- What's the other thing she said? (Signal.) *The pig showed that short is better.*
- Say everything the cow said in item 3. Get ready. (Signal.) *Well, the pig showed that short is better.*
- (Repeat until firm.)

g. Item 4: "You agreed to give up your hump," the cow said, "so give it up."
- (Call on a student.) Say everything the cow said. *[You agreed to give up your hump, so give it up.]*

h. Item 5: The cow said, "The camel showed that tall is better."
- Everybody, say everything the cow said. Get ready. (Signal.) *The camel showed that tall is better.*

i. Item 6: "Take back the things you gave up," the cow said, "but don't yell and fight."
- (Call on a student.) Say everything the cow said. *[Take back the things you gave up, but don't yell and fight.]*

j. Your turn: Underline everything the cow said in items 3 through 6. Pencils down when you've done that much.
  (Observe students and give feedback.)

k. Check your work. I'll call on different students to read everything you should have underlined in each item.

l. Item 3. *[Well, the pig showed that short is better.]*
- Everybody, write **X** next to item 3 if you got it wrong. ✓

m. Item 4. *[You agreed to give up your hump, so give it up.]*
- Everybody, write **X** next to item 4 if you got it wrong. ✓

n. Item 5. *[The camel showed that tall is better.]*
- Everybody, write **X** next to item 5 if you got it wrong. ✓

o. Item 6. *[Take back the things you gave up, but don't yell and fight.]*
- Everybody, write **X** next to item 6 if you got it wrong. ✓

Review Items

p. The rest of the items are review items from other lessons.

End-of-Lesson Activities

INDEPENDENT WORK

Now finish the independent work for lesson 8. Do the worksheet first, starting with item 7. For the textbook items, you'll write your answers on your lined paper. Raise your hand when you've finished the worksheet and textbook for lesson 8.
(Observe students and give feedback.)

WORKCHECK

Note: Worksheet items 3–6 have already been corrected.

a. (Direct students to take out their marking pencils.)

- We're going to check your independent work. Remember, if you got an item wrong, make an **X** next to the item. Don't change any answers.

b. (For each item: Read the item. Call on a student to answer it. If the answer is wrong, say the correct answer. Refer to the Answer Key for the correct answers.)

c. Now use your marking pencil to fix up any items you got wrong. Remember, all mistakes must be fixed up before you hand in your worksheet.

WRITING-SPELLING

(Present Writing-Spelling lesson 8 after completing Reading lesson 8. See Writing-Spelling Guide.)

Lesson 9

EXECISE 1
VOCABULARY REVIEW

a. You learned a sentence about how you measure your weight.
   - Everybody, say that sentence. Get ready. (Signal.) *You measure your weight in pounds.*
   - (Repeat until firm.)
b. Here's the last sentence you learned: They waded into the stream to remove tadpoles.
   - Everybody, say that sentence. Get ready. (Signal.) *They waded into the stream to remove tadpoles.*
   - (Repeat until firm.)
c. What word tells that they got rid of something? (Signal.) *Remove.*
   - What word names baby toads or frogs? (Signal.) *Tadpoles.*
   - What word tells that they walked through water that was not very deep? (Signal.) *Waded.*
   - (Repeat step c until firm.)
d. Once more. Say the sentence that tells where they waded. Get ready. (Signal.) *They waded into the stream to remove tadpoles.*

EXERCISE 2
READING WORDS

Column 1

a. Find lesson 9 in your textbook. ✓
   - Touch column 1. ✓
   - (Teacher reference:)

1. ruler	4. writing
2. thought	5. tipped
3. escape	6. stream

b. Word 1 is **ruler.** What word? (Signal.) *Ruler.*
   - A **ruler** is a tool that you use to measure inches or centimeters. Everybody, what do we call a tool that's used to measure inches or centimeters? (Signal.) *Ruler.*
c. Word 2 is **thought.** What word? (Signal.) *Thought.*
   - Something that you think about is a **thought.** Everybody, close your eyes and think about an ice-cream cone. Get a picture of an ice-cream cone. (Wait.)
   - What thought do you have? (Call on a student. Idea: *An ice-cream cone.*)
   - Everybody, what do we call something you think about? (Signal.) *A thought.*
d. Word 3 is **escape.** What word? (Signal.) *Escape.*
e. Word 4. What word? (Signal.) *Writing.*
   - (Repeat for words 5 and 6.)
f. Let's read those words again, the fast way.
   - Word 1. What word? (Signal.) *Ruler.*
   - (Repeat for words 2–6.)
g. (Repeat step f until firm.)

Column 2

h. Find column 2. ✓
   - (Teacher reference:)

1. dance	3. pencil
2. prance	4. fence

   - Some of these words have the letters **C-E.** What sound do those letters usually make? (Signal.) *sss.*
   - You'll spell each word and tell me the word.
i. Spell word 1. Get ready. (Signal.) *D-A-N-C-E.*
   - What word did you spell? (Signal.) *Dance.*
   - Spell word 2. Get ready. (Signal.) *P-R-A-N-C-E.*
   - What word did you spell? (Signal.) *Prance.*
   - Spell word 3. Get ready. (Signal.) *P-E-N-C-I-L.*
   - What word did you spell? (Signal.) *Pencil.*
   - Spell word 4. Get ready. (Signal.) *F-E-N-C-E.*
   - What word did you spell? (Signal.) *Fence.*
j. Let's read those words again the fast way.
   - Word 1. What word? (Signal.) *Dance.*
   - (Repeat for words 2–4.)
k. (Repeat step j until firm.)

Column 3

l. Find column 3. ✓
- (Teacher reference:)

1. Mary Williams	4. eraser
2. construction	5. escaping
3. apartment	6. waded

m. Number 1. What words? (Signal.) *Mary Williams.*
- Word 2. What word? (Signal.) *Construction.*
- (Repeat for words 3–6.)

n. (Repeat step m until firm.)

Column 4

o. Find column 4. ✓
- (Teacher reference:)

1. ink	4. shaft
2. erase	5. boast
3. cloth	6. boasted

p. Word 1. What word? (Signal.) *Ink.*
- (Repeat for words 2–6.)

q. (Repeat step p until firm.)

Individual Turns

(For columns 1–4: Call on individual students, each to read one to three words per turn.)

EXECISE 3
COMPREHENSION PASSAGE

a. Find part B in your textbook. ✓
- You're going to read a story about a felt-tipped pen. First you'll read the information passage. It gives some facts about felt-tipped pens.

b. Everybody, touch the title. ✓
- (Call on a student to read the title.) *[Felt-Tipped Pens.]*
- Everybody, what's this selection going to tell about? (Signal.) *Felt-tipped pens.*

c. (Call on individual students to read the passage, each student reading two or three sentences at a time. Ask the specified questions as the students read.)

> **Felt-Tipped Pens**
>
> You'll read a story about a felt-tipped pen.

- What do you do with a felt-tipped pen? (Call on a student. Ideas: *Write, draw pictures,* etc.)

> **Here are facts about felt-tipped pens:**
> • **Felt-tipped pens have tips that are made of felt. Felt is a kind of cloth.**

- What is felt? (Call on a student. Idea: *A kind of cloth.*)
- Listen to the fact about felt-tipped pens: Felt-tipped pens have tips that are made of felt.
- Everybody, say that fact. Get ready. (Signal.) *Felt-tipped pens have tips that are made of felt.*
- (Repeat until firm.)

> • **The shaft of the pen is filled with ink.**

- Listen to that fact again: The shaft of the pen is filled with ink.
- Everybody, say that fact. Get ready. (Signal.) *The shaft of the pen is filled with ink.*
- (Repeat until firm.)

> **The shaft is the long part of the pen that you hold when you write.**

- What is the shaft? (Call on a student. Idea: *The part of the pen that you hold.*)
- Who can show me the shaft of a pencil? (Call on a student.) Touch the shaft of your pencil. ✓

> • **The ink flows down to the tip. Ink is wet. The tip is made of cloth. So when ink gets on the tip, the tip gets wet with ink.**

- Everybody, listen to that part again: Ink is wet. The tip is made of cloth. So when ink gets on the tip, the tip gets wet with ink.
- What is the tip made of? (Call on a student. Ideas: *Felt; cloth.*)
- What happens to the tip when the wet ink gets on the tip? (Call on a student. Idea: *It gets wet.*)

> • **Most felt-tipped pens do not have an eraser. Ink is not easy to erase.**

- Why don't felt-tipped pens have erasers? (Call on a student. Idea: *Because ink is not easy to erase.*)

Lesson 9   53

What kind of writing tool does have an eraser?

- Tell me. (Call on a student. Ideas: *Pencil, erasable pen.*)

EXERCISE 4
STORY READING

a. Find part C in your textbook. ✓
- This is the first part of a new story. We're going to read this story two times. First you'll read it out loud and make no more than 6 errors. Then I'll read it and ask questions. Remember to follow along when someone else is reading.

b. Everybody, touch the title. ✓
- (Call on a student to read the title.) [*Joe Williams Wants a New Job.*]
- What do we know about Joe Williams? (Call on a student. Idea: *He wants a new job.*)

c. (Call on individual students to read the story, each student reading two or three sentences at a time.)

- (Correct errors: Tell the word. Direct the student to reread the sentence.)
- (If the group makes more than 6 errors, direct the students to reread the story.)

d. (After the group has read the selection making no more than 6 errors:) Now I'll read the story and ask questions. Follow along.

Joe Williams Wants a New Job

Joe Williams was a felt-tipped pen. He had a wide tip and his color was bright red.

- Everybody, is Joe Williams a person? (Signal.) *No.*
- What kind of thing is Joe Williams? (Call on a student. Idea: *A felt-tipped pen.*)
- What else do we know about him? (Call on a student. Ideas: *He has a wide tip; he is bright red; he wants a new job.*)

Joe's job was construction. He worked with other members of the construction team—pencils, paints, other pens, brushes, and erasers. Their construction job was to make pictures.

- What kind of job did Joe have? (Call on a student. Idea: *Construction.*)
- Who else was on the construction team? (Call on a student. Ideas: *Pencils, paints, other pens, brushes, and erasers.*)
- What job did the construction team have? (Call on a student. Idea: *Making pictures.*)

All day long, Joe worked with the others. They worked very fast. First, Joe would be sitting next to the other pens. Then somebody would pick him up, make a few marks with him, and toss him back with the other pens.

The work was hard, and everybody on the construction team was glad when it was time for lunch.

- Why was the construction team happy when lunchtime came? (Call on a student. Ideas: *They could stop working; the work was hard.*)

The members of the team would sit and talk about the picture they were making. Then, at one o'clock, work would start again, and it would keep going until the end of the day.

After the work was done, Joe would go to his apartment. He lived in the desk with his wife, Mary, who worked as a number-one pencil.

- Where did Joe and Mary live? (Call on a student. Idea: *In an apartment in the desk.*)
- What was Mary's job? (Call on a student. Idea: *She was a number-1 pencil.*)

Every day, the same thing happened. Joe worked on construction, laying down red lines and red marks. Then he went home. One day, Joe said to himself, "I'm tired of being a felt-tipped pen. I'm tired of laying down red lines. I want a new job."

- Why did Joe want a new job? (Call on a student. Idea: *He was tired of laying down red lines.*)

> When Joe told his wife that he was thinking of taking up a new job, she said, "Don't be silly, Joe. What else can you do?"

- Did Mary think that Joe could get a new job? (Call on a student. Idea: *No.*)
- Why not? (Call on a student. Idea: *Because she thought he couldn't do anything else.*)

> Joe looked at himself. He couldn't work as an eraser because he didn't have an eraser. He couldn't work as a pencil holder, because he didn't have the right shape. He couldn't work as a sheet of paper.

- Why not? (Call on a student. Ideas: *Because he wasn't made of the right material; he wasn't flat; etc.*)
- Why couldn't he work as a pencil holder? (Call on a student. Idea: *He wasn't the right shape.*)
- What's a pencil holder shaped like? (Call on a student. Ideas: *A cup; a glass.*)

> He said to himself, "Let's face it, Joe. You're just made to be a red felt-tipped pen." Then he said, "But I must be able to do something else."
> Joe felt sad, but he didn't stop thinking about a new job.
>
> **MORE NEXT TIME**

- Everybody, did Joe find a new job? (Signal.) *No.*
- Did Joe stop thinking about a new job? (Signal.) *No.*
- Is Joe Williams a **real pen** or a **make-believe pen**? (Signal.) *A make-believe pen.*
- How do you know? (Call on a student. Ideas: *A pen wouldn't have a job, live in an apartment, have a wife, think or talk, etc.*)
- In the next story, we'll find out if Joe gets a new job.

EXERCISE 5
PAIRED PRACTICE

a. You're going to work in pairs. Today, the **B** member of each pair will read first. They will read from the beginning of the title to the star in the middle of the story. Then the **A** members will read from the star to the end of the story.
b. Remember: The student who is not reading follows along. If there is a mistake, that student points out the error and tells the correct word.
- **B** members, start reading. When you're done, **A** members read. Raise your hand when your pair is finished. (Observe students and give feedback.)

EXERCISE 6
WRITTEN ITEMS
Comprehension Passage Items

a. Find part D in your textbook. ✓
- The questions in part D are about felt-tipped pens. I'll call on different students to read the items and say the answers. Follow along. Don't write anything until I tell you to write.
b. (For each item: Call on a student to read and answer the item.)
- Item 1. *[Felt is a kind of <u>cloth</u>.]*
- Item 2. *Most felt-tipped pens do not have an eraser because ink is <u>hard to erase</u>.]*
- (Teacher reference:)

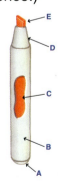

- Item 3. *[Which letter shows the ink? C.]*
- Item 4. *[Which letter shows the shaft? B.]*
- Item 5. *[Which letter shows the felt tip? E.]*
- Item 6. *[The pen in the picture does not have an eraser. Write the letter that shows where an eraser would go on the pen. A.]*

Lesson 9 55

Story Items

c. Find part E in your textbook. ✓
- The questions in part E are about today's story.

d. Item 7. [What color ink did Joe Williams have? *Red.*]
- Item 8. [What kind of tip did Joe Williams have? Idea: *Felt or felt-tipped.*]
- Item 9. [What kind of job did Joe have? *Making red lines.*]
- Item 10. [Write the names of 3 other members of the construction team. *Pencils, erasers, brushes.*]
- Item 11. [Where did Joe live? Ideas: *In a desk; in an apartment.*]
- Item 12. [His wife was named <u>Mary</u>.]
- Item 13. [Did she think that Joe could get a new job? *No.*]

- Item 14. [One of the things in the picture could be Joe's wife. Write the letter of the object that could be Joe's wife. *E.*]
- Item 15. [Object D could not be Joe's wife because Joe's wife is <u>a number-1 pencil</u>.]

Skill Items

e. **Find the skill items on your worksheet.** ✓
- I'll read. Here's a rule: Everybody on the construction team helps make pictures. Everybody, say the rule. Get ready. (Signal.) *Everybody on the construction team helps make pictures.*
- Listen: If the ink is on the construction team, what else do you know about the ink? (Signal.) *The ink helps make pictures.*
- Everybody, if the ruler is on the construction team, what else do you know about the ruler? (Signal.) *The ruler helps make pictures.*
- (Call on a student.) Read item 1. Don't say the answer. [The paint is on the construction team. So what else do you know about the paint?]
- Read item 2. Don't say the answer. [The pencil is on the construction team. So what else do you know about the pencil?]
- Everybody, write the answers to items 1 and 2. Raise your hand when you've done that much.
(Observe students and give feedback.)

f. For items 3 through 7 you'll underline everything Joe said in each item.
- Item 3: "Well," Joe said, "I'm tired of making red lines." Everybody, what's the first thing Joe said in that sentence? (Signal.) *Well.*
- Everybody, what's the other thing he said? (Signal.) *I'm tired of making red lines.*
- Everybody, say everything Joe said in item 3. Get ready. (Signal.) *Well, I'm tired of making red lines.*
- (Repeat until firm.)

g. Item 4: Joe said, "Our team works hard." Everybody, say everything Joe said in item 4. Get ready. (Signal.) *Our team works hard.*

h. Item 5: "Very soon," Joe said, "I must do something else." (Call on a student.) Say everything Joe said. [*Very soon, I must do something else.*]

i. Item 6: "What job can I get?" Joe asked. Everybody, say everything Joe said in item 6. Get ready. (Signal.) *What job can I get?*

j. Item 7: "Can you tell me," Joe asked, "how to find a new job?" (Call on a student.) Say everything Joe said. [*Can you tell me how to find a new job?*]

k. The sentence above item 8 says: They waded into the stream to remove tadpoles. Items 8 through 10 refer to that sentence.
- Item 8: What one word tells about taking things from the stream? Everybody, what word? (Signal.) *Remove.*
- Item 9: What one word names baby frogs or toads? Everybody, what word? (Signal.) *Tadpoles.*
- Item 10: What one word tells about walking in water that is not very deep? Everybody, what word? (Signal.) *Waded.*

Review Items

l. The rest of the items are review items from other lessons.

End-of-Lesson Activities

INDEPENDENT WORK

Now finish the independent work for lesson 9. Do the worksheet first. For the textbook items, you'll write your answers on your lined paper. Raise your hand when you've finished the worksheet and textbook for lesson 9.
(Observe students and give feedback.)

WORKCHECK

a. (Direct students to take out their marking pencils.)
- We're going to check your independent work. Remember, if you got an item wrong, make an **X** next to the item. Don't change any answers.

b. (For each item: Read the item. Call on a student to answer it. If the answer is wrong, say the correct answer. Refer to the Answer Key for the correct answers.)

c. Now use your marking pencil to fix up any items you got wrong. Remember, all mistakes must be fixed up before you hand in your worksheet.

Note: For lesson 10, each student will need a copy of the thermometer chart for lessons 10–50. (See Individual Reading Checkout in Teacher's Guide.)

Before presenting Literature lesson 2 (lesson 10), read the scheduled literature activity, secure the necessary materials, and run off the appropriate blackline masters. Reproducible blackline masters appear in the Literature Guide. (See Literature Guide.)

WRITING-SPELLING

(Present Writing-Spelling lesson 9 after completing Reading lesson 9. See Writing-Spelling Guide.)

Lesson 10

Materials: For all test lessons, each student will need a pencil, a textbook, lined paper and their copy of the thermometer chart.

For lesson 10, you will need materials for Literature lesson 1.

EXERCISE 1

READING CHECKOUTS

a. Today is a reading-checkout day. While you're writing answers, I'm going to call on you one at a time to read part of the story we read in lesson 9.

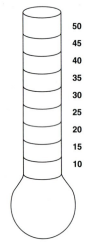

b. (Hold up a thermometer chart.) This is a thermometer chart. Write your name at the top of your thermometer chart. The numbers on the thermometer show the lessons for the checkouts from 10 through 50. The number at the bottom is 10. That's the checkout we'll do today. Touch the number 10. ✓
- When you pass a checkout, you color a space. Students who pass the checkout for lesson 10 today, get to color space 10 red.

c. You pass a checkout by reading the passage in less than a minute without making more than 2 mistakes. Remember, less than a minute and no more than 2 errors. If you don't pass the checkout today, you can try again next time. But you can't color in the space for 10 until you pass checkout 10. When I call on you to come and do your checkout, bring your thermometer chart.

Test 1

d. (Call on individual students to read the portion of story 9 marked with ✽. Time the student. Note words that are missed and total number of words read.)
- (Teacher reference:)

> ✽ When Joe told his wife that he was thinking of taking up a new job, she said, "Don't be silly, Joe. What else can you do?" Joe looked at himself. He couldn't work as an eraser because he **[50]** didn't have an eraser. He couldn't work as a pencil holder, because he didn't have the right shape. He couldn't work as a sheet of paper.
>
> He said to himself, "Let's face it, Joe. You're just made **[75]** to be a red felt-tipped pen." Then he said, "But I must be able to do something else."
>
> Joe felt sad, but he didn't stop ✽ **[100]** thinking about a new job.

- (If the student reads the passage in one minute or less and makes no more than 2 errors, direct the student to color in the bottom segment of the thermometer chart.)

- (If the student makes any mistakes, point to each word that was misread and identify it.)
- (If the student does not meet the time-error criterion for the passage, direct the student to practice reading the story with the assigned partner.)

EXERCISE 2

TEST

a. **Find lesson 10, test 1 in your textbook.** ✓
- This lesson is a test. You'll work items you've done before.
b. Read the items and write the answers on your lined paper. Work carefully. Raise your hand when you've completed all the items.

(Observe students, but do not give feedback on errors.)

EXERCISE 3

MARKING THE TEST

a. (Check students' work before beginning lesson 11. Refer to the Answer Key for the correct answers.)
b. (Record all test 1 results on the Test Summary Sheet and the Group Summary Sheet. Reproducible Summary Sheets are at the back of the Teacher's Guide.)

EXERCISE 4

TEST REMEDIES

- (Provide any necessary remedies for test 1 before presenting lesson 11. Test remedies are discussed in the Teacher's Guide.)

Test 1 Firming Table

Test Item	Introduced in lesson	Test Item	Introduced in lesson	Test Item	Introduced in lesson
1	1	9	4	17	8
2	1	10	5	18	7
3	3	11	5	19	4
4	3	12	6	20	4
5	3	13	6	21	7
6	3	14	7	22	7
7	4	15	7	23	4
8	4	16	8	24	4

LITERATURE

(Present Literature lesson 1 after completing Reading lesson 10. See Literature Guide.)

Lessons 11–15 • Planning Page

Looking Ahead

	Lesson 11	Lesson 12	Lesson 13	Lesson 14	Lesson 15
Lesson Events	Vocabulary Sentence Reading Words Vocabulary Review Comprehension Passage Story Reading Paired Practice Written Items Independent Work Workcheck Writing-Spelling Activity	Vocabulary Review Reading Words Comprehension Passage Story Reading Paired Practice Written Items Independent Work Workcheck Writing-Spelling	Vocabulary Review Reading Words Comprehension Passages Story Reading Paired Practice Written Items Independent Work Workcheck Writing-Spelling Activity	Vocabulary Sentence Reading Words Vocabulary Review Comprehension Passages Story Reading Paired Practice Written Items Independent Work Workcheck Writing-Spelling Activity	Vocabulary Review Reading Words Comprehension Passage Story Reading Written Items Reading Checkouts Independent Work Workcheck Writing-Spelling
Vocabulary Sentence	#3: The fly <u>boasted</u> about <u>escaping</u> from the spider.	#3: The fly <u>boasted</u> about <u>escaping</u> from the spider.	sentence #1 sentence #2 sentence #3	#4: The workers <u>propped up</u> the cage with <u>steel</u> bars.	#4: The workers <u>propped up</u> the cage with <u>steel</u> bars.
Reading Words: Word Types	modeled words proper nouns (names) mixed words	modeled words proper nouns (names) mixed words multi-syllable words "time" words	modeled words 2-syllable words mixed words	modeled words mixed words	modeled words compound words **o-a** words 2-syllable words mixed words
New Vocabulary	famous human expensive	Russia juggle		usually disappear	Alaska
Comprehension Passages	*Centimeters*	*Facts About Fleas*	1) *Learing About Time* 2) *Facts About Flea Circuses*	1) *Meters* 2) *Directions on a Map*	*Facts About Toads and Frogs*
Story	Joe Williams Gets a New Job	Aunt Fanny's Flea Circus	The Fleas Surprise Aunt Fanny	Aunt Fanny Changes Her Ways	Goad the Toad
Skill Items	Vocabulary sentences Quotations Deductions	Deductions Quotations	Titles Deductions Vocabulary sentence	Titles Vocabulary sentences Quotations	Deductions Titles
Special Materials	Metric and standard ruler, objects to measure for activity			Meterstick, yardstick, objects 1–3 meters long for activity	Thermometer charts
Special Projects/ Activities	Activity after lesson 11		Activity after lesson 13	Activity after lesson 14	

Lesson 11

EXERCISE 1
VOCABULARY

a. **Find page 338 in your textbook.** ✓
- Touch sentence 3. ✓
- This is a new vocabulary sentence. It says: The fly boasted about escaping from the spider. Everybody, read that sentence. Get ready. (Signal.) *The fly boasted about escaping from the spider.*
- Close your eyes and say the sentence. Get ready. (Signal.) *The fly boasted about escaping from the spider.*
- (Repeat until firm.)

b. When the fly **boasted,** it bragged. What did it tell its friends that it did? (Call on a student. Idea: *Escaped from the spider.*)

c. When you **escape** from something, you **get away** from it. What word tells about getting away from something? (Signal.) *Escaping.*

d. Listen to the sentence again: The fly boasted about escaping from the spider. Everybody, say that sentence. Get ready. (Signal.) *The fly boasted about escaping from the spider.*

e. What word tells that the fly bragged? (Signal.) *Boasted.*
- What word tells about getting away from something? (Signal.) *Escaping.*

EXERCISE 2
READING WORDS

Column 1

a. Find lesson 11 in your textbook. ✓
- Touch column 1. ✓
- (Teacher reference:)

1. circus	4. blood
2. famous	5. expensive
3. human	6. thousand

b. Word 1 is **circus.** What word? (Signal.) *Circus.*
- Spell **circus.** Get ready. (Tap for each letter.) *C-I-R-C-U-S.*

c. Word 2 is **famous.** What word? (Signal.) *Famous.*
- Spell **famous.** Get ready. (Tap for each letter.) *F-A-M-O-U-S.*
- If something is **famous**, it is **well-known**. Everybody, what's another way of saying **His father was well-known?** (Signal.) *His father was famous.*
- What's another way of saying **The river was well-known?** (Signal.) *The river was famous.*

d. Word 3 is **human.** What word? (Signal.) *Human.*
- Spell **human.** Get ready. (Tap for each letter.) *H-U-M-A-N.*
- A human is a person. Men, women, boys, girls, and babies are all humans.

e. Word 4 is **blood.** What word? (Signal.) *Blood.*
- Spell **blood.** Get ready. (Tap for each letter.) *B-L-O-O-D.*

f. Word 5 is **expensive.** What word? (Signal.) *Expensive.*
- Things that cost a lot of money are expensive. A vacation that costs a lot of money is an expensive vacation. Everybody, what do we call **clothes** that cost a lot of money? (Signal.) *Expensive clothes.*
- What do we call a **car** that costs a lot of money? (Signal.) *An expensive car.*

g. Word 6 is **thousand.** What word? (Signal.) *Thousand.*

h. Let's read those words again, the fast way.
- Word 1. What word? (Signal.) *Circus.*
- (Repeat for words 2–6.)

i. (Repeat step h until firm.)

Column 2

j. Find column 2. ✓
- (Teacher reference:)

| 1. Martha Jumpjump |
| 2. Henry Ouch |
| 3. Aunt Fanny |
| 4. Carl Goodscratch |

- These are all names of characters in the story you'll start reading in the next lesson.

k. Number 1. What name? (Signal.) *Martha Jumpjump.*
- (Repeat for: **2. Henry Ouch, 3. Aunt Fanny, 4. Carl Goodscratch.**)
l. (Repeat step k until firm.)

Column 3

m. Find column 3. ✓
- (Teacher reference:)

1. bread	4. fame
2. world	5. insect
3. flea	6. boasted

n. Word 1. What word? (Signal.) *Bread.*
- (Repeat for words 2–6.)
o. (Repeat step n until firm.)

Column 4

p. Find column 4. ✓
- (Teacher reference:)

1. round	4. hogged
2. ruler	5. thoughts
3. dancing	6. escaping

q. Word 1. What word? (Signal.) *Round.*
- (Repeat for words 2–6.)
r. (Repeat step q until firm.)

Individual Turns

(For columns 1–4: Call on individual students, each to read one to three words per turn.)

EXERCISE 3

VOCABULARY REVIEW

a. Here's the new vocabulary sentence: The fly boasted about escaping from the spider. Everybody, say that sentence. Get ready. (Signal.) *The fly boasted about escaping from the spider.*
b. What word tells about getting away from something? (Signal.) *Escaping.*
- What word tells that the fly bragged? (Signal.) *Boasted.*

EXECISE 4

COMPREHENSION PASSAGE

a. Find part B in your textbook. ✓
- You're going to read the next story about Joe Williams. First you'll read the information passage. It gives some facts about centimeters.

b. Everybody, touch the title. ✓
- (Call on a student to read the title.) *[Centimeters.]*
- Everybody, what's this selection going to tell about? (Signal.) *Centimeters.*
c. (Call on individual students to read the passage, each student reading two or three sentences at a time. Ask the specified questions as the students read.)

Centimeters

The story you'll read today tells about centimeters. Remember, <u>a centimeter is shorter than an inch.</u>

- Everybody, listen to that rule again: A centimeter is shorter than an inch. Say that rule. Get ready. (Signal.) *A centimeter is shorter than an inch.*
- (Repeat until firm.)

Every line in this row is one centimeter long:

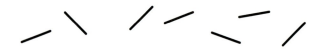

- Everybody, hold up your fingers and show me a space that is about one centimeter long. ✓

Every line in this row is one inch long:

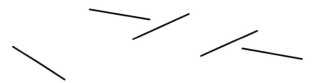

- Everybody, hold up your fingers and show me a space that is about one inch long. ✓

EXERCISE 5

STORY READING

a. Find part C in your textbook. ✓
- This is the last part of the story about Joe Williams. We're going to read this story two times. First you'll read it out loud and make no more than 6 errors. Then I'll read it and ask questions.
b. Everybody, touch the title. ✓
- (Call on a student to read the title.) *[Joe Williams Gets a New Job.]*

- Everybody, what's the title? (Signal.) *Joe Williams Gets a New Job.*
- What was Joe's first job? (Call on a student. Ideas: *Construction; as a red felt-tipped pen.*)
- Who else was on Joe's construction team? (Call on a student. Ideas: *Pencils, erasers, other pens, paints, and brushes.*)
- Why did Joe want a new job? (Call on a student. Idea: *He was tired of laying down red lines.*)

c. (Call on individual students to read the story, each student reading two or three sentences at a time.)

- (Correct errors: Tell the word. Direct the student to reread the sentence.)
- (If the group makes more than 6 errors, direct the students to reread the story.)

d. (After the group has read the selection making no more than 6 errors:)
Now I'll read the story and ask questions.

Joe Williams Gets a New Job

Every night, Joe went home and thought about jobs that he might do, but he didn't come up with any good thoughts. Then one night, Joe had a good thought. He was watching his wife, Mary. She was singing to herself, and she was dancing. When a number-one pencil dances, she makes a little line on the floor. Then she jumps and makes another little line right next to the first line. As Joe watched her make these lines, he jumped up from the chair and jumped across the floor. "I've got it," he yelled. "I've got it!"

- Joe had an idea. What do you think it had to do with? (Call on a student. Idea: *Mary dancing.*)

Mary stopped dancing and looked at Joe. "What are you thinking?"
Joe said, "I want you to make marks on me. Make marks that are one centimeter apart. Make marks all down the side of my shaft. If I have those marks on my shaft, I can work as a ruler.

- What did Joe want Mary to do? (Call on a student. Idea: *Make marks on him.*)
- Why did he want lines on his shaft? (Call on a student. Idea: *So he could work as a ruler.*)
- Everybody, show me how far apart those lines will be. ✓

Mary said, "Maybe that will work. Let's see."

- How do you think Mary is going to see if the idea works? (Call on a student. Idea: *Make marks on Joe and see if he can be a ruler.*)

She made the marks on Joe's side. Then she made numbers by the marks. When she was done, Joe jumped up and looked at himself. "Wow, that's nice," he said. He kept turning around and looking at himself. "I'll be the only round ruler on the construction team."
The next day, Joe didn't line up with the other pens. He went over with the rulers.

- Why did Joe go over with the rulers? (Call on a student. Ideas: *Because he wanted to work as a ruler; because he had lines on him.*)

One ruler said, "What do you think you're doing here, pen?"
"I'm now a ruler," Joe said.
Another ruler said, "We'll soon find out if you're really a ruler. It's just about time to work."
Pretty soon, somebody picked up Joe and said, "Let's see how this round ruler works." The person used Joe as a ruler. "This round ruler works very well," the person said. And from that day on, Joe had a new job. He was a round ruler. And he was happy.
THE END

- Everybody, did Joe get a new job? (Signal.) *Yes.*
- What was Joe's new job? (Call on a student. Idea: *Working as a ruler.*)

EXERCISE 6
PAIRED PRACTICE

a. You're going to work in pairs. Today, the **A** member of each pair will read first. They will read from the beginning of the title to the star in the middle of the story. Then the **B** members will read from the star to the end of the story.

b. Remember: The student who is not reading follows along. If there is a mistake, that student points out the error and tells the correct word.

- **A** members, start reading. When you're done, **B** members read. Raise your hand when your pair is finished.

(Observe students and give feedback.)

EXERCISE 7
WRITTEN ITEMS

Story Items

a. Take out a piece of lined paper and number it from 1 through 16. ✓
b. Find part D in your textbook. ✓
- Items 1 through 4 are about today's story. I'll call on different students to read the items, but don't say the answers.
c. (For each item: Call on a student to read the item.)
- (Teacher reference:)

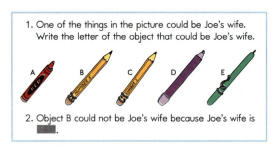

- Item 1. [One of the things in the picture could be Joe's wife. Write the letter of the object that could be Joe's wife.]
- Item 2. [Object B could not be Joe's wife because Joe's wife is blank.]
- (Teacher reference:)

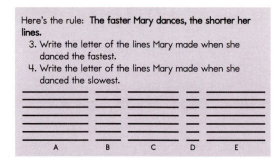

- Here's the rule: The faster Mary dances, the shorter her lines.
- Item 3. [Write the letter of the lines Mary made when she danced the fastest.]
- Item 4. [Write the letter of the lines Mary made when she danced the slowest.]

Skill Items

d. Item 5. They blank into the stream to blank blank. Raise your hand when you know which vocabulary sentence that's supposed to be. (Call on a student.) Say the sentence. [They waded into the stream to remove tadpoles.]
- Item 6. You blank your blank in blank. Raise your hand when you know which vocabulary sentence that's supposed to be. (Call on a student.) Say the sentence. [You measure your weight in pounds.]
- Everybody, write the sentences for items 5 and 6. Be sure to spell all the words correctly.

(Observe students and give feedback.)

Comprehension Passage Items

e. Find part A on your worksheet. ✓
- The questions in part A are about centimeters and inches.
f. (For each item: Call on a student to read the item.)
- Item 1. [Some of the lines in the box are one inch long. Some of the lines are one centimeter long. Circle every line that is one centimeter long.]
- Item 2. [Write the letter of every line that is one inch long.]

Story Items

g. Items 3 through 10 are about today's story.
- Item 3. [What color ink did Joe Williams have?]
- Item 4. [Who made marks on Joe?]
- Item 5. [Did Joe get a new job?]
- Item 6. [On his new job, Joe was blank.]
- Item 7. [How far apart were Joe's marks?]
- Item 8. [Circle the line that shows how far apart Joe's marks were.]
- Item 9. [Make an X on the picture that shows what Joe may have looked like after he got his new job.]
- Item 10. [Object D couldn't be Joe because it does not have blank.]

Skill Items

h. For items 11 through 14, you'll underline everything Joe said in each item.
- Item 11: "Doing the same thing every day," Joe said, "is very boring."
  Everybody, what's the first thing Joe said in that sentence? (Signal.) *Doing the same thing every day.*
- What's the other thing he said? (Signal.) *Is very boring.*
- Say everything Joe said in item 11. Get ready. (Signal.) *Doing the same thing every day is very boring.*
- (Repeat until firm.)

i. Item 12: "I've got an idea," Joe said loudly. "And it's a good one." Everybody, say everything Joe said in item 12. Get ready. (Signal.) *I've got an idea. And it's a good one.*

j. Item 13: Joe said, "Make marks on me. Make marks all down my side." Say everything Joe said. (Call on a student.) *[Make marks on me. Make marks all down my side.]*

k. Item 14: "Make marks," Joe told Mary, "that are one centimeter apart." Everybody, say everything Joe said in item 14. Get ready. (Signal.) *Make marks that are one centimeter apart.*

l. I'll read. Here's a rule: All the flat rulers work on Saturday. Everybody, say the rule. Get ready. (Signal.) *All the flat rulers work on Saturday.*
- Listen. If Pete is a flat ruler, what else do you know about Pete? (Signal.) *Pete works on Saturday.*
- If Jane is a flat ruler, what else do you know about Jane? (Signal.) *Jane works on Saturday.*
- Read item 15. Don't say the answer. (Call on a student.) *[Pete is a flat ruler. So what else do you know about Pete?]*
- Read item 16. Don't say the answer. *[Jane is a flat ruler. So what else do you know about Jane?]*

End-of-Lesson Activities

INDEPENDENT WORK

Now finish your independent work for lesson 11. Do the worksheet first and then the textbook. Raise your hand when you're finished.
(Observe students and give feedback.)

WORKCHECK

a. (Direct students to take out their marking pencils.)
- We're going to check your independent work. Remember, if you got an item wrong, make an **X** next to the item. Don't change any answers.

b. (For each item: Read the item. Call on a student to answer it. If the answer is wrong, say the correct answer. Refer to the Answer Key for the correct answers.)

c. Now use your marking pencil to fix up any items you got wrong. Remember, all mistakes must be fixed up before you hand in your independent work.

WRITING-SPELLING

(Present Writing-Spelling lesson 11 after completing Reading lesson 11. See Writing-Spelling Guide.)

ACTIVITY

(Present Activity 4 after completing Reading lesson 11. See Activities Across the Curriculum.)

Lesson 12

EXERCISE 1
VOCABULARY REVIEW

a. Here's the new vocabulary sentence: The fly boasted about escaping from the spider. Everybody, say that sentence. Get ready. (Signal.) *The fly boasted about escaping from the spider.*
b. What word tells that the fly bragged? (Signal.) *Boasted.*
- What word tells about getting away from something? (Signal.) *Escaping.*

EXERCISE 2
READING WORDS

Column 1

a. **Find lesson 12 in your textbook.** ✓
- Touch column 1. ✓
- (Teacher reference:)

1. Russia	3. surprise
2. great	4. tomorrow

b. Word 1 is **Russia.** What word? (Signal.) *Russia.*
- Spell **Russia.** Get ready. (Tap for each letter.) *R-U-S-S-I-A.*
- Russia is the name of a very large country. It's bigger than the United States.
c. Word 2 is **great.** What word? (Signal.) *Great.*
- Spell **great.** Get ready. (Tap for each letter.) *G-R-E-A-T.*
d. Word 3 is **surprise.** What word? (Signal.) *Surprise.*
- Spell **surprise.** Get ready. (Tap for each letter.) *S-U-R-P-R-I-S-E.*
e. Word 4 is **tomorrow.** What word? (Signal.) *Tomorrow.*
- Spell **tomorrow.** Get ready. (Tap for each letter.) *T-O-M-O-R-R-O-W.*
f. Let's read those words again, the fast way.
- Word 1. What word? (Signal.) *Russia.*
- (Repeat for words 2–4.)
g. (Repeat step f until firm.)

Column 2

h. Find column 2. ✓
- (Teacher reference:)

1. Aunt Fanny
2. Carl Goodscratch
3. Henry Ouch
4. Martha Jumpjump

- These are the names of the characters in today's story.
i. Number 1. What name? (Signal.) *Aunt Fanny.*
- (Repeat for names 2–4.)
j. (Repeat step i until firm.)

Column 3

k. Find column 3. ✓
- (Teacher reference:)

1. second	3. hour
2. minute	4. week

- These are names that tell about time.
l. Word 1. What word? (Signal.) *Second.*
- Word 2. What word? (Signal.) *Minute.*
- Word 3. What word? (Signal.) *Hour.*
- Word 4. What word? (Signal.) *Week.*
m. Let's read those words again.
- Word 1. What word? (Signal.) *Second.*
- (Repeat for words 2–4.)
n. (Repeat step m until firm.)

Column 4

o. Find column 4. ✓
- (Teacher reference:)

1. juggle	3. circus
2. ladies	4. famous

p. Word 1. What word? (Signal.) *Juggle.*
- When you juggle objects, you keep tossing the objects in the air and you make sure that at least two objects are always in the air at the same time.
- Word 2. What word? (Signal.) *Ladies.*
- (Repeat for words 3 and 4.)
q. Let's read those words again.
- Word 1. What word? (Signal.) *Juggle.*
- (Repeat for words 2–4.)
r. (Repeat step q until firm.)

Column 5

s. Find column 5. ✓
- (Teacher reference:)

1. blood	4. flea
2. bread	5. world
3. human	

t. Word 1. What word? (Signal.) *Blood.*
- (Repeat for words 2–5.)
u. (Repeat step t until firm.)

Column 6

v. Find column 6. ✓
- (Teacher reference:)

1. thousands	4. insect
2. gentlemen	5. hogged
3. expensive	

w. Word 1. What word? (Signal.) *Thousands.*
- (Repeat for words 2–5.)
x. (Repeat step w until firm.)

Individual Turns

(For columns 1–6: Call on individual students, each to read one to three words per turn.)

EXERCISE 3
COMPREHENSION PASSAGE

a. Find part B in your textbook. ✓
- You're going to read a story about a flea circus. First, you'll read the information passage. It gives some facts about fleas.
b. Everybody, touch the title. ✓
- (Call on a student to read the title.) *[Facts About Fleas.]*
- Everybody, what's the title? (Signal.) *Facts About Fleas.*
c. (Call on individual students to read the passage, each student reading two or three sentences at a time. Ask the specified questions as the students read.)

> **Facts About Fleas**
>
> You'll read about fleas in today's story. Here are some facts about fleas:
> Fleas are insects.
> All insects have six legs.
> So fleas have six legs.

- Listen to that again: Fleas are insects. All insects have six legs. So fleas have six legs.
- Everybody, what are fleas? (Signal.) *Insects.*
- How many legs do insects have? (Signal.) *Six.*
- So how many legs do fleas have? (Signal.) *Six.*

> **Fleas bite and suck blood.**

- Name another insect that bites and sucks blood. (Call on a student. Ideas: *Mosquitoes, ticks, lice.*)

> **A row of about five big fleas is one centimeter long.**

- Everybody, show me a space that is one centimeter long. ✓
- Everybody, about how many fleas would line up in that space? (Signal.) *Five.*

> **Different kinds of fleas live on different kinds of animals.**
> Cat fleas like to live on cats. Cat fleas are different from dog fleas. Dog fleas are different from human fleas. Human fleas are different from rat fleas.

- Everybody, what kind of things do dog fleas like to live on? (Signal.) *Dogs.*
- What kind of things do rat fleas like to live on? (Signal.) *Rats.*

> **The picture below shows a dog flea.**

- Everybody, does that big picture show the real size of the dog flea? (Signal.) *No.*
- The real size of the dog flea is shown inside the circle. The big picture shows what the flea would look like if the flea were very big. Everybody, touch the picture that shows the **real** size of the flea. ✓

Lesson 12 67

EXERCISE 4
STORY READING

a. Find part C in your textbook. ✓
- This is the first part of a new story.
- We're going to read this story two times. First, you'll read it out loud and make no more than 7 errors. Then I'll read it and ask questions.

b. Everybody, touch the title. ✓
- (Call on a student to read the title.) [Aunt Fanny's Flea Circus.]
- Everybody, what's the title? (Signal.) *Aunt Fanny's Flea Circus.*

c. (Call on individual students to read the story, each student reading two or three sentences at a time.)

- (Correct errors: Tell the word. Direct the student to reread the sentence.)
- (If the group makes more than 7 errors, direct the students to reread the story.)

d. (After the group has read the selection making no more than 7 errors:)
Now I'll read the story and ask questions.

Aunt Fanny's Flea Circus

Aunt Fanny's Flea Circus was formed in 1993. The circus had a great line-up of acts.

- What does that mean? (Call on a student. Idea: *The circus has lots of good acts.*)

Aunt Fanny had the most famous fleas in the world. One act was Carl Goodscratch, who dove 48 centimeters into two drops of water.

- Everybody, touch the picture on page 69. ✓
- If you look carefully, you can see Carl diving 48 centimeters into a tiny bucket. Everybody, touch Carl. ✓
- How many drops of water are in that bucket? (Signal.) *Two.*

When Carl did his dive, the people watching the show would sit without making a sound. Then they would cheer and stamp their feet.

- Show me what the people did. (Call on a student.) ✓

Another act that crowds loved was Martha Jumpjump, who skipped rope on a high wire. (The high wire was really a spider web that had been fixed up so that Martha wouldn't stick to it.)

- How could the spider web be fixed up so Martha wouldn't stick to it? (Call on a student. Idea: *It could be waxed.*)
- Why would it be bad for Martha to stick to the high wire? (Call on a student. Ideas: *She couldn't move; she might lose her balance;* etc.)
- Everybody, touch Martha in the picture. ✓
- What is Martha doing? (Call on a student. Idea: *Skipping rope on a high wire.*)

Then there was the French flea, Henry Ouch, the flea who trained rats. He would get into a cage with four or five rats and have them do all kinds of tricks. If they did not do what he told them to do, he would jump on their backs and bite them.

- Everybody, touch Henry in the picture. ✓
- What is Henry making the rats do? (Call on a student. Idea: *All kinds of tricks.*)

Aunt Fanny's Flea Circus went around the world, bringing in big crowds and making lots of money. But in 1999, Aunt Fanny and the fleas started to fight a lot. The fleas said that Aunt Fanny was hogging all the fame.

- When somebody hogs all the fame, the person acts like the biggest star of the show.

> Aunt Fanny said that she could do what she wanted because she owned the circus. The fleas were mad at Fanny because of the way she acted. After each show, people would come up to Fanny. "Great show, Fanny," they would say. The only thing Fanny did in the show was wave a stick at the fleas. The fleas did the real work.

- What did Aunt Fanny do during the show? (Call on a student. Idea: *Wave a stick at the fleas.*)
- What did the fleas do? (Call on a student. Idea: *The real work.*)

> Also, Aunt Fanny hogged all the money.

- What does that mean? (Call on a student. Idea: *Aunt Fanny kept all the money for herself.*)

> She kept the poor fleas locked in a little box while she lived in expensive apartments. She fed the fleas dry bread while she ate expensive food. She put thousands of dollars into the bank, but she didn't give the fleas a dime.

- Listen to that part again:
   She kept the poor fleas locked in a little box while she lived in expensive apartments. She fed the fleas dry bread while she ate expensive food. She put thousands of dollars into the bank, but she didn't give the fleas a dime.
- Where did the fleas live? (Call on a student. Idea: *In a little box.*)
- Where did Aunt Fanny live? (Call on a student. Idea: *In an expensive apartment.*)
- What did the fleas eat? (Call on a student. Idea: *Dry bread.*)
- What did Aunt Fanny eat? (Call on a student. Idea: *Expensive food.*)
- Name two things the fleas were mad about. (Call on a student. Ideas: *Aunt Fanny hogged all the money; Aunt Fanny lived in an expensive apartment; the fleas had to eat dry bread; etc.*)

> One night the fleas made up their minds that things had to change. "She's treating us like dirt," Carl said. "Are we going to take that?"
> "No," all the other fleas agreed. "Things must change."
> MORE NEXT TIME

- What does it mean when you treat someone like dirt? (Call on a student. Idea: *You don't treat them nicely.*)
- Everybody, were the fleas happy with how things were going? (Signal.) *No.*
- In the next Aunt Fanny story, we'll find out if things change.

EXERCISE 5

PAIRED PRACTICE

You're going to read aloud to your partner. Today the **B** members will read first. Then the **A** members will read from the star to the end of the story. (Observe students and give feedback. Praise teams that follow the rules.)

EXERCISE 6

WRITTEN ITEMS

Comprehension Passage Items

a. Find part A on your worksheet. ✓
- The questions in part A are about insects and spiders. I'll call on different students to read the items, but don't say the answers.

b. (For each item: Call on a student to read the item.)
- Item 1. *[A spider is not an insect because it doesn't have the right number of legs. Look at the picture of a spider. How many legs does a spider have?]*
- Item 2. *[How many legs does an insect have?]*
- Item 3. *[How many legs does a flea have?]*
- Item 4. *[If a fly is an insect, what else do you know about a fly?]*

Story Items

c. Items 5 through 13 are about today's story.
- Item 5. *[In what year was Aunt Fanny's Flea Circus formed?]*
- Item 6. *[In what year did Aunt Fanny and the fleas start to fight?]*

- Item 7. *[Underline the names of 3 fleas that were in the circus.]*
- Item 8. *[Draw a line from each flea's name to the objects the flea used in its act.]*
- Item 9. *[The fleas were mad at Aunt Fanny because she hogged all the <u>blank</u> and all the <u>blank</u>.]*
- Item 10. *[She made them live in a <u>blank</u>.]*
- Item 11. *[She fed them dry <u>blank</u>.]*
- Item 12. *[Where did Aunt Fanny live?]*
- Item 13. *[Circle the picture of the object where the fleas lived.]*

End-of-Lesson Activities

INDEPENDENT WORK

Now finish your independent work for lesson 12. Do the worksheet first and then the textbook. Raise your hand when you're finished.

(Observe students and give feedback.)

WORKCHECK

a. (Direct students to take out their marking pencils.)
- We're going to check your independent work. Remember, if you got an item wrong, make an **X** next to the item. Don't change any answers.

b. (For each item: Read the item. Call on a student to answer it. If the answer is wrong, say the correct answer. Refer to the Answer Key for the correct answers.)

c. Now use your marking pencil to fix up any items you got wrong. Remember, all mistakes must be fixed up before you hand in your independent work.

WRITING-SPELLING

(Present Writing-Spelling lesson 12 after completing Reading lesson 12. See Writing-Spelling Guide.)

Lesson 13

EXERCISE 1
VOCABULARY REVIEW

a. You learned a sentence about how you measure your weight.
- Everybody, say that sentence. Get ready. (Signal.) *You measure your weight in pounds.*
- (Repeat until firm.)

b. You learned a sentence that tells where they waded.
- Everybody, say that sentence. Get ready. (Signal.) *They waded into the stream to remove tadpoles.*
- (Repeat until firm.)

c. Here's the last sentence you learned: The fly boasted about escaping from the spider.
- Everybody, say that sentence. Get ready. (Signal.) *The fly boasted about escaping from the spider.*
- (Repeat until firm.)

d. What word tells that the fly bragged? (Signal.) *Boasted.*
- What word tells about getting away from something? (Signal.) *Escaping.*

e. Once more. Say the sentence that tells what the fly boasted about. Get ready. (Signal.) *The fly boasted about escaping from the spider.*

EXERCISE 2
READING WORDS

Column 1

a. Find lesson 13 in your textbook. ✓
- Touch column 1. ✓
- (Teacher reference:)

1. meter	3. directions
2. yea	4. Russia

b. Word 1 is **meter.** What word? (Signal.) *Meter.*
- Spell **meter.** Get ready. (Tap for each letter.) *M-E-T-E-R.*

c. Word 2 is **yea.** What word? (Signal.) *Yea.*
- Spell **yea.** Get ready. (Tap for each letter.) *Y-E-A.*

d. Word 3 is **directions.** What word? (Signal.) *Directions.*

e. Word 4 is **Russia.** What word? (Signal.) *Russia.*
- Spell **Russia.** Get ready. (Tap for each letter.) *R-U-S-S-I-A.*

f. Let's read those words again, the fast way.
- Word 1. What word? (Signal.) *Meter.*
- (Repeat for words 2–4.)

g. (Repeat step f until firm.)

Column 2

h. Find column 2. ✓
- (Teacher reference:)

1. <u>great</u>est	4. <u>mid</u>dle
2. <u>min</u>ute	5. <u>sur</u>prise
3. <u>fan</u>cy	6. <u>jug</u>gle

i. These words have more than one syllable. The first syllable is underlined.

j. Word 1. What's the first syllable? (Signal.) *great.*
- What's the whole word? (Signal.) *Greatest.*
- Word 2. What's the first syllable? (Signal.) *min.*
- What's the whole word? (Signal.) *Minute.*
- Word 3. What's the first syllable? (Signal.) *fan.*
- What's the whole word? (Signal.) *Fancy.*
- Word 4. What's the first syllable? (Signal.) *midd.*
- What's the whole word? (Signal.) *Middle.*
- Word 5. What's the first syllable? (Signal.) *sur.*
- What's the whole word? (Signal.) *Surprise.*
- Word 6. What's the first syllable? (Signal.) *jugg.*
- What's the whole word? (Signal.) *Juggle.*

k. Let's read those words again the fast way.
- Word 1. What word? (Signal.) *Greatest.*
- (Repeat for: **2. minute, 3. fancy, 4. middle, 5. surprise, 6. juggle.**)
l. (Repeat step k until firm.)

Column 3

m. Find column 3. ✓
- (Teacher reference:)

1. second	4. money
2. gentlemen	5. scared
3. tomorrow	6. propped

n. Word 1. What word? (Signal.) *Second.*
- (Repeat for words 2–6.)

o. (Repeat step n until firm.)

Column 4

p. Find column 4. ✓
- (Teacher reference:)

1. week	4. hour
2. ladies	5. hoop
3. cage	6. steel

q. Word 1. What word? (Signal.) *Week.*
- (Repeat for words 2–6.)

r. (Repeat step q until firm.)

Individual Turns

(For columns 1–4: Call on individual students, each to read one to three words per turn.)

EXERCISE 3

COMPREHENSION PASSAGES

Passage B

a. Find part B in your textbook. ✓
- You're going to read the next story about Aunt Fanny. First you'll read two information passages. This passage gives some facts about time.

b. Everybody, touch the title. ✓
- (Call on a student to read the title.) *[Learning About Time.]*
- Everybody, what's the title? (Signal.) *Learning About Time.*

c. (Call on individual students to read the passage, each student reading two or three sentences at a time.)

Learning About Time

Names that tell about time tell how long it takes for something to happen.

- Everybody, names that tell about time tell what? (Signal.) *How long it takes for something to happen.*

A week tells about time. A week is seven days long. So if something will happen a week from now, it will happen seven days from now.

- Everybody, how many days long is a week? (Signal.) *Seven.*

An hour is another name that tells about time. If you spent an hour watching TV, you may be able to watch two shows.

- What's your favorite cartoon show? (Call on a student. After student names a show:) You could watch two of those shows in one hour.

A second is a name that tells about time. When you count slowly, each number takes about one second.

- I'll count five seconds. Listen: 1...2...3...4...5. Your turn. Everybody, count five seconds with me. Get ready. 1...2...3...4...5.

A minute is a name that tells about time. A minute is much smaller than an hour.

- If you said the pledge to the flag three times in a row, it would take about a minute.

Remember, names that tell about time tell how long it takes for something to happen.

- Say four names that tell about time. (Call on individual students.) *[Minute, second, hour, week.]*

Passage C

d. Find part C in your textbook. ✓
- This passage gives some facts about flea circuses.

e. Everybody, touch the title. ✓
- (Call on a student to read the title.) [Facts About Flea Circuses.]
- Everybody, what's the title? (Signal.) *Facts About Flea Circuses.*

f. (Call on individual students to read the passage, each student reading two or three sentences at a time. Ask the specified questions as the students read.)

> **Facts About Flea Circuses**
>
> When we left Aunt Fanny in the last story, the fleas were mad at her. Name three things they were mad about.

- Tell me. (Call on a student. Idea: *Aunt Fanny hogged all the money, ate well, and lived in a nice apartment.*)

> The fleas in the story talk, so we know they are make-believe fleas. But there are such things as flea circuses. And these flea circuses do have fleas that put on acts.

- How do we know the fleas in the story are make-believe? (Call on a student. Idea: *Because they talk.*)
- Everybody, are there real flea circuses? (Signal.) *Yes.*
- Do the fleas really put on acts? (Signal.) *Yes.*

> Here are some facts about real flea circuses:
> Most fleas that are used in flea circuses come from Russia.

- Everybody, where do they come from? (Signal.) *Russia.*

> Fleas have been taught to juggle things.

- How do you juggle things? (Call on a student. Idea: *You keep things up in the air.* A demonstration is also acceptable.)

> Fleas have been taught to jump through hoops.
> Some fleas have been taught to pull things that weigh a hundred times more than a flea.

- Everybody, are fleas strong? (Signal.) *Yes.*
- How do you know? (Call on a student. Idea: *They can pull things that weigh a hundred times more than they do.*)

> The first trick a flea must be taught is to walk instead of hop.

- What's the first trick a flea must be taught? (Call on a student. Idea: *To walk instead of hop.*)

> Fleas like to take a great hop to go from place to place. But they can walk.
> After they have been taught to walk, they can be taught to walk on a high wire or to pull a cart.

- Name two things they can be taught after they learn to walk. (Call on a student. Idea: *To walk on a high wire and pull a cart.*)

EXERCISE 4

STORY READING

a. Find part D in your textbook. ✓
- We're going to read this story two times. First you'll read it out loud and make no more than 5 errors. Then I'll read it and ask questions.

b. Everybody, touch the title. ✓
- (Call on a student to read the title.) [The Fleas Surprise Aunt Fanny.]
- Everybody, what's the title? (Signal.) *The Fleas Surprise Aunt Fanny.*
- What do you think the fleas will do to surprise Aunt Fanny? (Call on a student. Ideas: *Go on strike; refuse to work; run away;* etc.)

c. (Call on individual students to read the story, each student reading two or three sentences at a time.)

- (Correct errors: Tell the word. Direct the student to reread the sentence.)
- (If the group makes more than 5 errors, direct the students to reread the story.)

Lesson 13 73

d. (After the group has read the selection making no more than 5 errors:)
Now I'll read the story and ask questions.

> **The Fleas Surprise Aunt Fanny**
>
> The fleas in Aunt Fanny's Flea Circus were tired of the way Aunt Fanny was treating them. They made up their minds to do something about it. Carl spoke for all the fleas. He went to Aunt Fanny and tried to tell her that she would have to change her ways. But she wouldn't even listen to him.

- When you change your ways, you do things differently.
- If she changed her ways, what would she do differently? (Call on different students. Ideas: *She'd be nicer to the fleas; she'd share the money,* etc.)
- Everybody, was Aunt Fanny willing to change her ways? (Signal.) *No.*

> "Please, Carl," she said. "Can't you see I'm late for dinner? Now be a good little flea and go back to your nice little box."
> "Go to your dinner," he yelled as loud as he could. "Things will be different tomorrow."
> Aunt Fanny was in for a great big surprise the next day. The circus was packed with people. Aunt Fanny picked up her stick and people clapped. "Ladies and gentlemen," she said. "You will see the greatest flea show in the world. The first act is the famous Martha Jumpjump skipping rope on the high wire."

- What kind of things would she say to introduce Martha's act? (Call on a student. Idea: *"For our first act, we have the amazing Martha Jumpjump. She can skip rope while up in the air on the high wire."*)

> Aunt Fanny waved her stick, and Martha went up to the high wire. But she didn't skip rope. She walked to the middle of the wire and fell off. "Booo," the crowd yelled.

- Why did Martha fall off the high wire? (Call on a student. Idea: *To teach Aunt Fanny a lesson.*)
- Everybody, did the crowd like Martha's act? (Signal.) *No.*

> The next act was Henry Ouch. He got in the cage with three rats. But he didn't make the rats do tricks. He hopped around the cage while the rats went to sleep. "Boooo," the crowd yelled.
> **MORE NEXT TIME**

- Why do you think Henry let the rats go to sleep? (Call on a student. Idea: *To teach Aunt Fanny a lesson.*)
- Everybody, did the crowd like Henry's act? (Signal.) *No.*

EXERCISE 5

PAIRED PRACTICE

You're going to read aloud to your partner. Today the **A** members will read first. Then the **B** members will read from the star to the end of the story. (Observe students and give feedback. Praise teams that follow the rules.)

EXERCISE 6

WRITTEN ITEMS

Skill Items

a. Find part E in your textbook. ✓
- I'll read. Here are titles for different stories: **100 Ways to Cook Turkey, Why Smoking Will Hurt You, A Funny Story.**
b. Read item 1. (Call on a student.) *[One story tells about reading something that makes you laugh. Write the letter of that title.]*
- Everybody, touch the title that names something that makes you laugh. ✓
- What's that title? (Signal.) *A Funny Story.*
c. Read item 2. (Call on a student.) *[One story tells about something that is bad for you. Write the letter of that title.]*
- Everybody, touch the title that tells about something that is bad for you. ✓
- What's that title? (Signal.) *Why Smoking Will Hurt You.*

d. Read item 3. (Call on a student.) *[One story tells about how to make different meals out of one thing. Write the letter of that title.]*
- Everybody, touch the title that tells about how to make different meals out of one thing. ✓
- What's that title? (Signal.) *100 Ways to Cook Turkey.*

Comprehension Passage Items

e. **Find part A on your worksheet.** ✓
- The item in part A is about time. I'll call on a student to read the item, but don't say the answers.
f. (Call on a student to read item 1.) *[Underline the 4 names that tell about time.]*
g. The questions in part B are about flea circuses.
h. (For each item: Call on a student to read the item.)
- Item 2. *[Were the fleas in Aunt Fanny's flea circus real fleas or make-believe fleas?]*
- Item 3. *[How do you know?]*
- Item 4. *[Where do the fleas in flea circuses usually come from?]*
- Item 5. *[What's the first thing that fleas must be taught?]*
- Item 6. *[Underline 2 other things that fleas have been taught to do.]*

Story Items

i. The questions in part C are about today's story.
j. (For each item: Call on a student to read the item.)
- Item 7. *[In what year was Aunt Fanny's Flea Circus formed?]*
- Item 8. *[In what year did Aunt Fanny and the fleas start to fight?]*
- Item 9. *[The fleas were mad at Aunt Fanny because she hogged all the <u>blank</u> and all the <u>blank</u>.]*
- Item 10. *[She made them live in a <u>blank</u>.]*
- Item 11. *[She fed them dry <u>blank</u>.]*
- The answers for items 12 through 15 are shown. You'll pick the right answer for each item.
- Item 12. *[What trick did Aunt Fanny want Martha to do?]*
- Item 13. *[What trick did Martha do?]*
- Item 14. *[What trick did Aunt Fanny want Henry Ouch to do?]*
- Item 15. *[What trick did Henry do?]*
- For items 16 through 18 the picture shows what each flea did. You'll write the name for each flea.
- Item 19. *[Which flea tried to get Aunt Fanny to change her ways?]*
- Item 20. *[Circle the picture that shows how Aunt Fanny probably looked after Martha fell off the wire.]*

End-of-Lesson Activities

INDEPENDENT WORK

Now finish your independent work for lesson 13. Do the worksheet first and then the textbook. Raise your hand when you're finished.
(Observe students and give feedback.)

WORKCHECK

a. (Direct students to take out their marking pencils.)
- We're going to check your independent work. Remember, if you got an item wrong, make an **X** next to the item. Don't change any answers.
b. (For each item: Read the item. Call on a student to answer it. If the answer is wrong, say the correct answer. Refer to the Answer Key for the correct answers.)
c. Now use your marking pencil to fix up any items you got wrong. Remember, all mistakes must be fixed up before you hand in your independent work.

WRITING-SPELLING

(Present Writing-Spelling lesson 13 after completing reading lesson 13. See Writing-Spelling Guide.)

ACTIVITY

(Present Activity 5 after completing Reading lesson 13. See Activities Across the Curriculum.)

Lesson 14

EXERCISE 1
VOCABULARY

a. **Find page 338 in your textbook.** ✓
- Touch sentence 4. ✓
- This is a new vocabulary sentence. It says: The workers propped up the cage with steel bars. Everybody, read that sentence. Get ready. (Signal.) *The workers propped up the cage with steel bars.*
- Close your eyes and say the sentence. Get ready. (Signal.) *The workers propped up the cage with steel bars.*
- (Repeat until firm.)

b. Listen: The workers propped up the cage with steel bars. When you **prop up** something, you **support** the thing so it will stay in place. What did the workers prop up in the sentence? (Signal.) *The cage.*
- So what stayed in place? (Signal.) *The cage.*
- What held the cage in place? (Signal.) *Steel bars.*

c. The workers propped up the cage with steel bars. Steel is a very tough metal. **Steel** bars are strong.

d. Listen to the sentence again: The workers propped up the cage with steel bars.

e. What are the words that mean **supported?** (Signal.) *Propped up.*
- What word names a very tough metal? (Signal.) *Steel.*
- What were the bars made of? (Signal.) *Steel.*
- What did the bars prop up? (Signal.) *The cage.*

f. (Repeat step e until firm.)

EXERCISE 2
READING WORDS

Column 1

a. Find lesson 14 in your textbook. ✓
- Touch column 1. ✓
- (Teacher reference:)

| 1. scared | 3. fancy |
| 2. usually | 4. disappear |

b. Word 1 is **scared.** What word? (Signal.) *Scared.*
- Spell **scared.** Get ready. (Tap for each letter.) *S-C-A-R-E-D.*

c. Word 2 is **usually.** What word? (Signal.) *Usually.*
- Spell **usually.** Get ready. (Tap for each letter.) *U-S-U-A-L-L-Y.*
- Things that **usually** happen are things that happen **most of the time.** If Jenny wears black shoes most of the time, Jenny **usually** wears black shoes.

d. Word 3 is **fancy.** What word? (Signal.) *Fancy.*
- Spell **fancy.** Get ready. (Tap for each letter.) *F-A-N-C-Y.*

e. Word 4 is **disappear.** What word? (Signal.) *Disappear.*
- When something disappears, you can't see it anymore. If an animal disappears, you can't see that animal anymore.

f. Let's read those words again, the fast way.
- Word 1. What word? (Signal.) *Scared.*
- (Repeat for words 2–4.)

g. (Repeat step f until firm.)

Column 2

h. Find column 2. ✓
- (Teacher reference:)

1. south	4. directions
2. measure	5. money
3. crowd	6. propped

i. Word 1. What word? (Signal.) *South.*
- (Repeat for words 2–6.)

j. (Repeat step i until firm.)

Column 3

k. Find column 3. ✓
- (Teacher reference:)

1. pillow	4. yea
2. north	5. loop
3. meter	6. steel

l. Word 1. What word? (Signal.) *Pillow.*
- (Repeat for: **2. north, 3. meter, 4. yea, 5. loop, 6. steel.**)

m. (Repeat step l until firm.)

Individual Turns

(For columns 1–3: Call on individual students, each to read one to three words per turn.)

EXERCISE 3
VOCABULARY REVIEW

a. Here's the new vocabulary sentence: The workers propped up the cage with steel bars.
- Everybody, say that sentence. Get ready. (Signal.) *The workers propped up the cage with steel bars.*
- (Repeat until firm.)

b. What two words mean **supported?** (Signal.) *Propped up.*
- What word names a tough metal? (Signal.) *Steel.*
- What was made of steel? (Signal.) *Bars.*
- What did the bars prop up? (Signal.) *The cage.*

EXERCISE 4
COMPREHENSION PASSAGES

Passage B

a. Find part B in your textbook. ✓
- You're going to read the last story about Aunt Fanny. First you'll read two information passages. This passage gives some facts about meters.

b. Everybody, touch the title. ✓
- (Call on a student to read the title.) [*Meters.*]
- Everybody, what's the title? (Signal.) *Meters.*

c. (Call on individual students to read the passage, each student reading two or three sentences at a time. Ask the specified questions as the students read.)

> **Meters**
>
> You're going to read about meters. We use meters to measure how long things are.
>
> A meter is 100 centimeters long.

- Everybody, which is longer, a centimeter or a meter? (Signal.) *Meter.*
- How many centimeters long is a meter? (Signal.) *100.*
- Hold up your fingers to show me how long a centimeter is.
  (Observe children and give feedback.)
- I'll show you how long a meter is. (Hold up your hands about 3 feet apart.)
- Your turn. Show me how long a meter is. (Observe children and give feedback.)

Passage C

d. Find part C in your textbook. ✓
- This information passage gives some facts about maps.

e. Everybody, touch the title. ✓
- (Call on a student to read the title.) [*Directions on a Map.*]
- Everybody, what's the title? (Signal.) *Directions on a Map.*

f. (Call on individual students to read the passage, each student reading two or three sentences at a time. Ask the specified questions as the students read.)

Note: Make sure all students are facing the same direction.

> **Directions on a Map**
>
> You are going to read about 4 directions: north, south, east, and west.

- Everybody, how many directions? (Signal.) *Four.*
- Name them. Get ready. (Signal.) *North, south, east, west.*
- (Repeat until firm.)

> Maps always show: north on the top.
> south on the bottom.
> east on this side: →
> west on this side: ←

- Everybody, what's on the top? (Signal.) *North.*
- What's on the bottom? (Signal.) *South.*
- (Repeat until firm.)

> If something on a map goes north, it goes this way: ↑

Lesson 14   77

> *Note:* To correct, you must face the same direction the students are facing.

- Everybody, pretend your finger is an arrow. Touch your paper to show which way north is on a map. ✓

> If something on a map goes south, it goes this way: ↓

- Everybody, pretend your finger is an arrow. Touch your paper to show which way south is on a map. ✓

> If something on a map goes this way → which direction is it going?

- Everybody, what's the answer? (Signal.) *East.*

> If something on a map goes this way ← which direction is it going?

- Everybody, what's the answer? (Signal.) *West.*

EXERCISE 5

STORY READING

a. Find part D in your textbook. ✓
- This is the last story about Aunt Fanny.
- We're going to read this story two times. First you'll read it out loud and make no more than 6 errors. Then I'll read it and ask questions.

b. Everybody, touch the title. ✓
- (Call on a student to read the title.) [*Aunt Fanny Changes Her Ways.*]
- What's going to happen in this story? (Call on a student. Ideas: *Aunt Fanny will change her ways; Aunt Fanny will do things differently.*)

c. (Call on individual students to read the story, each student reading two or three sentences at a time.)

- (Correct errors: Tell the word. Direct the student to reread the sentence.)
- (If the group makes more than 6 errors, direct the students to reread the story.)

d. (After the group has read the selection making no more than 6 errors:)
Now I'll read the story and ask questions.

Aunt Fanny Changes Her Ways

The fleas had given Aunt Fanny a surprise. Martha Jumpjump did not do her act. Henry Ouch did not do his act.

- What was Martha Jumpjump supposed to do? (Call on a student. Idea: *Skip rope on a high wire.*)
- What did she do instead of skipping rope on the high wire? (Call on a student. Idea: *Fell off the high wire.*)
- What was Henry Ouch supposed to do? (Call on a student. Idea: *Make the rats do tricks.*)
- What did he do instead? (Call on a student. Idea: *Went to sleep.*)

The crowd did not like the show at all, and Aunt Fanny was getting scared. If the rest of the fleas did not do their acts, Aunt Fanny would have to give money back to the people who paid to see the show.

- What would happen if none of the fleas did their act? (Call on a student. Idea: *Aunt Fanny would have to give money back to the people at the show.*)
- Even if the people got their money back, do you think they would be very happy? (Call on a student. Idea: *No.*)

The next act was Carl Goodscratch. He went up to the top of his 48 centimeter ladder. Then he looked up at Aunt Fanny and said, "Don't you think that you should treat us better? Don't you think that you should give us more money and give us a better place to live?"

Aunt Fanny looked at the little flea. Then she looked at the crowd. They looked mad. "Yes, Carl, yes, yes, yes," she said. "Do the dive and I will share everything with you."

- What will she share? (Call on a student. Ideas: *The money; the fame.*)

> "Do you really mean that?" Carl asked.
> "Yes, yes, yes, yes, yes," Aunt Fanny said. Her hand was shaking so much that the stick was making a wind.

- Why was her hand shaking so much? (Call on a student. Idea: *Because she was upset.*)

> So Carl did a dive. People say it was the best dive he ever did. He turned around five times. He made seven loops. And he landed in the water without making any splash at all.

- Why did Carl do such a good dive? (Call on a student. Idea: *Because Aunt Fanny decided to share.*)

> The crowd went wild. "Yea, yea," the people cheered. "What a show!" they shouted.

- Everybody, did the crowd like Carl's act? (Signal.) *Yes.*

> Now everybody in Aunt Fanny's Flea Circus is happy. Aunt Fanny is happy because the fleas work harder and put on a better show. The fleas are happy because they live in a great big fancy dog house that is a meter high and a meter wide. And they have lots and lots of money.
> **THE END**

- Everybody, did Aunt Fanny change her ways? (Signal.) *Yes.*
- Why is Aunt Fanny happy? (Call on a student. Idea: *Because the fleas work harder and put on a better show.*)
- Why do the fleas work harder? (Call on a student. Idea: *Because Aunt Fanny is being fair and sharing with them.*)
- Where do the fleas live? (Call on a student. Idea: *In a big fancy dog house.*)
- Where did they used to live? (Call on a student. Idea: *In a little box.*)
- Everybody, tell me how high that dog house was. Get ready. (Signal.) *One meter.*
- Show me how high that dog house was. ✓

EXECISE 6
PAIRED PRACTICE

You're going to read aloud to your partner. Today the **B** members will read first. Then the **A** members will read from the star to the end of the story. (Observe students and give feedback. Praise teams that follow the rules.)

EXERCISE 7
WRITTEN ITEMS
Skill Items

a. Find part E in your textbook. ✓
- I'll read. Here are titles for different stories: **Jane Goes on a Train, The Hot Summer, My Dog Likes Cats, The Best Meal.**

b. Read item 1. (Call on a student.) *[One story tells about eating good food. Write the letter of that title.]*
- Everybody, touch the title that tells about eating. ✓
- What's that title? (Signal.) *The Best Meal.*

c. Read item 2. (Call on a student.) *[One story tells about somebody taking a trip. Write the letter of that title.]*
- Everybody, touch the title that tells about taking a trip. ✓
- What's that title? (Signal.) *Jane Goes on a Train.*

d. Read item 3. (Call on a student.) *[One story tells about a time of year when people go swimming a lot. Write the letter of that title.]*
- Everybody, touch the title that names a time of year. ✓
- What's that title? (Signal.) *The Hot Summer.*

e. Read item 4. (Call on a student.) *[One story tells about pets. Write the letter of that title.]*
- Everybody, touch the title that names pets. ✓
- What's that title? (Signal.) *My Dog Likes Cats.*

f. Item 5. They blank into the stream to blank blank. Raise your hand when you know which vocabulary sentence that's supposed to be. (Call on a student.) Say the sentence. *[They waded into the stream to remove tadpoles.]*

Lesson 14

- Item 6. The fly blank about blank from the spider. Raise your hand when you know which vocabulary sentence that's supposed to be. (Call on a student.) Say the sentence. [The fly boasted about escaping from the spider.]
- When you write your sentences, be sure to spell all the words correctly.

Comprehension Passage Items

g. **Find part A on your worksheet.** ✓
- The questions in part A are about meters. I'll call on different students to read the items, but don't say the answers.

h. (For each item: Call on a student to read the item.)
- Item 1. [Which is longer, a centimeter or a meter?]
- Item 2. [How many centimeters long is a meter?]

i. The questions in part B are about the directions on a map.

j. (For each item: Call on a student to read the item.)
- Item 3. [Write **north, south, east,** and **west** in the right boxes.]
- Item 4. [Touch the **X**. An arrow goes from the **X**. Which direction is that arrow going?]
- Item 5. [Touch the **Y**. An arrow goes from the **Y**. Which direction is that arrow going?]
- Item 6. [Touch the **B**. An arrow goes from the **B**. Which direction is that arrow going?]

Story Items

k. Items 7 through 17 are about today's story.
- Item 7. [The fleas were mad at Aunt Fanny because she hogged all the blank and all the blank.]
- Item 8. [She fed them dry blank.]
- For items 9 through 11 the picture shows what each flea did. You'll write the name for each flea.
- Item 12. [Did Aunt Fanny change her ways?]
- Item 13. [Which flea made Aunt Fanny say she would change?]
- Item 14. [Underline 2 reasons why Aunt Fanny is happy now.]
- Item 15. [Where do the fleas live now?]
- Item 16. [Where did they used to live?]
- Item 17. [Underline 2 reasons why the fleas are happy now.]

End-of-Lesson Activities

INDEPENDENT WORK

Now finish your independent work for lesson 14. Raise your hand when you're finished. (Observe students and give feedback.)

WORKCHECK

a. (Direct students to take out their marking pencils.)
- We're going to check your independent work. Remember, if you got an item wrong, make an **X** next to the item. Don't change any answers.

b. (For each item: Read the item. Call on a student to answer it. If the answer is wrong, say the correct answer. Refer to the Answer Key for the correct answers.)

c. Now use your marking pencil to fix up any items you got wrong. Remember, all mistakes must be fixed up before you hand in your independent work.

WRITING-SPELLING

(Present Writing-Spelling lesson 14 after completing Reading lesson 14. See Writing-Spelling Guide.)

ACTIVITY

(Present Activity 6 after completing Reading lesson 14. See Activities Across the Curriculum.)

Lesson 15

Materials: Each student will need their thermometer chart for exercise 6.

EXERCISE 1
VOCABULARY REVIEW

a. Here's the vocabulary sentence you learned in the last lesson: The workers propped up the cage with steel bars.
  • Everybody, say that sentence. Get ready. (Signal.) *The workers propped up the cage with steel bars.*
  • (Repeat until firm.)
b. What word names a tough metal? (Signal.) *Steel.*
  • What was made of steel? (Signal.) *Bars.*
  • What two words mean **supported?** (Signal.) *Propped up.*
  • What did the bars prop up? (Signal.) *The cage.*

EXERCISE 2
READING WORDS
Column 1
a. **Find lesson 15 in your textbook.** ✓
  • Touch column 1. ✓
  • (Teacher reference:)

  1. Alaska   4. favorite
  2. escape   5. opposite
  3. rough

b. Word 1 is **Alaska.** What word? (Signal.) *Alaska.*
  • Spell **Alaska.** Get ready. (Tap for each letter.) *A-L-A-S-K-A.*
  • Alaska is the largest state. It is far north of the other states.
c. Word 2 is **escape.** What word? (Signal.) *Escape.*
  • Spell **escape.** Get ready. (Tap for each letter.) *E-S-C-A-P-E.*
  • What do you do when you escape from somebody? (Call on a student. Idea: *You get away from the person.*)
d. Word 3 is **rough.** What word? (Signal.) *Rough.*
  • Spell **rough.** Get ready. (Tap for each letter.) *R-O-U-G-H.*
e. Word 4 is **favorite.** What word? (Signal.) *Favorite.*
f. Word 5 is **opposite.** What word? (Signal.) *Opposite.*
g. Let's read those words again, the fast way.
  • Word 1. What word? (Signal.) *Alaska.*
  • (Repeat for words 2–5.)
h. (Repeat step g until firm.)

Column 2
i. Find column 2. ✓
  • (Teacher reference:)

  1. <u>tad</u>poles   3. <u>gold</u>fish
  2. <u>some</u>times   4. <u>any</u>body

  • These words are compound words. The first part of each word is underlined.
j. Word 1. What's the first part? (Signal.) *tad.*
  • What's the whole word? (Signal.) *Tadpoles.*
  • Everybody, what are tadpoles? (Signal.) *Baby frogs or toads.*
k. Word 2. What's the first part? (Signal.) *some.*
  • What's the whole word? (Signal.) *Sometimes.*
l. Word 3. What's the first part? (Signal.) *gold.*
  • What's the whole word? (Signal.) *Goldfish.*
m. Word 4. What's the first part? (Signal.) *any.*
  • What's the whole word? (Signal.) *Anybody.*
n. Let's read those words again.
  • Word 1. What word? (Signal.) *Tadpoles.*
  • (Repeat for words 2–4.)
o. (Repeat step n until firm.)

Column 3

p. Find column 3. ✓
- (Teacher reference:)

1. boast	3. toaster
2. Goad	4. floating

- These words have the letters **O-A** in them. What sound does **O-A** usually make? (Signal.) *Oh.*
q. Word 1. What word? (Signal.) *Boast.*
- What do you do when you boast about something? (Call on a student. Idea: *You brag about it.*)
- Word 2 is a name. What name? (Signal.) *Goad.*
- Word 3. What word? (Signal.) *Toaster.*
- Word 4. What word? (Signal.) *Floating.*
r. Let's read those words again.
- Word 1. What word? (Signal.) *Boast.*
- (Repeat for words 2–4.)
s. (Repeat step r until firm.)

Column 4

t. Find column 4. ✓
- (Teacher reference:)

1. <u>mem</u>bers	3. <u>hunt</u>ers
2. <u>pill</u>ow	4. <u>doll</u>ars

- These words have more than one syllable.
  The first syllable is underlined.
u. Word 1. What's the first syllable? (Signal.) *mem.*
- What's the whole word? (Signal.) *Members.*
v. Word 2. What's the first syllable? (Signal.) *pill.*
- What's the whole word? (Signal.) *Pillow.*
w. Word 3. What's the first syllable? (Signal.) *hunt.*
- What's the whole word? (Signal.) *Hunters.*
x. Word 4. What's the first syllable? (Signal.) *doll.*
- What's the whole word? (Signal.) *Dollars.*
y. Let's read those words again.
- Word 1. What word? (Signal.) *Members.*
- (Repeat for words 2–4.)
z. (Repeat step y until firm.)

Column 5

a. Find column 5. ✓
- (Teacher reference:)

1. full-grown	4. strong
2. family	5. disappears
3. thousands	6. covered

b. Word 1. What word? (Signal.) *Full-grown.*
- (Repeat for words 2–6.)
c. Let's read those words again.
- (Repeat step b until firm.)

Column 6

d. Find column 6. ✓
- (Teacher reference:)

1. rich	4. hound
2. shore	5. front
3. circus	

e. Word 1. What word? (Signal.) *Rich.*
- (Repeat for words 2–5.)
f. (Repeat step e until firm.)

Individual Turns

(For columns 1–6: Call on individual students, each to read one to three words per turn.)

EXERCISE 3

COMPREHENSION PASSAGE

a. Find part B in your textbook. ✓
- You're going to read a story about a toad. First you'll read the information passage. It gives some facts about toads.
b. Everybody, touch the title. ✓
- (Call on a student to read the title.) *[Facts About Toads and Frogs.]*
- Everybody, what's the title? (Signal.) *Facts About Toads and Frogs.*
c. (Call on individual students to read the passage, each student reading two or three sentences at a time.)

Facts About Toads and Frogs

Toads and frogs are members of the same family. Here are facts about toads and frogs:
They are born in water, and they live in the water until they are full-grown. Then they move onto the land.

- Everybody, where are they born? (Signal.) *In water.*
- Where do they live until they are full-grown? (Signal.) *In water.*
- And then where do they go? (Signal.) *Onto land.*

> **At first toads and frogs are tadpoles that have no legs.**

- Everybody, what are toads and frogs when they are first born? (Signal.) *Tadpoles.*
- The pictures show tadpoles. Touch the picture of the tadpole that has no legs. ✓
- That's how the tadpole looks when it is first born. What will that tadpole grow into? (Call on a student. Idea: *Toad or frog.*)

> **Then the tadpoles grow two back legs.**

- Everybody, what do they grow first? (Signal.) *Two back legs.*

> **Then they grow two front legs.**

- Everybody, what do they grow next? (Signal.) *Two front legs.*

> **Then the tail disappears and they are full-grown toads or frogs.**

- What's the last thing that happens before they are full-grown toads or frogs? (Signal.) *The tail disappears.*

> **Now that their legs are big and strong, frogs and toads live on the land.**
> **Remember, they are born in the water and grow up in the water. Then they move to the land.**

EXERCISE 4
STORY READING

a. Find part C in your textbook. ✓
- We're going to read this story two times. First you'll read it out loud and make no more than 6 errors. Then I'll read it and ask questions.

b. Everybody, touch the title. ✓
- (Call on a student to read the title.) [*Goad the Toad.*]
- Everybody, what's the title? (Signal.) *Goad the Toad.*

c. (Call on individual students to read the story, each student reading two or three sentences at a time.)

- (Correct errors: Tell the word. Direct the student to reread the sentence.)
- (If the group makes more than 6 errors, direct the students to reread the story.)

d. (After the group has read the selection making no more than 6 errors:)
Now I'll read the story and ask questions.

> **Goad the Toad**
>
> Once there was a toad named Goad. Goad was the biggest toad you have ever seen. Goad was bigger than a baseball. She was even bigger than a toaster.

- Everybody, show me with your hands how big a toaster is. ✓
- Are there really toads that big? (Signal.) *No.*
- Real toads are about as big as my fist. So is Goad a real toad or a make-believe toad? (Signal.) *Make-believe toad.*

> **Goad was not only big. She was smart. She was smarter than a trained seal. Not only was Goad big and smart, Goad was fast. She was faster than a cat chasing a mouse.**

- We know three things about Goad. Let me read that part again. You listen and get ready to tell the three things:
    Goad was not only big. She was smart. She was smarter than a trained seal. Not only was Goad big and smart, Goad was fast. She was faster than a cat chasing a mouse.
- Everybody, Goad was big and smart and what else? (Signal.) *Fast.*

> **Goad lived near a large lake called Four Mile Lake. It was four miles from one end of the lake to the other.**

- Why was it called Four Mile Lake? (Call on a student. Idea: *Because it was four miles from one end to the other.*)

Lesson 15 83

- The map shows Four Mile Lake. Touch the west bank of the lake. ✓
- There's a dotted line that goes through the lake. Follow that line and see how many miles you go before you reach the east bank. ✓
- Everybody, how many miles? (Signal.) *Four.*

> Goad liked to visit places on Four Mile Lake. Sometimes, she would hop over to the logs near the north shore of the lake.

- Everybody, touch the letter at the north shore of the lake in the picture. ✓
- What letter? (Signal.) *T.*

> Sometimes, she would hop over the hills on the south shore.

- Everybody, touch the letter at the south shore of the lake. ✓
- What letter? (Signal.) *B.*

> Sometimes, she would go for a dip near the east shore of the lake.

- Everybody, touch the letter at the east shore of the lake. ✓
- What letter? (Signal.) *W.*

> When Goad was in the water, she was not fast. She could not swim as fast as a seal or a goldfish. In fact, she could not swim as fast as a very slow frog.

- Everybody, was Goad fast on land? (Signal.) *Yes.*
- Was she fast in water? (Signal.) *No.*

> When Goad was in the water, she looked like a floating pillow with two big eyes.
> Because Goad was so big, and so fast, and so smart, thousands of hunters went to Four Mile Lake every year to see if they could catch Goad.

- Why did they want to catch her? (Call on a student. Ideas: *Because she was different from the other toads; because she was so big, fast, and smart.*)

> People from the circus knew that if they had Goad, they could put on a show that would bring thousands of people to the circus.

- Would a great big smart toad make a good circus act? (Call on a student. Idea: *Yes.*)

> Hunters from zoos knew that people would come from all over to visit any zoo that had a toad like Goad. Some hunters came because they wanted to become rich.

- How could they become rich by catching Goad? (Call on a student. Ideas: *Make people pay to see her; sell her to the zoo.*)

> Goad was worth thousands of dollars to anybody who could catch her. But nobody was able to catch her.
> **More next time**

- Why do you suppose that nobody was able to catch Goad? (Call on a student. Ideas: *She was too smart; she was too fast.*)

EXERCISE 5

WRITTEN ITEMS
Skill Items

a. Find part D in your textbook. ✓
- Number your lined paper from 1 through 16. Pencils down when you've finished. ✓
- The rule for item 1 says: Frogs have smooth skin. That rule tells you something about any frog. It doesn't tell you anything about things that are not frogs.
- Everybody, does the rule tell about toads? (Signal.) *No.*
- Does the rule tell about birds? (Signal.) *No.*
- Does the rule tell about snakes that have smooth skin? (Signal.) *No.*
- The only thing the rule tells about is frogs.
- Listen: Frogs have smooth skin. What's the only thing that rule tells about? (Signal.) *Frogs.*

b. Find the rule for item 2. ✓
- The rule says: **Birds have two feet.**

- Does that rule tell you anything about humans? (Signal.) *No.*
- Does it tell you anything about monkeys? (Signal.) *No.*
- What's the only thing the rule tells about? (Signal.) *Birds.*

c. Find the rule for item 6. ✓
- The rule says: **The largest mountains were covered with snow.**
- What's the only thing that rule tells about? (Signal.) *The largest mountains.*
- Does that rule tell about the smaller mountains? (Signal.) *No.*
- Does that rule tell about the valley? (Signal.) *No.*
- Does that rule tell about the snow near the lake? (Signal.) *No.*

d. Your turn. Write answers to items 1 through 8. Raise your hand when you've done that much.
(Observe students and give feedback.)

Comprehension Passage Items

e. **Find part A on your worksheet.** ✓
- The questions in part A are about tadpoles, toads, and frogs. I'll call on different students to read the items, but don't say the answers.

f. (For each item: Call on a student to read the item.)
- Item 1. *[Circle what happens first.]*
- Item 2. *[Underline what happens last.]*
- Item 3. *[Make a box around the animals that live on the land.]*

Story Items

g. Items 4 through 11 are about today's story.
- Item 4. *[What kind of animal was Goad?]*
- Item 5. *[Name the lake that Goad lived near.]*
- Item 6. *[Why did the lake have that name?]*
- Item 7. *[Was Goad fast or slow on land?]*
- Item 8. *[Was Goad fast or slow in the water?]*
- Item 9. *[Underline 2 reasons people wanted to catch Goad.]*
- Item 10. *[Make a box around the animal that could be Goad.]*
- Item 11. *[Hunters from a zoo said 2 of the things below. Underline those 2 things.]*

EXERCISE 6

Note: There is a reading checkout in this lesson; therefore, there is no paired practice.

READING CHECKOUTS

a. Today is a reading-checkout day. While you're writing answers to your worksheet and textbook items, I'm going to call on you one at a time to read part of the story we read in lesson 14.

b. (Hold up a thermometer chart.) ✓
- Remember, when you pass a checkout, you color that space red. Students who pass the checkout for lesson 15 get to color space 15 red.

c. You pass a checkout by reading the passage in less than a minute without making more than 2 mistakes. Remember, less than a minute and no more than 2 errors. If you don't pass the checkout today, you can try again next time. But you can't color in the space for 15 until you pass checkout 15. When I call on you to come and do your checkout, bring your thermometer chart.

d. (Call on individual students to read the portion of story 14 marked with ❀.)
- (Time the student. Note words that are missed and total number of words read.)
- (Teacher reference:)

> ❀ So Carl did a dive. People say it was the best dive he ever did. He turned around five times. He made seven loops. And he landed in the water without making any splash at all.
> The crowd went wild. "Yea, yea," the people cheered. "What a show!" they shouted. **[50]**
> Now everybody in Aunt Fanny's Flea Circus is happy. Aunt Fanny is happy because the fleas work harder and put on a better show. The **[75]** fleas are happy because they live in a great big fancy dog house that is a meter high and a meter wide. And they have ❀ **[100]** lots and lots of money.

- (If the student reads the passage in one minute or less and makes no more than 2 errors, direct the student to color in space 15 of the thermometer chart.)

- (If the student makes any mistakes, point to each word that was misread and identify it.)
- (If the student does not meet the time-error criterion for the passage, direct the student to practice reading the story with the assigned partner.)

End-of-Lesson Activities

INDEPENDENT WORK

Now finish your independent work for lesson 15. Raise your hand when you're finished. (Observe students and give feedback.)

WORKCHECK

a. (Direct students to take out their marking pencils.)
- We're going to check your independent work. Remember, if you got an item wrong, make an **X** next to the item. Don't change any answers.

b. (For each item: Read the item. Call on a student to answer it. If the answer is wrong, say the correct answer. Refer to the Answer Key for the correct answers.)

c. Now use your marking pencil to fix up any items you got wrong. Remember, all mistakes must be fixed up before you hand in your worksheet.

WRITING-SPELLING

(Present Writing-Spelling lesson 15, after completing Reading lesson 15. See Writing-Spelling Guide.)

Lessons 16–20 • Planning Page
Looking Ahead

	Lesson 16	Lesson 17	Lesson 18	Lesson 19	Lesson 20
Lesson Events	Vocabulary Sentences Reading Words Vocabulary Review Comprehension Passages Story Reading Paired Practice Written Items Independent Work Workcheck Writing-Spelling	Vocabulary Sentences Reading Words Vocabulary Review Comprehension Passages Story Reading Paired Practice Written Items Independent Work Workcheck Writing-Spelling	Vocabulary Review Reading Words Comprehension Passages Story Reading Paired Practice Written Items Independent Work Workcheck Writing-Spelling	Vocabulary Review Reading Words Comprehension Passages Story Reading Paired Practice Written Items Independent Work Workcheck Writing-Spelling Activity	Reading Checkouts Test Marking the Test Test Remedies Literature Lesson
Vocabulary Sentence	sentence #1 sentence #2 sentence #3	#5: Hunters were <u>stationed</u> at <u>opposite</u> ends of the field.		sentence #1 sentence #2 sentence #3	
Reading Words: Word Types	–ed words multi-syllable words mixed words	modeled words –y words multi-syllable words mixed words	modeled words –ed words mixed words	–tion and –sion words 2-syllable words mixed words	
New Vocabulary	warts	England	binoculars stationed		
Comprehension Passages	More Facts About Toads and Frogs	1) How Far Apart Things Are 2) How Toads Catch Flies	1) Facts About Moles 2) The Opposite Direction	1) Binoculars 2) How Fast Things Move	
Story	Goad Uses Her First Trick	Food Traps	Goad's Four Tricks	The Brown Family Comes to Catch Goad	
Skill Items	Vocabulary Same Vocabulary sentence	Deductions Vocabulary Titles Vocabulary sentences	Deductions Same Vocabulary	Deductions Same Quotations Vocabulary sentence	Test: Vocabulary sentences #3, 4; Deductions
Special Materials					Thermometer charts, * materials for literature project
Special Projects/Activities				Activity after lesson 19	

* Literature anthology; blackline masters 2A, 2B, 2C; lined paper; scissors; tape or paste; drawing materials.

Lesson 16

EXERCISE 1
VOCABULARY REVIEW

a. You learned a sentence that tells where they waded.
- Everybody, say that sentence. Get ready. (Signal.) *They waded into the stream to remove tadpoles.*
- (Repeat until firm.)

b. You learned a sentence that tells what the fly boasted about.
- Everybody, say that sentence. Get ready. (Signal.) *The fly boasted about escaping from the spider.*
- (Repeat until firm.)

c. Here's the last sentence you learned: The workers propped up the cage with steel bars.
- Everybody, say that sentence. Get ready. (Signal.) *The workers propped up the cage with steel bars.*
- (Repeat until firm.)

d. What word names a very tough metal? (Signal.) *Steel.*
- What are the words that mean **supported?** (Signal.) *Propped up.*

e. Once more. Say the sentence that tells what the workers did to the cage. Get ready. (Signal.) *The workers propped up the cage with steel bars.*

EXERCISE 2
READING WORDS

Column 1

a. Find lesson 16 in your textbook. ✓
- Touch column 1. ✓
- (Teacher reference:)

1. covered	4. noticed
2. visited	5. removed
3. escaped	6. stationed

- All the words in column 1 end with the letters **E-D.**

b. Word 1. What word? (Signal.) *Covered.*
- Spell **covered.** Get ready. (Tap for each letter.) *C-O-V-E-R-E-D.*

c. Word 2. What word? (Signal.) *Visited.*
- Spell **visited.** Get ready. (Tap for each letter.) *V-I-S-I-T-E-D.*

d. Word 3. What word? (Signal.) *Escaped.*
- Spell **escaped.** Get ready. (Tap for each letter.) *E-S-C-A-P-E-D.*

e. Word 4. What word? (Signal.) *Noticed.*
f. (Repeat for words 5 and 6.)

g. Let's read those words again.
- Word 1. What word? (Signal.) *Covered.*
- (Repeat for words 2–6.)

h. (Repeat step g until firm.)

Column 2

i. Find column 2. ✓
- (Teacher reference:)

1. **favor**ite	3. **Toads**ville
2. **eve**ning	4. **hun**dreds

- Part of each word is underlined.

j. Word 1. What's the underlined part? (Signal.) *favor.*
- What's the whole word? (Signal.) *Favorite.*

k. Word 2. What's the underlined part? (Signal.) *eve.*
- What's the whole word? (Signal.) *Evening.*

l. Word 3. What's the underlined part? (Signal.) *toads.*
- What's the whole word? (Signal.) *Toadsville.*

m. Word 4. What's the underlined part? (Signal.) *hun.*
- What's the whole word? (Signal.) *Hundreds.*

n. Let's read those words again.
- Word 1. What word? (Signal.) *Favorite.*
- (Repeat for words 2–4.)

o. (Repeat step n until firm.)

Column 3

p. Find column 3. ✓
- (Teacher reference:)

1. warts	4. first
2. belly	5. opposite
3. Alaska	

q. Word 1. What word? (Signal.) *Warts.*
- Warts are little bumps that some people have on their body.
- Word 2. What word? (Signal.) *Belly.*
- (Repeat for: **3. Alaska, 4. first, 5. opposite.**)

Column 4

r. Find column 4. ✓
- (Teacher reference:)

1. shovels	4. there
2. tongue	5. underground
3. rough	

s. Word 1. What word? (Signal.) *Shovels.*
- (Repeat for words 2–5.)

t. (Repeat step s until firm.)

Individual Turns

(For columns 1–4: Call on individual students, each to read one to three words per turn.)

EXERCISE 3

COMPREHENSION PASSAGE

a. Find part B in your textbook. ✓
- The information passage gives some facts about toads and frogs.

b. Everybody, touch the title. ✓
- (Call on a student to read the title.) *[More Facts About Toads and Frogs.]*
- Everybody, what's the title? (Signal.) *More Facts About Toads and Frogs.*

c. (Call on individual students to read the passage, each student reading two or three sentences at a time.)

> **More Facts About Toads and Frogs**
>
> Toads and frogs are members of the same family. But toads are different from frogs. Here are some facts about how toads and frogs are different:
> Toads have skin that is rough and covered with warts.

- Everybody, what is a toad's skin covered with? (Signal.) *Warts.*
- Warts are like rough bumps. Everybody, do **frogs** have skin that is rough and covered with warts? (Signal.) *No.*

> No toads have teeth, but some frogs have teeth.

- Everybody, listen to that fact again: No toads have teeth, but some frogs have teeth.
- Say that fact. Get ready. (Signal.) *No toads have teeth, but some frogs have teeth.*
- (Repeat until firm.)
- Do any toads have teeth? (Signal.) *No.*
- Do any frogs have teeth? (Signal.) *Yes.*

> The back legs of toads are not as big or strong as the back legs of frogs.

- Everybody, whose back legs are stronger, toads' or frogs'? (Signal.) *Frogs'.*
- So which animal could jump farther, a toad or a frog? (Signal.) *A frog.*

EXERCISE 4

STORY READING

a. Find part C in your textbook. ✓
- We're going to read this story two times. First you'll read it out loud and make no more than 6 errors. Then I'll read it and ask questions.

b. Everybody, touch the title. ✓
- (Call on a student to read the title.) *[Goad Uses Her First Trick.]*
- Everybody, what's Goad going to do in this story? (Signal.) *Her first trick.*

c. (Call on individual students to read the story, each student reading two or three sentences at a time.)
- (Correct errors: Tell the word. Direct the student to reread the sentence.)
- (If the group makes more than 6 errors, direct the students to reread the story.)

d. (After the group has read the selection making no more than 6 errors:) Now I'll read the story and ask questions.

> **Goad Uses Her First Trick**
>
> Goad lived near Four Mile Lake. Down the road from the lake was a town. The name of that town was Toadsville. It was named Toadsville because so many people who visited the town had come to hunt for a big, smart, fast toad.

- Everybody, who is that big, smart, fast toad? (Signal.) *Goad.*

Lesson 16 89

And in the evening you could find hundreds of people sitting around Toadsville talking about Goad. First they would talk about some of the traps that had been made to catch Goad. Then they would tell how Goad escaped. One of their favorite stories is the one of the great big net.

- How could you use a great big net to catch a toad? (Call on a student. Idea: *Drop it on top of the toad.*)

Five hunters from Alaska had come to Four Mile Lake with a net that was nearly a mile wide. They waited until Goad was on a hill where there were no trees, just some white rocks. Then they flew over the hill in a plane and dropped the great big net over the hill.

Goad was under the net. The five hunters rushed to the place where Goad had last been seen. But there was no Goad. There was some grass and five large white rocks. The hunters removed the net and began to go over every centimeter of the ground.

- The picture on the next page shows the hunters looking for Goad. You can see the trick that Goad is using. What is she doing? (Call on a student. Idea: *Pretending to be a rock.*)

Suddenly, one of the hunters noticed that the biggest rock was moving. The biggest rock wasn't a rock at all. It was Goad.

She had moved near the other rocks. Then she had turned over on her back so that her white belly was showing. That belly looked like a white rock. Suddenly she turned over. "There she is," one of the hunters yelled, but before the others could turn around, Goad hopped down the side of the hill and was gone.

MORE NEXT TIME

- Why didn't those hunters just grab her when she was hopping down the hill? (Call on a student. Idea: *Goad was too fast.*)

EXERCISE 5
PAIRED PRACTICE

You're going to read aloud to your partner. Today the **A** members will read first. Then the **B** members will read from the star to the end of the story. (Observe students and give feedback. Praise teams that follow the rules.)

EXERCISE 6
WRITTEN ITEMS
Skill Items

a. Find part D in your textbook. ✓
- Number your lined paper from 1 through 16. Pencils down when you're finished. ✓

> Write the word from the box that means the same thing as the underlined part of each sentence.
>
> | weight | measure | leaves | paws |
> |--------|---------|--------|------|
> | grove | family | hooves | evening |
>
> 1. The deer ran into the <u>small group of trees</u> to hide.
> 2. The horse's <u>feet</u> were covered with mud.
> 3. She used a ruler to <u>see</u> how long the rope was.

b. Touch item 1. ✓
- This is a new type of item. The underlined part of each sentence tells about one of the words in the box.
c. Item 1: The deer ran into the <u>small group of trees</u> to hide.
- Everybody, what words are underlined? (Signal.) *Small group of trees.*

- Raise your hand when you've found the word in the box that means **small group of trees.**
- Everybody, what word means **small group of trees?** (Signal.) *Grove.*
- Say sentence 1 with the word **grove** instead of **small group of trees.** Get ready. (Signal.) *The deer ran into the grove to hide.*

d. Item 2: The horse's <u>feet</u> were covered with mud.
- Everybody, what word is underlined? (Signal.) *Feet.*
- Raise your hand when you've found the word in the box that means **feet.** ✓
- Everybody, what word? (Signal.) *Hooves.*
- Say sentence 2 with the word **hooves** instead of **feet.** Get ready. (Signal.) *The horse's hooves were covered with mud.*

e. Item 3: She used a ruler to <u>see</u> how long the rope was.
- Everybody, what word is underlined? (Signal.) *See.*
- Raise your hand when you've found the word in the box that can replace the word **see.** ✓
- Everybody, what word? (Signal.) *Measure.*
- Say sentence 3 with the word **measure** instead of **see.** Get ready. (Signal.) *She used a ruler to measure how long the rope was.*

f. Everybody, write the answers to items 1 through 3. Remember, write the words from the box that mean the same thing as the underlined part of each sentence. Raise your hand when you've finished items 1 through 3.
(Observe students and give feedback.)

g. Read item 4. (Call on a student.) *[Look at object A, object B, and object C. Write at least 2 ways all 3 objects are the same.]*
- Read the choices for item 4. (Call on a student.) *[They are all big. They are pink. They are not round. They are striped. They are circles.]*
- Name one way they're the same. (Call on a student.) *[They are pink.]* or *[They are striped.]* or *[They are circles.]*
- Name another way they're the same. (Call on a student.)
- Name another way they're the same. (Call on a student.)

h. **Find part A on your worksheet.** ✓
- (Teacher reference:)

1. At each dot, draw an arrow to show which way the string will move when the girl pulls it.

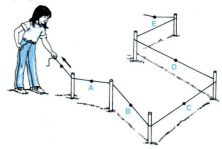

i. The picture shows somebody pulling on the end of the string. Touch the arrow near the dot by the girl's hand. ✓
- The arrow shows the way the string will move at that point when the girl pulls on the end. There are five other dots along the string. Touch dot A. ✓
- When the girl pulls on the end of the string, the string will move at dot A. Move your finger to show me which way the dot will move.
(Observe students and give feedback.)
- You should be moving toward the girl. Draw an arrow to show the dot moving in that direction.
(Observe students and give feedback.)

j. At each of the other dots draw an arrow to show which way the string will move. Pencils down when you're finished.
(Observe students and give feedback.)

Story Items

k. Items 6 through 10 are about today's story. I'll call on different students to read the items, but don't say the answers.

l. (For each item: Call on a student to read the item.)
- Item 6. *[Goad was hard to catch because she was very <u>blank</u>.]*
- Item 7. *[What did the hunters from Alaska use when they tried to catch Goad?]*
- Item 8. *[Goad fooled the hunters from Alaska by making herself look like a <u>blank</u>.]*
- Item 9. *[What part of Goad is white?]*
- Item 10. *[Underline the picture of Goad using her first trick.]*

End-of-Lesson Activities

INDEPENDENT WORK

Now finish your independent work for lesson 16. Raise your hand when you're finished. (Observe students and give feedback.)

WORKCHECK

a. (Direct students to take out their marking pencils.)
- We're going to check your independent work. Remember, if you got an item wrong, make an **X** next to the item.

b. (For each item: Read the item. Call on a student to answer it. If the answer is wrong, say the correct answer. Refer to the Answer Key for the correct answers.)

c. Now use your marking pencil to fix up any items you got wrong. Remember, all mistakes must be fixed up before you hand in your independent work.

WRITING-SPELLING

(Present Writing-Spelling lesson 16 after completing Reading lesson 16. See Writing-Spelling Guide.)

Lesson 17

EXERCISE 1
VOCABULARY

a. **Find page 338 in your textbook.** ✓
- Touch sentence 5. ✓
- This is a new vocabulary sentence. It says: Hunters were stationed at opposite ends of the field. Everybody, read that sentence. Get ready. (Signal.) *Hunters were stationed at opposite ends of the field.*
- Close your eyes and say the sentence. Get ready. (Signal.) *Hunters were stationed at opposite ends of the field.*
- (Repeat until firm.)

b. Listen: Hunters were **stationed** at opposite ends of the field. When someone is stationed in a place, the person is supposed to stay in that place.

c. Everybody, where were the hunters stationed? (Signal.) *At opposite ends of the field.*
- That means some hunters had a place at one end of the field and other hunters had a place at the other end of the field.

d. Hunters were stationed at opposite ends of the field. If one end of the field was the north end, what was the opposite end? (Signal.) *The south end.*
- If one end of the field was the east end, what was the opposite end? (Signal.) *The west end.*

e. Listen to the sentence again: Hunters were stationed at opposite ends of the field. Say that sentence. Get ready. (Signal.) *Hunters were stationed at opposite ends of the field.*

f. The hunters had to stay where they were placed. So the hunters were . . . (Signal.) *Stationed.*
- What word tells which ends of the field? (Signal.) *Opposite.*

EXERCISE 2
READING WORDS

Column 1

a. Find lesson 17 in your textbook. ✓
- Touch column 1. ✓
- (Teacher reference:)

1. famous	4. tongue
2. women	5. England
3. breath	6. silence

b. Word 1 is **famous.** What word? (Signal.) *Famous.*
- Spell **famous.** Get ready. (Tap for each letter.) *F-A-M-O-U-S.*

c. Word 2 is **women.** What word? (Signal.) *Women.*
- Spell **women.** Get ready. (Tap for each letter.) *W-O-M-E-N.*

d. Word 3 is **breath.** What word? (Signal.) *Breath.*
- Spell **breath.** Get ready. (Tap for each letter.) *B-R-E-A-T-H.*

e. Word 4 is **tongue.** What word? (Signal.) *Tongue.*
- Spell **tongue.** Get ready. (Tap for each letter.) *T-O-N-G-U-E.*

f. Word 5 is **England.** What word? (Signal.) *England.*
- England is a country that is almost 4 thousand miles from the United States.

g. Word 6 is **silence.** What word? (Signal.) *Silence.*

h. Let's read those words again, the fast way.
- Word 1. What word? (Signal.) *Famous.*
- (Repeat for words 2–6.)

i. (Repeat step h until firm.)

Column 2

j. Find column 2. ✓
- (Teacher reference:)

1. family	4. already
2. belly	5. sixty
3. sticky	6. stubby

- These words all end with the letter **Y.**

k. Word 1. What word? (Signal.) *Family.*
- (Repeat for words 2–6.)

l. (Repeat step k until firm.)

Column 3

m. Find column 3. ✓
- (Teacher reference:)

1. <u>shov</u>els	4. <u>un</u>derground
2. <u>sec</u>onds	5. <u>half</u>way
3. <u>wood</u>en	

- These words have more than one syllable.
  The first syllable is underlined.

n. Word 1. What's the first syllable? (Signal.) *shove.*
- What's the whole word? (Signal.) *Shovels.*
o. Word 2. What's the first syllable? (Signal.) *sec.*
- What's the whole word? (Signal.) *Seconds.*
p. Word 3. What's the first syllable? (Signal.) *wood.*
- What's the whole word? (Signal.) *Wooden.*
q. Word 4. What's the first syllable? (Signal.) *un.*
- What's the whole word? (Signal.) *Underground.*
r. Word 5. What's the first syllable? (Signal.) *half.*
- What's the whole word? (Signal.) *Halfway.*
s. Let's read those words again.
- Word 1. What word? (Signal.) *Shovels.*
- (Repeat for words 2–5.)
t. (Repeat step s until firm.)

Column 4

u. Find column 4. ✓
- (Teacher reference:)

1. length	4. noticed
2. blue	5. evening
3. hundred	

v. Word 1. What word? (Signal.) *Length.*
- (Repeat for words 2–5.)
w. Let's read those words again.
- Word 1. What word? (Signal.) *Length.*
- (Repeat for words 2–5.)
x. (Repeat step w until firm.)

Column 5

y. Find column 5. ✓
- (Teacher reference:)

1. distance	3. swallow
2. balloon	4. fourth

z. Word 1. What word? (Signal.) *Distance.*
- (Repeat for words 2–4.)
a. (Repeat step z until firm.)

Individual Turns

(For columns 1–5: Call on individual students, each to read one to three words per turn.)

EXERCISE 3

VOCABULARY REVIEW

a. Here's the new vocabulary sentence: Hunters were stationed at opposite ends of the field.
- Everybody, say that sentence. Get ready. (Signal.) *Hunters were stationed at opposite ends of the field.*
- (Repeat until firm.)
b. What word tells which ends of the field? (Signal.) *Opposite.*
- The hunters had to stay where they were placed. So the hunters were . . . (Signal.) *Stationed.*

EXERCISE 4

COMPREHENSION PASSAGES

Passage B

a. Find part B in your textbook. ✓
- You're going to read the next story about Goad. First you'll read two information passages. The first one tells about distance and length.
b. Everybody, touch the title. ✓
- (Call on a student to read the title.) [How Far Apart Things Are.]
- Everybody, what's the title? (Signal.) *How Far Apart Things Are.*
c. (Call on individual students to read the passage, each student reading two or three sentences at a time.)

How Far Apart Things Are

Names that tell about length or distance tell how far apart things are. The book your teacher is holding is one foot tall. A ruler is one foot long.

- Everybody, hold up your hands so they are about one foot apart. ✓

A <u>mile</u> is a name that tells how far apart things are. If two things are a mile apart, they are more than 5 thousand feet apart.

- Everybody, a mile is more than how many feet? (Signal.) *5 thousand.*
- That's a long distance.

A <u>meter</u> is a name that tells about length.

- Everybody, hold up your hands so they are about a meter apart. ✓

A <u>centimeter</u> is a name that tells about length.

- Everybody, hold up your fingers so they are about a centimeter apart. ✓

Remember, miles, feet, meters, centimeters, and inches are names that tell about length. They tell how far apart things are.

Passage C

d. Find part C in your textbook. ✓
  - This information passage tells more about toads.
e. Everybody, touch the title. ✓
  - (Call on a student to read the title.) [*How Toads Catch Flies.*]
  - Everybody, what's the title? (Signal.) *How Toads Catch Flies.*
f. (Call on individual students to read the passage, each student reading two or three sentences at a time.)

How Toads Catch Flies

Toads eat flies. A toad catches flies with its long, long tongue. A toad's tongue is almost as long as the toad.

- Everybody, show me your tongue. ✓
- Is your tongue almost as long as you are? (Signal.) *No.*
- Show me how long a real toad is. ✓
- If a toad is that long, show me how long its tongue would be. ✓

A toad's tongue is covered with sticky goo. The tongue moves so fast that it hits a fly before the fly can move. The fly sticks to the tongue.

- Why doesn't the fly just fall off the tongue? (Call on a student. Idea: *Because it's stuck to the sticky goo.*)

When the toad pulls its tongue back, the fly comes with it.
   The pictures below show a toad's tongue catching a fly.

A   B   C   D   E

- Everybody, touch picture A. ✓
- The tongue is just coming out in picture A.
- Touch picture B. ✓
- Is the tongue longer in that picture? (Signal.) *Yes.*
- Is the tongue touching the fly? (Signal.) *No.*
- Touch picture C. ✓
- Is the tongue touching the fly? (Signal.) *Yes.*
- What's happening in picture D? (Call on a student. Idea: *The toad is putting its tongue back into its mouth.*)
- Where is the fly in picture E? (Call on a student. Idea: *Inside the toad.*)

EXERCISE 5

STORY READING

a. Find part D in your textbook. ✓
  - We're going to do this story two times. First you'll read it out loud and make no more than 6 errors. Then I'll read it and ask questions.
b. Everybody, touch the title. ✓
  - (Call on a student to read the title.) [*Food Traps.*]
  - Everybody, what's the title? (Signal.) *Food Traps.*

c. (Call on individual students to read the story, each student reading two or three sentences at a time.)
- (Correct errors: Tell the word. Direct the student to reread the sentence.)
- (If the group makes more than 6 errors, direct the students to reread the story.)

d. (After the group has read the selection making no more than 6 errors:)
Now I'll read the story and ask questions.

Food Traps

The people in Toadsville like to tell stories about Goad and how she escaped from traps. They tell about how she once escaped from the great big net.

- What trick did she use to escape from the net? (Call on a student. Idea: *She pretended she was a rock.*)

The people also tell how Goad got away from food traps. One of the hunters' favorite tricks was to make food traps.

All food traps work the same way. You put out some food that a toad likes. Maybe you put some blue flies on the ground. My, my, how toads love those blue flies. Then you make a trap that closes on the toad when it goes for the food.

PICTURE 1

PICTURE 2

PICTURE 3

- The pictures show how the trap works. Picture 1 shows how the trap looks before the trap falls on the toad. Touch the pole that's standing straight up. ✓
- The pole is straight up. And it holds the net up.
- Touch picture 2. ✓
- The toad is pulling on the end of the string and the pole is falling over. The net is coming down.
- Touch picture 3. ✓
- The pole is lying down. And the net is over the toad.

If the pole tips over, the toad is trapped in the net. Hunters put blue flies at the end of the string. When the toad eats the flies, the string moves and the pole falls over.

PICTURE 4

- Touch the fly in picture 4. It's at letter A. ✓
- The arrow shows which way the end of the string will move when the toad pulls on the fly. ✓
- Follow the string along to B. ✓
- Point and show me which way the string will move at B. ✓
- Point and show me which way the pole will move at C. ✓
- (Repeat sequence until firm.)

Remember, a fly is on the end of the string. So when the fly moves, the string moves. And when the string moves, the pole moves. That pole holds up a net. So when the fly moves, the string moves. And when the string moves, the pole moves. And when the pole moves, the net falls over the toad.

If you believe the stories they tell in the town of Toadsville, Goad has escaped from over five hundred food traps. Not all these stories are true. Goad has really escaped from four hundred food traps, but that's a lot of escaping for one toad. How did she do it? You already know one of her tricks. You'll find out about more of her tricks in the next story.

- What trick do you already know about?
  (Call on a student. Idea: *Pretending to be a rock.*)
- Listen to that last part again:

And when the string moves, the pole moves. That pole holds up a net. So when the fly moves, the string moves. And when the string moves, the pole moves. And when the pole moves, the net falls over the toad.

If you believe the stories they tell in the town of Toadsville, Goad has escaped from over five hundred food traps. Not all these stories are true. Goad has really escaped from four hundred food traps, but that's a lot of escaping for one toad. How did she do it? You already know one of her tricks. You'll find out about more of her tricks in the next story.

EXERCISE 6
PAIRED PRACTICE

You're going to read aloud to your partner. Today the **B** members will read first. Then the **A** members will read from the star to the end of the story. (Observe students and give feedback. Praise teams that follow the rules.)

EXERCISE 7
WRITTEN ITEMS
Skill Items

a. Find part E in your textbook. ✓
- Number your lined paper from 1 through 17. Pencils down when you're finished. ✓

b. The rule for item 1 says: Dogs have four legs. That rule tells you something about any dog. It doesn't tell you anything about things that are not dogs.
- Everybody, does the rule tell about cats? (Signal.) *No.*
- Does the rule tell about birds? (Signal.) *No.*
- Does the rule tell about cows that have four legs? (Signal.) *No.*
- The only thing the rule tells about is dogs.
- Listen: Dogs have four legs. What's the only thing that rule tells about? (Signal.) *Dogs.*

c. Your turn. Write the answers for item 1. Raise your hand when you've done that much.
   (Observe students and give feedback.)

> Write the word or words from the box that mean the same thing as the underlined part of each sentence.
>
> | danger | million | a meter | half | bark |
> | great | during | ruler | measure | an inch |
>
> 2. The <u>tree's covering</u> was full of holes.
> 3. She went on a <u>wonderful</u> trip.
> 4. The string was <u>100 centimeters</u> long.

d. Pencils down. ✓
- I'll read the instructions above the box: Write the word or words from the box that mean the same thing as the underlined part of each sentence.

e. Item 2: The <u>tree's covering</u> was full of holes.
- Everybody, what words are underlined? (Signal.) *Tree's covering.*
- Raise your hand when you've found the word in the box that means **tree's covering.** ✓
- Everybody, what word? (Signal.) *Bark.*
- Say sentence 1 with the word **bark** instead of **tree's covering.** Get ready. (Signal.) *The bark was full of holes.*

f. Item 3: She went on a <u>wonderful</u> trip.
- Everybody, what word is underlined? (Signal.) *Wonderful.*
- Raise your hand when you've found the word in the box that means **wonderful.** ✓
- Everybody, what word? (Signal.) *Great.*
- Say sentence 2 with the word **great** instead of **wonderful.** Get ready. (Signal.) *She went on a great trip.*

g. Item 4: The string was <u>100 centimeters</u> long.
- Everybody, what's underlined? (Signal.) *100 centimeters.*
- Raise your hand when you've found the words in the box that mean **100 centimeters.** ✓
- Everybody, what words mean **100 centimeters?** (Signal.) *A meter.*
- Say sentence 3 with the words **a meter** instead of **100 centimeters.** Get ready. (Signal.) *The string was a meter long.*

h. Everybody, write the answers to items 2 through 4. Remember, write the words from the box that mean the same thing as the underlined part of each sentence. Raise your hand when you've finished items 2 through 4.
   (Observe students and give feedback.)

Lesson 17   97

Story Items

j. Item 10 is a question about today's story. (Call on a student to read item 10.) [People in Toadsville said that Goad had escaped from over five hundred food traps. But Goad had really escaped from <u>blank</u> food traps.]

k. **Find part C on your worksheet.** ✓

- Items 6 through 11 are about today's story. I'll call on different students to read the items, but don't say the answers.

l. For items 6 through 9, you'll underline the word **make-believe** after each statement that could not be true.

- (For each item: Call on a student to read the item.)
- Item 6. *[A toad was as big as a pillow.]*
- Item 7. *[A toad could hop.]*
- Item 8. *[A toad ate flies.]*
- Item 9. *[A toad is smarter than a person.]*
- For items 10 and 11, there's a picture of a food trap. The arrow at **A** shows the way the fly will move when the toad grabs it.
- Item 10. *[Draw an arrow to show which way the string will move at B.]*
- Item 11. *[Draw an arrow to show which way the pole will move at C.]*

End-of-Lesson Activities

INDEPENDENT WORK

Now finish your independent work for lesson 17. Raise your hand when you're finished.
(Observe students and give feedback.)

WORKCHECK

a. (Direct students to take out their marking pencils.)
- We're going to check your independent work. Remember, if you got an item wrong, make an **X** next to the item.

b. (For each item: Read the item. Call on a student to answer it. If the answer is wrong, say the correct answer. Refer to the Answer Key for the correct answers.)

c. Now use your marking pencil to fix up any items you got wrong. Remember, all mistakes must be fixed up before you hand in your independent work.

WRITING-SPELLING

(Present Writing-Spelling lesson 17 after completing Reading lesson 17. See Writing-Spelling Guide.)

Lesson 18

EXERCISE 1
VOCABULARY REVIEW

a. Here's the new vocabulary sentence: **Hunters were stationed at opposite ends of the field.**
- Everybody, say that sentence. Get ready. (Signal.) *Hunters were stationed at opposite ends of the field.*
- (Repeat until firm.)
- The hunters had to stay where they were placed. So the hunters were . . . (Signal.) *Stationed.*

b. What word tells which ends of the field? (Signal.) *Opposite.*

EXERCISE 2
READING WORDS

Column 1

a. **Find lesson 18 in your textbook.** ✓
- Touch column 1. ✓
- (Teacher reference:)

| 1. decide | 3. binoculars |
| 2. group | 4. instructions |

b. Word 1 is **decide.** What word? (Signal.) *Decide.*
- Spell **decide.** Get ready. (Tap for each letter.) *D-E-C-I-D-E.*

c. Word 2 is **group.** What word? (Signal.) *Group.*
- Spell **group.** Get ready. (Tap for each letter.) *G-R-O-U-P.*

d. Word 3 is **binoculars.** What word? (Signal.) *Binoculars.*
- Binoculars are powerful glasses that you can look through. Binoculars make far-off things look close.

e. Word 4 is **instructions.** What word? (Signal.) *Instructions.*

f. Let's read those words again, the fast way.
- Word 1. What word? (Signal.) *Decide.*
- (Repeat for words 2–4.)

g. (Repeat step f until firm.)

Column 2

h. Find column 2. ✓
- (Teacher reference:)

1. tion	4. al
2. sion	5. aw
3. ar	

i. Combination 1 is spelled **T-I-O-N.**
- That combination usually makes the sound **shun.** What sound? (Signal.) *shun.*

j. Spell combination 2. Get ready. (Tap for each letter.) *S-I-O-N.*
- That combination makes the same sound as combination 1. What sound? (Signal.) *shun.*

k. Tell me the sound for the rest of the combinations.
- Combination 3. What sound? (Signal.) *are.*
- Combination 4. What sound? (Signal.) *all.*
- Combination 5. What sound? (Signal.) *awe.*

l. Let's do those combinations again.
- Combination 1. What sound? (Signal.) *shun.*
- (Repeat for combinations 2–5.)

m. (Repeat step l until firm.)

Column 3

n. Find column 3. ✓
- (Teacher reference:)

1. propped	4. swallowed
2. stationed	5. decided
3. boasted	

- These words all end with the letters **E-D.**

o. Word 1. What word? (Signal.) *Propped.*
- What do you do when you prop up something? (Call on a student. Idea: *Support it so it stays in place.*)

p. Word 2. What word? (Signal.) *Stationed.*
- Everybody, if you are stationed in a place, is it okay to move away from that place? (Signal.) *No.*

q. Word 3. What word? (Signal.) *Boasted.*
- (Repeat for words 4 and 5.)

r. Let's read those words again.
- Word 1. What word? (Signal.) *Propped.*
- (Repeat for: **2. stationed, 3. boasted, 4. swallowed, 5. decided.**)
s. (Repeat step r until firm.)

Column 4
t. Find column 4. ✓
- (Teacher reference:)

1. steel	4. breath
2. third	5. famous
3. sixty	6. wild

u. Word 1. What word? (Signal.) *Steel.*
- Name something that could be made of steel. (Call on a student. Ideas: *Cage, bars, knife,* etc.)
- Word 2. What word? (Signal.) *Third.*
- (Repeat for words 3–6.)
v. Let's read those words again.
- Word 1. What word? (Signal.) *Steel.*
- (Repeat for words 2–6.)
w. (Repeat step v until firm.)

Column 5
x. Find column 5. ✓
- (Teacher reference:)

1. gulp	4. blast
2. fourth	5. silence
3. England	6. tramping

y. Word 1. What word? (Signal.) *Gulp.*
- (Repeat for words 2–6.)
z. (Repeat step y until firm.)
a. Let's read those words again.
- Word 1. What word? (Signal.) *Gulp.*
- (Repeat for words 2–6.)
b. (Repeat step a until firm.)

Individual Turns
(For columns 1–5: Call on individual students, each to read one to three words per turn.)

EXERCISE 3
COMPREHENSION PASSAGES

Passage B
a. Find part B in your textbook. ✓
- You're going to read the next story about Goad. First you'll read two information passages.
b. Everybody, touch the title. ✓
- (Call on a student to read the title.) *[Facts About Moles.]*

- Everybody, what's the title? (Signal.) *Facts About Moles.*
c. (Call on individual students to read the passage, each student reading two or three sentences at a time.)

> **Facts About Moles**
>
> Today's story tells something about moles. Here are some facts about moles:
> Moles are animals that spend nearly all their time underground.

- Everybody, where do moles spend most of their time? (Signal.) *Underground.*
- They dig holes and live in the holes.

> There are different types of moles. Some are big. Some have almost no hair.

- Are all moles the same? (Signal.) *No.*
- How do some of them look? (Call on a student. Ideas: *Some are big; some have almost no hair.*)

> Bigger moles are about the same size as toads.

- Everybody, show me how big they are. ✓

> Moles cannot see very well. Some types of moles cannot see at all. They even have skin growing over their eyes.

- Not all moles are totally blind. But no moles see well because they don't have to use their eyes. Why don't they have to use their eyes? (Call on a student. Idea: *Because they live underground.*)

> Moles have legs that work like shovels.

- Everybody, say that fact. (Signal.) *Moles have legs that work like shovels.*
- You can see a mole's legs in the picture. Moles' legs work like shovels. What do they help the mole do? (Call on a student. Idea: *Dig.*)

Passage C
d. Find part C in your textbook. ✓
e. Everybody, touch the title. ✓
- (Call on a student to read the title.) *[The Opposite Direction.]*

- Everybody, what's the title? (Signal.) *The Opposite Direction.*
f. (Call on individual students to read the passage, each student reading two or three sentences at a time.)

> **The Opposite Direction**
>
> You're going to learn about things that move the opposite direction. If you move north, the opposite direction is south.

- Everybody, what's the opposite direction of north? (Signal.) *South.*
- What's the opposite direction of south? (Signal.) *North.*
- Yes, north and south are opposites.

> If you move up, the opposite direction is down.

- Everybody, what's the opposite direction of up? (Signal.) *Down.*
- What's the opposite direction of down? (Signal.) *Up.*

> If you move to the left, the opposite direction is to the right.

- Everybody, what's the opposite direction of left? (Signal.) *Right.*
- What's the opposite direction of right? (Signal.) *Left.*

> **What's the opposite direction of north?**

- Everybody, what is it? (Signal.) *South.*

> **What's the opposite direction of down?**

- Everybody, what is it? (Signal.) *Up.*

> **What's the opposite of east?**

- Everybody, what is it? (Signal.) *West.*

> **Point to the front of the room.**

- Everybody, do it. ✓

> **Now point in the opposite direction.**

- Everybody, do it. ✓

> **Point to the floor.**

- Everybody, do it. ✓

> **Now point in the opposite direction.**

- Everybody, do it. ✓

EXERCISE 4
STORY READING

a. Find part D in your textbook. ✓
 - We're going to do this story two times. First you'll read it out loud and make no more than 8 errors. Then I'll read it and ask questions.
b. Everybody, touch the title. ✓
 - (Call on a student to read the title.) [*Goad's Four Tricks.*]
 - Everybody, how many tricks does Goad have? (Signal.) *Four.*
 - You already know one trick. What's that? (Call on a student. Idea: *Goad pretended to be a rock.*)
c. (Call on individual students to read the story, each student reading two or three sentences at a time.)
 - (Correct errors: Tell the word. Direct the student to reread the sentence.)
 - (If the group makes more than 8 errors, direct the students to reread the story.)
d. (After the group has read the selection making no more than 8 errors:) Now I'll read the story and ask questions.

> **Goad's Four Tricks**
>
> Goad has escaped from four hundred food traps. She has four tricks that she uses to escape from those traps. One trick is to make herself look like a rock, the way she did when she escaped from the great net. Her second trick is to dig.

- Everybody, what's the second trick? (Signal.) *To dig.*
- Remember that.

> You wouldn't think that a toad the size of a pillow could dig very fast, but you have never seen Goad dig. She can dig so fast that worms get mad at her. She can dig faster than a snake. She can even dig faster than a mole. And moles have legs like shovels.

Lesson 18 101

- Everybody, who could dig faster, Goad or a mole? (Signal.) *Goad.*
- Why would a worm get mad at Goad? (Call on a student. Idea: *Because she could dig so fast.*)

Goad's third trick is to eat the trap.

- Everybody, what's her third trick? (Signal.) *To eat the trap.*
- Now you know three tricks that Goad uses. What's the first trick? (Call on a student. Idea: *She pretends to be a rock.*)
- What's the second? (Call on a student. Idea: *She digs.*)
- What's the third? (Call on a student. Idea: *She eats the trap.*)

If the food trap is a big wooden box that drops over Goad, that fat toad just smiles to herself and starts eating.
Her fourth trick is to blow the trap away.

- What's her fourth trick? (Call on a student. Idea: *To blow the trap away.*)

That's right. She takes in a big breath of air. When she does this, she gets bigger.

- (Call on a student.) Show me how to take in air so you get bigger. ✓

She gets so big that she looks just like a brown and green and white balloon. When she is nearly two times the size of a pillow, she blows. The wind comes out of her mouth so fast that she can blow most traps a hundred meters away.

- Everybody, show me how you take in a big breath and then blow. ✓
- How far could Goad blow a trap when she blew air out? (Signal.) *A hundred meters.*

That's how she got away from the famous steel trap.

- What did she do to get away from the famous steel trap? (Call on a student. Idea: *Blew the trap away.*)

A man came from England. The man boasted that he had made a trap that could hold any toad. "No toad can eat through this trap," he said. "And no toad can dig under this trap if I put it on hard rock."
And that's just what he did.

- Why did he put it on hard rock? (Call on a student. Idea: *So Goad couldn't dig to get out.*)

He propped up the steel trap next to the road, where there was no dirt, just hard rock. Then he put sixty blue flies under the trap.
There is no toad in the world that can stay away from sixty blue flies. So before very long, out popped Goad. Her tongue came out. In one gulp, she had swallowed half of the flies. She was ready for her second gulp, when BONG.
MORE NEXT TIME

- What made that BONG sound? (Call on a student. Idea: *The trap falling over Goad.*)
- Who can remember Goad's first trick? (Call on a student. Idea: *Pretends to be a rock.*)
- Who can remember Goad's second trick? (Call on a student. Idea: *Digs.*)
- Who can remember Goad's third trick? (Call on a student. Idea: *Eats the trap.*)
- Who can remember Goad's fourth trick? (Call on a student. Idea: *Blows the trap away.*)

EXERCISE 5

PAIRED PRACTICE

You're going to read aloud to your partner. Today the **A** members will read first. Then the **B** members will read from the star to the end of the story. (Observe students and give feedback. Praise teams that follow the rules.)

EXERCISE 6

WRITTEN ITEMS
Skill Items

a. Find part E in your textbook. ✓
- Number your lined paper from 1 through 12.

b. **Find item 1.** ✓
- There's a rule and some questions. The rule is: **Tadpoles have a tail.**
- Everybody, what's the only thing that rule tells about? (Signal.) *Tadpoles.*
- Listen: Hilda is a tadpole. So what does the rule tell you about Hilda? (Signal.) *She has a tail.*
- Listen: Herman is not a tadpole. So what does the rule tell you about Herman? (Signal.) *Nothing.*
- Listen: Oliver is a dog. So what does the rule tell you about Oliver? (Signal.) *Nothing.*
- Listen: A cat is not a tadpole. So what does the rule tell you about a cat? (Signal.) *Nothing.*

c. Your turn: Write answers to items 1 through 4 on your lined paper. Items 3 and 4 use a different rule. Raise your hand when you've done that much. (Observe students and give feedback.)

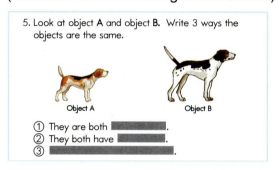

d. I'll read item 5. Look at object A and object B. Write 3 ways the objects are the same.
- Name one way they're the same. Start with the words **they are both.** (Call on a student. Ideas: *They are both dogs; they are both standing; they are both facing right;* etc.)
- Name another way they're the same. Start with the words **they both have.** (Call on a student. Ideas: *They both have four legs; they both have more than one color;* etc.)
- Name another way they're the same. (Call on a student. Ideas: *They both have long ears; they both eat; they both need water;* etc.)

Story Items

e. **Find item 4 on your worksheet.** ✓
- Items 4 through 10 are about today's story. I'll call on different students to read the items, but don't say the answers.

f. (For each item: Call on a student to read the item.)
- I'll read. Here are Goad's four tricks for escaping from hunters: eat the trap, blow the trap away, look like a rock, dig.
- Item 4. *[Goad's first trick was to blank.]*
- Item 5. *[Goad's second trick was to blank.]*
- Item 6. *[Goad's third trick was to blank.]*
- Item 7. *[Goad's fourth trick was to blank.]*
- Item 8. *[A mole's legs work like blank.]*
- Item 9. *[The man from England put his steel trap on a rock. He put it there so that Goad could not blank.]*
- Item 10. *[What did the man from England put in his trap?]*

End-of-Lesson Activities

INDEPENDENT WORK

Now finish your independent work for lesson 18. Do your worksheet first. Raise your hand when you're finished.
(Observe students and give feedback.)

WORKCHECK

a. (Direct students to take out their marking pencils.)
- We're going to check your independent work. Remember, if you got an item wrong, make an **X** next to the item.

b. (For each item: Read the item. Call on a student to answer it. If the answer is wrong, say the correct answer. Refer to the Answer Key for the correct answers.)

c. Now use your marking pencil to fix up any items you got wrong. Remember, all mistakes must be fixed up before you hand in your independent work.

WRITING-SPELLING

(Present Writing-Spelling lesson 18 after completing Reading lesson 18. See Writing-Spelling Guide.)

Lesson 19

EXERCISE 1
VOCABULARY REVIEW

a. You learned a sentence that tells what the fly boasted about.
- Everybody, say that sentence. Get ready. (Signal.) *The fly boasted about escaping from the spider.*
- (Repeat until firm.)

b. You learned a sentence that tells what the workers did to the cage.
- Everybody, say that sentence. Get ready. (Signal.) *The workers propped up the cage with steel bars.*
- (Repeat until firm.)

c. Here's the last sentence you learned: Hunters were stationed at opposite ends of the field.
- Everybody, say that sentence. Get ready. (Signal.) *Hunters were stationed at opposite ends of the field.*
- (Repeat until firm.)

d. What word tells they were not at the same ends of the field? (Signal.) *Opposite.*
- What word tells that the hunters had to stay where they were placed? (Signal.) *Stationed.*

e. Once more. Say the sentence that tells where hunters were stationed. Get ready. (Signal.) *Hunters were stationed at opposite ends of the field.*

EXERCISE 2
READING WORDS

Column 1

a. **Open your textbook to lesson 19.** ✓
- Touch column 1. ✓
- The ending sounds at the top of column 1 both say **shun.** How is the first **shun** spelled? (Signal.) *T-I-O-N.*
- How is the other **shun** spelled? (Signal.) *S-I-O-N.*

- (Teacher reference:)

> tion
> sion
> 1. impres<u>sion</u>
> 2. sta<u>tion</u>
> 3. instruc<u>tion</u>
> 4. ac<u>tion</u>
> 5. vaca<u>tion</u>
> 6. men<u>tion</u>

b. The words in column 1 have the ending **T-I-O-N** or **S-I-O-N.** I'll read the words: **impression, station, instruction, action, vacation, mention.**

c. Your turn to read and spell the words.
- Word 1. What word? (Signal.) *Impression.*
- Spell **impression.** Get ready. (Tap for each letter.) *I-M-P-R-E-S-S-I-O-N.*
- (Repeat for words 2–6.)

d. Let's read those words again.
- Word 1. What word? (Signal.) *Impression.*
- (Repeat for words 2–6.)

e. (Repeat step d until firm.)

Column 2

f. Find column 2. ✓
- (Teacher reference:)

> 1. <u>tramp</u>ing   4. <u>prob</u>lem
> 2. <u>weak</u>ness   5. <u>mid</u>dle
> 3. <u>stub</u>by

- These words have more than one syllable. The first syllable is underlined.

g. Word 1. What's the first syllable? (Signal.) *tramp.*
- What's the whole word? (Signal.) *Tramping.*

h. Word 2. What's the first syllable? (Signal.) *weak.*
- What's the whole word? (Signal.) *Weakness.*

i. Word 3. What's the first syllable? (Signal.) *stub.*
- What's the whole word? (Signal.) *Stubby.*

j. Word 4. What's the first syllable? (Signal.) *prob.*
- What's the whole word? (Signal.) *Problem.*

k. Word 5. What's the first syllable? (Signal.) *mid.*
- What's the whole word? (Signal.) *Middle.*

l. Let's read those words again.
- Word 1. What word? (Signal.) *Tramping.*
- (Repeat for: **2. weakness, 3. stubby, 4. problem, 5. middle.**)

m. (Repeat step l until firm.)

Column 3

n. Find column 3. ✓
- (Teacher reference:)

1. women	4. wild
2. dreams	5. binoculars
3. group	6. decided

o. Word 1. What word? (Signal.) *Women.*
- (Repeat for words 2–6.)

p. Let's read those words again.
- Word 1. What word? (Signal.) *Women.*
- (Repeat for words 2–6.)

q. (Repeat step p until firm.)

Column 4

r. Find column 4. ✓
- (Teacher reference:)

1. wolves	4. either
2. holler	5. fifteen
3. torch	6. motion

s. Word 1. What word? (Signal.) *Wolves.*
- (Repeat for words 2–6.)

t. (Repeat step s until firm.)

Individual Turns

(For columns 1–4: Call on individual students, each to read one to three words per turn.)

EXERCISE 3

COMPREHENSION PASSAGES

Passage B

a. Find part B in your textbook. ✓
- You're going to read the next story about Goad. First you'll read two information passages. The first one tells about binoculars.

b. Everybody, touch the title. ✓
- (Call on a student to read the title.) [Binoculars.]
- Everybody, what's the title? (Signal.) *Binoculars.*

c. (Call on individual students to read the passage, each student reading two or three sentences at a time.)

> **Binoculars**
>
> Here is a picture of binoculars: Follow these instructions:
> 1. Hold your hands so they make circles.

- Everybody, do it. ✓

> 2. Now look through the circles made by your hands.

- Everybody, do it. ✓

> Looking through binoculars is like looking through the circles made by your hands. But when you look through binoculars, things look very, very big. Things may look ten times as big as they look through the circles made by your hands.

- How do things look when you look through binoculars? (Call on a student. Idea: *Very big.*)

> If you see this through the circles made by your hands,

> you would see this through a strong pair of binoculars.

- Everybody, which looks bigger, the horse through the hands or the horse through the binoculars? (Signal.) *The horse through the binoculars.*

> If you saw something that looked one centimeter tall through the circles made by your hands, that thing would look ten centimeters tall through strong binoculars.

- Everybody, if something looked one inch tall through the circles made by your hands, how tall would it look through strong binoculars? (Signal.) *Ten inches tall.*

Passage C

d. Find part C in your textbook. ✓
- This passage gives some facts about how fast things move.
e. Everybody, touch the title. ✓
- (Call on a student to read the title.) *[How Fast Things Move.]*
- Everybody, what's the title? (Signal.) *How Fast Things Move.*
f. (Call on individual students to read the passage, each student reading two or three sentences at a time.)

> **How Fast Things Move**
>
> Here's the rule: Names that tell how fast things move have two parts.

- Everybody, say the rule. Get ready. (Signal.) *Names that tell how fast things move have two parts.*

> Here's a name that tells how fast things move: <u>miles per hour</u>. The two parts are <u>miles</u> and <u>hour</u>.

- Everybody, say the whole name. Get ready. (Signal.) *Miles per hour.*
- What's the first part? (Signal.) *Miles.*
- What's the last part? (Signal.) *Hour.*

> Here's another name that tells how fast things move: <u>meters per second</u>. The two parts are <u>meters</u> and <u>second</u>.

- Everybody, say the whole name. Get ready. (Signal.) *Meters per second.*
- What's the first part? (Signal.) *Meters.*
- What's the second part? (Signal.) *Second.*

> Here's a name that does not tell how fast things move: <u>meters</u>.
> Here's another name that does not tell how fast things move: <u>hours</u>.

- Everybody, how many parts does the name **hours** have? (Signal.) *One.*
- How many parts are in names that tell how fast things move? (Signal.) *Two.*
- So **hours** can't be a name that tells how fast things move.
- Everybody, names that tell how fast things move have how many parts? (Signal.) *Two.*

EXERCISE 4

STORY READING

a. Find part D in your textbook. ✓
- We're going to do this story two times. First you'll read it out loud and make no more than 6 errors. Then I'll read it and ask questions.
b. Everybody, touch the title. ✓
- (Call on a student to read the title.) *[The Brown Family Comes to Catch Goad.]*
- Everybody, who's going to come to catch Goad? (Signal.) *The Brown Family.*
c. (Call on individual students to read the story, each student reading two or three sentences at a time.)

- (Correct errors: Tell the word. Direct the student to reread the sentence.)
- (If the group makes more than 6 errors, direct the students to reread the story.)

d. (After the group has read the selection making no more than 6 errors:)
Now I'll read the story and ask questions.

> **The Brown Family Comes to Catch Goad**
>
> The famous steel trap came down over Goad. "I told you I could catch her," the man from England boasted as he ran down the road toward the trap. But before he was halfway there, something happened. You could hear the sound of wind. It sounded like air leaking from a tire. Then there was silence. Then there was a great blast of wind, and the famous steel trap went sailing through the air. Goad had used her fourth trick.

- The sound like air leaking from a tire was Goad taking in a big breath. What made the blast of wind? (Call on a student. Idea: *Goad blowing.*)
- That was Goad's fourth trick.
- Who can remember Goad's first trick? (Call on a student. Idea: *She pretended to be a rock.*)
- Who can remember Goad's second trick? (Call on a student. Idea: *She dug.*)
- Who can remember Goad's third trick? (Call on a student. Idea: *She ate the trap.*)
- Who can remember Goad's fourth trick? (Call on a student. Idea: *She blew away the trap.*)

Everybody agreed that steel traps couldn't catch Goad, and nets couldn't hold her either. Hundreds of men, women, boys, and girls came tramping over the hills every summer, but they couldn't catch her. Even trained hunters and trappers failed.

- What does that mean, they failed? (Call on a student. Idea: *They couldn't catch Goad.*)

But Goad has one weakness, and if you listen to the groups of people talking in the town of Toadsville, you know what her only weakness is. She can't swim fast. When she's in the water, she's like a great fat lump, with stubby legs that can hardly push her along.

- What are stubby legs? (Call on a student. Idea: *Legs that are short and fat.*)

At least a thousand people must have said, "If we could just find her when she's swimming, there's no way she could get away."
That sounds like an easy thing to do, but there is one problem. You first have to find Goad when she is in the water.

- Everybody, is she in the water all the time? (Signal.) *No.*

There's an old man in the town of Toadsville who shows pictures of Goad swimming in the lake. The old man took the pictures from high above the lake. Everyone who sees the pictures says the same sort of thing. They say, "If I saw that toad swimming in the lake like that, I'd get in a boat and catch her."
Sometimes in the summer you can count hundreds of people stationed around the lake, ready for action.

- When they're stationed, they're standing around waiting for something. What are they waiting for? (Call on a student. Ideas: *Goad to go swimming; action.*)
- What kind of action are they ready for? (Call on a student. Idea: *Catching Goad.*)

Some of the people have binoculars. They sit hour after hour, looking through the binoculars. Their great hope is that they will see Goad swimming far from the shore of the lake.
Last summer, a group of wild hunters had the chance that everybody dreams about. They spotted Goad swimming in the middle of the lake. And they were ready for action.

- Where was Goad? (Call on a student. Idea: *Swimming in the middle of the lake.*)
- It says that the hunters were ready for action. How would they be ready if they wanted to catch Goad in the water? (Call on a student. Idea: *They'd have a net or something to catch her with.*)

These wild hunters were part of the famous Brown family. The Brown family was made up of 40 people. Fifteen of them were on vacation at Four Mile Lake, and they decided to spend all their time looking for Goad.
MORE NEXT TIME

- Everybody, what family did they come from? (Signal.) *The Brown family.*

- Imagine, they planned to spend all their vacation time looking for Goad. Does that sound like a fun way to spend a vacation? (Call on individual students. Responses: Student preference.)

EXERCISE 5
PAIRED PRACTICE

You're going to read aloud to your partner. Today the **B** members will read first. Then the **A** members will read from the star to the end of the story.

(Observe students and give feedback.)

EXERCISE 6
WRITTEN ITEMS
Skill Items

a. Find part E in your textbook. ✓
- Number your lined paper from 1 through 18. ✓

b. Touch item 1. ✓
- There's a rule and some questions. The rule is: **Trees have leaves.**
- Everybody, what's the only thing that rule tells about? (Signal.) *Trees.*
- Listen: An alder is a tree. So what does the rule tell you about an alder? (Signal.) *It has leaves.*
- Listen: A rosebush is not a tree. So what does the rule tell you about a rosebush? (Signal.) *Nothing.*
- Listen: A daisy is a flower. So what does the rule tell you about a daisy? (Signal.) *Nothing.*

c. Your turn. Write answers to items 1 through 3 on your lined paper. Raise your hand when you've done that much. (Observe students and give feedback.)

Story Items

d. Items 4 through 11 are about today's story. I'll call on different students to read the items, but don't say the answers.

e. (For each item: Call on a student to read the item.)
- Item 4. *[What is Goad's only weakness?]*
- Item 5. *[People hoped they could be around when Goad was swimming in the lake because blank.]*
- Item 6. *[There were 40 people in the Brown family. How many of them were going to try to catch Goad?]*
- Read what it says above item 7. *[Here are Goad's four tricks for escaping from hunters: blow the trap away, dig, look like a rock, eat the trap.]*
- Item 7. *[Goad's first trick was to <u>blank</u>.]*
- Item 8. *[Goad's second trick was to <u>blank</u>.]*
- Item 9. *[Goad's third trick was to <u>blank</u>.]*
- Item 10. *[Goad's fourth trick was to <u>blank</u>]*
- Item 11. *[How did Goad get away from the famous steel trap?]*

Comprehension Passage Items

f. Find item 1 on your worksheet. ✓
- The picture shows what you would see if you looked through the circles made by your hands. In the empty circle, you'll draw what you would see if you looked at the same triangle through binoculars.
- Find item 2. ✓
- The picture shows what you would see through strong binoculars. You'll draw what the same square would look like if you looked at it through the circles made by your hands.

End-of-Lesson Activities

INDEPENDENT WORK

Now finish your independent work for lesson 19. Raise your hand when you're finished. (Observe students and give feedback.)

WORKCHECK

a. (Direct students to take out their marking pencils.)
- We're going to check your independent work. Remember, if you got an item wrong, make an **X** next to the item.

b. (For each item: Read the item. Call on a student to answer it. If the answer is wrong, say the correct answer. Refer to the Answer Key for the correct answers.)

c. Now use your marking pencil to fix up any items you got wrong. Remember, all mistakes must be fixed up before you hand in your independent work.

Note: Before presenting lesson 20, you will need to:
- Reproduce blackline masters for the Fact Game;
- Preview Literature lesson 3, secure materials, and reproduce blackline masters. (See the Literature Guide.)

WRITING-SPELLING

(Present Writing-Spelling lesson 19 after completing Reading lesson 19. See Writing-Spelling Guide.)

ACTIVITY

(Present Activity 7 after completing Reading lesson 19. See Activities Across the Curriculum.)

Lesson 20

Test 2

Materials: Each student will need their thermometer chart.
You will need materials for Literature lesson 2.

EXERCISE 1
READING CHECKOUTS

a. Today is a test day and a reading-checkout day. While you're writing answers, I'm going to call on you one at a time to read part of the story we read in lesson 19.
  - Remember, you pass the checkout by reading the passage in less than a minute without making more than 2 mistakes. And when you pass the checkout, you color the space for lesson 20 on your thermometer chart. When I call on you to come and do your checkout, bring your thermometer chart.
b. (Call on individual students to read the portion of story 19 marked with ✿.)
  - (Time the student. Note words that are missed and total number of words read.)
  - (Teacher reference:)

> ✿ That sounds like an easy thing to do, but there is one problem. You first have to find Goad when she is in the water.
> There's an old man in the town of Toadsville who shows pictures of Goad swimming in the lake. The old man took the pictures from [50] high above the lake. Everyone who sees the pictures says the same sort of thing. They say, "If I saw that toad swimming in the [75] lake like that, I'd get in a boat and catch her."
> Sometimes in the summer you can count hundreds of people stationed around the lake, ✿ [100] ready for action.

- (If the student reads the passage in one minute or less and makes no more than 2 errors, direct the student to color in the space for lesson 20 on the thermometer chart.)
- (If the student makes any mistakes, point to each word that was misread and identify it.)
- (If the student does not meet the time-error criterion for the passage, direct the student to practice reading the story with the assigned partner.)

EXERCISE 2
TEST

a. **Find lesson 20, test 2 in your textbook.** ✓
  - This lesson is a test. You'll work items you've done before.
b. Read the items and write the answers on your lined paper. Work carefully. Raise your hand when you've completed all the items.
  (Observe students but do not give feedback on errors.)

EXERCISE 3
MARKING THE TEST

a. (Check students' work before beginning lesson 21. Refer to the Answer Key for the correct answers.)
b. (Record all test 2 results on the Test Summary Sheet and the Group Summary Sheet. Reproducible Summary Sheets are at the back of the Teacher's Guide.)

EXERCISE 4

TEST REMEDIES

- (Provide any necessary remedies for test 2 before presenting lesson 21. Test remedies are discussed in the Teacher's Guide.)

Test 2 Firming Table

Test Item	Introduced in lesson
1	12
2	12
3	12
4	13
5	14
6	14
7	16
8	16

Test Item	Introduced in lesson
9	17
10	17
11	17
12	17
13	18
14	14
15	14
16	14

Test Item	Introduced in lesson
17	14
18	11
19	11
20	14
21	15
22	15

LITERATURE

(Present Literature lesson 2 after completing Reading lesson 20. See Literature Guide.)

Lessons 21–25 • Planning Page

Looking Ahead

	Lesson 21	Lesson 22	Lesson 23	Lesson 24	Lesson 25
Lesson Events	Vocabulary Review Reading Words Comprehension Passages Story Reading Paired Practice Written Items Independent Work Workcheck Writing-Spelling	Vocabulary Review Reading Words Comprehension Passages Story Reading Paired Practice Written Items Independent Work Workcheck Writing-Spelling	Vocabulary Review Reading Words Comprehension Passage Story Reading Paired Practice Written Items Independent Work Workcheck Writing-Spelling	Vocabulary Review Reading Words Comprehension Passage Story Reading Paired Practice Written Items Independent Work Workcheck Writing-Spelling	Vocabulary Sentence Reading Words Vocabulary Review Comprehension Passage Story Reading Reading Checkouts Written Items Independent Work Workcheck Writing-Spelling
Vocabulary Sentence	#1: You measure your weight in pounds.	#2: They waded into the stream to remove tadpoles.	#3: The fly boasted about escaping from the spider.	#4: The workers propped up the cage with steel bars.	#6: He motioned to the flight attendant ahead of him.
Reading Words: Word Types	modeled words –tion and –sion words –ed words 2-syllable words compound words mixed words	–y words –ing words 2-syllable words mixed words	o-i words 2-syllable words –ed words mixed words	modeled words words with endings multi-syllable words mixed words	modeled words –y words compound words e words mixed words
New Vocabulary	engine impression motioned	New York	moist boiled broiled	spoiled completely apart	
Comprehension Passages	1) *Animals and Fire* 2) *Smoke and Wind*	1) *Names That Tell How Fast Things Move* 2) *How Air Moves an Object*	*Facts About Miles*	*More Facts About Miles*	*Telling How Two Things Are Different*
Story	*The Browns Make Up a Plan*	*Goad in the Water*	*A Big Picnic*	*Jack and Lisa Have a Race*	*Nancy Wants to Stay Little*
Skill Items	Deductions Vocabulary	Vocabulary Same	Deductions	Deductions Titles	Different
Special Materials		Balloon	* Materials for project		Thermometer charts
Special Projects			Project after lesson 23		

* Large sheet of butcher paper or poster board; color markers; construction paper; paste; possibly paints or crayons.

Lesson 21

EXERCISE 1
VOCABULARY REVIEW

a. You learned a sentence about how you measure your weight.
- Everybody, say that sentence. Get ready. (Signal.) *You measure your weight in pounds.*
- (Repeat until firm.)

b. I'll say part of the sentence. When I stop, you say the next word. Listen: You measure your . . . Everybody, what's the next word? (Signal.) *Weight.*

c. Listen: You measure your weight in . . . Everybody, what's the next word? (Signal.) *Pounds.*
- Say the whole sentence. Get ready. (Signal.) *You measure your weight in pounds.*

d. Listen: You . . . Everybody, what's the next word? (Signal.) *Measure.*

EXERCISE 2
READING WORDS

Column 1

a. **Find lesson 21 in your textbook.** ✓
- Touch column 1. ✓
- (Teacher reference:)

| 1. trouble | 3. engine |
| 2. exactly | 4. ordering |

b. Word 1 is **trouble.** What word? (Signal.) *Trouble.*
- Spell **trouble.** Get ready. (Tap for each letter.) *T-R-O-U-B-L-E.*

c. Word 2 is **exactly.** What word? (Signal.) *Exactly.*
- Spell **exactly.** Get ready. (Tap for each letter.) *E-X-A-C-T-L-Y.*

d. Word 3 is **engine.** What word? (Signal.) *Engine.*
- Spell **engine.** Get ready. (Tap for each letter.) *E-N-G-I-N-E.*
- The part of a car or a plane that makes it move is the engine. When the engine doesn't work, the vehicle doesn't move. Everybody, what's the part of a vehicle that makes it move? (Signal.) *Engine.*

e. Spell word 4. Get ready. (Tap for each letter.) *O-R-D-E-R-I-N-G.*
- What word? (Signal.) *Ordering.*

f. Let's read those words again, the fast way.
- Word 1. What word? (Signal.) *Trouble.*
- (Repeat for words 2–4.)

g. (Repeat step f until firm.)

Column 2

h. Find column 2. ✓
- (Teacher reference:)

| 1. impression | 3. mention |
| 2. direction | 4. question |

- These words end in **T-I-O-N** or **S-I-O-N.** What sound does that part make? (Signal.) *shun.*

i. Word 1. What word? (Signal.) *Impression.*
- When you have an impression about something, you have an idea about that thing. If you have the impression that somebody is watching you, you have the idea that somebody is watching you. Everybody, what's another way of saying **She had the idea that she was working slowly?** (Signal.) *She had the impression that she was working slowly.*

j. Word 2. What word? (Signal.) *Direction.*
- Spell **direction.** Get ready. (Tap for each letter.) *D-I-R-E-C-T-I-O-N.*
- (Repeat for words 3 and 4.)

k. Let's read those words again.
- Word 1. What word? (Signal.) *Impression.*
- (Repeat for words 2–4.)

l. (Repeat step k until firm.)

Column 3

m. Find column 3. ✓
- (Teacher reference:)

1. motioned	4. settled
2. stationed	5. arrived
3. interested	

- These words end in **E-D.** You'll read the whole words.

n. Word 1. What word? (Signal.) *Motioned.*
- Here's how you motion to come over here. (Motion.)
- Show me how you motion for somebody to move back. (Call on a student.)

o. Word 2. What word? (Signal.) *Stationed.*
- (Repeat for words 3–5.)

p. Let's read those words again.
- Word 1. What word? (Signal.) *Motioned.*
- (Repeat for: **2. stationed, 3. interested, 4. settled, 5. arrived.**)

q. (Repeat step p until firm.)

Column 4

r. Find column 4. ✓
- (Teacher reference:)

> 1. <u>holl</u>er 3. <u>smok</u>y
> 2. <u>sim</u>ple 4. <u>torch</u>es

- These words have two syllables. The first syllable is underlined.

s. Word 1. What's the first syllable? (Signal.) *holl.*
- What's the whole word? (Signal.) *Holler.*

t. Word 2. What's the first syllable? (Signal.) *sim.*
- What's the whole word? (Signal.) *Simple.*

u. Word 3. What's the first syllable? (Signal.) *smoke.*
- What's the whole word? (Signal.) *Smoky.*

v. Word 4. What's the first syllable? (Signal.) *torch.*
- What's the whole word? (Signal.) *Torches.*

w. Let's read those words again.
- Word 1. What word? (Signal.) *Holler.*
- (Repeat for words 2–4.)

x. (Repeat step w until firm.)

Column 5

y. Find column 5. ✓
- (Teacher reference:)

> 1. <u>to</u>ward   4. <u>snap</u>shots
> 2. <u>out</u>smart 5. <u>back</u>ward
> 3. <u>grand</u>mother

- The words in this column are compound words. The first part of each word is underlined.

z. Word 1. What's the underlined part? (Signal.) *to.*
- What's the whole word? (Signal.) *Toward.*
- Yes, they moved toward the lake.

a. Word 2. What's the underlined part? (Signal.) *out.*
- What's the whole word? (Signal.) *Outsmart.*
- Yes, when you outsmart somebody, you win in a contest that shows who is smartest.

b. Word 3. What's the underlined part? (Signal.) *grand.*
- What's the whole word? (Signal.) *Grandmother.*

c. Word 4. What's the underlined part? (Signal.) *snap.*
- What's the whole word? (Signal.) *Snapshots.*

d. Word 5. What's the underlined part? (Signal.) *back.*
- What's the whole word? (Signal.) *Backward.*

e. Let's read those words again.
- Word 1. What word? (Signal.) *Toward.*
- (Repeat for words 2–5.)

f. (Repeat step e until firm.)

Column 6

g. Find column 6. ✓
- (Teacher reference:)

> 1. wolves 3. solid
> 2. great   4. twenty

h. Word 1. What word? (Signal.) *Wolves.*
- (Repeat for word 2–4.)

i. (Repeat step h until firm.)

Individual Turns

(For columns 1–6: Call on individual students, each to read one to three words per turn.)

EXERCISE 3

COMPREHENSION PASSAGES

Passage B

a. Find part B in your textbook. ✓
- You're going to read the next story about Goad. First you'll read two information passages. The first one gives some facts about animals and fire.

b. Everybody, touch the title. ✓
- (Call on a student to read the title.) *[Animals and Fire.]*

- Everybody, what's the title? (Signal.) *Animals and Fire.*
c. (Call on individual students to read the passage, each student reading two or three sentences at a time.)

Animals and Fire

You're going to read about how animals act when there is a fire. Here is the rule: <u>**When there is a fire, all animals try to get away from the fire.**</u>

- Everybody, what do all animals do when there is a fire? (Signal.) *Try to get away.*
- (Repeat until firm.)

The animals are not interested in hunting for food. The animals are not interested in fighting with other animals. Deer don't like wolves, but when a fire is near, wolves and deer may run side by side. They do not fight or bother each other.

- Do you know why deer don't like wolves? (Call on a student. Idea: *Because wolves hunt and eat deer.*)

Passage C

d. Find part C in your textbook. ✓
- The next information passage gives some facts about smoke and wind.
e. Everybody, touch the title. ✓
- (Call on a student to read the title.) [*Smoke and Wind.*]
- Everybody, what's the title? (Signal.) *Smoke and Wind.*
f. (Call on individual students to read the passage, each student reading two or three sentences at a time.)

Smoke and Wind

You're going to read about smoke and wind in today's story. Here's the rule: <u>**The smoke moves in the same direction the wind moves.**</u>

- Everybody, listen to that rule again: The smoke moves in the same direction the wind moves.
- Say that rule. Get ready. (Signal.) *The smoke moves in the same direction the wind moves.*
- (Repeat until firm.)

**If the wind blows to the north, the smoke moves to the north.
If the wind blows in this direction ↗, the smoke blows in this direction ↗.**

- Everybody, let's say the wind is blowing to the north. In which direction does the smoke move? (Signal.) *North.*
- In which direction does the smoke move if the wind blows to the east? (Signal.) *East.*

EXERCISE 4

STORY READING

a. Find part D in your textbook. ✓
- We're going to read this story two times. First you'll read it out loud and make no more than 8 errors. Then I'll read it and ask questions.
b. Everybody, touch the title. ✓
- (Call on a student to read the title.) [*The Browns Make Up a Plan.*]
- Everybody, what's the title? (Signal.) *The Browns Make Up a Plan.*
c. (Call on individual students to read the story, each student reading two or three sentences at a time.)

- (Correct errors: Tell the word. Direct the student to reread the sentence.)
- (If the group makes more than 8 errors, direct the students to reread the story.)

d. (After the group has read the selection making no more than 8 errors:) Now I'll read the story and ask questions.

The Browns Make Up a Plan

- Everybody, how many Browns are vacationing at Four Mile Lake? (Signal.) *Fifteen.*

The grandmother in the Brown family gave the impression that she was very mean. She was always ordering the other Browns around.

- What would she do to give the impression of being mean? (Call on a student. Ideas: *Act mean; be bossy; yell at people.*)

Lesson 21 115

- **What kinds of things would she say to order them around?** (Call on a student. Ideas: *Go get me the paper; Fix me some dinner;* etc.)

And the other Browns did a lot of yelling. But there's one thing you have to say about the Browns. They were the best hunters that ever came to Toadsville.

- **What's so special about the Browns?** (Call on a student. Idea: *They were the best hunters that ever came to Toadsville.*)
- **Goad better watch out.**

   When fourteen Browns went running down the hill after something that looked like a great toad, it was something to see. And it was something to hear. That grandmother wasn't far away, yelling at everybody. "Come on, Billy," she'd holler.
   Then she'd holler some more. "Run faster. Keep up. Don't look down, Doris. Keep your head up." When Grandmother Brown was on the east side of the lake, the people on the west side of the lake could hear everything she yelled.

- **Everybody, how many Browns went down the hill?** (Signal.) *Fourteen.*
- **Which Brown wasn't running down the hill?** (Call on a student. Idea: *The grandmother.*)
- **Everybody, how far is it from the west side of Four Mile Lake to the east side?** (Signal.) *Four miles.*
- **So how far away could you hear her voice?** (Signal.) *Four miles away.*
- **So what do you know about her voice?** (Call on a student. Idea: *It was very loud.*)

   After spending three days running after everything that moved, the Browns settled down. They had a plan. They didn't mention anything about what they were going to do, but everybody knew that they had a plan. People would question them. "What are you going to do?" But the Browns didn't answer these questions. The grandmother would usually say, "Stop asking questions. We've got work to do."
   Their plan was simple. First they stationed Browns around the places that Goad liked the most. Everybody knew where these places were. In fact, you can buy little books in the town of Toadsville that show maps of Goad's favorite spots.

- **What were some of her favorite spots?** (Call on a student. Ideas: *Logs near the north shore; hills on the south shore; the east shore.*)

   The first Brown to spot Goad was Mike. When he saw Goad near the south shore of the lake, he didn't try to rush down and catch her. Instead, he motioned for the other Browns to join him.

- **Show me how he might motion to the other Browns to come.** (Call on a student.)
- **Show me how he would motion to show where Goad is.** (Call on a student.)

When the other Browns arrived, they put their plan into action.

- **What does that mean, put their plan into action?** (Call on a student. Idea: *They started using their plan.*)

They gave Goad the impression that the hills were on fire.

- **How could they give that impression?** (Call on a student. Ideas: *By setting little fires; by lighting torches.*)

The wind was blowing toward the lake. So six Browns lit big smoky torches.

- **Everybody, was the wind blowing toward the lake or away from the lake?** (Signal.) *Toward the lake.*
- **Which way will the smoke from the torches move?** (Signal.) *Toward the lake.*
- **How many Browns lit torches?** (Signal.) *Six.*

> These torches made great clouds of smoke. The smoke rolled down the hills toward Goad, who was resting in the grass after eating one bee and sixteen blue flies. Goad was very smart and when she smelled the smoke, she did just what the Browns hoped she would do.

- What do animals do when a fire is near? (Call on a student. Idea: *Try to get away from the fire.*)

> She hopped toward the lake. Slowly, the fourteen Browns moved down the hill. Hop, hop. Goad moved closer to the water. As the Browns moved closer, Goad thought that the fire was coming closer. Hop, hop. Splash.
>
> **MORE NEXT TIME**

- What made that splash sound? (Call on a student. Idea: *Goad jumping into the water.*)
- Listen to this last part again:
  > The wind was blowing toward the lake. So six Browns lit big smoky torches. These torches made great clouds of smoke. The smoke rolled down the hills toward Goad, who was resting in the grass after eating one bee and sixteen blue flies. Goad was very smart and when she smelled the smoke, she did just what the Browns hoped she would do. She hopped toward the lake. Slowly, the fourteen Browns moved down the hill. Hop, hop. Goad moved closer to the water. As the Browns moved closer, Goad thought that the fire was coming closer. Hop, hop. Splash.
- Everybody, which way was the wind blowing? (Signal.) *Toward the lake.*
- So which way did the smoke blow? (Signal.) *Toward the lake.*
- What did Goad think the smoke came from? (Call on a student. Idea: *A fire on the hill.*)
- Everybody, did she move **toward the smoke** or **away from the smoke**? (Signal.) *Away from the smoke.*
- I think the Browns tricked her.

EXERCISE 5
PAIRED PRACTICE

You're going to read aloud to your partner. Today the **A** members will read first. Then the **B** members will read from the star to the end of the story.

(Observe students and give feedback.)

EXERCISE 6
WRITTEN ITEMS
Story Items

a. **Find part C on your worksheet.** ✓
  - The questions in part C are about today's story. I'll call on different students to read the items, but don't say the answers.
b. (For each item: Call on a student to read the item.)
  - Item 3. *[What is Goad's only weakness?]*
  - Item 4. *[Why did people use binoculars to look for Goad?]*
  - Item 5. *[How many Browns went to Four Mile Lake?]*
  - Item 6. *[What did the grandmother do most of the time?]*
  - Item 7. *[Underline the names of 2 members of the Brown family.]*
  - Item 8. *[Did the people in Toadsville know the Browns' plan for catching Goad?]*
  - Item 9. *[The Browns wanted to make Goad think that there was a <u>blank</u>.]*
  - Item 10. *[What did the Browns burn to make the smoke?]*

End-of-Lesson Activities

INDEPENDENT WORK

Now finish your independent work for lesson 21. Raise your hand when you're finished.
(Observe students and give feedback.)

WORKCHECK

a. (Direct students to take out their marking pencils.)
  - We're going to check your independent work. Remember, if you got an item wrong, make an **X** next to the item.

b. (For each item: Read the item. Call on a student to answer it. If the answer is wrong, say the correct answer. Refer to the Answer Key for the correct answers.)

c. Now use your marking pencil to fix up any items you got wrong. Remember, all mistakes must be fixed up before you hand in your independent work.

Note: You will need a balloon for a demonstration in lesson 22.

WRITING-SPELLING

(Present Writing-Spelling lesson 21 after completing Reading lesson 21. See Writing-Spelling Guide.)

Lesson 22

Materials: You will need a balloon for a demonstration in exercise 3.

EXERCISE 1
VOCABULARY REVIEW

a. You learned a sentence that tells why they waded into the stream.
- Everybody, say that sentence. Get ready. (Signal.) *They waded into the stream to remove tadpoles.*
- (Repeat until firm.)

b. I'll say part of the sentence. When I stop, you say the next word. Listen: They waded into the stream to remove . . . Everybody, what's the next word? (Signal.) *Tadpoles.*

c. Listen: They . . . Everybody, what's the next word? (Signal.) *Waded.*
- Say the whole sentence. Get ready. (Signal.) *They waded into the stream to remove tadpoles.*

d. Listen: They waded into the stream to . . . Everybody, what's the next word? (Signal.) *Remove.*

EXERCISE 2
READING WORDS

Column 1

a. **Find lesson 22 in your textbook.** ✓
- **Touch column 1.** ✓
- (Teacher reference:)

1. twenty	4. exactly
2. crazy	5. smoky
3. fuzzy	

- These words end in **Y**. The **Y** makes the sound **ee** at the end of these words.

b. Word 1. What word? (Signal.) *Twenty.*
- Spell **twenty**. Get ready. (Tap for each letter.) *T-W-E-N-T-Y.*
- (Repeat step b for words 2–5.)

c. Let's read those words again.
- Word 1. What word? (Signal.) *Twenty.*
- (Repeat for words 2–5.)

d. (Repeat step c until firm.)

Column 2

e. **Find column 2.** ✓
- (Teacher reference:)

1. boasting	4. screaming
2. roaring	5. believing
3. ringing	6. paddling

- These words end in **I-N-G**.

f. Word 1. What word? (Signal.) *Boasting.*
- What's another word that means the same thing as **boasting**? (Signal.) *Bragging.*
- What's another way of saying **He was always bragging about how smart he was**? (Signal.) *He was always boasting about how smart he was.*

g. Word 2. What word? (Signal.) *Roaring.*
- (Repeat for words 3–6.)

h. Let's read those words again.
- Word 1. What word? (Signal.) *Boasting.*
- (Repeat for words 2–6.)

i. (Repeat step h until firm.)

Column 3

j. **Find column 3.** ✓
- (Teacher reference:)

1. <u>dot</u>ted	4. <u>stick</u>ing
2. <u>snap</u>shots	5. <u>happen</u>ed
3. <u>sol</u>id	6. <u>upp</u>er

- These words have more than one syllable. The first part of each word is underlined.

k. Word 1. What's the underlined part? (Signal.) *dot.*
- What's the whole word? (Signal.) *Dotted.*

l. Word 2. What's the underlined part? (Signal.) *snap.*
- What's the whole word? (Signal.) *Snapshots.*

m. Word 3. What's the underlined part? (Signal.) *sol.*
- What's the whole word? (Signal.) *Solid.*

n. Word 4. What's the underlined part? (Signal.) *stick.*

- What's the whole word? (Signal.) *Sticking.*
o. Word 5. What's the underlined part? (Signal.) *hap.*
- What's the whole word? (Signal.) *Happened.*
p. Word 6. What's the underlined part? (Signal.) *up.*
- What's the whole word? (Signal.) *Upper.*
q. Let's read those words again.
- Word 1. What word? (Signal.) *Dotted.*
- (Repeat for: **2. snapshots, 3. solid, 4. sticking, 5. happened, 6. upper.**)
r. (Repeat step q until firm.)

Column 4
s. Find column 4. ✓
- (Teacher reference:)

1. New York	3. impression
2. trouble	4. grown-ups

t. Word 1 is the name of a place. What place? (Signal.) *New York.*
- New York is the name of one of the largest cities in the world. New York is also the name of the state where you'll find New York City.
- Word 2. What word? (Signal.) *Trouble.*
- (Repeat for words 3 and 4.)
u. Let's read those words again.
- Number 1. What words? (Signal.) *New York.*
- Word 2. What word? (Signal.) *Trouble*
- (Repeat for words 3 and 4.)
v. (Repeat step u until firm.)

Column 5
w. Find column 5. ✓
- (Teacher reference:)

1. engine	3. skip
2. picnic	4. unload

x. Word 1. What word? (Signal.) *Engine.*
- (Repeat for words 2–4.)
y. (Repeat step x until firm.)

Column 6
z. Find column 6. ✓
- (Teacher reference:)

1. wrinkle	3. movies
2. diving	4. arrow

a. Word 1. What word? (Signal.) *Wrinkle.*
- (Repeat for words 2–4.)
b. (Repeat step a until firm.)

Individual Turns
(For columns 1–6: Call on individual students, each to read one to three words per turn.)

EXERCISE 3

COMPREHENSION PASSAGES
Passage B
a. Find part B in your textbook. ✓
- You're going to read the next story about Goad. First you'll read two information passages.
b. Everybody, touch the title in part B. ✓
- (Call on a student to read the title.) *[Names That Tell How Fast Things Move.]*
- Everybody, what's the title? (Signal.) *Names That Tell How Fast Things Move.*
c. (Call on individual students to read the passage, each student reading two or three sentences at a time. Ask the specified questions as the students read.)

> **Names That Tell How Fast Things Move**
>
> Names that tell how fast things move have two parts. The first part of the name tells about length. The second part tells about time.

- Everybody, names that tell how fast things move have how many parts? (Signal.) *Two.*
- What does the first part of the name tell about? (Signal.) *Length.*
- What does the second part of the name tell about? (Signal.) *Time.*
- (Repeat until firm.)

> Here is a name that tells how fast things move: <u>centimeters per minute.</u> The first part of the name is <u>centimeters.</u> That part tells about length. The second part of the name is <u>minute.</u> That part tells about time.

- Everybody, listen: centimeters per minute. How many parts does that name have? (Signal.) *Two.*

- What's the first part? (Signal.) *Centimeters.*
- That part tells about length.
- What's the second part of the name **centimeters per minute?** (Signal.) *Minute.*
- That part tells about time.
- Once more: centimeters per minute. What's the first part? (Signal.) *Centimeters.*
- What does that part tell about? (Signal.) *Length.*
- What's the second part of the name? (Signal.) *Minute.*
- What does that part tell about? (Signal.) *Time.*
- Remember, the first part tells about length. The second part tells about time.

Passage C

> *Note:* You will need a balloon.

d. Find part C in your textbook. ✓
- This information passage tells about how air moves an object.

e. Everybody, touch the title. ✓
- (Call on a student to read the title.) *[How Air Moves an Object.]*
- Everybody, what's the title? (Signal.) *How Air Moves an Object.*

f. (Call on individual students to read the passage, each student reading two or three sentences at a time.)

> **How Air Moves an Object**
>
> In the story for today, you'll read about how air can move an object. You've seen it happen with balloons. When you fill them with air and let them go, they fly around until they run out of air.

- (Blow up a balloon and let it go so the students can see that it will fly around until it runs out of air.)

> Here's the rule about how the balloon moves: **The balloon moves the opposite direction the air moves.**

- Everybody, which way does the balloon move? (Signal.) *The opposite direction the air moves.*
- (Repeat until firm.)

> Touch the dotted arrow in the picture.

- Everybody, do it. ✓

> The dotted arrow shows the direction the air moves from the balloon.

- Everybody, put your finger on the page and point to show the direction of the dotted arrow. ✓
- Remember, that's the direction the air moves from the balloon.

> The balloon moves the opposite direction the air moves. The solid arrow shows the direction the balloon will fly through the air.

- Everybody, put your finger on the solid arrow and show the direction the balloon will move when the air comes out. ✓
- (Point up.) If the air comes out of the balloon this way, the balloon will move in the opposite direction. Point to show me which way the balloon will move. ✓
- (Point left.) If the air moves out of the balloon in this direction, which direction will the balloon move? Everybody, show me. ✓
- (Repeat until firm.)

EXERCISE 4

STORY READING

a. Find part D in your textbook. ✓
- We're going to read this story two times. First you'll read it out loud and make no more than 7 errors. Then I'll read it and ask questions.

b. Everybody, touch the title. ✓
- (Call on a student to read the title.) *[Goad in the Water.]*
- Everybody, what's the title? (Signal.) *Goad in the Water.*

c. (Call on individual students to read the story, each student reading two or three sentences at a time.)

- (Correct errors: Tell the word. Direct the student to reread the sentence.)
- (If the group makes more than 7 errors, direct the students to reread the story.)

d. (After the group has read the selection making no more than 7 errors:)

Lesson 22 121

Now I'll read the story and ask questions.

Goad in the Water

- What problem does Goad have when she's in the water? (Call on a student. Idea: *She can't swim fast.*)

The Browns had given Goad the impression that a fire was coming down the hill. What really came down the hill were fourteen Browns. The six grown-ups were each carrying a smoky torch.

- The wind was blowing toward the lake, so which way was the smoke moving? (Call on a student.) [*Toward the lake.*]

Goad went into the water, thinking that she was getting away from a fire. But she was doing just what the Browns wanted her to do.

- What did the Browns want her to do? (Call on a student. Idea: *Get into the water.*)
- Why? (Call on a student. Idea: *Because she'd be easier to catch in the water.*)

Her stubby little legs paddled her out into the lake.
When Goad was about twenty meters from the shore, the grandmother motioned to the Browns, and the Browns came roaring down the hill.

- Show me how the grandmother might have motioned to the Browns. (Call on a student.)

The hills were ringing with noise. Every Brown was yelling, "We've got her." But a much louder voice rang above the others. "Mark, move faster." Of course, it was Grandmother Brown, yelling orders to everybody.

It seemed that Goad would never get away from these fourteen screaming Browns. Her little legs were paddling as fast as they could, but she knew that she was in trouble. Browns were running into the water now, diving, splashing, yelling, coming at Goad like fourteen crazy people.

- Listen to that part again and get a picture of what's happening.
  The hills were ringing with noise. Every Brown was yelling, "We've got her." But a much louder voice rang above the others. "Mark, move faster." Of course, it was Grandmother Brown, yelling orders to everybody.
  It seemed that Goad would never get away from these fourteen screaming Browns. Her little legs were paddling as fast as they could, but she knew that she was in trouble. Browns were running into the water now, diving, splashing, yelling, coming at Goad like fourteen crazy people.
- How do you think poor Goad feels? (Call on a student. Ideas: *Frightened; confused.*)

The next part of the story is the part that some people still have trouble believing, because there are still a lot of questions about it. Nobody has movies to show exactly what happened, but a boy from New York who was on vacation took snapshots that show what happened.

- Everybody, the snapshots that he took are on the next page. Touch them. ✓

- Everybody, can you see Goad in the top snapshot? (Signal.) *Yes.*
- Can you see her in the middle snapshot? (Signal.) *Yes.*
- What's happened to her in the middle snapshot? (Call on a student. Idea: *She's gotten bigger.*)
- What is she doing in the bottom snapshot? (Call on a student. Idea: *Flying away.*)

> The first snapshot shows the Browns splashing toward Goad. In the second snapshot Goad is loading up with air. She looks like a balloon with a lot of air in it. She is almost round, with her stubby little legs sticking out to the sides.

- What does Goad do to make herself get bigger? (Call on a student. Idea: *Fills up with air.*)
- Everybody, touch Goad in the second picture. ✓
- Do you see her stubby little legs sticking out to the side? (Call on a student.) [*Yes.*]

> In the same picture, there are two or three Browns reaching out for her. One Brown is diving at her, and he looks like he is very close to her.
> In the third snapshot, the Browns are standing in the water, pointing up in the air. In the upper corner of the picture, you can see a little fuzzy mark. That's Goad, flying away from the Browns.

- Goad made herself work just like a balloon. When the air moved from her mouth, she flew in the opposite direction.

EXERCISE 5
PAIRED PRACTICE

You're going to read aloud to your partner. Today the **B** members will read first. Then the **A** members will read from the star to the end of the story.
(Observe students and give feedback.)

EXERCISE 6
WRITTEN ITEMS
Story Items
a. **Find part C on your worksheet.** ✓
- The questions in part C are about today's story. I'll call on different students to read the items, but don't say the answers.
b. (For each item: Call on a student to read the item.)
- Item 10. [When the Brown family tricked Goad, what did Goad think was coming down the hill?]
- Item 11. [What was really coming down the hill?]
- Item 12. [What did Goad do when she smelled the smoke?]
- Item 13. [Air rushes out of Goad this way. Draw an arrow to show which way Goad will move.]
- Item 14. [How do people know how Goad got away from the Browns?]
- Item 15. [What was Goad doing in the second snapshot?]
- Item 16. [What was Goad doing in the third snapshot?]
- Item 17. [The picture shows Goad filled up with air. Arrow A shows air leaving Goad this way. Write the letter of the arrow that shows the way Goad will move.]

End-of-Lesson Activities

INDEPENDENT WORK

Now finish your independent work for lesson 22. Raise your hand when you're finished. (Observe students and give feedback.)

WORKCHECK

a. (Direct students to take out their marking pencils.)
- We're going to check your independent work. Remember, if you got an item wrong, make an **X** next to the item.
b. (For each item: Read the item. Call on a student to answer it. If the answer is wrong, say the correct answer. Refer to the Answer Key for the correct answers.)

c. Now use your marking pencil to fix up any items you got wrong. Remember, all mistakes must be fixed up before you hand in your independent work.

Note: A special project occurs after lesson 23. See page 130 for the materials you'll need.

WRITING-SPELLING

(Present Writing-Spelling lesson 22 after completing Reading lesson 22. See Writing-Spelling Guide.)

Lesson 23

EXERCISE 1
VOCABULARY REVIEW

a. You learned a sentence that tells what the fly boasted about.
- Everybody, say that sentence. Get ready. (Signal.) *The fly boasted about escaping from the spider.*
- (Repeat until firm.)

b. I'll say part of the sentence. When I stop, you say the next word. Listen: The fly boasted about . . . Everybody, what's the next word? (Signal.) *Escaping.*

c. Listen: The fly . . . Everybody, what's the next word? (Signal.) *Boasted.*
- Say the whole sentence. Get ready. (Signal.) *The fly boasted about escaping from the spider.*

EXERCISE 2
READING WORDS

Column 1

a. **Find lesson 23 in your textbook.** ✓
- Touch column 1. ✓
- (Teacher reference:)

1. moist	3. broiled
2. boiled	4. noise

- All the words in column 1 have the letter combination **O-I**. What sound does that combination make? (Signal.) *oy.*

b. Word 1. What word? (Signal.) *Moist.*
- Spell **moist.** Get ready. (Tap for each letter.) *M-O-I-S-T.*
- Things that are moist are slightly wet, not dripping wet.

c. Word 2. What word? (Signal.) *Boiled.*
- Spell **boiled.** Get ready. (Tap for each letter.) *B-O-I-L-E-D.*
- When things are boiled, they cook in bubbling hot water.

d. Word 3. What word? (Signal.) *Broiled.*
- Spell **broiled.** Get ready. (Tap for each letter.) *B-R-O-I-L-E-D.*
- Things that are broiled are cooked over an open fire.

e. Word 4. What word? (Signal.) *Noise.*
- Spell **noise.** Get ready. (Tap for each letter.) *N-O-I-S-E.*

f. Let's read those words again.
- Word 1. What word? (Signal.) *Moist.*
- (Repeat for words 2–4.)

g. (Repeat step f until firm.)

Column 2

h. Find column 2. ✓
- (Teacher reference:)

1. **backward**	4. **picnic**
2. **laughing**	5. **loaded**
3. **louder**	

- These words have two syllables. The first syllable is underlined.

i. Word 1. What's the first syllable? (Signal.) *back.*
- What's the whole word? (Signal.) *Backward.*

j. Word 2. What's the first syllable? (Signal.) *laugh.*
- What's the whole word? (Signal.) *Laughing.*

k. Word 3. What's the first syllable? (Signal.) *loud.*
- What's the whole word? (Signal.) *Louder.*

l. Word 4. What's the first syllable? (Signal.) *pic.*
- What's the whole word? (Signal.) *Picnic.*

m. Word 5. What's the first syllable? (Signal.) *load.*
- What's the whole word? (Signal.) *Loaded.*

n. Let's read those words again.
- Word 1. What word? (Signal.) *Backward.*
- (Repeat for words 2–5.)

o. (Repeat step n until firm.)

Column 3

p. Find column 3. ✓
- (Teacher reference:)

1. waded	4. unloaded
2. skipped	5. outsmarted
3. soaked	

- These words end in **E-D**.
q. Word 1. What word? (Signal.) *Waded.*
- What do you do when you wade? (Call on a student. Idea: *You walk in water that is not very deep.*)
r. Word 2. What word? (Signal.) *Skipped.*
- (Repeat for: **3. soaked, 4. unloaded, 5. outsmarted.**)
s. Let's read those words again.
- Word 1. What word? (Signal.) *Waded.*
- (Repeat for words 2–5.)
t. (Repeat step s until firm.)

Column 4
u. Find column 4. ✓
- (Teacher reference:)

1. strange	4. crows
2. families	5. gathered
3. smiled	

- These are words that are in your story.
v. Word 1. What word? (Signal.) *Strange.*
- (Repeat for words 2–5.)
w. Let's read those words again.
- Word 1. What word? (Signal.) *Strange.*
- (Repeat for words 2–5.)
x. (Repeat step w until firm.)

Column 5
y. Find column 5. ✓
- (Teacher reference:)

1. flight attendant	4. completely
2. wrinkled	5. worry
3. caught	

z. Number 1. Those words are **flight attendant.** What words? (Signal.) *Flight attendant.*
a. Word 2. What word? (Signal.) *Wrinkled.*
- (Repeat for words 3–5.)
b. (Repeat step z until firm.)

Individual Turns
(For columns 1–5: Call on individual students, each to read one to three words per turn.)

EXERCISE 3
COMPREHENSION PASSAGE
a. Find part B in your textbook. ✓

- You're going to read the last story about Goad. First you'll read an information passage that gives some facts about miles.
b. Everybody, touch the title. ✓
- (Call on a student to read the title.) [Facts About Miles.]
- Everybody, what's the title? (Signal.) *Facts About Miles.*
c. (Call on individual students to read the passage, each student reading two or three sentences at a time.)

> **Facts About Miles**
>
> The story in this lesson will tell about miles. Here are some facts about miles:
> We use miles to tell how far it is between places that are far apart.

- Everybody, we use miles to tell how far it is between what kind of places? (Signal.) *Places that are far apart.*

> A mile is a little more than five thousand feet.

- Everybody, listen to that fact again. A mile is a little more than five thousand feet.
- Say that fact. (Signal.) *A mile is a little more than five thousand feet.*
- (Repeat until firm.)
- How long is a mile? (Signal.) *A little more than five thousand feet.*

> Look at the map. The numbers on the arrows tell how many miles it is from one place to another place.

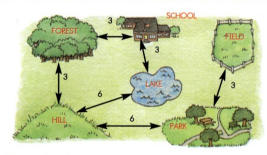

- Everybody, touch the arrow that goes from the forest to the hill. ✓
- The number on the arrow is 3, so it is 3 miles from the forest to the hill.
- Touch the arrow that goes from the hill to the lake. ✓
- How far is it from the hill to the lake? (Signal.) *6 miles.*

- Touch the arrow that goes from the hill to the park. ✓
- How far is it from the hill to the park? (Signal.) *6 miles.*
- Touch the arrow that goes from the park to the field. ✓
- How far is it from the park to the field? (Signal.) *3 miles.*

EXERCISE 4

STORY READING

a. Find part C in your textbook. ✓
- We're going to read this story two times. First you'll read it out loud and make no more than 8 errors. Then I'll read it and ask questions.

b. Everybody, touch the title. ✓
- (Call on a student to read the title.) *[A Big Picnic.]*
- Everybody, what's the title? (Signal.) *A Big Picnic.*

c. (Call on individual students to read the story, each student reading two or three sentences at a time.)

- (Correct errors: Tell the word. Direct the student to reread the sentence.)
- (If the group makes more than 8 errors, direct the students to reread the story.)

d. (After the group has read the selection making no more than 8 errors:)
Now I'll read the story and ask questions.

A Big Picnic

The three snapshots of the Browns trying to catch Goad showed Goad in the water, Goad getting bigger, and Goad flying into the air. She had loaded up with air and when the Browns were about to grab her, she unloaded.

- Everybody, let's say the air rushed out of Goad this way. (Point left.) Show me which way Goad would move. ✓

A great gust of wind came out of her mouth, and she went flying backward. She skipped over the water two times, and then she went straight up into the air. She looked just like a great balloon when you let the air out of it. The Browns just stood there and looked.

One of the Browns said, "Oh nuts," but they seemed to know that Goad had outsmarted them. They didn't run after her.

- Everybody, did the Browns' plan work? (Signal.) *No.*
- Why do you think they didn't run after Goad? (Call on a student. Ideas: *People can't fly; Goad was going too fast; they knew they'd been beaten.*)

Fourteen Browns stood around in the water watching the great toad land in the weeds about a hundred meters away. Then fourteen soaked Browns waded from the water. They moved slowly.

- Everybody, how far away did Goad land? (Signal.) *About a hundred meters away.*
- Why do you think the Browns were moving slowly? (Call on a student. Ideas: *Tired; sad that Goad got away.*)

When they joined the grandmother at the top of the hill, she did something that was very strange. She smiled. Nobody had ever seen her do that before. She had a few missing teeth, but she had a warm smile. It was the kind of old wrinkled smile that makes <u>you</u> want to smile. And that's just what happened. When she smiled, one of the little Browns smiled. Then another Brown smiled, and before you knew it, one of the soaking wet Browns began to laugh. Well, before you knew it, they were all laughing. "That's some toad," one of them yelled, and they all laughed harder.

- Listen to that part again and get a picture of it. See if you feel like laughing.

    When they joined the grandmother at the top of the hill, she did something that was very strange. She smiled. Nobody had ever seen her do that before. She had a few missing teeth, but she had a warm smile. It was the kind of old wrinkled smile that makes <u>you</u> want to smile. And that's just what happened.

Lesson 23 127

> When she smiled, one of the little Browns smiled. Then another Brown smiled, and before you knew it, one of the soaking wet Browns began to laugh. Well, before you knew it, they were all laughing. "That's some toad," one of them yelled, and they all laughed harder.

- One of the Browns said, "That's some toad." What did that person mean? (Call on a student. Ideas: *Goad was smart; Goad was amazing.*)

> **There's something about seeing fifteen Browns laughing and slapping each other on the back. It makes you start laughing too.**

- Why are there fifteen Browns now? (Call on a student. Idea: *Because the fourteen Browns joined the grandmother.*)

> **A lot of people had gathered to see the Browns try to catch Goad. The first thing you know, the hills were loaded with people who were laughing. Their cheeks were moist because big tears were running down their cheeks.**

- Why did they have tears running down their cheeks? (Call on a student. *Idea: Because they were laughing so hard.*)

> **The sound of the laughing was very loud, but pretty soon, a much louder voice rang above the laughing. "Let's have a picnic and forget about that fat old toad."**

- Everybody, who do you think had a voice that you could hear over all that laughter? (Signal.) *The grandmother.*

> **And that's just what everybody did.**

- What did they do? (Call on a student. Idea: *Had a picnic.*)

> **All those people with binoculars and nets who had been watching. All the little kids and the families, and the old people, and dogs and cats and pet crows, and fifteen Browns. They all had a picnic. They ate boiled corn and broiled hot dogs.**

- How do you fix boiled corn? (Call on a student. Idea: *Cook the corn in boiling water.*)
- How do you fix broiled hot dogs? (Call on a student. Idea: *Cook the hot dogs over a campfire without a pot or a pan.*)

> **They did a lot of laughing. And some people say that they could hear somebody else laughing. They say that it sounded like a laughing toad.**

- Everybody, touch that laughing toad in the picture. ✓
- Who do you think that laughing toad was? (Signal.) *Goad.*

EXERCISE 5

PAIRED PRACTICE

You're going to read aloud to your partner. Today the **A** members will read first. Then the **B** members will read from the star to the end of the story.
(Observe students and give feedback.)

EXERCISE 6

WRITTEN ITEMS

Story Items

a. Find part D in your textbook. ✓
- The questions in part D are about today's story. I'll call on different students to read the items, but don't say the answers.
b. (For each item: Call on a student to read the item.)
- Item 1. [*A boy from New York took three snapshots of Goad getting away from the Browns. What was Goad doing in the second snapshot?*]

128 Lesson 23

- Item 2. *[What was Goad doing in the third snapshot?]*
- Item 3. *[Did the Browns catch Goad?]*
- Item 4. *[What happened right after the grandmother smiled?]*
- Item 5. *[Why were so many other people around the lake?]*
- Item 6. *[Write 2 things that the people ate at the picnic.]*
- Item 7. *[Air rushes out of Goad this way. Draw an arrow to show which way Goad will move.]*
- Item 8. *[Air rushes out of Goad this way. Draw an arrow to show which way Goad will move.]*

Comprehension Passage Items

c. **Open your workbook to lesson 23.** ✓
- Find item 1 on your worksheet. ✓

d. I'll read the directions: Things that are this far apart on the map are 1 mile apart.
- Everybody, hold up your fingers to show me how far apart one mile is on the map. (Observe students and give feedback.)

e. I'll read again: Things that are this far apart on the map are 2 miles apart.
- Everybody, hold up your fingers to show me how far apart two miles are. (Observe students and give feedback.)

f. Remember, the longer arrows show two miles. You'll write **1** or **2** in the circle that is on each arrow.

End-of-Lesson Activities

INDEPENDENT WORK

Note: The special project on textbook page 143 is not part of the independent work.

Now finish your independent work for lesson 23. Raise your hand when you're finished. (Observe students and give feedback.)

WORKCHECK

a. (Direct students to take out their marking pencils.)
- We're going to check your independent work. Remember, if you got an item wrong, make an **X** next to the item.

b. (For each item: Read the item. Call on a student to answer it. If the answer is wrong, say the correct answer. Refer to the Answer Key for the correct answers.)

c. Now use your marking pencil to fix up any items you got wrong. Remember, all mistakes must be fixed up before you hand in your independent work.

WRITING-SPELLING

(Present Writing-Spelling lesson 23 after completing Reading lesson 23. See Writing-Spelling Guide.)

Special Project

Note: After completing lesson 23, do this special project with the students. You may do the project during another part of the day.

Materials: Large sheet of butcher paper or poster board (at least 5 feet x 4 feet), color marker, scissors, construction paper, possibly paints or crayons, paste

a. Find page 143 in your textbook. ✔
  - This section tells about a special project we're going to do.
  - (Call on individual students to read two or three sentences at a time.)
  - (Teacher reference:)

   ### Special Project

   Make a large map of Four Mile Lake. Show the directions **north, south, east,** and **west.** Make pictures and labels for the following places:
   - logs
   - hills
   - where the Browns almost caught Goad (Show 6 smoky torches.)
   - Toadsville
   - where you think the Browns had their picnic (Show a picnic table or a hot dog.)

b. (Divide students into groups, each of which is responsible for part of the project:
  - Group 1 is to make the map of the lake. The group is to show the scale on the map and follow the specifications the textbook provides in lesson 15;
  - Group 2 is to make pictures and labels for the logs, hills, and Toadsville;
  - Group 3 is to show where the Browns almost caught Goad, and where they had their picnic.)

Lesson 24

EXERCISE 1
VOCABULARY REVIEW

a. You learned a sentence that tells what the workers used to prop up the cage.
- Everybody, say that sentence. Get ready. (Signal.) *The workers propped up the cage with steel bars.*
- (Repeat until firm.)

b. I'll say part of the sentence. When I stop, you say the next word. Listen: The workers . . . Everybody, what's the next word? (Signal.) *Propped.*

c. Listen: The workers propped up the cage with . . . Everybody, what's the next word? (Signal.) *Steel.*
- Say the whole sentence. Get ready. (Signal.) *The workers propped up the cage with steel bars.*

EXERCISE 2
READING WORDS

Column 1

a. **Find lesson 24 in your textbook.** ✓
- **Touch column 1.** ✓
- (Teacher reference:)

1. mirror	4. spoiled
2. CD	5. wrong
3. Nancy	6. arrows

b. Word 1 is **mirror.** What word? (Signal.) *Mirror.*
- Spell **mirror.** Get ready. (Tap for each letter.) *M-I-R-R-O-R.*

c. Word 2 is **CD.** What word? (Signal.) *CD.*

d. Word 3 is a name. What name? (Signal.) *Nancy.*
- Spell **Nancy.** Get ready. (Tap for each letter.) *N-A-N-C-Y.*

e. Word 4. What word? (Signal.) *Spoiled.*
- Spell **spoiled.** Get ready. (Tap for each letter.) *S-P-O-I-L-E-D.*
- Spoiled children cry and act like babies to make people do things for them. Everybody, what do we call children who act like babies? (Signal.) *Spoiled.*

f. Word 5 is **wrong.** What word? (Signal.) *Wrong.*
- Spell **wrong.** Get ready. (Tap for each letter.) *W-R-O-N-G.*

g. Word 6 is **arrows.** What word? (Signal.) *Arrows.*

h. Let's read those words again, the fast way.
- Word 1. What word? (Signal.) *Mirror.*
- (Repeat for words 2–6.)

i. (Repeat step h until firm.)

Column 2

j. Find column 2. ✓
- (Teacher reference:)

1. completely	4. argued
2. hanging	5. reached
3. heavier	6. smiling

- All these words have an ending.

k. Word 1. What word? (Signal.) *Completely.*
- **Completely** is another word for **totally.** Here's another way of saying **She totally finished her homework: She completely finished her homework.**
- Your turn. What's another way of saying **She totally finished her homework?** (Signal.) *She completely finished her homework.*
- What's another way of saying **They totally rebuilt the engine?** (Signal.) *They completely rebuilt the engine.*

l. Word 2. What word? (Signal.) *Hanging.*
- (Repeat for words 3–6.)

m. (Repeat step l until firm.)

Column 3

n. Find column 3. ✓
- (Teacher reference:)

1. <u>a</u>head	4. <u>any</u>how
2. <u>a</u>part	5. <u>with</u>in
3. <u>a</u>greed	6. <u>won</u>der

- These words are compound words. The first part of each word is underlined.

o. Word 1. What's the underlined part? (Signal.) *a.*

Lesson 24 131

- What's the whole word? (Signal.) *Ahead.*
p. Word 2. What's the underlined part? (Signal.) *a.*
- What's the whole word? (Signal.) *Apart.*
- Things that are not close to each other are far apart. Things that **are** close to each other are **not** far apart. Hold your hands so they are not far apart. ✓
- Hold your hands so they are as far apart as they can get. Be careful that you don't hit your neighbor. ✓
q. Word 3. What's the underlined part? (Signal.) *a.*
- What's the whole word? (Signal.) *Agreed.*
r. Word 4. What's the underlined part? (Signal.) *any.*
- What's the whole word? (Signal.) *Anyhow.*
s. Word 5. What's the underlined part? (Signal.) *with.*
- What's the whole word? (Signal.) *Within.*
t. Word 6. What's the underlined part? (Signal.) *Won.*
- What's the whole word? (Signal.) *Wonder.*
u. Let's read those words again.
- Word 1. What word? (Signal.) *Ahead.*
- (Repeat for: **2. apart, 3. agreed, 4. anyhow, 5. within, 6. wonder.**)
v. (Repeat step u until firm.)

Column 4

w. Find column 4. ✓
- (Teacher reference:)

1. United States	4. pant
2. Lisa	5. Saturday
3. morning	6. caught

x. Number 1. What words? (Signal.) *United States.*
- How many states are in the United States? (Signal.) *50.*
y. Word 2 is a name. What name? (Signal.) *Lisa.*
z. Word 3. What word? (Signal.) *Morning.*
- (Repeat for words 4–6.)

a. Let's read those words again.
- Number 1. What words? (Signal.) *United States.*
- Word 2. What word? (Signal.) *Lisa.*
- (Repeat for words 3–6.)
b. (Repeat step a until firm.)

Column 5

c. Find column 5. ✓
- (Teacher reference:)

1. school	4. write
2. worry	5. bridge
3. motioned	6. thousand

d. Word 1. What word? (Signal.) *School.*
- (Repeat for words 2–6.)
e. Let's read those words again.
- Word 1. What word? (Signal.) *School.*
- (Repeat for words 2–6.)
f. (Repeat step e until firm.)

Individual Turns

(For columns 1–5: Call on individual students, each to read one to three words per turn.)

EXERCISE 3

COMPREHENSION PASSAGE

a. Find part B in your textbook. ✓
- You're going to read a story about a brother and sister who have a race. First you'll read the information passage. It gives some facts about miles.
b. Everybody, touch the title. ✓
- (Call on a student to read the title.) *[More Facts About Miles.]*
- Everybody, what's the title? (Signal.) *More Facts About Miles.*
c. (Call on individual students to read the passage, each student reading two or three sentences at a time.)

> **More Facts About Miles**
>
> Some places are many miles apart. If you flew from the east side of the United States to the west side of the United States, you would go about 25 hundred miles.

- Everybody, about how many miles is it from the east side to the west side? (Signal.) *25 hundred miles.*

132 Lesson 24

If you flew from the north side of the United States to the south side of the United States, you would go about 13 hundred miles.

- Everybody, about how many miles is it from the north side to the south side? (Signal.) *13 hundred miles.*

The map shows the United States.

- Everybody, what part of the world does the map show? (Signal.) *The United States.*
- Touch the arrow that goes from the east side to the west side of the United States. ✓
- Everybody, about how far is it from the east side to the west side? (Signal.) *25 hundred miles.*
- Touch the east end of that arrow. ✓
- Now go along the arrow to the west end. ✓
- Touch the arrow that goes from the north side to the south side of the United States. ✓
- Everybody, about how far is it from the north side to the south side? (Signal.) *13 hundred miles.*
- Touch the north end of that arrow. ✓
- Now go along the arrow to the south end. ✓

EXERCISE 4

STORY READING

a. Find part C in your textbook. ✓
- We're going to read this story two times. First you'll read it out loud and make no more than 8 errors. Then I'll read it and ask questions.
b. Everybody, touch the title. ✓
- (Call on a student to read the title.) *[Jack and Lisa Have a Race.]*
- Everybody, what's the title? (Signal.) *Jack and Lisa Have a Race.*
c. (Call on individual students to read the story, each student reading two or three sentences at a time.)
- (Correct errors: Tell the word. Direct the student to reread the sentence.)
- (If the group makes more than 8 errors, direct the students to reread the story.)
d. (After the group has read the selection making no more than 8 errors:)
Now I'll read the story and ask questions.

Jack and Lisa Have a Race

Jack was two years older than his sister Lisa. Jack could do most things better than Lisa. Jack could read better and write better. Jack could lift heavier things than Lisa could lift. And Jack could run faster than Lisa.

But Lisa did something that Jack didn't do. Every morning Lisa got up and ran three miles. While Lisa was running, Jack was still sleeping.

- Everybody, what are the names of the children? (Signal.) *Jack and Lisa.*
- Who was older? (Signal.) *Jack.*
- Who was better at doing most things? (Signal.) *Jack.*
- How far did Lisa run every morning? (Signal.) *Three miles.*
- That's a pretty long distance.

One day Jack and Lisa were on their way to school. Jack said, "You're always running in the morning, but I can still run faster than you. I'll show you. Come on, let's race to the corner."

Before Lisa could say anything, Jack said, "Get ready. Go," and started to run. Lisa ran, too, but she could not keep up with her brother. When Lisa reached the corner, Jack was waiting and smiling, but he was out of breath. He said, "I told you (pant, pant), I could beat you (pant, pant)."

- Everybody, who won the race? (Signal.) *Jack.*
- Who was out of breath? (Signal.) *Jack.*

Lesson 24 133

- I'll read the part that Jack said at the end when he was panting. I won't say, "Pant, pant." I'll actually pant the way he did.

  "I told you [pant 2 times] I could beat you [pant 2 times]."

> Lisa said, "You are fast in a short race, but I'll bet I can run a mile faster than you can."
> Jack said, "That's a joke (pant, pant). I can run a lot faster than you (pant). So I could beat you in a mile (pant)."
> Lisa said, "You're already out of breath and we only ran a thousand feet. Remember, a mile is over 5 thousand feet. So your tongue will be hanging out long before you've run a mile."
> Jack said, "That's not (pant) so. I'm faster than you, no matter how far we run."

- Everybody, a mile is more than how many feet? (Signal.) *5 thousand.*
- How many feet had the children just raced? (Signal.) *A thousand.*
- The mile race is over five times that long.

> The children argued some more. Then they agreed to race a mile on Saturday.
> On Saturday, Jack and Lisa went to a bike path near the river. They started at a place that was one mile from the big white bridge. Jack said, "By the time you get to the bridge, you'll see me there, resting in the grass."
> The race started and Jack was soon far ahead of Lisa. He looked back and smiled. "Come on," he called. "Is that as fast as you can run?"
> Lisa did not answer.
> By the time Jack could clearly see the white bridge, he was running much slower. Lisa was now right behind him, running quite a bit faster than he was.

> By the time Jack was close enough to read the large signs over the bridge, Lisa was two hundred feet ahead of him. She was pulling away, and he was panting like a sick dog.

- Everybody, who was ahead right after the race started? (Signal.) *Jack.*
- Who was ahead when Jack could read the large signs over the bridge? (Signal.) *Lisa.*
- How far ahead was she? (Signal.) *2 hundred feet.*
- Who was running faster? (Signal.) *Lisa.*

> Lisa won the race by a thousand feet. After Jack caught his breath and was able to speak without panting, he said to Lisa, "You were right. I can't run a mile as fast as you. So I'll have to start running with you in the mornings."
> And that's what he did.
> **THE END**

- Everybody, who won the race? (Signal.) *Lisa.*
- By how much? (Signal.) *One thousand feet.*
- That's a lot.
- Do you think Jack will get faster and in better shape after he runs every morning for a few weeks? (Call on students.)

EXERCISE 5
PAIRED PRACTICE

You're going to read aloud to your partner. Today the **B** members will read first. Then the **A** members will read from the star to the end of the story.
(Observe students and give feedback.)

EXERCISE 6
WRITTEN ITEMS
Story Items

a. **Find item 4 on your worksheet.** ✓
- Items 4 through 12 are about today's story. I'll call on different students to read the items, but don't say the answers.

b. (For each item: Call on a student to read the item.)
- Item 4. *[On the way to school, the children raced. Which child won the race?]*
- Item 5. *[Who was out of breath?]*
- Item 6. *[How far did they race on their way to school?]*
- Item 7. *[On Saturday, the children had another race. How long was that race?]*
- Item 8. *[Who was ahead right after the race started?]*
- Item 9. *[Who was ahead when Jack could read the signs over the bridge?]*
- Item 10. *[Who won the race?]*
- Item 11. *[How far ahead was the winner at the end of the race?]*
- Item 12. *[What did Jack decide to do after losing the race?]*

End-of-Lesson Activities

INDEPENDENT WORK

Now finish your independent work for lesson 24. Raise your hand when you're finished. (Observe students and give feedback.)

WORKCHECK

a. (Direct students to take out their marking pencils.)
- We're going to check your independent work. Remember, if you got an item wrong, make an **X** next to the item.

b. (For each item: Read the item. Call on a student to answer it. If the answer is wrong, say the correct answer. Refer to the Answer Key for the correct answers.)

c. Now use your marking pencil to fix up any items you got wrong. Remember, all mistakes must be fixed up before you hand in your independent work.

WRITING-SPELLING

(Present Writing-Spelling lesson 24 after completing Reading lesson 24. See Writing-Spelling Guide.)

Lesson 25

Materials: Each student will need their thermometer chart for exercise 6.

EXERCISE 1
VOCABULARY

a. **Find page 338 in your textbook.** ✓
- Touch sentence 6. ✓
- This is a new vocabulary sentence. It says: He motioned to the flight attendant ahead of him. Everybody, say that sentence. Get ready. (Signal.) *He motioned to the flight attendant ahead of him.*
- Close your eyes and say the sentence. Get ready. (Signal.) *He motioned to the flight attendant ahead of him.*
- (Repeat until firm.)

b. When you **motion** to another person, you use your hands or body to show the person what to do. Show me how you would motion for me to come over to where you are. (Call on a student.)
- Everybody, when you use your hands to show someone what to do, what are you doing? (Signal.) *Motioning.*

c. He motioned to the **flight attendant** ahead of him. The flight attendant is somebody who works on a plane and takes care of the passengers.
- Everybody, what's the name of a person who takes care of passengers on a plane? (Signal.) *Flight attendant.*

d. If the flight attendant is **ahead** of him, the attendant is **in front** of him. What's another way of saying **in front of him**? (Signal.) *Ahead of him.*

e. Listen to the sentence again: He motioned to the flight attendant ahead of him. Everybody, say that sentence. Get ready. (Signal.) *He motioned to the flight attendant ahead of him.*

f. What two words name a person who takes care of passengers on a plane? (Signal.) *Flight attendant.*
- What word means that a person used his hands to show what the attendant should do? (Signal.) *Motioned.*
- What word means **in front**? (Signal.) *Ahead.*
- (Repeat step f until firm.)

EXERCISE 2
READING WORDS
Column 1

a. **Find lesson 25 in your textbook.** ✓
- Touch column 1. ✓
- (Teacher reference:)

> 1. police officer 4. badge
> 2. horrible   5. edge
> 3. heard

b. Number 1 is **police officer.** What words? (Signal.) *Police officer.*

c. Word 2 is **horrible.** What word? (Signal.) *Horrible.*
- Spell **horrible.** Get ready. (Tap for each letter.) *H-O-R-R-I-B-L-E.*

d. Word 3 is **heard.** What word? (Signal.) *Heard.*
- I **heard** the bell. Spell **heard.** Get ready. (Tap for each letter.) *H-E-A-R-D.*

e. Word 4 is **badge.** What word? (Signal.) *Badge.*
- Spell **badge.** Get ready. (Tap for each letter.) *B-A-D-G-E.*

f. Word 5 is **edge.** What word? (Signal.) *Edge.*
- Spell **edge.** Get ready. (Tap for each letter.) *E-D-G-E.*

g. Let's read those words again, the fast way.
- Number 1. What words? (Signal.) *Police officer.*
- Word 2. What word? (Signal.) *Horrible.*
- (Repeat for words 3–5.)

h. (Repeat step g until firm.)

Column 2

i. Find column 2. ✓
- (Teacher reference:)

> 1. tiny   3. thirsty
> 2. silly   4. Nancy

- All these words end with the letter **Y.**

j. Word 1. What word? (Signal.) *Tiny.*
- (Repeat for words 2–4.)

k. (Repeat step j until firm.)

136 Lesson 25

Column 3

l. Find column 3. ✓
- (Teacher reference:)

1. **door**way	3. **doll**house
2. **good**bye	4. **out**fit

- All these words are compound words. The first part of each word is underlined.
m. Word 1. What's the underlined part? (Signal.) *door.*
- What's the whole word? (Signal.) *Doorway.*
n. Word 2. What's the underlined part? (Signal.) *good.*
- What's the whole word? (Signal.) *Goodbye.*
o. Word 3. What's the underlined part? (Signal.) *doll.*
- What's the whole word? (Signal.) *Dollhouse.*
p. Word 4. What's the underlined part? (Signal.) *out.*
- What's the whole word? (Signal.) *Outfit.*
q. Let's read those words again, the fast way.
- Word 1. What word? (Signal.) *Doorway.*
- (Repeat for words 2–4.)
r. (Repeat step q until firm.)

Column 4

s. Find column 4. ✓
- (Teacher reference:)

1. peanut	3. screamed
2. treat	4. greeting

- All these words have the sound **EEE**.
t. Word 1. What word? (Signal.) *Peanut.*
- (Repeat for words 2–4.)
u. (Repeat step t until firm.)

Column 5

v. Find column 5. ✓
- (Teacher reference:)

1. hurt	3. wearing
2. mirror	4. CD

w. Word 1. What word? (Signal.) *Hurt.*
- (Repeat for words 2–4.)
x. (Repeat step w until firm.)

Column 6

y. Find column 6. ✓
- (Teacher reference:)

1. spoiled	3. stamping
2. shrunk	4. tight

z. Word 1. What word? (Signal.) *Spoiled.*
- (Repeat for words 2–4.)
a. (Repeat step z until firm.)

Individual Turns

(For columns 1–6: Call on individual students, each to read one to three words per turn.)

EXERCISE 3
VOCABULARY REVIEW

a. Here's the new vocabulary sentence you learned: He motioned to the flight attendant ahead of him.
- Everybody, say that sentence. Get ready. (Signal.) *He motioned to the flight attendant ahead of him.*
- (Repeat until firm.)
b. What word means **in front?** (Signal.) *Ahead.*
- What word means to show somebody what to do by using your hands? (Signal.) *Motioned.*
- What words refer to a person who takes care of passengers on a plane? (Signal.) *Flight attendant.*

EXERCISE 4
COMPREHENSION PASSAGE

a. Find part B in your textbook. ✓
- You're going to read a story about a girl named Nancy. First you'll read the information passage. It gives some information about objects that are different.
b. Everybody, touch the title. ✓
- (Call on a student to read the title.) *[Telling How Two Things Are Different.]*
- Everybody, what's the title? (Signal.) *Telling How Two Things Are Different.*
c. (Call on individual students to read the passage, each student reading two or three sentences at a time. Ask the specified questions as the students read.)

Lesson 25 137

Telling How Two Things Are Different

You're going to tell how things are different. When you tell how things are different, you must name **both** the objects you're talking about. The things in the picture are object A **and** object B. When you tell how they are different, you must name object A and object B.

Here's a sentence that does **not** tell how they are different: Object A is big. That sentence does not tell about object B.

Here's a right way of telling about that difference: Object A is big, but object B is small.

- Everybody, say that way that they're different. Get ready. (Signal.) *Object A is big, but object B is small.*

Remember, to tell one way the objects are different, you have to name **both** objects. Name another way object A and object B are different. Remember to name **both** objects.

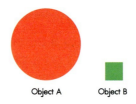

- Do it. (Call on a student. Praise descriptions that name both objects and that tell about a difference. Ideas: *A is round, but B is square; A is red, but B is green; A is big, but B is not.*)

EXERCISE 5
STORY READING

Note: Ask questions marked 1 during the first reading. Ask questions marked 2 during the second reading.

a. Find part C in your textbook. ✓
- The error limit for this story is 10.
- Read carefully and don't make more than 10 errors. I'm going to ask some questions as you read the story. Then I'll read the story and ask more questions.

b. Everybody, touch the title. ✓
- (Call on a student to read the title.) [*Nancy Wants to Stay Little.*]
- Everybody, who is this story about? (Signal.) *Nancy.*
- What do we know about Nancy? (Call on a student. Idea: *She wants to stay little.*)

c. (Call on individual students to read the story, each student reading two or three sentences at a time. Ask questions marked **1.**)

- (Correct errors: Tell the word. Direct the student to reread the sentence.)
- (If the group makes more than 10 errors, direct the students to reread the story.)

d. (After the group has read the selection making no more than 10 errors, read the story to the students and ask questions marked **2.**)

Nancy Wants to Stay Little

Nancy was a spoiled little girl.

2. How do spoiled children act? (Call on a student. Ideas: *They have temper tantrums; they whine; they always want their way; like babies;* etc.)

She liked being little because she could get her way by crying, stamping her feet, turning red in the face, and making lots of noise. When she acted this way, her mother would say, "If you stop crying, I'll give you a treat." Nancy got lots and lots of treats by crying and acting like a little baby girl.

2. Everybody, if Nancy wanted a treat from her mother, would Nancy just ask for it? (Signal.) *No.*
2. What would Nancy do to get a treat? (Call on a student. Ideas: *Cry; stamp her feet; turn red in the face; make lots of noise.*)

Then one day something happened. Nancy's dad came home from work. He picked her up and said, "How is my big girl?"

Big girl? Who wants to be a big girl? Nancy knew that if you're a big girl you can't get your way by crying and kicking and stamping and making noise.

2. Everybody, did Nancy want to become a big girl? (Signal.) *No.*
2. Why not? (Call on a student. Idea: *Because big girls can't get their way by crying, kicking,* etc.)

After her dad put her down, she went to her room and looked in the mirror. She could see that what her dad said was right.

2. What was her dad right about? (Call on a student. Idea: *She was growing.*)

She was getting bigger. The shoes she was wearing were a little tight but when she got these shoes a few months back, they were almost too big for her. Her new striped shirt looked a little small on her.

2. Everybody, were her clothes getting smaller, or was she getting bigger? (Signal.) *She was getting bigger.*
2. Why were her shoes and her shirt too small? (Call on a student. Idea: *Because she was getting bigger.*)

"Oh nuts," she said in a loud voice. "I don't want to be a big girl." She kicked the mirror and hurt her foot. Then she began to cry and scream and stamp her feet and jump up and down.

That night she had a very bad dream. In her dream she was getting bigger and bigger. When she woke up the next morning she saw something on her bed. It was a CD. She rubbed her eyes, picked up the CD, and looked at it.

"I don't know how this CD got on my bed," she said to herself. "Maybe it is something from Daddy."

2. Who did she think left the CD on her bed? (Call on a student. Idea: *Her father.*)

She put the CD in the CD player. A strange voice sang this song:

**"If you hate to be tall, tall, tall,
And you want to be small, small, small,
Just say these words in a good loud voice:
Broil, boil, dump that oil."**

1. That is a strange song.
1. Do you think her daddy left that CD on the bed? (Call on a student. Student preference.)
2. Listen to the words of that song again.
   If you hate to be tall, tall, tall,
   And you want to be small, small, small,
   Just say these words in a good loud voice:
   Broil, boil, dump that oil.
2. Everybody, what words do you say if you want to be small? (Signal.) *Broil, boil, dump that oil.*
- (Repeat until firm.)

Nancy played the CD two times. Then she said, "That's the worst song in the world."

1. Do you think she remembers the words that you say to be small? (Call on a student. Student preference.)
2. Everybody, did she like the song? (Signal.) *No.*

Later that day she was playing with her friend Sally. Sally was doing tricks that Nancy couldn't do. Sally jumped rope. Then she was throwing a ball in the air and catching it.

Nancy was getting very mad because she could not do those things.

2. What things couldn't Nancy do? (Call on a student. Ideas: *Jump rope; play catch with a ball.*)

At last she said, "Well, I can do something you can't do. I can make myself small by saying some words that you don't know."

2. Everybody, tell me the words she's talking about. Get ready. (Signal.) *Broil, boil, dump that oil.*

Lesson 25 139

> "No, you can't make yourself small," Sally said.
> "Yes, I can," Nancy said. "But I don't feel like doing it now."

1. Did Nancy really think that she could make herself small? (Call on a student. Idea: *No.*)

> Nancy didn't really think that she could make herself small, but she wouldn't tell that to Sally.
> "You don't know any words that could make you small," Sally said.
> Nancy was very mad. "Just listen to this," she said. Then she continued in a loud voice, "Broil, boil, dump that oil."
> **MORE NEXT TIME**

1. Go back to the beginning of the story. Follow along while I read.
2. Everybody, did she remember the words? (Signal.) *Yes.*
2. Do you think anything will happen to her? (Call on a student. Student preference.)
2. We'll find out in the next story.

EXERCISE 6

Note: There is a reading checkout in this lesson; therefore, there is no paired practice.

READING CHECKOUTS

a. Today is a reading-checkout day. While you're doing your independent work, I'm going to call on you one at a time to read part of the story from lesson 24. When I call you to come and do your checkout, bring your thermometer chart.
- Remember, you pass the checkout by reading the passage in less than a minute without making more than 2 mistakes. And when you pass the checkout, you'll color the space for lesson 25 on your thermometer chart.

b. (Call on individual students to read the portion of story 24 marked with ❋.)
- (Time the student. Note words that are missed and total number of words read.)
- (Teacher reference:)

> ❋ On Saturday, Jack and Lisa went to a bike path near the river. They started at a place that was one mile from the big white bridge. Jack said, "By the time you get to the bridge, you'll see me there, resting in the grass."
> The race started and Jack [50] was soon far ahead of Lisa. He looked back and smiled. "Come on," he called. "Is that as fast as you can run?"
> Lisa did [75] not answer.
> By the time Jack could clearly see the white bridge, he was running much slower. Lisa was now right behind him, running quite ❋ [100] a bit faster than he was.

- (If the student reads the passage in one minute or less and makes no more than 2 errors, direct the student to color in the space for lesson 25 on the thermometer chart.)
- (If the student makes any mistakes, point to each word that was misread and identify it.)
- (If the student does not meet the time-error criterion for the passage, direct the student to practice reading the story with the assigned partner.)

EXERCISE 7

WRITTEN ITEMS

Comprehension Passage

a. **Find part A on your worksheet.** ✓
- **Touch part A.** ✓
- **I'll read: Write 3 ways that tell how object A is different from object B.** ✓
- **For items 1 through 3, you'll fill in the blanks to tell how the objects are different.**
- **Read item 1 and say words to go in the blanks.** (Call on a student. Ideas: *Object A is round, but object B is square; Object A is gray, but object B is black; Object A is big, but object B is small.*)

Story Items

b. **Items 4 through 11 are about today's story. I'll call on different students to read the items, but don't say the answers.**

c. (For each item: Call on a student to read the item.)
- Item 4. *[What 2 things would Nancy do to get her own way?]*
- Item 5. *[Nancy didn't want to become bigger because she wouldn't be able to blank.]*
- Item 6. *[Nancy knew that she was getting bigger because blank.]*
- Item 7. *[What did Nancy find on her bed?]*
- Item 8. *[The voice told the words to say if you want to stay small. Write those words.]*
- Item 9. *[Who could do tricks that Nancy couldn't do?]*
- Item 10. *[How did that make Nancy feel?]*
- Item 11. *[Did Nancy really think that the words would make her small?]*

End-of-Lesson Activities

INDEPENDENT WORK

Now finish your independent work for lesson 25. Raise your hand when you're finished. (Observe students and give feedback.)

WORKCHECK

a. (Direct students to take out their marking pencils.)
- We're going to check your independent work. Remember, if you got an item wrong, make an **X** next to the item. Don't change any answers.

b. (For each item: Read the item. Call on a student to answer it. If the answer is wrong, say the correct answer. Refer to the Answer Key for the correct answers.)

c. Now use your marking pencil to fix up any items you got wrong. Remember, all mistakes must be fixed up before you hand in your independent work.

WRITING-SPELLING

(Present Writing-Spelling lesson 25 after completing Reading lesson 25. See Writing-Spelling Guide.)

Lessons 26–30 • Planning Page

Looking Ahead

	Lesson 26	**Lesson 27**	**Lesson 28**	**Lesson 29**	**Lesson 30**
Lesson Events	Vocabulary Review Reading Words Comprehension Passage Story Reading Paired Practice Written Items Independent Work Workcheck Writing-Spelling Activity Optional Activity	Vocabulary Review Reading Words Story Reading Paired Practice Written Items Independent Work Workcheck Writing-Spelling Activity	Vocabulary Review Reading Words Comprehension Passage Story Reading Paired Practice Written Items Independent Work Workcheck Writing-Spelling	**Vocabulary Sentence** Reading Words Vocabulary Review Comprehension Passages Story Reading Paired Practice Written Items Independent Work Workcheck Writing-Spelling Activity	Fact Game Reading Checkouts Test Marking the Test Test Remedies Literature Lesson
Vocabulary Sentence	#6: He <u>motioned</u> to the <u>flight attendant ahead</u> of him.	sentence #4 sentence #5 sentence #6	#5: Hunters were <u>stationed</u> at <u>opposite</u> ends of the field.	#7: The <u>traffic</u> was moving forty miles <u>per</u> hour.	
Reading Words: Word Types	modeled words -mb words mixed words	multi-syllable words mixed words	modeled words words with endings mixed words	-ly words words with endings mixed words multi-syllable words	
New Vocabulary	boom		catch your breath hoist stale	water strider lawn	
Comprehension Passages	*Facts About Ants*		*Sugar Shines*	1) *Water Has a Skin* 2) *Facts About Dew*	
Story	*A Green Man Visits Nancy*	*Nancy is Still Tiny*	*Nancy Finds Something to Eat*	*Nancy Tries to Get Some Water*	
Skill Items	Different Deductions	Different Vocabulary sentence	Different Vocabulary sentences	Different Deductions	Test: Deductions; Vocabulary sentences #5, 6
Special Materials	Drawing materials for activity				Thermometer charts, dice, Fact Game 30, Fact Game Answer Key, scorecard sheets, *materials for literature project
Special Projects/ Activities	Activity after lesson 26	Activity after lesson 27		Activity after lesson 29	

* Literature anthology; blackline masters 3A, 3B, 3C, 3D, 3E; 2 each; hard-boiled eggs, carrots, celery sticks, tomatoes, oranges, peaches; scissors and paste; lined paper; crayons; copy of *Julie Rescues Big Mack*.

Lesson 26

EXERCISE 1
VOCABULARY REVIEW

a. Here's the new vocabulary sentence you learned: He motioned to the flight attendant ahead of him.
- Everybody, say that sentence. Get ready. (Signal.) *He motioned to the flight attendant ahead of him.*
- (Repeat until firm.)

b. What word means to show somebody what to do by using your hands? (Signal.) *Motioned.*
- What words refer to a person who takes care of passengers on a plane? (Signal.) *Flight attendant.*
- What word means **in front**? (Signal.) *Ahead.*

EXERCISE 2
READING WORDS

Column 1

a. **Find lesson 26 in your textbook.** ✓
- Touch column 1. ✓
- (Teacher reference:)

1. piece	4. cabinet
2. giant	5. although
3. brought	6. decide

b. Word 1 is **piece**. What word? (Signal.) *Piece.*
- Spell **piece**. Get ready. (Tap for each letter.) *P-I-E-C-E.*

c. Word 2 is **giant**. What word? (Signal.) *Giant.*
- Spell **giant**. Get ready. (Tap for each letter.) *G-I-A-N-T.*

d. Word 3 is **brought**. What word? (Signal.) *Brought.*
- Spell **brought**. Get ready. (Tap for each letter.) *B-R-O-U-G-H-T.*

e. Word 4 is **cabinet**. What word? (Signal.) *Cabinet.*
- Spell **cabinet**. Get ready. (Tap for each letter.) *C-A-B-I-N-E-T.*

f. Word 5 is **although**. What word? (Signal.) *Although.*

g. Word 6 is **decide**. What word? (Signal.) *Decide.*

h. Let's read those words again, the fast way.
- Word 1. What word? (Signal.) *Piece.*
- (Repeat for words 2–6.)

i. (Repeat step h until firm.)

Column 2

j. Find column 2. ✓
- (Teacher reference:)

1. climb	3. dumb
2. crumb	4. thumb

- All these words end with the letters **M-B**. The **B** doesn't make any sound in the words.

k. Word 1. What word? (Signal.) *Climb.*
- (Repeat for words 2–4.)

l. (Repeat step k until firm.)

Column 3

m. Find column 3. ✓
- (Teacher reference:)

1. police officer	4. horrible
2. flight attendant	5. badge
3. heard	6. peanut

n. Number 1. What words? (Signal.) *Police officer.*
- Number 2. What words? (Signal.) *Flight attendant.*

o. Word 3. What word? (Signal.) *Heard.*
- (Repeat for words 4–6.)

p. (Repeat steps n and o until firm.)

Column 4

q. Find column 4. ✓
- (Teacher reference:)

1. boom	4. cookie
2. shrunk	5. goodbye
3. doorway	6. beyond

r. Word 1. What word? (Signal.) *Boom.*
- When a voice booms, it's very loud. Who can say something in a booming voice? (Call on a student.)

s. Word 2. What word? (Signal.) *Shrunk.*
• (Repeat for: **3. doorway, 4. cookie, 5. goodbye, 6. beyond.**)

t. Let's read those words again.
• Word 1. What word? (Signal.) *Boom.*
• (Repeat for words 2–6.)

u. (Repeat step t until firm.)

Column 5

v. Find column 5. ✓
• (Teacher reference:)

1. outfit	4. bathroom
2. edge	5. screamed
3. dollhouse	6. plastic

w. Word 1. What word? (Signal.) *Outfit.*
• (Repeat for words 2–6.)

x. (Repeat step w until firm.)

Individual Turns

(For columns 1–5: Call on individual students, each to read one to three words per turn.)

EXERCISE 3

COMPREHENSION PASSAGE

a. Find part B in your textbook. ✓
• You're going to read the next story about Nancy. First you'll read the information passage. It gives some facts about ants.

b. Everybody, touch the title. ✓
• (Call on a student to read the title.) *[Facts About Ants.]*
• Everybody, what's the title? (Signal.) *Facts About Ants.*

c. (Call on individual students to read the passage, each student reading two or three sentences at a time. Ask the specified questions as the students read.)

> **Facts About Ants**
>
> The story you'll read today tells about ants. Here are some facts about ants:
> Ants are insects.
> All insects have six legs.
> So ants have six legs.

• Listen to that again: Ants are insects. All insects have six legs. So ants have six legs.
• You learned about another insect that Goad likes to eat. Everybody, what insect? (Signal.) *A fly.*
• Everybody, how many legs does a fly have? (Signal.) *Six.*
• How many legs does a flea have? (Signal.) *Six.*
• How many legs does an ant have? (Signal.) *Six.*
• How many legs does any insect have? (Signal.) *Six.*

> **Some ants are red and some ants are black.**

• Everybody, listen to that fact again: Some ants are red and some ants are black.
• Say that fact. Get ready. (Signal.) *Some ants are red and some ants are black.*
• (Repeat until firm.)

> **Ants are very strong for their size.**

• Everybody, listen to that fact again: Ants are very strong for their size.
• Say that fact. Get ready. (Signal.) *Ants are very strong for their size.*
• (Repeat until firm.)

> Here's a rule: <u>**An ant can carry an object that weighs ten times as much as the ant.**</u>

• Everybody, an ant can carry an object that weighs how much? (Signal.) *Ten times as much as the ant.*
• (Repeat until firm.)

> **If an ant weighed as much as an elephant, the ant could carry ten elephants.**
> **Ants are very light. It would take about one hundred ants to weigh as much as a peanut.**

EXERCISE 4

STORY READING

a. Find part C in your textbook. ✓
• We're going to read this story two times. First you'll read it out loud and make no more than 9 errors. Then I'll read it and ask questions.

b. Everybody, touch the title. ✓
• (Call on a student to read the title.) *[A Green Man Visits Nancy.]*

144 Lesson 26

- What's going to happen in this story? (Call on a student. Idea: *A green man will visit Nancy.*)
c. (Call on individual students to read the story, each student reading two or three sentences at a time.)
- (Correct errors: Tell the word. Direct the student to reread the sentence.)
- (If the group makes more than 9 errors, direct the students to reread the story.)
d. (After the group has read the selection making no more than 9 errors:) Now I'll read the story and ask questions.

A Green Man Visits Nancy

Nancy had just said some words that she had heard on a CD.

- Everybody, what words did she say? (Signal.) *Broil, boil, dump that oil.*
- What were those words supposed to do? (Call on a student. Idea: *Make Nancy small.*)
- Did she really think that she would become small? (Call on a student.) *No.*

All at once, the world began to spin around and around. Then Sally started to grow bigger, bigger, and bigger. Sally wasn't the only thing that began to grow. The jump rope that Sally was holding began to get larger.

- Everybody, were things really getting bigger? (Signal.) *No.*
- Why did things seem to get bigger and bigger? (Call on a student. Idea: *Because Nancy was getting smaller and smaller.*)

Sally's voice boomed out, "Oh, what's wrong? Oh, what's wrong?"

- Why did Sally's voice seem to boom? (Call on a student. Idea: *Because Nancy was so small.*)
- Who can say "Oh, what's wrong" the way it sounded to Nancy? (Call on individual students.)

The world was still turning and spinning and things were getting larger and larger. Now Nancy was no taller than the grass next to the sidewalk.

- Everybody, show me how tall that grass would be. ✓

Sally was looking down at Nancy. "Oh, Nancy, what's wrong? You're just a little tiny thing. I'll get somebody to help."

Sally dropped her jump rope and ran away.

- How would you feel if you were Sally and saw your friend shrink up the way Nancy did? (Call on a student. Ideas: *Surprised; afraid.*)

Each step that Sally took shook the ground. Nancy looked around. She was too afraid to cry. And besides, it wouldn't do any good. There was nobody around to treat her like a baby.

- There were two reasons she didn't cry. Listen to that part again:
  She was too afraid to cry. And besides, it wouldn't do any good. There was nobody around to treat her like a baby.
- Why didn't she cry? (Call on a student. Idea: *She was too afraid, and it wouldn't do any good.*)

An ant came running along the sidewalk. When Nancy looked at the size of the ant, she knew that she had grown even smaller. To her, that ant was the size of a horse.

- How did Nancy know that she was still getting smaller? (Call on a student. Idea: *Because she was smaller than an ant.*)

Lesson 26 145

> The ant looked very mean—with its round shiny head and six legs running.
> Nancy was so frightened that she screamed, but her voice did not sound like it should. Her voice had become smaller as she grew smaller. Now her voice was so small that it sounded like a little squeak. You couldn't hear her voice five meters away. "Squeak," she screamed.

- What had happened to her voice as she became smaller? (Call on a student. Idea: *It got smaller.*)

> At that moment, a voice behind her said, "Go away, ant." The ant turned and ran off down the sidewalk. Nancy turned around and saw a little green man no taller than she was. "Greetings," the man said. "I am the one who made the CD."
> "Hello," Nancy said slowly. Then she said, "Why did you give me that funny CD?"
> The little man said, "You didn't want anybody to call you a big girl. And you got your wish. Nobody would call a tiny thing like you a big girl."

- Why did the little green man give her the CD? (Call on a student. Idea: *Because Nancy didn't want anybody to call her a big girl.*)

> "I guess you're right," Nancy said. "But I really didn't want to be this little. I'm so little now that . . . "

- Those dots mean that Nancy didn't finish what she started to say. Who can finish her sentence? "I'm so little now that . . ." (Call on different students. Ideas: *I can't do anything; I'll get hurt;* etc.)
- Everybody, was Nancy happy about being so little? (Signal.) *No.*

> "Now, now," the green man said. "You should be very, very happy. Even if you grow two times the size you are now, you'll be smaller than a blue fly. Even if you grow twenty times the size you are now, you'll be smaller than a mouse. So you should be very glad."
> "Well, I don't . . . "

- The dots mean that she didn't finish talking. The green man interrupted her.
- What do you think Nancy was going to say? (Call on a student. Idea: *Well, I don't like being this small.*)

> "I'll walk to your house with you and then I must go," the green man said. "Don't stay outside too long. There are cats and rats and loads of toads that love to eat things your size."
> **MORE NEXT TIME**

- Name some other things that Nancy would have to watch out for. (Call on different students. Ideas: *People's feet, bicycles, birds,* etc.)

EXERCISE 5

PAIRED PRACTICE

You're going to read aloud to your partner. Today the **A** members will read first. Then the **B** members will read from the star to the end of the story.
(Observe students and give feedback.)

EXERCISE 6

WRITTEN ITEMS

Story Items

a. **Find item 7 on your worksheet.** ✓
- Items 7 through 14 are about today's story. I'll call on different students to read the items, but don't say the answers.

b. (For each item: Call on a student to read the item.)
- Item 7. [*Did Nancy say the words on the CD?*]
- Item 8. [*Write the words Nancy said.*]
- Item 9. [*So what happened to Nancy?*]
- Item 10. [*Why did Nancy think that the jump rope got bigger?*]

- Item 11. *[How big did the ant seem to Nancy?]*
- Item 12. *[Nancy's voice sounded like a little squeak because she was so <u>blank</u>.]*
- Item 13. *[Who gave the CD to Nancy?]*
- Item 14. *[Why did he give her the CD?]*

Skill Items

c. Item 15. *[Write 2 ways that tell how object A is different from object B. Remember, you must name both objects.]*
- Name one way object A is different from object B. (Call on a student. Ideas: *Object A is tall, but object B is short; object A is striped, but object B is not striped;* etc.)

End-of-Lesson Activities

INDEPENDENT WORK

Now finish your independent work for lesson 26. Raise your hand when you're finished. (Observe students and give feedback.)

WORKCHECK

a. (Direct students to take out their marking pencils.)
- We're going to check your independent work. Remember, if you got an item wrong, make an **X** next to the item. Don't change any answers.

b. (For each item: Read the item. Call on a student to answer it. If the answer is wrong, say the correct answer. Refer to the Answer Key for the correct answers.)

c. Now use your marking pencil to fix up any items you got wrong. Remember, all mistakes must be fixed up before you hand in your independent work.

WRITING-SPELLING

(Present Writing-Spelling lesson 26 after completing Reading lesson 26. See Writing-Spelling Guide.)

ACTIVITY

(Present Activity 8 after completing Reading lesson 26. See Activities Across the Curriculum.)

OPTIONAL ACTIVITY

(Sing the song "The Ants Go Marching" with the students.)

Lesson 27

EXERCISE 1
VOCABULARY REVIEW

a. You learned a sentence that tells what the workers did to the cage.
- Everybody, say that sentence. Get ready. (Signal.) *The workers propped up the cage with steel bars.*
- (Repeat until firm.)

b. You learned a sentence that tells where hunters were stationed.
- Everybody, say that sentence. Get ready. (Signal.) *Hunters were stationed at opposite ends of the field.*
- (Repeat until firm.)

c. Here's the last sentence you learned: He motioned to the flight attendant ahead of him.
- Everybody, say that sentence. Get ready. (Signal.) *He motioned to the flight attendant ahead of him.*
- (Repeat until firm.)

d. What word means **in front?** (Signal.) *Ahead.*
- What's the name of a person who takes care of passengers on a plane? (Signal.) *Flight attendant.*
- What word means **showed somebody what to do by using your hands?** (Signal.) *Motioned.*
- (Repeat step d until firm.)

e. Once more. Say the sentence that tells who he motioned to. Get ready. (Signal.) *He motioned to the flight attendant ahead of him.*

EXERCISE 2
READING WORDS

Column 1

a. Find lesson 27 in your textbook. ✓
- Touch column 1. ✓
- (Teacher reference:)

1. decide	3. bathroom
2. cabinet	4. cookie

b. Word 1. What word? (Signal.) *Decide.*
- (Repeat for words 2–4.)

c. (Repeat step b until firm.)

Column 2

d. Find column 2. ✓

1. flight attendant	4. badge
2. police officer	5. horrible
3. plastic	

e. Number 1. What words? (Signal.) *Flight attendant.*
- Number 2. What words? (Signal.) *Police officer.*

f. Word 3. What word? (Signal.) *Plastic.*
- (Repeat for words 4 and 5.)

g. (Repeat step f until firm.)

Column 3

h. Find column 3. ✓

1. although	4. pieces
2. brought	5. grain
3. bedroom	

i. Word 1. What word? (Signal.) *Although.*
- (Repeat for words 2–5.)

j. (Repeat step i until firm.)

Column 4

k. Find column 4. ✓
- (Teacher reference:)

1. dollhouse	4. beyond
2. outfit	5. crumb
3. shrunk	

l. Word 1. What word? (Signal.) *Dollhouse.*
- (Repeat for words 2–5.)

m. (Repeat step l until firm.)

Individual Turns

(For columns 1–4: Call on individual students, each to read one to three words per turn.)

EXERCISE 3
STORY READING

Note: Ask questions marked **1** during the first reading. Ask questions marked **2** during the second reading.

a. Find part B in your textbook. ✓
- The error limit for this story is 10.
- Read carefully and don't make more than 10 errors. I'm going to ask some questions as you read the story. Then I'll read the story and ask more questions.

b. Everybody, touch the title. ✓
- (Call on a student to read the title.) [*Nancy Is Still Tiny.*]
- What do you think is going to happen in this part of the story? (Call on a student. Idea: *Nancy will still be tiny.*)

c. (Call on individual students to read the story, each student reading two or three sentences at a time. Ask questions marked **1**.)

- (Correct errors: Tell the word. Direct the student to reread the sentence.)
- (If the group makes more than 10 errors, direct the students to reread the story.)

d. (After the group has read the selection making no more than 10 errors, read the story to the students and ask questions marked **2**.)

Nancy Is Still Tiny

The green man walked with Nancy into her house. They didn't open the door. They walked right through the crack at the bottom of the door.

2. Everybody, show me how big the crack under a door is. ✓
2. Show me how big Nancy is. ✓

Then Nancy and the green man walked to Nancy's room. As soon as they were inside the room, the green man said, "Goodbye," and he left.

So there was Nancy, all alone in her room. When she had been bigger, she loved to spend time in her room. She had her dolls, her dollhouse, and her toy trains. She had a TV set, and she had CDs. Things were not the same now that she was so small.

Nancy couldn't play with her dolls because they were at least one hundred times bigger than she was.

2. Everybody, show me how big a small doll is. ✓
2. Show me how big Nancy is. ✓

In fact, the dollhouse was so big that Nancy almost got lost walking around inside it. She tried to turn on her TV, but she couldn't make the button move.

2. Why not? (Call on a student. Idea: *She wasn't big enough.*)

That button was five times as big as she was.

Somehow, she made the CD player work. It already had a CD in it, and when she turned on the player, a great voice came from the player. The voice was so loud that it knocked Nancy down. "If you hate to be tall, tall, tall," the voice boomed. Nancy held her hands over her ears and tried to get away from the horrible noise.

2. Everybody, do you think the CD player would sound loud to you? (Signal.) *No.*
2. Why did it sound so loud to Nancy? (Call on a student. Idea: *Because she was so tiny.*)

It seemed as if a long time passed before the CD ended, but suddenly it was quiet in the room again.

2. Everybody, do you think Nancy will want to play her CD player again? (Signal.) *No.*

Nancy's head hurt and she felt very tired. She went back into the dollhouse and found a bed. The bed was far too big for Nancy but she curled up in a corner of the bed and took a nap.

2. Tell me how you take a nap. (Call on a student. Idea: *You go to sleep for a little while.*)

She slept for about an hour and when she woke up, she heard voices in the room. One voice was her mother's. The other voice belonged to a man who looked bigger than three mountains. He was dressed in a dark blue outfit, and he wore a shiny badge.

Lesson 27 149

1. Who would be dressed up in a blue outfit and wear a shiny badge? (Call on a student. Idea: *A police officer.*)

> Nancy's mother was crying.

1. Why do you think she was crying? (Call on a student. Idea: *Because she didn't know where Nancy was.*)

> Nancy's mother said, "I don't know where she went. We've looked all over for her, but nobody's seen her."

1. Everybody, who are they talking about? (Signal.) *Nancy.*

> The police officer said, "Now, let me make sure I understand this. The last time Nancy was seen she was playing with Sally Allen. Is that right?"

1. What story do you think Sally told about Nancy? (Call on a student. Idea: *That she was playing with Nancy and then Nancy yelled some words and started to shrink.*)
1. Do you think that Nancy's mother and the police officer believe that story? (Call on a student. Student preference.)

> Nancy's mother said, "That's right, she was playing with Sally."
> The police officer said, "And Sally Allen claims that Nancy shrunk up until she was less than one centimeter tall."
> A large tear fell down and almost hit Nancy.

2. Everybody, show me how big a tear is. ✓
2. Tell me how big that tear would look to Nancy. (Call on a student. Idea: *Very big.*)

> The tear was bigger than she was. "I don't know what made Sally make up such a crazy story," Nancy's mother said.

2. Why does she call it a crazy story? (Call on a student. Idea: *Because it sounds impossible.*)

> "But all I know is that my dear little Nancy is gone and I miss her. I love her very much."
> "Here I am, Mom," Nancy shouted from the doorway of her dollhouse. But her voice was so small that it sounded like a tiny, tiny squeak that wasn't as loud as the sound a new shoe makes when it squeaks.
> **MORE NEXT TIME**

1. Go back to the beginning of the story. Follow along while I read.
2. Everybody, will her mother hear her? (Signal.) *No.*
2. Why not? (Call on a student. Idea: *Because Nancy's voice sounds like only a squeak when she yells.*)

EXERCISE 4
PAIRED PRACTICE

You're going to read aloud to your partner. Today the **B** members will read first. Then the **A** members will read from the star to the end of the story.
(Observe students and give feedback.)

EXERCISE 5
WRITTEN ITEMS
Story Items

a. **Find item 1 on your worksheet.** ✓
- Items 1 through 9 are about today's story. I'll call on different students to read the items, but don't say the answers.
b. (For each item: Call on a student to read the item.)
- Item 1. [Could Nancy turn on the TV set?]
- Item 2. [Where was the bed that Nancy napped in?]
- Item 3. [Whose voices did Nancy hear when she woke up from her nap?]
- Item 4. [Nancy's mother was crying because she could not find blank.]
- Item 5. [Sally told what happened to Nancy. Did Nancy's mother believe the story?]
- Item 6. [Nancy shouted at her mother. Her mother couldn't hear Nancy because Nancy's voice was too blank.]

- Here's a rule: If you get smaller, your voice gets higher. Item 7. *[Circle the picture that shows when Nancy's voice would be highest.]*
- Item 8. *[Cross out the picture that shows when Nancy's voice would be lowest.]*
- Item 9. *[Look at object A and object E. Write one way that tells how both objects are the same.]*

End-of-Lesson Activities

INDEPENDENT WORK

Now finish your independent work for lesson 27. Raise your hand when you're finished. (Observe students and give feedback.)

WORKCHECK

a. (Direct students to take out their marking pencils.)
- We're going to check your independent work. Remember, if you got an item wrong, make an **X** next to the item. Don't change any answers.

b. (For each item: Read the item. Call on a student to answer it. If the answer is wrong, say the correct answer. Refer to the Answer Key for the correct answers.)

c. Now use your marking pencil to fix up any items you got wrong. Remember, all mistakes must be fixed up before you hand in your independent work.

WRITING-SPELLING

(Present Writing-Spelling lesson 27 after completing Reading lesson 27. See Writing-Spelling Guide.)

ACTIVITY

(Present Activity 9 after completing Reading lesson 27. See Activities Across the Curriculum.)

Lesson 28

EXERCISE 1
VOCABULARY REVIEW

a. You learned a sentence that tells where hunters were stationed.
- Everybody, say that sentence. Get ready. (Signal.) *Hunters were stationed at opposite ends of the field.*
- (Repeat until firm.)

b. I'll say part of the sentence. When I stop, you say the next word. Listen: Hunters were stationed at . . . Everybody, what's the next word? (Signal.) *Opposite.*

c. Listen: Hunters were . . . Everybody, what's the next word? (Signal.) *Stationed.*
- Say the whole sentence. Get ready. (Signal.) *Hunters were stationed at opposite ends of the field.*

EXERCISE 2
READING WORDS

Column 1

a. Find lesson 28 in your textbook. ✓
- Touch column 1. ✓
- (Teacher reference:)

> 1. probably 4. learn
> 2. tough   5. umbrella
> 3. sweater

b. Word 1 is **probably.** What word? (Signal.) *Probably.*
- Spell **probably.** Get ready. (Tap for each letter.) *P-R-O-B-A-B-L-Y.*

c. Word 2 is **tough.** What word? (Signal.) *Tough.*
- Spell **tough.** Get ready. (Tap for each letter.) *T-O-U-G-H.*

d. Word 3 is **sweater.** What word? (Signal.) *Sweater.*
- Spell **sweater.** Get ready. (Tap for each letter.) *S-W-E-A-T-E-R.*

e. Word 4 is **learn.** What word? (Signal.) *Learn.*
- Spell **learn.** Get ready. (Tap for each letter.) *L-E-A-R-N.*

f. Word 5 is **umbrella.** What word? (Signal.) *Umbrella.*

g. Let's read those words again, the fast way.
- Word 1. What word? (Signal.) *Probably.*
- (Repeat for words 2–5.)

h. (Repeat step g until firm.)

Column 2

i. Find column 2. ✓
- (Teacher reference:)

> 1. closely   4. stretched
> 2. wobbled 5. building
> 3. easily   6. decided

- All these words have endings.

j. Word 1. What word? (Signal.) *Closely.*
- (Repeat for words 2–6.)

k. (Repeat step j until firm.)

Column 3

l. Find column 3. ✓
- (Teacher reference:)

> 1. catch your breath 4. although
> 2. hoist   5. bedroom
> 3. crumb   6. traffic

m. Number 1. What words? (Signal.) *Catch your breath.*
- When you catch your breath, you breathe very hard. Everybody, what are you doing when you breathe very hard? (Signal.) *Catching your breath.*

n. Word 2. What word? (Signal.) *Hoist.*
- When you hoist something, you pull hard and lift it up. Everybody, what are you doing to something when you pull hard and lift it up? (Signal.) *Hoisting it.*

o. Word 3. What word? (Signal.) *Crumb.*
- (Repeat for words 4–6.)

p. Let's read those words again.
- Number 1. What words? (Signal.) *Catch your breath.*

q. Word 2. What word? (Signal.) *Hoist.*
- (Repeat for words 3–6.)

r. (Repeat steps p and q until firm.)

Column 4

s. Find column 4. ✓
- (Teacher reference:)

1. stale	4. grain
2. cabinet	5. squirrel
3. piece	6. scary

t. Word 1. What word? (Signal.) *Stale.*
- Food that is stale is old and not very good to eat. Here's another way of saying **The bread was old and not very good to eat: The bread was stale.**
- Your turn. What's another way of saying **The bread was old and not very good to eat?** (Signal.) *The bread was stale.*
- (Repeat until firm.)
- What's another way of saying **The crumb was old and not very good to eat?** (Signal.) *The crumb was stale.*

u. Word 2. What word? (Signal.) *Cabinet.*
- (Repeat for words 3–6.)

v. Let's read those words again.
- Word 1. What word? (Signal.) *Stale.*
- (Repeat for words 2–6.)

w. (Repeat step v until firm.)

Column 5

x. Find column 5. ✓
- (Teacher reference:)

1. bathroom	4. strider
2. cookie	5. tube
3. beyond	6. dew

y. Word 1. What word? (Signal.) *Bathroom.*
- (Repeat for words 2–6.)

z. (Repeat step y until firm.)

Individual Turns

(For columns 1–5: Call on individual students, each to read one to three words per turn.)

EXERCISE 3

COMPREHENSION PASSAGE

a. Find part B in your textbook. ✓
- You're going to read the next story about Nancy. First you'll read the information passage. It gives some facts about sugar.

b. Everybody, touch the title. ✓
- (Call on a student to read the title.) *[Sugar Shines.]*
- Everybody, what's the title? (Signal.) *Sugar Shines.*

c. (Call on individual students to read the passage, each student reading two or three sentences at a time. Ask the specified questions as the students read.)

> **Sugar Shines**
>
> The story you'll read today talks about how sugar shines.

- What will the story tell about? (Call on a student. Idea: *How sugar shines.*)

> **A grain of sugar is much smaller than an ant. It is no bigger than a grain of sand.**

- How big is a grain of sugar? (Call on a student. Ideas: *Smaller than an ant; no bigger than a grain of sand.*)

> **The picture shows what a grain of sugar would look like if it were big.**

- Everybody, touch the picture. ✓
- It looks like a big piece of glass.

> **The grain in the picture has sharp corners. Each side is very smooth. The sugar looks like glass. And the sugar shines like glass.**

- If you look at a pile of sugar in bright light, you will see that it sparkles and shines. Why does it shine? (Call on a student. Idea: *Because it's like glass.*)

EXERCISE 4

STORY READING

a. Find part C in your textbook. ✓
- We're going to read this story two times. First you'll read it out loud and make no more than 7 errors. Then I'll read it and ask questions.

b. Everybody, touch the title. ✓
- (Call on a student to read the title.) *[Nancy Finds Something to Eat.]*
- What's going to happen in this story? (Call on a student. Idea: *Nancy will find something to eat.*)

c. (Call on individual students to read the story, each student reading two or three sentences at a time.)

- (**Correct errors:** Tell the word. Direct the student to reread the sentence.)
- (If the group makes more than 7 errors, direct the students to reread the story.)

d. (After the group has read the selection making no more than 7 errors:)
Now I'll read the story and ask questions.

Nancy Finds Something to Eat

Nancy was shouting and waving her arms, but her mother and the police officer didn't see her as they walked from the room.

- Why didn't they see her? (Call on a student. Idea: *Because she was so small.*)
- Why couldn't they hear her voice? (Call on a student. Idea: *Because her voice was a tiny squeak.*)
- The first thing that Nancy learned about being very small has to do with the sound of your voice.
- Everybody, what happens to your voice when you get smaller? (Signal.) *It gets higher.*
- (Repeat until firm.)

Although Nancy ran as fast as her tiny legs could move, she couldn't keep up with them. By the time she reached the doorway to her bedroom, she was tired. For her mother and the police officer, the walk to the doorway took only a few steps. But for Nancy it was a long, long run.

- How far was it for her mother and the police officer? (Call on a student. Idea: *Only a few steps.*)
- How far was it for Nancy? (Call on a student. Idea: *A long, long run.*)
- Why was it so much farther for Nancy? (Call on a student. Idea: *Because she had such tiny legs.*)

Nancy decided not to follow her mother beyond the bedroom door. Nancy didn't want to get lost.

- Why would she get lost in her own house? (Call on a student. Idea: *Because her house was so big for her.*)

So she stood there trying to catch her breath.

- Everybody, show me how you catch your breath. ✓

Then she walked slowly back toward her dollhouse. On the way, she looked at all the bits and pieces of things that were stuck in the carpet. Between those giant ropes of blue and green were giant pieces of dirt and giant crumbs.

- What are the giant ropes of blue and green? (Call on a student. Idea: *The rug.*)
- Everybody, are they really giant ropes? (Signal.) *No.*
- Why are they called giant ropes? (Call on a student. Idea: *Because compared to Nancy, they are giant.*)

One crumb was the size of a bucket next to Nancy.

- Everybody, show me how big that crumb looked to Nancy. ✓

It was a cookie crumb. "I wonder how long it's been here," Nancy said to herself. "I wonder if it's stale."

- Everybody, would it taste good if it's stale? (Signal.) *No.*
- Would it taste good to Nancy if it's not stale? (Signal.) *Yes.*

She felt silly for the thought that was going through her head. She was thinking, "If that cookie crumb is any good, I'll eat the whole thing. It will be like eating the world's biggest cookie."
So she bent over and sniffed the cookie crumb.

- Why did she do that? (Call on a student. Idea: *To find out if it's stale.*)

Then she tapped it with her fist. Then she broke off a little piece. That piece sparkled with shiny sugar.

- Everybody, look at the picture. Touch the giant ropes. ✓

154 Lesson 28

- What are those ropes? (Call on a student. Idea: *The rug.*)
- Everybody, touch the cookie crumb that is as big as a bucket. ✓
- How big would that crumb look to you? (Call on a student. Idea: *Very small.*)
- Why are parts of the cookie shiny? (Call on a student. Idea: *Because there's sugar on it.*)

> **Slowly, she brought the piece of cookie to her mouth and took a tiny bite from it. "Not bad," she said to herself.**

- What did she mean by "not bad"? (Call on a student. Idea: *She thought it tasted fine.*)

> **"Not bad at all." She took a big bite and another. With two hands she lifted up the whole crumb and began to eat it. She ate about half of it, and then she stopped. She wasn't hungry any more.**
>   **"I need a glass of water," she said to herself.**

- Everybody, did she feel hungry? (Signal.) *No.*
- How did she feel? (Call on a student. Idea: *Thirsty.*)
- Everybody, show me how big a glass of water is. ✓
- Could Nancy drink that much water? (Signal.) *No.*

> **She didn't really need a glass of water. She needed much less than a drop of water.**

- How much water did she need? (Call on a student. Ideas: *A tiny amount; less than a drop.*)
- Everybody, could she drink a whole drop of water? (Signal.) *No.*

> **But how do you get water when you're smaller than a fly? How do you get water if you can't reach something as high as a sink?**

- Why does the story say a sink is high? (Call on a student. Idea: *Because compared to Nancy's size, a bathroom sink would be high.*)

> **"Water," Nancy said to herself. "I must find water."**
>   **MORE NEXT TIME**

- What do you think she'll do? (Call on a student. Student preference.)
- Nancy has already found out one thing about being very small. What is that? (Call on a student. Idea: *Small things have very high voices.*)

EXERCISE 5
PAIRED PRACTICE

You're going to read aloud to your partner. Today the **A** members will read first. Then the **B** members will read from the star to the end of the story.
(Observe students and give feedback.)

EXERCISE 6
WRITTEN ITEMS
Story Items

a. **Find item 4 on your worksheet.** ✓
- Items 4 through 14 are about today's story. I'll call on different students to read the items, but don't say the answers.
b. (For each item: Call on a student to read the item.)
- Item 4. *[What did Nancy say to get small?]*
- Item 5. *[The walk to the bedroom doorway was much longer for Nancy than for her mother because Nancy blank.]*
- Item 6. *[In this story, Nancy found something to eat. What did she find?]*
- Item 7. *[To Nancy it was the size of blank.]*
- Item 8. *[Why did she sniff it before she started eating it?]*
- Item 9. *[How much of it did she eat?]*
- Item 10. *[Why didn't she eat the whole thing?]*
- Item 11. *[After Nancy finished eating, she wanted something. What did she want?]*
- Item 12. *[Did she know how she was going to get it?]*
- Item 13. *[Circle the picture that could be Nancy standing next to the big crumb she found.]*

Lesson 28 155

- Item 14. *[Underline what Nancy has learned about being so small.]*

End-of-Lesson Activities

INDEPENDENT WORK

Now finish your independent work for lesson 28. Raise your hand when you're finished. (Observe students and give feedback.)

WORKCHECK

a. (Direct students to take out their marking pencils.)
- We're going to check your independent work. Remember, if you got an item wrong, make an **X** next to the item. Don't change any answers.

b. (For each item: Read the item. Call on a student to answer it. If the answer is wrong, say the correct answer. Refer to the Answer Key for the correct answers.)

c. Now use your marking pencil to fix up any items you got wrong. Remember, all mistakes must be fixed up before you hand in your independent work.

WRITING-SPELLING

(Present Writing-Spelling lesson 28 after completing Reading lesson 28. See Writing-Spelling Guide.)

Lesson 29

EXERCISE 1
VOCABULARY

a. **Find page 338 in your textbook.** ✓
- Touch sentence 7. ✓
- This is a new vocabulary sentence. It says: The traffic was moving forty miles per hour. Everybody, say that sentence. Get ready. (Signal.) *The traffic was moving forty miles per hour.*
- Close your eyes and say the sentence. Get ready. (Signal.) *The traffic was moving forty miles per hour.*
- (Repeat until firm.)

b. All the vehicles that are driving on a street are the **traffic.**

c. Forty miles **per** hour means forty miles **each** hour. A car that is moving forty miles per hour is moving forty miles **each** hour.
- Everybody, what's another way of saying **71 miles each hour?** (Signal.) *71 miles per hour.*

d. Listen: The traffic was moving forty miles per hour. Everybody, say the sentence. Get ready. (Signal.) *The traffic was moving forty miles per hour.*

e. What word refers to all the cars and trucks that are moving on a street? (Signal.) *Traffic.*
- What word means **each?** (Signal.) *Per.*

EXERCISE 2
READING WORDS

Column 1

a. Find lesson 29 in your textbook. ✓
- Touch column 1. ✓
- (Teacher reference:)

1. finally	4. slowly
2. easily	5. probably
3. closely	6. early

- All these words end with the letters **L-Y.**

b. Word 1. What word? (Signal.) *Finally.*
- (Repeat for words 2–6.)

c. (Repeat step b until firm.)

Column 2

d. Find column 2. ✓
- (Teacher reference:)

1. building	4. thirsty
2. wobbled	5. weighs
3. stretched	6. moving

- All these words have endings.

e. Word 1. What word? (Signal.) *Building.*
- (Repeat for words 2–6.)

f. (Repeat step e until firm.)

Column 3

g. Find column 3. ✓
- (Teacher reference:)

1. hoist	4. squirrel
2. tough	5. dew
3. sweater	6. forty

h. Word 1. What word? (Signal.) *Hoist.*
- (Repeat for words 2–6.)

i. (Repeat step h until firm.)

Column 4

j. Find column 4. ✓
- (Teacher reference:)

1. cover	4. finished
2. discover	5. umbrella
3. discovered	

k. Word 1. What word? (Signal.) *Cover.*
- (Repeat for words 2–5.)

l. (Repeat step k until firm.)

Column 5

m. Find column 5. ✓
- (Teacher reference:)

1. water strider	4. tube
2. lawn	5. traffic
3. learn	

n. Number 1. What words? (Signal.) *Water strider.*
- A water strider is an insect that can walk on the top of water. Everybody, what's the name of an insect that can walk on water? (Signal.) *Water strider.*

o. Word 2. What word? (Signal.) *Lawn.*
- **Lawn** is the name for grass that is well-kept and mowed. Everybody, what's the name for grass that is well-kept and mowed? (Signal.) *Lawn.*
p. Word 3. What word? (Signal.) *Learn.*
- (Repeat for: **4. tube, 5. traffic.**)
q. Let's read those words again.
- Number 1. What words? (Signal.) *Water strider.*
r. Word 2. What word? (Signal.) *Lawn.*
- (Repeat for: **3. learn, 4. tube, 5. traffic.**)
s. (Repeat steps q and r until firm.)

Individual Turns
(For columns 1–5: Call on individual students, each to read one to three words per turn.)

EXERCISE 3
VOCABULARY REVIEW

a. Here's the new vocabulary sentence: The traffic was moving forty miles per hour.
- Everybody, say that sentence. Get ready. (Signal.) *The traffic was moving forty miles per hour.*
- (Repeat until firm.)
b. What word means **each**? (Signal.) *Per.*
- What word refers to all the cars and trucks that are moving on a street? (Signal.) *Traffic.*

EXERCISE 4
COMPREHENSION PASSAGES
Passage B
a. Find part B in your textbook. ✓
- You're going to read the next story about Nancy. First you'll read two information passages. The first passage gives some facts about water.
b. Everybody, touch the title. ✓
- (Call on a student to read the title.) *[Water Has a Skin.]*
- Everybody, what's the title? (Signal.) *Water Has a Skin.*
c. (Call on individual students to read the passage, each student reading two or three sentences at a time. Ask the specified questions as the students read.)

> **Water Has a Skin**
>
> The next story tells about the skin that water has.

- What will it tell about? (Call on a student. Idea: *The skin water has.*)

> You can see how that skin works by filling a small tube with water. Here's a picture of what you will see.
> The top of the water is not flat. The skin bends up in the middle.

- The first picture shows somebody filling the tube. The second picture shows the tube filled all the way to the top.
- Everybody, touch the top of the water in the full tube. ✓
- That's where the skin is. Everybody, which part of the skin bends up? (Signal.) *The middle.*
- Which part of the skin is the lowest? (Call on a student. Idea: *The part near the sides of the tube.*)

Passage C
d. Find part C in your textbook. ✓
- This passage gives some facts about dew.
e. Everybody, touch the title. ✓
- (Call on a student to read the title.) *[Facts About Dew.]*
- Everybody, what's the title? (Signal.) *Facts About Dew.*
f. (Call on individual students to read the passage, each student reading two or three sentences at a time. Ask the specified questions as the students read.)

> **Facts About Dew**
>
> The story you'll read today talks about dew.

- Everybody, what will the story tell about? (Signal.) *Dew.*

The drops of water that you see on grass and cars early in the morning is called dew.

- Name two places you find dew. (Call on a student. Ideas: *On grass; on cars; on bushes;* etc.)
- When do you find it there? (Call on a student. Idea: *Early in the morning.*)

Here are some facts about dew: Dew forms at night.

- Everybody, listen to that fact again: Dew forms at night.
- Say that fact. Get ready. (Signal.) *Dew forms at night.*
- (Repeat until firm.)

Dew forms when the air gets cooler.

- Everybody, listen to that fact again: Dew forms when the air gets cooler.
- Say that fact. Get ready. (Signal.) *Dew forms when the air gets cooler.*
- (Repeat until firm.)
- Why does dew form at night and not during the daytime? (Call on a student. Idea: *Because the air is cool at night.*)

Dew disappears in the morning when the air warms up.

- What makes the dew disappear? (Call on a student. Idea: *The warm air.*)

EXERCISE 5
STORY READING

Note: Ask questions marked **1** during the first reading. Ask questions marked **2** during the second reading.

a. Find part D in your textbook. ✓
- The error limit for this story is 9.
- Read carefully and don't make more than 9 errors. I'm going to ask some questions as you read the story. Then I'll read the story and ask more questions.
b. Everybody, touch the title. ✓
- (Call on a student to read the title.) [*Nancy Tries to Get Some Water.*]
- What's going to happen in this story? (Call on a student. Idea: *Nancy will try to get some water.*)
- What's Nancy's problem about getting water? (Call on a student. Idea: *She doesn't know how to reach high places like a sink.*)
- How do you think she feels about climbing to high places? (Call on a student. Idea: *Scared.*)
c. (Call on individual students to read the story, each student reading two or three sentences at a time. Ask questions marked **1.**)

- (Correct errors: Tell the word. Direct the student to reread the sentence.)
- (If the group makes more than 9 errors, direct the students to reread the story.)

d. (After the group has read the selection making no more than 9 errors, read the story to the students and ask questions marked **2.**)

Nancy Tries to Get Some Water

If Nancy knew more about very small things, she wouldn't have been so afraid of climbing to high places to find water. Here's the rule. <u>If tiny animals fall from high places, they don't get hurt.</u>

2. Everybody, what happens to tiny animals if they fall from high places? (Signal.) *They don't get hurt.*

If we dropped an ant from a high airplane, the ant would not be hurt at all when it landed on the ground. A mouse wouldn't be hurt either.

2. Why wouldn't these animals be hurt if they fell from an airplane? (Call on a student. Idea: *Because they're tiny.*)

A squirrel wouldn't be badly hurt. A dog would probably be killed. And you can imagine what would happen to an elephant.

2. What would happen to an elephant? (Call on a student. Idea: *It would die.*)

Nancy was thirsty, so thirsty that she wanted to yell and scream and stamp her feet like a baby.

1. Everybody, do you think she'll do that? (Signal.) *No.*

1. Why not? (Call on a student. Idea: *Because nobody could hear her.*)

> Nancy knew that it wouldn't do any good to act like a baby. So she made up her mind to start thinking. She was pretty smart. She said to herself, "If it were early morning, I could go out and drink dew from the lawn."

2. What is dew on the lawn? (Call on a student. Idea: *Drops of water on the grass.*)
2. When do you see dew? (Call on a student. Idea: *In the morning.*)

> But the grass was not moist with dew, and Nancy couldn't wait until morning.

2. Why couldn't she wait until morning? (Call on a student. Idea: *Because she is thirsty now.*)

> So she went to the bathroom, looking for water. She had walked from her bedroom to the bathroom hundreds of times before, but this time it wasn't a walk. It was a long, long trip. She finally arrived in the bathroom. She walked around as she made up a plan for getting water. Here's the plan: She would climb up the corner strip of the cabinet. That strip was made of rough wood and it was easy to grip. It went straight to the top of the cabinet.

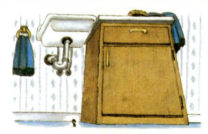

2. Listen to her plan again. Here's that plan:
   > She would climb up the corner strip of the cabinet. That strip was made of rough wood and it was easy to grip. It went straight to the top of the cabinet.
2. Why was the corner strip of the cabinet easy to grip? (Call on a student. Idea: *Because it was made of rough wood.*)
2. Everybody, touch the cabinet in the picture. ✓
2. Run your finger up and down the corner strip she would climb. ✓
2. What's next to the top of the cabinet? (Signal.) *The sink.*

> Nancy didn't know what kind of problem would meet her at the top of the cabinet. But first she had to get to the top. So up she went. She hoisted herself up one centimeter, two centimeters. Slowly, up. Then she began moving faster and faster. "This isn't too hard," she said to herself. When she was almost at the top, she reached a spot where the strip was moist with oil. And she slipped.

2. Everybody, touch the place on the strip where she was when she fell. ✓

> She fell all the way to the floor.

1. Everybody, look at the picture. What's happening in that picture? (Call on a student. Idea: *Nancy's falling.*)
1. Everybody, will she hurt herself? (Signal.) *No.*
1. Why not? (Call on a student. Ideas: *Because tiny things don't hurt themselves when they fall from high places; because she's so small.*)

> The fall scared her. She landed on her back. For a moment she didn't move. Then she got up slowly, testing her arms and legs to make sure that they weren't hurt. She had fallen from something that was a hundred times taller than she was, but she wasn't hurt.

2. She had just fallen from a cabinet. Everybody, show me how high that cabinet would be if it were in this room. ✓
2. That cabinet is a hundred times taller than Nancy.

160 Lesson 29

> She wasn't hurt at all, not one broken bone. Not one scratch. Not even an ouch.
> "I don't know what's happening," Nancy said to herself. "But I'm not afraid to try climbing that cabinet again."
> This time she got to the top.
> MORE NEXT TIME

1. Go back to the beginning of the story. Follow along while I read.
2. If you were Nancy climbing the cabinet the second time, would you be very, very careful? (Call on a student. Idea: *Not necessarily.*)
2. Why not? (Call on a student. Ideas: *Because tiny things don't hurt themselves when they fall from high places; because Nancy is so small.*)
2. Nancy has now learned two things about being very small. What's the thing she learned about talking? (Call on a student. Idea: *Small things have very high voices.*)
2. What's the thing she learned about high places? (Call on a student. Ideas: *Small things don't hurt themselves when they fall from high places; high places aren't scary.*)

EXERCISE 6
PAIRED PRACTICE

You're going to read aloud to your partner. Today the **B** members will read first. Then the **A** members will read from the star to the end of the story.
(Observe students and give feedback.)

EXERCISE 7
WRITTEN ITEMS
Story Items

a. **Find item 6 on your worksheet.** ✓
 - Items 6 through 18 are about today's story. I'll call on different students to read the items, but don't say the answers.
b. (For each item: Call on a student to read the item.)
 - Item 6. [*If tiny animals fall from high places, they don't blank.*]
 - Item 7. [*When Nancy was thirsty, she didn't scream and yell and stamp her feet. Why not?*]
 - Item 8. [*There wasn't any dew on the grass because it was not blank.*]
 - Item 9. [*Where did Nancy go to look for water?*]
 - Item 10. [*Nancy slipped on the strip of wood because it was blank.*]
 - Item 11. [*The cabinet was a blank times taller than Nancy.*]
 - Item 12. [*Did Nancy get hurt when she fell?*]
 - Item 13. [*Why not?*]
c. Items 14 through 18 are about animals that fell from a cliff. You'll underline the words that tell what happened to each animal. The choices are **not hurt, hurt** or **killed.**

End-of-Lesson Activities

INDEPENDENT WORK

Now finish your independent work for lesson 29. Raise your hand when you're finished. (Observe students and give feedback.)

WORKCHECK

a. (Direct students to take out their marking pencils.)
 - We're going to check your independent work. Remember, if you got an item wrong, make an **X** next to the item. Don't change any answers.
b. (For each item: Read the item. Call on a student to answer it. If the answer is wrong, say the correct answer. Refer to the Answer Key for the correct answers.)
c. Now use your marking pencil to fix up any items you got wrong. Remember, all mistakes must be fixed up before you hand in your independent work.

> **Note:** Before presenting lesson 30:
> - Reproduce blackline masters for the Fact Game;
> - Preview Literature lesson 4, secure materials and reproduce blackline masters. (See the Literature Guide.)

WRITING-SPELLING

(Present Writing-Spelling lesson 29 after completing Reading lesson 29. See Writing-Spelling Guide.)

ACTIVITY

(Present Activity 10 after completing Reading lesson 29. See Activities Across the Curriculum.)

Test 3

Lesson 30

Materials for Lesson 30

Fact Game

For each team (4 or 5 students):
- pair of number cubes (or dice)
- copy of Fact Game 30

For each student:
- their copy of the scorecard sheet

For each monitor:
- a pencil
- Fact Game 30 answer key (at end of textbook A)

Reading Checkout

Each student needs their thermometer chart.

Literature Lesson 3

See Literature Guide for the materials you will need.

EXERCISE 1
FACT GAME

a. You're going to play a game that uses the facts you have learned. You will take turns. When it is your turn, you'll read a question out loud and then you'll answer it. If you answer all parts of the question correctly, you earn one point.

b. I'll show you how to play the game.
- (Choose four students to sit at a table.)
- I'll be the monitor for now. First the monitor hands the number cubes to the person to the left. That person rolls the number cubes.
- (Hand the number cubes to the student on your left. Tell the student:) Roll the number cubes.

c. The person who rolls the number cubes tells the number of dots that are showing.
- (Tell the student who rolled the number cubes:) Count up the dots and tell us how many. ✓

d. Now the person who rolled the number cubes reads the question for that number out loud.
- (Ask the student who rolled the number cubes:) What question are you going to read out loud? ✓

- Read your question and then answer it. ✓

e. The monitor uses the Fact Game Answer Key. The monitor compares the player's answer with the correct answer. If the answer is correct, the monitor tells the player that the answer is correct. Then the monitor gives the player one point by putting a check mark on the player's scorecard. The first check mark goes in box 1. Every time a player answers a question correctly, the monitor puts a check mark in the next box on that player's card. If the player's answer is not correct, the monitor says the correct answer. The player does not get a point.

- (If the student answered the item correctly, say:) That's the right answer. (Then record one point on the student's scorecard.)

- (If the student answered the item incorrectly, say:) That's the wrong answer. The answer is _____.

f. The player passes the number cubes to the person to the left and that player rolls the number cubes. Remember, roll the number cubes, figure out the number of the question, read that question out loud, and answer it. The monitor gives the points and tells the correct answers. Do not argue with the monitor. If you argue, you lose your next turn.

g. (Divide the students into groups of four or five each. Identify a monitor for each group. Give each group a pair of number cubes.)

h. (Direct each monitor to the Lesson 30 Fact Game Answer Key at the back of textbook A. Tell each monitor:) That page gives the correct answers for this game. Don't show the answers to the other players.

i. **Everybody write your name on your scorecard and find lesson 30.** ✓

- You have 10 minutes to play the game. Keep taking turns until I tell you to stop.
- (Permit the game to be played for 10 minutes. When 5 minutes have elapsed, remind the group that 5 minutes remain.)

j. (After the game has been played for 10 minutes, have all the students who earned more than 5 points stand up. Praise these players for doing a very good job.)
- (Award points to monitors. Monitors receive the number of points earned by the highest performer in the monitor's group.)
- (For each game that ran smoothly, tell the monitor:) Your group did a good job.

EXERCISE 2
READING CHECKOUTS

a. Today is a test day and a reading-checkout day. While you're writing answers, I'm going to call on you one at a time to read part of the story we read in lesson 29. When I call on you to come and do your checkout, bring your thermometer chart.
- Remember, you pass the checkout by reading the passage in less than a minute without making more than 2 mistakes. And when you pass the checkout, you color the space for lesson 30 on your thermometer chart.

b. (Call on individual students to read the portion of story 29 marked with ✿.)
- (Time the student. Note words that are missed and number of words read.)
- (Teacher reference:)

> ✿ If Nancy knew more about very small things, she wouldn't have been so afraid of climbing to high places to find water. Here's the rule: <u>If tiny animals fall from high places, they don't get hurt.</u> If we dropped an ant from a high airplane, the ant would not be [50] hurt at all when it landed on the ground. A mouse wouldn't be hurt either. A squirrel wouldn't be badly hurt. A dog would probably [75] be killed. And you can imagine what would happen to an elephant.
>   Nancy was thirsty, so thirsty that she wanted to yell and scream and ✿ [100] stamp her feet like a baby.

- (If the student reads the passage in one minute or less and makes no more than 2 errors, direct the student to color in the space for lesson 30 on the thermometer chart.)
- (If the student makes any mistakes, point to each word that was misread and identify it.)
- (If the student does not meet the time-error criteria for the passage, direct the student to practice reading the story with the assigned partner.)

EXERCISE 3
TEST

a. **Find page 179 in your textbook.** ✓
- This is a test. You'll work items you've done before.
b. Work carefully. Raise your hand when you've completed all the items. (Observe students but do not give feedback on errors.)

EXERCISE 4
MARKING THE TEST

a. (Check students' work before beginning lesson 31. Refer to the Answer Key for the correct answers.)
b. (Record all test 3 results on the Test Summary Sheet and the Group Summary Sheet. Reproducible Summary Sheets are at the back of the Teacher's Guide.)

EXERCISE 5
TEST REMEDIES

- (Provide any necessary remedies for test 3 before presenting lesson 31. Test remedies are discussed in the Teacher's Guide.)

Test 3 Firming Table

Test Item	Introduced in lesson	Test Item	Introduced in lesson	Test Item	Introduced in lesson
1	21	10	23	19	21
2	22	11	23	20	21
3	22	12	23	21	25
4	22	13	24	22	17
5	22	14	24	23	25
6	22	15	24	24	25
7	22	16	26	25	17
8	23	17	29		
9	23	18	29		

Note: Before presenting lesson 31, exercise 3, read the exercise and decide if you want to demonstrate the experiment. If so, secure the necessary materials.

LITERATURE

(Present Literature lesson 3 after completing Reading lesson 30. See Literature Guide.)

Lessons 31–35 • Planning Page

Looking Ahead

	Lesson 31	Lesson 32	Lesson 33	Lesson 34	Lesson 35
Lesson Events	Vocabulary Review Reading Words Comprehension Passage Story Reading Paired Practice Written Items Independent Work Workcheck Writing-Spelling	Vocabulary Review Reading Words Comprehension Passage Story Reading Paired Practice Written Items Independent Work Workcheck Writing-Spelling	Vocabulary Sentence Reading Words Vocabulary Review Comprehension Passage Story Reading Paired Practice Written Items Independent Work Workcheck Writing-Spelling Activity	Vocabulary Review Reading Words Story Reading Paired Practice Written Items Independent Work Workcheck Writing-Spelling Activity	Vocabulary Review Reading Words Comprehension Passage Story Reading Reading Checkouts Written Items Independent Work Wordcheck Writing-Spelling
Vocabulary Sentence	#7: The traffic was moving forty miles per hour.	sentence #5 sentence #6 sentence #7	#8: He is supposed to make a decision in a couple of days.	#8: He is supposed to make a decision in a couple of days.	sentence #6 sentence #7 sentence #8
Reading Words: Word Types	modeled words –ed words multi-syllable words words with endings mixed words	–ed words compound words mixed words	modeled words words with endings multi-syllable words mixed words	modeled words –ed words 2-syllable words mixed words	modeled words mixed words multi-syllable words
New Vocabulary	gram	decision	expression	manage	several distance
Comprehension Passages	*More About the Skin That Water Has*	*Grams*	*More About Grams*		*Sounds That Objects Make*
Story	*Nancy Gets Some Water*	*Nancy is Hungry Again*	*Nancy Finds Some More Food*	*The Green Man Visits Nancy Again*	*Nancy Becomes Regular Size*
Skill Items	Vocabulary Same and Different	Deductions Same and Different	Vocabulary sentences Same and Different	Vocabulary Deductions	Vocabulary sentence Same and Different
Special Materials	Dish of water, 3 hairs.				* Materials for project
Special Projects/ Activities			Activity after lesson 33	Activity after lesson 34	Project after lesson 35

* Steel wool (preferably without soap); a transparent bowl; water; several steel objects, like a wrench, screw, or nails.

Lesson 31

Materials: (Optional) A clear dish, water, and strand of hair for demonstration in exercise 3.

EXERCISE 1
VOCABULARY REVIEW

a. Here's the new vocabulary sentence: The traffic was moving forty miles per hour.
- Everybody, say that sentence. Get ready. (Signal.) *The traffic was moving forty miles per hour.*
- (Repeat until firm.)

b. What word refers to all the cars and trucks that are moving on a street? (Signal.) *Traffic.*
- What word means **each**? (Signal.) *Per.*

EXERCISE 2
READING WORDS
Column 1

a. **Find lesson 31 in your textbook.** ✓
- Touch column 1. ✓
- (Teacher reference:)

1. unit	5. supposed
2. search	6. decision
3. complain	7. couple
4. refrigerator	

b. Word 1 is **unit**. What word? (Signal.) *Unit.*
- Spell **unit**. Get ready. (Tap for each letter.) *U-N-I-T.*

c. Word 2 is **search**. What word? (Signal.) *Search.*
- Spell **search**. Get ready. (Tap for each letter.) *S-E-A-R-C-H.*

d. Word 3 is **complain**. What word? (Signal.) *Complain.*
- Spell **complain**. Get ready. (Tap for each letter.) *C-O-M-P-L-A-I-N.*

e. Word 4 is **refrigerator**. What word? (Signal.) *Refrigerator.*

f. Word 5 is **supposed**. What word? (Signal.) *Supposed.*

g. Word 6 is **decision**. What word? (Signal.) *Decision.*

h. Word 7 is **couple**. What word? (Signal.) *Couple.*

i. Let's read those words again, the fast way.
- Word 1. What word? (Signal.) *Unit.*
- (Repeat for words 2–7.)

j. (Repeat step i until firm.)

Column 2

k. Find column 2. ✓
- (Teacher reference:)

1. stretched	4. finished
2. discovered	5. learned
3. weighed	

- All these words end with the letters **E-D**.
l. Word 1. What word? (Signal.) *Stretched.*
- (Repeat for words 2–5.)

m. (Repeat step l until firm.)

Column 3

n. Find column 3. ✓
- (Teacher reference:)

1. <u>house</u>fly	3. <u>dark</u>ness
2. <u>bee</u>tles	4. <u>um</u>brella

- These words have more than one syllable. The first syllable is underlined.

o. Word 1. What's the first syllable? (Signal.) *house.*
- What's the whole word? (Signal.) *Housefly.*

p. Word 2. What's the first syllable? (Signal.) *bee.*
- What's the whole word? (Signal.) *Beetles.*

q. Word 3. What's the first syllable? (Signal.) *dark.*
- What's the whole word? (Signal.) *Darkness.*

r. Word 4. What's the first syllable? (Signal.) *um.*
- What's the whole word? (Signal.) *Umbrella.*

s. Let's read those words again, the fast way.
- Word 1. What word? (Signal.) *Housefly.*
- (Repeat for: **2. beetles, 3. darkness, 4. umbrella.**)

t. (Repeat step s until firm.)

Column 4

u. Find column 4. ✓
- (Teacher reference:)

1. easily	4. wondering
2. strider	5. sweater
3. scary	

- All these words have endings.

v. Word 1. What word? (Signal.) *Easily.*
- (Repeat for words 2–5.)

w. (Repeat step v until firm.)

Column 5

x. Find column 5. ✓
- (Teacher reference:)

1. gram	4. frightened
2. fright	5. tough
3. frighten	6. scale

y. Word 1. What word? (Signal.) *Gram.*
- A gram is a very small unit of weight. A large paper clip weighs about one gram.

z. Word 2. What word? (Signal.) *Fright.*
- (Repeat for words 3–6.)

a. Let's read those words again.
- Word 1. What word? (Signal.) *Gram.*
- (Repeat for words 2–6.)

b. (Repeat step a until firm.)

Individual Turns

(For columns 1–5: Call on individual students, each to read one to three words per turn.)

EXERCISE 3

COMPREHENSION PASSAGE

Note: Optional demonstration in step c.

a. Find part B in your textbook. ✓
- You're going to read the next story about Nancy. First you'll read the information passage. It gives some more information about water.

b. Everybody, touch the title. ✓
- (Call on a student to read the title.) [More About the Skin That Water Has.]
- Everybody, what's the title? (Signal.) *More About the Skin That Water Has.*

c. We'll read about another way to show the skin of water. (Indicate if you will demonstrate the experiment described in the passage.)

d. (Call on individual students to read the passage, each student reading two or three sentences at a time. Ask the specified questions as the students read.)

> **More About the Skin That Water Has**
>
> When we fill a tube with water, you can see that the water has a skin. You can use a dish of water and a hair to show that water has a skin.
>
> First you can float a hair on water. If you're careful, the hair won't even get wet. It will just rest on the skin of the water.
>
> Hair A in the picture is resting on the water.

- Why won't the hair get wet? (Call on a student. Idea: *Because it's only touching the skin of the water.*)
- Everybody touch hair A. ✓
- You can see the water around the hair bending down. The hair is dry.

> Look at hair B. The end of that hair is pushed down through the skin of the water. As the hair goes down, the skin of the water bends down around the hair. Look at the skin around hair B.

- Everybody, what's happening to the skin around hair B? (Signal.) *It's bending down.*

> The end of hair C is under the water. But hair C is moving up. When the hair moves up slowly, the skin hangs onto the hair and bends up.

- Everybody, touch hair C. ✓
- When the hair moves up, does the skin bend **up** or **down**? (Signal.) *Up.*

Remember, when the hair goes up, the skin bends up. When the hair goes down, the skin bends down.

EXERCISE 4
STORY READING

Note: Ask questions marked **1** during the first reading. Ask questions marked **2** during the second reading.

a. Find part C in your textbook. ✓
- The error limit for this story is 9.
- Read carefully and don't make more than 9 errors. I'm going to ask some questions as you read the story. Then I'll read the story and ask more questions.

b. Everybody, touch the title. ✓
- (Call on a student to read the title.) *[Nancy Gets Some Water.]*
- What's going to happen in this story? (Call on a student. Idea: *Nancy will get some water.*)
- Where did we leave Nancy at the end of the last story? (Call on a student. Idea: *At the top of the cabinet.*)

c. (Call on individual students to read the story, each student reading two or three sentences at a time. Ask questions marked **1**.)

- (Correct errors: Tell the word. Direct the student to reread the sentence.)
- (If the group makes more than 9 errors, direct the students to reread the story.)

d. (After the group has read the selection making no more than 9 errors, read the story to the students and ask questions marked **2**.)

Nancy Gets Some Water

Nancy had climbed to the top of the cabinet. She was ready to have a nice drink of water. Next to the sink there were lots of drops of water. Some drops were bigger than she was. Some drops were about the size of an open umbrella top.

2. Everybody, show me how big those smaller drops looked to Nancy. ✓

**She rushed over to them.
Nancy didn't know much about water drops. Here's the rule: <u>Water drops have a skin that goes all the way around them.</u>**

2. Everybody, what do water drops have? (Signal.) *Skin that goes all the way around them.*

**That skin is tough. If you are at a pond, you may see little insects called water striders that walk right on top of the water. They are walking on the skin of the water.
If you look closely, you can see that the legs of water striders make little dents in the water but their legs do not go into the water. The legs just bend the skin of the water down without going through the skin.**

2. When the legs of the water strider push down, what does the skin of the water do? (Call on a student. Idea: *Bends down.*)

Nancy had seen water striders, but she didn't think about how tough the skin of water must be if you are very small. She ran over to one drop of water. The drop of water came up to her knees. Then she bent over and touched the water drop with her hands. It felt like a water balloon.

2. Everybody, did it feel wet to Nancy? (Signal.) *No.*
2. Why not? (Call on a student. Idea: *Because it had a skin.*)
2. Everybody, look at the picture. You can see her hands pushing down on the water drop. Are her hands wet? (Signal.) *No.*
2. Why not? (Call on a student. Idea: *Because they're only touching the skin of the water.*)

> When she pushed, the skin moved in. But her hands didn't go through the skin. "How do insects drink water?" she thought for an instant. Then she got back to her problem. "How am I going to drink?"

1. **What would you do?** (Call on individual students. Student preference.)

> "I'll just hit it harder," she thought. She made a fist, wound up and swung as hard as she could swing. Her fist went right through the skin of the drop.

2. **Everybody, did she get through the skin?** (Signal.) *Yes.*

> Her hand was wet and her arm was wet. She pulled her hand back, but it didn't come out easily. It stuck at the wrist.

2. **Everybody, show me where the skin of the water held onto Nancy.** ✓

> She pulled and tugged, and the skin of the water stretched out. Finally, **pop.**

1. **What made that "pop" sound?** (Call on a student. Idea: *The water skin, when Nancy's hand came out of it.*)

> Her hand came out, and the skin of the drop wobbled back into its round shape.

2. **What did the water drop do?** (Call on a student. Idea: *Got back into its round shape.*)

> Nancy thought about the best way of getting water from the drop. At last, she backed up a few steps, put her head down, and charged the drop of water. Her head hit the water drop and **pop.** Her head went through the skin.

1. **Everybody, was her head in water now?** (Signal.) *Yes.*
1. **Look at the picture on the next page. You can see her head inside the water drop. The skin of the water drop is around her neck.**

> She drank quickly, trying not to get water in her nose. Then she pulled her head back.

1. **What's going to happen when she tries to pull her head out?** (Call on a student. Idea: *It'll get stuck.*)

> The skin of the water tugged at her neck. The water pulled at her neck the way a tight sweater pulls on your neck when you try to take it off.

2. **Everybody, show me where a tight sweater would stick when you try to pull it over your head.** ✓

> Nancy pulled hard, and **pop.** Her head came out of the drop.
> "That was scary," she said out loud.
> **MORE NEXT TIME**

1. **Go back to the beginning of the story. Follow along while I read.**
2. **I'll bet that was scary. What would have happened to her if she didn't get her head out of the water drop?** (Call on a student. Idea: *She would have drowned.*)
2. **Nancy has learned three things about being very small. What's the thing she learned about talking?** (Call on a student. Idea: *Small things have very high voices.*)
2. **What's the thing she learned about high places?** (Call on a student. Idea: *Small things do not hurt themselves when they fall from high places.*)
2. **What's the thing she learned about water?** (Call on a student. Idea: *Water has a skin.*)

EXERCISE 5
PAIRED PRACTICE

You're going to read aloud to your partner. Today the **A** members will read first. Then the **B** members will read from the star to the end of the story.

(Observe students and give feedback.)

EXERCISE 6
WRITTEN ITEMS
Story Items

a. Find part D in your textbook. ✓
- Items 1 through 15 are about today's story. I'll call on different students to read the items, but don't say the answers.

b. (For each item: Call on a student to read the item.)
- Item 1. *[Some drops of water were <u>blank</u> than Nancy.]*
- Item 2. *[When Nancy first touched the water drop, did her hand get wet?]*
- Item 3. *[What did Nancy have to do to get her hand inside the water drop?]*
- Item 4. *[Did Nancy get her head inside the water drop?]*
- Item 5. *[What happened when Nancy tried to pull her head back out of the water drop?]*
- Item 6. *[Write the letters of the water striders.]*
- List the 3 things that Nancy has learned about being very small.
  Item 7. *[Small animals have a voice that is <u>blank</u>.]*
- Item 8. *[Small animals don't get hurt when they <u>blank</u>.]*
- Item 9. *[Water has a <u>blank</u>.]*
- Item 10. *[Is a water strider an insect?]*
- Item 11. *[How many legs does a water strider have?]*
- Item 12. *[How many legs does an ant have?]*
- Item 13. *[How many legs does a spider have?]*
- Item 14. *[How many legs does a flea have?]*
- Item 15. *[How many legs does a cat have?]*

Skill Items

c. Item 16. *[Write one way that tells how both objects are the same.]*
- Tell me a way they're the same. (Call on individual students. Ideas: *They're both dogs; they both have tails; they're both standing;* etc.)

d. Read item 17. *[Write 2 ways that tell how object A is different from object B.]*
- Tell me a way that object A is different from object B. (Call on individual students. Ideas: *A has a long tail, but B has a short tail; A is a beagle, but B is a poodle; A is facing right, but B is facing left,* etc.)

End-of-Lesson Activities

INDEPENDENT WORK

Now finish your textbook and worksheet items independent work for lesson 31. Raise your hand when you're finished. (Observe students and give feedback.)

WORKCHECK

a. (Direct students to take out their marking pencils.)
- We're going to check your independent work. Remember, if you got an item wrong, make an **X** next to the item. Don't change any answers.

b. (For each item: Read the item. Call on a student to answer it. If the answer is wrong, say the correct answer. Refer to the Answer Key for the correct answers.)

c. Now use your marking pencil to fix up any items you got wrong. Remember, all mistakes must be fixed up before you hand in your independent work.

WRITING-SPELLING

(Present Writing-Spelling lesson 31 after completing Reading lesson 31. See Writing-Spelling Guide.)

Lesson 32

Materials: You will need a full-length pencil for a demonstration in Exercise 3.

EXERCISE 1
VOCABULARY REVIEW

a. You learned a sentence that tells where hunters were stationed.
- Everybody, say that sentence. Get ready. (Signal.) *Hunters were stationed at opposite ends of the field.*
- (Repeat until firm.)

b. You learned a sentence that tells who he motioned to.
- Everybody, say that sentence. Get ready. (Signal.) *He motioned to the flight attendant ahead of him.*
- (Repeat until firm.)

c. Here's the last sentence you learned: The traffic was moving forty miles per hour.
- Everybody, say that sentence. Get ready. (Signal.) *The traffic was moving forty miles per hour.*
- (Repeat until firm.)

d. What word means **each**? (Signal.) *Per.*
- What word refers to all the cars and trucks that are on the street? (Signal.) *Traffic.*

e. Once more. Say the sentence that tells how fast the traffic was moving. Get ready. (Signal.) *The traffic was moving forty miles per hour.*

EXERCISE 2
READING WORDS

Column 1

a. Find lesson 32 in your textbook. ✓
- Touch column 1. ✓
- (Teacher reference:)

> 1. discovered   5. complained
> 2. frightened   6. learned
> 3. wondered   7. supposed
> 4. finished

- All these words end with the letters **E-D**.

b. Word 1. What word? (Signal.) *Discovered.*
- (Repeat for words 2–7.)
c. (Repeat step b until firm.)

Column 2

d. Find column 2. ✓
- (Teacher reference:)

> 1. **house**flies   3. **base**ball
> 2. **for**ever   4. **foot**ball

- All these words are compound words. The first part of each word is underlined.

e. Word 1. What's the first syllable? (Signal.) *house.*
- What's the whole word? (Signal.) *Houseflies.*

f. Word 2. What's the first syllable? (Signal.) *for.*
- What's the whole word? (Signal.) *Forever.*

g. Word 3. What's the first syllable? (Signal.) *base.*
- What's the whole word? (Signal.) *Baseball.*

h. Word 4. What's the first syllable? (Signal.) *foot.*
- What's the whole word? (Signal.) *Football.*

i. Let's read those words again, the fast way.
- Word 1. What word? (Signal.) *Houseflies.*
- (Repeat for words 2–4.)
j. (Repeat step i until firm.)

Column 3

k. Find column 3. ✓
- (Teacher reference:)

> 1. stale   5. traffic
> 2. grams   6. forty
> 3. search   7. couple
> 4. moving

l. Word 1. What word? (Signal.) *Stale.*
- (Repeat for words 2–7.)
m. (Repeat step l until firm.)

Column 4

n. Find column 4. ✓
- (Teacher reference:)

1. decision	4. dining
2. refrigerator	5. chunk
3. weighs	6. toast

o. Word 1. What word? (Signal.) *Decision.*
- Spell **decision.** Get ready. (Tap for each letter.) *D-E-C-I-S-I-O-N.*
- When you make a decision to do something, you make up your mind to do it. To make a decision to play, you make up your mind to play. To make a decision to work, you make up your mind to work.
- Your turn. What do you do to make a decision to work? (Signal.) *Make up your mind to work.*
- (Repeat until firm.)
- What do you do to make a decision to read? (Signal.) *Make up your mind to read.*

p. Word 2. What word? (Signal.) *Refrigerator.*
- (Repeat for words 3–6.)

q. Let's read those words again.
- Word 1. What word? (Signal.) *Decision.*
- (Repeat for words 2–6.)

r. (Repeat step q until firm.)

Column 5

s. Find column 5. ✓
- (Teacher reference:)

1. hoist	4. replied
2. lawn	5. thirty
3. reply	6. unit

t. Word 1. What word? (Signal.) *Hoist.*
- (Repeat for words 2–6.)

u. (Repeat step t until firm.)

Individual Turns

(For columns 1–5: Call on individual students, each to read one to three words per turn.)

EXERCISE 3
COMPREHENSION PASSAGE

Note: You will need a full-length pencil for a demonstration.

a. Find part B in your textbook. ✓
- You're going to read the next story about Nancy. First you'll read the information passage. It gives some facts about grams.

b. Everybody, touch the title. ✓
- (Call on a student to read the title.) [*Grams.*]
- Everybody, what's the title? (Signal.) *Grams.*

c. (Call on individual students to read the passage, each student reading two or three sentences at a time. Ask the specified questions as the students read.)

> **Grams**
>
> In some stories, you've read about things that do not weigh very much. When we weigh very small things, the unit we use is grams.

- Everybody, what is the unit we use to weigh small things? (Signal.) *Grams.*

> Here's a rule about grams: **All grams are the same weight.**

- Everybody, listen to that fact again: All grams are the same weight.
- Say that fact. Get ready. (Signal.) *All grams are the same weight.*
- (Repeat until firm.)

> If you had a block of water that was one centimeter on all sides, that block would weigh one gram.

- Everybody, how much does a block of water 1 centimeter on all sides weigh? (Signal.) *1 gram.*

> A pencil weighs more than a gram. A long pencil weighs about five grams. A short pencil weighs about two grams.

Lesson 32   173

- Everybody, about how much does a long pencil weigh? (Signal.) *5 grams.*
- About how much does a short pencil weigh? (Signal.) *2 grams.*
- (Hold up a long pencil.) Everybody, about how much does this pencil weigh? (Signal.) *5 grams.*
- Let's say you're holding a long pencil. Close your eyes and feel how much it weighs. (Pause.) How much does a long pencil weigh? (Signal.) *5 grams.*

EXERCISE 4
STORY READING

Note: Ask questions marked **1** during the first reading. Ask questions marked **2** during the second reading.

a. Find part C in your textbook. ✓
- The error limit for this story is 8.
- Read carefully and don't make more than 8 errors. I'm going to ask some questions as you read the story. Then I'll read the story and ask more questions.

b. Everybody, touch the title. ✓
- (Call on a student to read the title.) [*Nancy Is Hungry Again.*]
- What's going to happen in this story? (Call on a student. Idea: *Nancy will get hungry again.*)
- Where did we leave Nancy last time? (Call on a student. Idea: *On the top of the bathroom cabinet drinking water drops.*)

c. (Call on individual students to read the story, each student reading two or three sentences at a time. Ask questions marked **1.**)

- (Correct errors: Tell the word. Direct the student to reread the sentence.)
- (If the group makes more than 8 errors, direct the students to reread the story.)

d. (After the group has read the selection making no more than 8 errors, read the story to the students and ask questions marked **2.**)

Nancy Is Hungry Again

Nancy found out three things about being very small.

1. What's the thing she learned about talking? (Call on a student. Idea: *Small things have very high voices.*)
1. What's the thing she learned about high places? (Call on a student. Idea: *Small things do not get hurt when they fall from high places.*)
1. What's the thing she learned about water? (Call on a student. Idea: *Water has a skin.*)

She found out that small things have very high voices. She also discovered that very small things do not hurt themselves when they fall from high places. The third thing she discovered was that a drop of water is very different to someone who is quite small.

2. How is it different? (Call on a student. Ideas: *You can feel its skin; it seems quite big;* etc.)

During her first night of being small, Nancy found out a fourth fact about being small. Here's the rule: The food that a very small animal eats each day weighs more than the animal.

2. How much does the food weigh? (Call on a student. Idea: *More than the animal.*)
2. Let's say that you are a very small animal, and next to you is the pile of food you will eat in one day. Everybody, show me how big the pile would look to you. ✓

Let's say a small animal weighs one gram.

1. Everybody, is that a very small animal? (Signal.) *Yes.*
1. How much would the food weigh that the animal eats in one day? (Call on a student. Idea: *More than 1 gram.*)

The food that the animal eats each day weighs more than one gram. The food that bigger animals eat each day does not weigh as much as the animals.

2. You are a big animal. Raise your hand if you weigh more than 50 pounds. (Call on a student who raised a hand.) Could you eat more than 50 pounds of food in one day? *No.*

> An elephant may eat two hundred pounds of food each day, but the elephant may weigh more than a thousand pounds. An adult human may eat five pounds of food each day, but the adult weighs much more than five pounds. A large dog may eat three pounds of food every day but the dog may weigh more than 80 pounds.
>
> Nancy learned this rule during the first night that she was very small.

1. Which rule did she learn about? (Call on a student. Idea: *The food that a very small animal eats each day weighs more than the animal.*)

> She woke up in the middle of the night. She was very hungry. So she got up from her dollhouse bed and went looking for another chunk of cookie that was on her rug. She found one and ate it. Then she felt thirsty, so she went back to the bathroom, climbed to the top of the cabinet, and drank from a drop of water.
>
> "That's scary," she said when she finished.

2. Why is it scary for Nancy to drink from a drop of water? (Call on a student. Idea: *Because the skin of the water pulls around Nancy's neck.*)

> She went back to bed in her dollhouse, but before the sun came up, she woke up again.

1. Why do you think she woke up? (Call on individual students. Student preference.)

> She was hungry. The cookie crumbs were gone so she couldn't eat cookie crumbs. She tried to forget about how hungry she was. She knew that she had already eaten a chunk of cookie that weighed almost as much as she did. She wondered, "How can I still be hungry?"
>
> The feeling of hunger did not go away. After a few minutes, she got out of bed. "Oh nuts," she said. "I'm going to have to go hunting for food."
>
> MORE NEXT TIME

1. Go back to the beginning of the story. Follow along while I read.
2. Everybody, if you were a very small animal, would you eat more often than you eat now? (Signal.) *Yes.*
2. Nancy has now learned four things about being very small. What's the thing she learned about talking? (Call on a student. Idea: *Small things have very high voices.*)
2. What's the thing she learned about high places? (Call on a student. Idea: *Small things do not get hurt when they fall from high places.*)
2. What's the thing she learned about water? (Call on a student. Idea: *Water has a skin.*)
2. What's the thing she learned about how much food small animals eat? (Call on a student. Idea: *The food that a very small animal eats each day weighs more than the animal.*)

EXERCISE 5

PAIRED PRACTICE

You're going to read aloud to your partner. Today the **B** members will read first. Then the **A** members will read from the star to the end of the story.

(Observe students and give feedback.)

Lesson 32

EXERCISE 6
WRITTEN ITEMS

Skill Items

a. **Find part D in your textbook.** ✓
- **Read item 1.** (Call on a student.) *[Write one way that tells how both objects are the same.]*
- **Tell me a way they're the same.** (Call on individual students. Ideas: *They're both squares; they're both yellow; they both have dots;* etc.)

b. **Read item 2.** (Call on a student.) *[Write 2 ways that tell how object A is different from object B.]*
- **Tell me a way that object A is different from object B.** (Call on individual students. Ideas: *A is small, but B is big; A has black dots, but B has blue dots;* etc.)

Story Items

c. **Find Part B on your worksheet.** ✓
- **Items 8 through 20 are about today's story. I'll call on different students to read the items, but don't say the answers.**

d. (For each item: Call on a student to read the item.)
- **Item 8.** *[The food that a very small animal eats each day weighs blank.]*
- **Item 9.** *[Is a mouse a small animal?]*
- **Item 10.** *[Does the food a mouse eats each day weigh more than the mouse?]*
- **Item 11.** *[Are you a small animal?]*
- **Item 12.** *[Does the food that you eat each day weigh as much as you do?]*
- **Item 13.** *[How many times did Nancy wake up during the night?]*
- **Item 14.** *[Why did she wake up?]*
- **Item 15.** *[What did Nancy eat the first time she woke up?]*
- **Item 16.** *[Why didn't Nancy eat a cookie crumb the second time she woke up?]*
- **Item 17.** *[The food that three of the animals eat each day weighs more than those animals. Circle those animals.]*
- **Item 18.** *[Small animals don't get hurt when they blank.]*
- **Item 19.** *[Small animals have a voice that is blank.]*
- **Item 20.** *[Water has a blank.]*

End-of-Lesson Activities

INDEPENDENT WORK

Now finish your independent work for lesson 32. Raise your hand when you're finished. (Observe students and give feedback.)

WORKCHECK

a. (Direct students to take out their marking pencils.)
- **We're going to check your independent work. Remember, if you got an item wrong, make an X next to the item. Don't change any answers.**

b. (For each item: Read the item. Call on a student to answer it. If the answer is wrong, say the correct answer. Refer to the Answer Key for the correct answers.)

c. **Now use your marking pencil to fix up any items you got wrong. Remember, all mistakes must be fixed up before you hand in your independent work.**

WRITING-SPELLING

(Present Writing-Spelling lesson 32 after completing Reading lesson 32. See Writing-Spelling Guide.)

Lesson 33

EXERCISE 1
VOCABULARY

a. **Find page 338 in your textbook.** ✓
- Touch sentence 8. ✓
- This is a new vocabulary sentence. It says: He is supposed to make a decision in a couple of days.
- Everybody, read that sentence. Get ready. (Signal.) *He is supposed to make a decision in a couple of days.*
- Close your eyes and say the sentence. Get ready. (Signal.) *He is supposed to make a decision in a couple of days.*
- (Repeat until firm.)

b. Here's what that sentence means: He should make up his mind about what to do in two days. Listen again: He should make up his mind about what to do in two days.

c. Here's another way of saying **He is supposed to make a decision: He should make a decision.**
- When you make a decision, you make up your mind about what to do.

d. **A couple** is **two.** A couple of days is two days. A couple of oranges is two oranges. What word means **two**? (Signal.) *Couple.*

e. Listen: He is supposed to make a decision in a couple of days. Everybody, say the sentence. Get ready. (Signal.) *He is supposed to make a decision in a couple of days.*

f. What part means **should**? (Signal.) *Supposed to.*
- What part means **make up his mind**? (Signal.) *Make a decision.*
- What word means **two**? (Signal.) *Couple.*
- (Repeat step f until firm.)

EXERCISE 2
READING WORDS

Column 1

a. Find lesson 33 in your textbook. ✓
- Touch column 1. ✓
- (Teacher reference:)

1. instead	3. expression
2. couple	4. important

b. Word 1 is **instead.** What word? (Signal.) *Instead.*
- Spell **instead.** Get ready. (Tap for each letter.) *I-N-S-T-E-A-D.*

c. Word 2 is **couple.** What word? (Signal.) *Couple.*
- Spell **couple.** Get ready. (Tap for each letter.) *C-O-U-P-L-E.*

d. Word 3 is **expression.** What word? (Signal.) *Expression.*
- Spell **expression.** Get ready. *E-X-P-R-E-S-S-I-O-N.*
- The expression on your face shows what you're feeling. A surprised expression means that you are surprised. A happy expression means that you're happy.

e. Word 4 is **important.** What word? (Signal.) *Important.*

f. Let's read those words again, the fast way.
- Word 1. What word? (Signal.) *Instead.*
- (Repeat for words 2–4.)

g. (Repeat step f until firm.)

Column 2

h. Find column 2. ✓
- (Teacher reference:)

1. soundly	4. frightened
2. moments	5. baseballs
3. wondering	

- All these words have endings.

i. Word 1. What word? (Signal.) *Soundly.*
- When you sleep soundly, it is not easy for something to wake you up.

j. Word 2. What word? (Signal.) *Moments.*
- (Repeat for words 3–5.)

k. Let's read those words again.
- Word 1. What word? (Signal.) *Soundly.*
- (Repeat for words 2–5.)

l. (Repeat step k until firm.)

Column 3

m. Find column 3. ✓
- (Teacher reference:)

1. forever	4. decision
2. refrigerator	5. answered
3. footballs	

n. Word 1. What word? (Signal.) *Forever.*
- (Repeat for words 2–5.)

o. (Repeat step n until firm.)

Column 4

p. Find column 4. ✓
- (Teacher reference:)

1. chunk	4. cherry
2. search	5. toast
3. scale	

q. Word 1. What word? (Signal.) *Chunk.*
- Spell **chunk.** Get ready. (Tap for each letter.) *C-H-U-N-K.*

r. Word 2. What word? (Signal.) *Search.*
- Spell **search.** Get ready. (Tap for each letter.) *S-E-A-R-C-H.*

s. Word 3. What word? (Signal.) *Scale.*
- (Repeat for words 4 and 5.)

t. Let's read those words again.
- Word 1. What word? (Signal.) *Chunk.*
- (Repeat for words 2–5.)

u. (Repeat step t until firm.)

Column 5

v. Find column 5. ✓
- (Teacher reference:)

1. yourself	4. learned
2. whirl	5. dining
3. swirl	

w. Word 1. What word? (Signal.) *Yourself.*
- (Repeat for words 2–5.)

x. (Repeat step w until firm.)

Individual Turns

(For columns 1–5: Call on individual students, each to read one to three words per turn.)

EXERCISE 3

VOCABULARY REVIEW

a. Here's the new vocabulary sentence: He is supposed to make a decision in a couple of days.
- Everybody, say the sentence. Get ready. (Signal.) *He is supposed to make a decision in a couple of days.*
- (Repeat until firm.)

b. What part means **make up his mind?** (Signal.) *Make a decision.*
- What part means **should?** (Signal.) *Supposed to.*
- What word means **two?** (Signal.) *Couple.*
- (Repeat step b until firm.)

EXERCISE 4

COMPREHENSION PASSAGE

a. Find part B in your textbook. ✓
- You're going to read the next story about Nancy. First you'll read the information passage. It gives some more information about grams.

b. Everybody, touch the title. ✓
- (Call on a student to read the title.) [More About Grams.]
- Everybody, what's the title? (Signal.) *More About Grams.*

c. (Call on individual students to read the passage, each student reading two or three sentences at a time. Ask the specified questions as the students read.)

> **More About Grams**
>
> You learned about grams. You know that grams are used to weigh some kinds of things.

- What kinds of things? (Call on a student. Ideas: *Small things; light things.*)

> You know how much water it takes to weigh one gram.

- How big would a block of water be if it weighed 1 gram? (Call on a student. Idea: *1 centimeter on all sides.*)

> You know how much a long pencil weighs.

- Everybody, how much? (Signal.) *5 grams.*

> You know how much a short pencil weighs.

- Everybody, how much? (Signal.) *2 grams.*

> **Here are some facts about how much other things weigh. A big cherry weighs about ten grams.**

- Everybody, about how much does a big cherry weigh? (Signal.) *10 grams.*

> **An apple weighs about two hundred grams.**

- Everybody, about how much does an apple weigh? (Signal.) *200 grams.*

> **Most insects weigh much less than a gram. Even a very big spider like the spider in the picture weighs less than a gram.**

- Everybody, look at the spider in the picture. Does that spider weigh **more than a gram** or **less than a gram**? (Signal.) *Less than a gram.*

> **It would take about one hundred ants to weigh one gram.**

- Everybody, about how many ants does it take to weigh 1 gram? (Signal.) *100.*
- The picture of the ants shows a gram of water on one side of the scale. Everybody, touch the gram of water. ✓
- What kind of insects are on the other side of the scale? (Signal.) *Ants.*
- About how many ants? (Signal.) *100.*
- The weight is the same on both sides of the scale. The gram of water weighs the same as about 100 ants.

> **It would take about thirty houseflies to weigh one gram.**

- Everybody, about how many houseflies does it take to weigh 1 gram? (Signal.) *30.*
- Touch the gram of water on the scale with the houseflies. ✓
- About how many houseflies are on the other side of the scale? (Signal.) *30.*
- The weight is the same on both sides of the scale. So how much do the houseflies weigh? (Signal.) *1 gram.*

> **It would take about two hundred fleas from Russia to weigh one gram.**

- Everybody, about how many fleas does it take to weigh 1 gram? (Signal.) *200.*
- Touch the gram of water on the scale with the fleas. ✓
- About how many fleas are on the other side of the scale? (Signal.) *200.*
- The weight is the same on both sides of the scale. So how much do the fleas weigh? (Signal.) *1 gram.*

> **The picture below shows how much a big beetle weighs. How many grams of water are on the scale?**

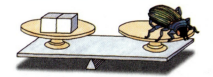

- Everybody, how many grams are on the scale? (Signal.) *2.*
- Touch them. ✓

> **So how much weight is on the side of the scale with the beetle?**

- The weight is the same on both sides of the scale. So how much weight is on the side with the beetle? (Signal.) *2 grams.*

EXERCISE 5
STORY READING

> **Note:** Ask questions marked **1** during the first reading. Ask questions marked **2** during the second reading.

a. Find part C in your textbook. ✓
- The error limit for this story is 8.
- Read carefully and don't make more than 8 errors. I'm going to ask some questions as you read the story. Then I'll read the story and ask more questions.
b. Everybody, touch the title. ✓
- (Call on a student to read the title.) *[Nancy Finds Some More Food.]*

- What's going to happen in this story? (Call on a student. Idea: *Nancy will find some more food.*)
- How did Nancy feel at the end of the last story? (Call on a student. Idea: *Hungry.*)
- Why was she hungry again? (Call on a student. Ideas: *Because she needed more food; her stomach was empty; because she was such a small animal.*)

c. (Call on individual students to read the story, each student reading two or three sentences at a time. Ask questions marked **1**.)

- (Correct errors: Tell the word. Direct the student to reread the sentence.)
- (If the group makes more than 8 errors, direct the students to reread the story.)

d. (After the group has read the selection making no more than 8 errors, read the story to the students and ask questions marked **2**.)

Nancy Finds Some More Food

Nancy went toward the kitchen. The walk seemed to take forever. The house was dark and Nancy couldn't see well, so she felt the walls and walked slowly toward the kitchen. When she was in the dining room, she could hear the sound of the refrigerator. In fact, she could feel the refrigerator. It shook the floor.

Finally, Nancy reached the kitchen. By now, she was so hungry that she wanted to scream and cry and kick and roll around on the floor like a baby.

1. Everybody, do you think she'll do that? (Signal.) *No.*
1. Why not? (Call on a student. Idea: *Because nobody would hear her, so it wouldn't do any good.*)

But she didn't do any of those things because she knew that acting like a baby wouldn't do any good. So she opened her eyes wide and tried to look for scraps of food.

Near the refrigerator, she found something. She bent over and sniffed it. She wasn't sure what it was, but it smelled bad. "I'm not that hungry," she said. "I'll bet that chunk of food has been on the floor for a week."

Nancy walked nearly all the way around the kitchen, but she couldn't find any other food. "I'll bet there's food on the counter," she said to herself.

1. What do you think she'll do? (Call on individual students. Student preference.)

Up she went, without feeling frightened.

2. What's the counter? (Call on a student. Idea: *The place in the kitchen where you get food ready/set dishes.*)
2. Why wasn't she frightened? (Call on a student. Ideas: *Because she knew it wouldn't hurt if she fell; because she'd climbed up on a counter before.*)

She reached the top and began to search the counter.

She smelled it before she saw it—toast. She followed her nose.

1. What does that mean? (Call on a student. Idea: *She walked toward the smell.*)

In the darkness, she could just see the toast.

2. Everybody, could she see it clearly? (Signal.) *No.*

Three pieces of toast were piled on a plate. To Nancy, the pile of toast looked like a giant ten-story building.

2. Everybody, how high did the three pieces of toast seem to her? (Signal.) *As high as a 10-story building.*

Nancy was wondering how to climb onto the plate so that she could reach the toast. But when she started to walk around the plate, she found crumbs all over the counter.

1. What do you think she'll do? (Call on a student. Idea: *Eat the crumbs.*)

> **There were crumbs that seemed as big as baseballs and crumbs as big as footballs. There was even one crumb that was the size of a chair.**
>
> **Nancy picked up a crumb that was the size of a football.**

2. Everybody, show me how she held that crumb. ✓

> **She ate it with a loud, "Chomp, chomp, chomp."**

2. What made that "chomp, chomp" noise? (Call on a student. Idea: *Nancy chewing the toast.*)

> **When Nancy had been full-sized, she hated toast. She complained when her mother served it. "Oh, not that stuff," she used to say. "I hate toast."**
>
> **Now that she was small and hungry all the time, she didn't hate toast. In fact, that crumb of toast tasted so good that she ate another piece the size of a football.**
>
> **Nancy weighed much less than a gram.**

2. Everybody, did Nancy weigh as much as a centimeter of water? (Signal.) *No.*

> **In one day, she had eaten food that weighed a gram.**
>   **MORE NEXT TIME**

1. Go back to the beginning of the story. Follow along while I read.
2. Listen to that part again. Nancy weighed much less than a gram. In one day, she had eaten food that weighed a gram.
2. Everybody, which weighed more—Nancy or the food that she ate in one day? (Signal.) *The food that she ate in one day.*
2. Nancy has learned four things about being very small. What's the thing she learned about talking? (Call on a student. Idea: *Small things have high voices.*)
2. What's the thing she learned about high places? (Call on a student. Idea: *Small things do not get hurt when they fall from high places.*)
2. What's the thing she learned about water? (Call on a student. Idea: *It has a skin.*)
2. What's the thing she learned about how much small animals eat? (Call on a student. Idea: *The food that a very small animal eats each day weighs more than the animal.*)

EXERCISE 6

PAIRED PRACTICE

You're going to read aloud to your partner. Today the **A** members will read first. Then the **B** members will read. ✓

EXERCISE 7

WRITTEN ITEMS

Story Items

a. **Find item 1 on your worksheet.** ✓
- I'll call on different students to read items 1 through 18. Don't say the answers.
b. (Call on a student to read each item.)
- Item 1. [Why couldn't Nancy see very well when she walked to the kitchen?]
- Item 2. [Why didn't Nancy act like a baby when she was very hungry?]
- Item 3. [Was Nancy frightened when she climbed the kitchen counter?]
- Item 4. [If she fell, she wouldn't get *blank*.]
- Item 5. [What did Nancy smell on the kitchen counter?]
- Item 6. [How many pieces of toast were on the plate?]
- Item 7. [That pile looked as tall as a *blank* to Nancy.]
- Item 8. [Did Nancy have to climb the pile of toast to get something to eat?]
- Item 9. [What did she find to eat on the counter?]
- Item 10. [How many toast crumbs did Nancy eat?]
- Item 11. [Each crumb was as big as *blank*.]
- Item 12. [Nancy hated toast when she was full-sized. Why doesn't she hate toast now?]

Lesson 33   **181**

- Item 13. *[How much does Nancy weigh?]*
- Item 14. *[Nancy ate a lot of food in one day. How much did that food weigh?]*
- Item 15. *[Water has a <u>blank</u>.]*
- Item 16. *[Small animals don't get hurt when they <u>blank</u>.]*
- Item 17. *[The food that a small animal eats each day weighs <u>blank</u>.]*
- Item 18. *[Small animals have a voice that is <u>blank</u>.]*

End-of-Lesson Activities

INDEPENDENT WORK

Now finish your independent work for lesson 33. Raise your hand when you're finished. (Observe students and give feedback.)

WORKCHECK

a. (Direct students to take out their marking pencils.)
- We're going to check your independent work. Remember, if you got an item wrong, make an **X** next to the item. Don't change any answers.

b. (For each item: Read the item. Call on a student to answer it. If the answer is wrong, say the correct answer. Refer to the Answer Key for the correct answers.)

c. Now use your marking pencil to fix up any items you got wrong. Remember, all mistakes must be fixed up before you hand in your independent work.

WRITING-SPELLING

(Present Writing-Spelling lesson 33 after completing Reading lesson 33. See Writing-Spelling Guide.)

ACTIVITY

(Present Activity 11 after completing Reading lesson 33. See Activities Across the Curriculum.)

Lesson 34

EXERCISE 1
VOCABULARY REVIEW

a. Here's the new vocabulary sentence: He is supposed to make a decision in a couple of days.
- Everybody, say the sentence. Get ready. (Signal.) *He is supposed to make a decision in a couple of days.*
- (Repeat until firm.)

b. What part means **make up his mind?** (Signal.) *Make a decision.*
- What word means **two?** (Signal.) *Couple.*
- What part means **should?** (Signal.) *Supposed to.*

c. (Repeat step b until firm.)

EXERCISE 2
READING WORDS
Column 1

a. **Find lesson 34 in your textbook.** ✓
- Touch column 1. ✓
- (Teacher reference:)

1. neither	3. manage
2. remind	4. prove

b. Word 1 is **neither.** What word? (Signal.) *Neither.*
- Spell **neither.** Get ready. (Tap for each letter.) *N-E-I-T-H-E-R.*

c. Word 2 is **remind.** What word? (Signal.) *Remind.*
- Spell **remind.** Get ready. (Tap for each letter.) *R-E-M-I-N-D.*

d. Word 3 is **manage.** What word? (Signal.) *Manage.*
- Spell **manage.** Get ready. (Tap for each letter.) *M-A-N-A-G-E.*
- When you work hard to do something, you manage to do it. Here's another way of saying **He worked hard to keep swimming: He managed to keep swimming.**
- Your turn. What's another way of saying **He worked hard to keep swimming?** (Signal.) *He managed to keep swimming.*
- What's another way of saying **The baby worked hard to walk?** (Signal.) *The baby managed to walk.*

e. Word 4 is **prove.** What word? (Signal.) *Prove.*
- Spell **prove.** Get ready. (Tap for each letter.) *P-R-O-V-E.*
- When you prove something, you show that it is true. When you prove that you can stand up, you show it's true that you can stand up.
- What would you have to do to prove that they are serving spaghetti for lunch? (Call on a student. Idea: *Show it's true that they are serving spaghetti for lunch.*)
- What would you have to do to prove that it is raining outside? (Call on a student. Idea: *Show it's true that it's raining outside.*)

f. Let's read those words again, the fast way.
- Word 1. What word? (Signal.) *Neither.*
- (Repeat for words 2–4.)

g. (Repeat step f until firm.)

Column 2

h. Find column 2. ✓
- (Teacher reference:)

1. answered	3. worried
2. learned	4. managed

- All these words end with the letters **E-D.**

i. Word 1. What word? (Signal.) *Answered.*
- (Repeat for words 2–4.)

j. (Repeat step i until firm.)

Column 3

k. Find column 3. ✓
- (Teacher reference:)

1. <u>be</u>come	4. <u>sound</u>ly
2. <u>sob</u>bing	5. <u>dar</u>ling
3. <u>your</u>self	6. <u>in</u>stead

- These words have more than one syllable. The first syllable is underlined.

l. Word 1. What's the first syllable? (Signal.) *be.*

Lesson 34 183

- What's the whole word? (Signal.) *Become.*
m. Word 2. What's the first syllable? (Signal.) *sob.*
- What's the whole word? (Signal.) *Sobbing.*
n. Word 3. What's the first syllable? (Signal.) *your.*
- What's the whole word? (Signal.) *Yourself.*
o. Word 4. What's the first syllable? (Signal.) *sound.*
- What's the whole word? (Signal.) *Soundly.*
p. Word 5. What's the first syllable? (Signal.) *dar.*
- What's the whole word? (Signal.) *Darling.*
q. Word 6. What's the first syllable? (Signal.) *in.*
- What's the whole word? (Signal.) *Instead.*
r. Let's read those words again, the fast way.
- Word 1. What word? (Signal.) *Become.*
- (Repeat for words 2–6.)
s. (Repeat step r until firm.)

Column 4

t. Find column 4. ✓
- (Teacher reference:)

1. couple	4. important
2. whirl	5. expression
3. moments	6. swirl

u. Word 1. What word? (Signal.) *Couple.*
- (Repeat for words 2–6.)
v. (Repeat step u until firm.)

Individual Turns

(For columns 1–4: Call on individual students, each to read one to three words per turn.)

EXERCISE 3

STORY READING

Note: Ask questions marked **1** during the first reading. Ask questions marked **2** during the second reading.

a. Find part B in your textbook. ✓
- The error limit for this story is 9.
- Read carefully and don't make more than 9 errors. I'm going to ask some questions as you read the story. Then I'll read the story and ask more questions.
b. Everybody, touch the title. ✓
- (Call on a student to read the title.) [*The Green Man Visits Nancy Again.*]
- What's going to happen in this story? (Call on a student. Idea: *The green man is going to visit Nancy again.*)
c. (Call on individual students to read the story, each student reading two or three sentences at a time. Ask questions marked **1**.)

- (Correct errors: Tell the word. Direct the student to reread the sentence.)
- (If the group makes more than 9 errors, direct the students to reread the story.)

d. (After the group has read the selection making no more than 9 errors, read the story to the students and ask questions marked **2**.)

The Green Man Visits Nancy Again

Nancy was full.

2. Why was she full? (Call on a student. Idea: *Because she'd eaten bread crumbs the size of footballs.*)

She didn't feel like climbing down from the counter top, so she just jumped.

2. Everybody, will she hurt herself? (Signal.) *No.*
2. Why not? (Call on a student. Ideas: *Because very small things don't hurt themselves when they fall from high places; because she's so small.*)

For Nancy, it was like jumping from the top of a building that is more than one hundred stories tall. But she landed on her feet as easily as you would if you jumped from a chair to the floor.

2. Would it be hard for you to jump from a chair to the floor? (Call on a student.) *No.*
2. That's how easy it was for Nancy to jump down from the counter.

184 Lesson 34

She walked back to her dollhouse. By the time she got back in bed, it was almost time for the sun to come up. She wasn't very tired, but she made a decision to sleep.

2. What does it mean that she made a decision to sleep? (Call on a student. Idea: *She made up her mind to sleep.*)

She closed her eyes, and in a few moments, she was sleeping soundly.

2. Everybody, if you sleep soundly, is it easy for something to wake you up? (Signal.) *No.*

"Wake up, wake up," a loud voice said. Nancy opened her eyes. For a moment she didn't know where she was or what was standing in front of her. It was green and it was speaking in a loud voice, "Come on and wake up. Wake up."

1. What do you think it was? (Call on a student. Idea: *The green man.*)

"I'm awake," Nancy said. Her voice sounded thick and sleepy. The room was light. In fact, things looked so bright that Nancy had to cover her eyes.

2. Everybody, show me how you cover your eyes when things look very bright. ✓
2. If the room was very bright, was it still nighttime? (Signal.) *No.*

"Is that you?" she asked.
The little green man answered, "Of course it's me. I've come to see if you're happy."
"No, I'm not happy," Nancy said.
"And why not?" the green man asked.
"Because I don't like being so little."
"Oh," the green man said and sat down. "I thought you never wanted to get big."
"I was wrong," Nancy replied. "I want to get big. I want to grow up. I want to be back with my parents and my friends."

The little green man said, "I can change you back to your regular size if I want to. But I'm not going to change you unless you tell me some things that you learned." The green man stood up and stared at Nancy. "What have you learned about kicking and screaming and acting like a baby?"
Nancy smiled. "I don't have to act like a baby because I can take care of myself."

2. Nancy learned that she doesn't have to act like a baby. Why not? (Call on a student. Idea: *Because she can take care of herself.*)

The man said, "And when nobody is around, what do you do instead of kicking and crying?"
Nancy said, "You have to take care of yourself."
"Good," the green man said. "I'm glad that you learned things about yourself. But have you learned things about the world you live in?"

1. Did she? (Call on a student. Idea: *Yes.*)
1. Name something she learned. (Call on different students. Ideas: *Small things don't hurt themselves when they fall from high places; water has a skin; small things have very high voices; the food that a small animal eats each day weighs more than the animal.*)

"Lots of things," Nancy said, and she began to list them. "I've learned that little things don't hurt themselves when they fall from high places. I've learned that. . ." Suddenly everything seemed to whirl and swirl around. Nancy tried to keep talking. "I've learned . . ." She felt very dizzy.
MORE NEXT TIME

1. Go back to the beginning of the story. Follow along while I read.
2. What do you think is happening? (Call on a student. Idea: *Nancy's getting bigger.*)

Lesson 34 185

2. Everybody, show me her regular size. ✓
2. Show me her size when the green man talked to her. ✓

EXERCISE 4
PAIRED PRACTICE

You're going to read aloud to your partner. Today the **B** members will read first. Then the **A** members will read from the star to the end of the story.
(Observe students and give feedback.)

EXERCISE 5
WRITTEN ITEMS
Story Items

a. **Find item 1 on your worksheet.** ✓
- Items 1 through 11 are about today's story. I'll call on different students to read the items, but don't say the answers.

b. (For each item: Call on a student to read the item.)
- Item 1. [Was Nancy afraid to jump down from the counter top?]
- Item 2. [Did she get hurt when she jumped?]
- Item 3. [Tell why.]
- Item 4. [Who woke Nancy?]
- Item 5. [Was Nancy happy about being so little?]
- Item 6. [Did Nancy change her mind about growing up?]
- Item 7. [Nancy learned that she doesn't have to act like a baby because <u>blank</u>.]
- Item 8. [Small animals don't get hurt when they <u>blank</u>.]
- Item 9. [Small animals have a voice that is <u>blank</u>.]
- Item 10. [Water has a <u>blank</u>.]
- Item 11. [The food that a small animal eats each day weighs <u>blank</u>.]

End-of-Lesson Activities

INDEPENDENT WORK

Now finish your independent work for lesson 34. Raise your hand when you're finished.
(Observe students and give feedback.)

WORKCHECK

a. (Direct students to take out their marking pencils.)
- We're going to check your independent work. Remember, if you got an item wrong, make an **X** next to the item. Don't change any answers.
b. (For each item: Read the item. Call on a student to answer it. If the answer is wrong, say the correct answer. Refer to the Answer Key for the correct answers.)
c. Now use your marking pencil to fix up any items you got wrong. Remember, all mistakes must be fixed up before you hand in your independent work.

Note: A special project occurs after lesson 35. See page 192 for the materials you'll need.

WRITING-SPELLING

(Present Writing-Spelling lesson 34 after completing Reading lesson 34. See Writing-Spelling Guide.)

ACTIVITY

(Present Activity 12 after completing Reading lesson 34. See Activities Across the Curriculum.)

Lesson 35

Materials: You will need a firm plastic ruler for a demonstration in exercise 3. Each student will need their thermometer chart for exercise 5.

EXERCISE 1
VOCABULARY REVIEW

a. You learned a sentence that tells who he motioned to.
- Everybody, say the sentence. Get ready. (Signal.) *He motioned to the flight attendant ahead of him.*
- (Repeat until firm.)

b. You learned a sentence that tells how fast the traffic was moving.
- Everybody, say that sentence. Get ready. (Signal.) *The traffic was moving forty miles per hour.*
- (Repeat until firm.)

c. Here's the last sentence you learned: He is supposed to make a decision in a couple of days.
- Everybody, say the sentence. Get ready. (Signal.) *He is supposed to make a decision in a couple of days.*
- (Repeat until firm.)

d. What part means **make up his mind?** (Signal.) *Make a decision.*
- What word means **two?** (Signal.) *Couple.*
- What part means **should?** (Signal.) *Supposed to.*
- (Repeat step d until firm.)

e. Once more. Say the sentence that tells what he is supposed to do. Get ready. (Signal.) *He is supposed to make a decision in a couple of days.*

EXERCISE 2
READING WORDS

Column 1

a. **Find lesson 35 in your textbook.** ✓
- Touch column 1. ✓
- (Teacher reference:)

1. several	4. sobbing
2. continue	5. worried
3. distance	6. couple

b. Word 1 is **several.** What word? (Signal.) *Several.*
- Spell **several.** Get ready. (Tap for each letter.) *S-E-V-E-R-A-L.*
- Several is more than two, but is not a lot. If you have several pieces of paper, could you have two? (Signal.) *No.*
- Could you have 200? (Signal.) *No.*
- Could you have four? (Signal.) *Yes.*

c. Word 2 is **continue.** What word? (Signal.) *Continue.*

d. Word 3 is **distance.** What word? (Signal.) *Distance.*
- Spell **distance.** Get ready. (Tap for each letter.) *D-I-S-T-A-N-C-E.*
- The farther apart things are, the bigger the distance between them. Hold your hands up in front of you.
- Now make a bigger distance between your hands. ✓
- Now make a smaller distance between your hands. ✓

e. Word 4. What word? (Signal.) *Sobbing.*
- (Repeat for words 5 and 6.)

f. (Repeat step e until firm.)

Column 2

g. Find column 2. ✓
- (Teacher reference:)

1. desk	4. instead
2. snaps	5. managed
3. prove	6. reminds

h. Word 1. What word? (Signal.) *Desk.*
- (Repeat for words 2–6.)

i. (Repeat step h until firm.)

Column 3

j. Find column 3. ✓
- (Teacher reference:)

1. expression	4. becoming
2. darling	5. important
3. neither	

k. Word 1. What word? (Signal.) *Expression.*
- (Repeat for words 2–5.)

l. (Repeat step k until firm.)

Individual Turns

(For columns 1–3: Call on individual students, each to read one to three words per turn.)

EXERCISE 3
COMPREHENSION PASSAGE

Note: You will need a firm plastic ruler.

a. Find part B in your textbook. ✓
- You're going to read the last story about Nancy. First you'll read the information passage. It gives some information about sound.

b. Everybody, touch the title. ✓
- (Call on a student to read the title.) *[Sounds That Objects Make.]*
- Everybody, what's the title? (Signal.) *Sounds That Objects Make.*

c. (Call on individual students to read the passage, each student reading two or three sentences at a time. Ask the specified questions as the students read.)

> **Sounds That Objects Make**
>
> In lesson 26 you read about Nancy's voice and what happened to it when she became smaller and smaller.

- What happened to her voice? (Call on a student. Ideas: *It got smaller; it sounded like a squeak.*)
- Everybody, is the story about Nancy a **true story** or a **make-believe story?** (Signal.) *A make-believe story.*
- But if Nancy did get smaller, her voice really would get higher.

> Here's the rule about your voice: <u>If you get smaller, your voice gets higher.</u>

- Everybody, listen to that rule again. If you get smaller, your voice gets higher.
- Say that rule. Get ready. (Signal.) *If you get smaller, your voice gets higher.*
- (Repeat until firm.)

> Follow these instructions and you will see how sounds get higher when things get smaller.

- First we'll read the instructions. Then you'll tell me how to follow the instructions. These instructions will show you how the sound gets higher when things get smaller.

> 1. Place a plastic ruler so that one end of it is on your desk and the other end hangs over the edge of the desk. Make sure that most of the ruler hangs over the desk. Picture 1 on the next page shows how to place the ruler on your desk.

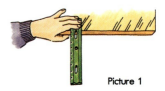

Picture 1

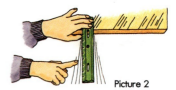

Picture 2

- Everybody, touch picture 1. ✓
- Look at how much of the ruler hangs over the desk.

> 2. Hold down the end of the ruler that is on the desk.
> 3. Bend the other end of the ruler down. Then let it go so it snaps back. The ruler will make a sound.
> 4. Now move the ruler so a smaller part of the ruler hangs over the edge of the desk. The ruler will make a sound that is higher.
> 5. Now move the ruler so that even less of the ruler hangs over the edge of the desk. The ruler will make a sound that is even higher.

- Now you have to tell me how to follow the instructions.
- What do I do first? (Call on a student. Idea: *Place the ruler on the desk so most of the ruler hangs over the edge of the desk.*)
- (After carrying out each direction, ask, "What do I do next?" and call on a student. Continue until the demonstration is completed.)

- How does the sound change when less and less of the ruler hangs over the desk? (Call on a student. Idea: *The sound gets higher.*)

> **The ruler works just like your voice. When your body gets smaller, the sound of your voice gets higher.**

- Listen to that again. When your body gets smaller, the sound of your voice gets higher. Everybody, say that. Get ready. (Signal.) *When your body gets smaller, the sound of your voice gets higher.*
- What happens to your voice when you get smaller? (Signal.) *It gets higher.*
- What happens to the sound when the part of the ruler that hangs over the desk gets smaller? (Signal.) *It gets higher.*

EXERCISE 4
STORY READING

Note: Ask questions marked **1** during the first reading. Ask questions marked **2** during the second reading.

a. Find part C in your textbook. ✓
- The error limit for this story is 9.
- Read carefully and don't make more than 9 errors. I'm going to ask some questions as you read the story. Then I'll read the story and ask more questions.

b. Everybody, touch the title. ✓
- (Call on a student to read the title.) [*Nancy Becomes Regular Size.*]
- What's going to happen in this story? (Call on a student. Idea: *Nancy will become regular size.*)
- Everybody, show me her regular size. ✓
- Show me how big she was when we left her in the last story. ✓

c. (Call on individual students to read the story, each student reading two or three sentences at a time. Ask questions marked **1**.)

- (Correct errors: Tell the word. Direct the student to reread the sentence.)
- (If the group makes more than 9 errors, direct the students to reread the story.)

d. (After the group has read the selection making no more than 9 errors, read the story to the students and ask questions marked **2**.)

> **Nancy Becomes Regular Size**
>
> The whole room seemed to be turning and swirling. Nancy felt so dizzy that she was afraid she would fall over. She kept trying to tell the little green man about the things she had learned. Finally, she managed to say, "I learned that water has a skin."
>
> Nancy closed her eyes and talked very loudly. She hoped that she could stop the dizzy feeling by talking loudly.
>
> Suddenly, Nancy opened her eyes. But she didn't see the little green man. She saw the face of a woman.

1. Who do you think it is? (Call on a student. Idea: *Nancy's mom.*)

> **The expression on that woman's face was one of shock. Her eyes were wide open and so was her mouth.**

2. Everybody, show me the expression of the face. ✓

> "Where . . . ," the woman said, "where have you been?"
>
> The expression changed. Tears began to form in the woman's eyes. Then Nancy's mother threw her arms around Nancy. "Oh, Nancy," she said. Her voice was sobbing, and she was holding Nancy very tightly. "Oh, darling," she said. "We've been so worried . . . "

2. Why was her mother crying? (Call on a student. Idea: *Because she was so happy to see Nancy.*)

> **Nancy started to cry. She didn't want to cry, but she was so glad to see her mother, and it felt so good to have her mother hold her. She couldn't hold back the tears. "Oh, Mother," she said.**

2. Everybody, was Nancy crying because she felt bad? (Signal.) *No.*

> For a few minutes, neither Nancy nor her mother said anything.

1. Everybody, who talked? (Signal.) *Nobody.*

> Then, her mother grabbed Nancy's hands and held them tightly as she said, "Nancy, where have you been? The police have been looking for you and . . . And Sally told a crazy story about you becoming very small."

2. Everybody, did her mother believe the story? (Signal.) *No.*
2. Why wouldn't her mother believe a story about Nancy shrinking up into a tiny thing? (Call on a student. Idea: *Because it sounded crazy.*)

> "It's true," Nancy said. "I know it sounds crazy, but I can prove to you that it really happened. I can tell you where the crumbs of toast are on the counter. I can tell you about the drops of water in the bathroom." Nancy said. "And I can tell you other things."

2. Name two things Nancy could tell about to prove that she had been small. (Call on a student. Ideas: *The crumbs of toast on the kitchen counter; the drops of water in the bathroom.*)
2. What else could she tell? (Call on different students. Ideas: *Tiny things have very high voices; tiny things don't get hurt when they fall from high places; the food a small animal eats each day may weigh as much as the animal; water has a skin.*)

> Nancy's mother was smiling and crying and laughing at the same time. "Oh, Nancy, I don't know what to believe, but I'm very glad to have my darling little baby back."

1. Everybody, does Nancy want to be a darling little baby anymore? (Signal.) *No.*

> Nancy said, "I'm not a baby. That's the most important thing I learned when I was less than one centimeter tall. I can take care of myself. And I don't mind growing up at all."
> That story took place a couple of years ago. Nancy is still growing up. And she's doing a fine job. She doesn't act like a baby—not even when things go wrong. Instead, she reminds herself, "I can take care of myself." And that's just what she does.
>
> THE END

1. Go back to the beginning of the story. Follow along while I read.
2. What does she tell herself when things go wrong? (Call on a student. Idea: *I can take care of myself.*)
2. Do you think she's a nicer girl than she was before? (Call on a student. Idea: *Yes.*)

EXERCISE 5

READING CHECKOUTS

Note: There is a reading checkout in this lesson; therefore, there is no paired practice.

a. Today is a reading-checkout day. While you're doing your independent work, I'm going to call on you one at a time to read part of the story from lesson 34. When I call you to come and do your checkout, bring your thermometer chart.
- Remember, you pass the checkout by reading the passage in less than a minute without making more than 2 mistakes. And when you pass the checkout, you'll color the space for lesson 35 on your thermometer chart.
b. (Call on individual students to read the portion of story 34 marked with ✦.)
- (Time the student. Note words that are missed and total number of words read.)
- (Teacher reference:)

> 🌼 The little green man answered, "Of course it's me. I've come to see if you're happy."
> "No, I'm not happy," Nancy said.
> "And why not?" the green man asked.
> "Because I don't like being so little."
> "Oh," the green man said and sat down. "I thought you never wanted to [50] get big."
> "I was wrong," Nancy replied. "I want to get big. I want to grow up. I want to be back with my parents [75] and my friends."
> The little green man said, "I can change you back to your regular size if I want to. But I'm not going 🌼 [100] to change you unless you tell me some things that you learned."

- (If the student reads the passage in one minute or less and makes no more than 2 errors, direct the student to color in the space for lesson 35 on the new thermometer chart.)
- (If the student makes any mistakes, point to each word that was misread and identify it.)
- (If the student does not meet the time-error criterion for the passage, direct the student to practice reading the story with the assigned partner.)

EXERCISE 6

WRITTEN ITEMS

Story Items

a. **Find item 5 on your worksheet.** ✓
- Items 5 through 11 are about today's story. I'll call on different students to read the items, but don't say the answers.
b. (For each item: Call on a student to read the item.)
- Item 5. [Why did Nancy cry when she saw her mother?]
- Nancy told about two things to prove that she had been very small. Item 6. [There were crumbs of blank on the counter.]
- Item 7. [There were drops of blank in the blank.]
- Item 8. [Does Nancy want to be called a baby now?]
- Item 9. [Does Nancy want to grow up now?]
- Item 10. [When things go wrong, Nancy tells herself, "I can take blank."]
- Item 11. [One of these pictures shows Nancy when she was very small. Which picture is that?]

End-of-Lesson Activities

INDEPENDENT WORK

Now finish your independent work for lesson 35. Raise your hand when you're finished. (Observe students and give feedback.)

WORKCHECK

a. (Direct students to take out their marking pencils.)
- We're going to check your independent work. Remember, if you got an item wrong, make an **X** next to the item. Don't change any answers.
b. (For each item: Read the item. Call on a student to answer it. If the answer is wrong, say the correct answer. Refer to the Answer Key for the correct answers.)
c. Now use your marking pencil to fix up any items you got wrong. Remember, all mistakes must be fixed up before you hand in your independent work.

WRITING-SPELLING

(Present Writing-Spelling lesson 35 after completing Reading lesson 35. See Writing-Spelling Guide.)

Special Project

Note: After completing Lesson 35, do this special project with the students. You may do the project during another part of the school day.

Purpose: To conduct an experiment to show that substances like steel can float on water.

Materials: Steel wool (preferably without soap), a transparent bowl, water, and several steel objects, like a wrench, screw, or nails.

a. You're going to show how strong the skin on top of water is by floating something that is made of steel.
- (Present larger steel objects and a transparent container nearly filled with water.)
- All these objects are made of steel, and things made of steel sink in water. No matter how careful you are, you can't float these objects on water.
- (Direct individual students to try floating the larger objects on the water.)

b. Make a small tight wad of steel wool, about 1/4" in diameter. This material is steel wool. It is thin hairs of steel. The steel is just like the steel in the other objects, so this little ball of steel wool should sink, just like the other steel objects did.
- (Challenge individual students to see if they can make the small ball float.)

c. (After students conclude that the steel won't float:) The Nancy stories told us that if something is small enough, it will float on water.
- (Present students with strands of steel wool. Each strand should be about three inches long. Challenge students to see if they can float the single strands on the water. Remind them:) Put the steel wool down very carefully. Remember, if it breaks the skin on top of the water, it will sink.

d. (After students have confirmed that they can float single strands on the water, have a challenge game.)
- Let's see who can float the most spokes of steel wool.
- (To make spokes, a student first floats one strand, then makes an X by crossing the first strand with a second, then continues to add strands that cross in the same place. Make a "Best Steel Floater" award for the winner.)

e. (Alternative demonstration: For this demonstration you will need a small piece of filter paper and a small needle or a straight pin.)
- (Have students try to float a small needle. They probably will not be able to do it. [Make sure the needle is perfectly dry before each trial.])
- (Tell students that you think you can float the needle. Place the needle on a round piece of filter paper (the type used for coffee filters). The filter will float at first and then, as it gets wet, sink. As the filter sinks, the needle will probably continue to float. Point out the way the skin of the water bends down around the needle. It will be quite visible.)
- (Ask students why the needle floated when it started out on the filter paper but didn't float when they tried placing it directly on the surface of the water. [Idea: The chances are that they could not place it on the water without putting part of the needle below the surface of the water. When the needle is on the filter paper, it is positioned so that no part of it breaks the surface skin of the water.])
- (After the demonstration, direct the students to write a report in which they describe the experiments and tell what they learned.)

Lessons 36–40 • Planning Page

Looking Ahead

	Lesson 36	Lesson 37	Lesson 38	Lesson 39	Lesson 40
Lesson Events	Vocabulary Review Reading Words Comprehension Passage Story Reading Paired Practice Independent Work Workcheck Writing-Spelling Activity	**Vocabulary Sentence** Reading Words Vocabulary Review Comprehension Passage Story Reading Paired Practice Independent Work Workcheck Writing-Spelling Activity	Vocabulary Review Reading Words Comprehension Passage Story Reading Paired Practice Independent Work Workcheck Writing-Spelling	Vocabulary Review Reading Words Comprehension Passage Story Reading Globe Paired Practice Independent Work Workcheck Writing-Spelling	Fact Game Reading Checkouts Test Marking the Test Test Remedies Literature Lesson
Vocabulary Sentence	#7: The <u>traffic</u> was moving forty miles <u>per</u> hour.	#9: <u>Several</u> paths <u>continued</u> for a great <u>distance</u>.	#9: <u>Several</u> paths <u>continued</u> for a great <u>distance</u>.	sentence #7 sentence #8 sentence #9	
Reading Words: Word Types	modeled words mixed words	modeled words –ed words words with endings mixed words	modeled words **e-w** words compound words mixed words	modeled words words with endings mixed words multi-syllable words	
New Vocabulary	a record	Kennedy Airport speedometer realized	San Francisco passenger realized	insect engine passengers brewed	
Comprehension Passages	Miles Per Hour	More About Pushes in the Opposite Direction	Speedometers	Airplane Crew Members	
Story	A Push in the Opposite Direction	Herman the Fly	Herman Goes to Kennedy Airport	Herman Ends Up on a Jumbo Jet	
Skill Items	Titles Vocabulary sentences	Same and Different	Deductions Vocabulary	Vocabulary sentence	Test: Same and Different; Vocabulary sentences #7, 8
Special Materials		Drawing materials for Activity		Globe	Thermometer charts, dice, Fact Game 40, Fact Game Answer Key, scorecard sheets, *materials for literature project.
Special Projects/ Activities	Activity after lesson 36	Activity after lesson 37			

* Literature anthology; blackline masters 4A, 4B, 4C; lined paper; scissors; tape or paste; drawing materials; poster making materials.

Lesson 36

EXERCISE 1
VOCABULARY REVIEW

a. You learned a sentence that tells how fast the traffic was moving.
- Everybody, say that sentence. Get ready. (Signal.) *The traffic was moving forty miles per hour.*
- (Repeat until firm.)

b. I'll say part of the sentence. When I stop, you say the next word. Listen: The . . . Everybody, what's the next word? (Signal.) *Traffic.*

c. Listen: The traffic was moving forty miles . . . Everybody, what's the next word? (Signal.) *Per.*
- Say the whole sentence. Get ready. (Signal.) *The traffic was moving forty miles per hour.*

EXERCISE 2
READING WORDS

Column 1

a. Find lesson 36 in your textbook. ✓ Touch column 1. ✓
- (Teacher reference:)

1. a record	4. space
2. cabbage	5. Herman
3. maggot	

b. Number 1 is **a record.** What words? (Signal.) *A record.*
- Somebody who sets a record does something better than anybody has done before. The person who swims the fastest sets a record for fast swimming.

c. Word 2 is **cabbage.** What word? (Signal.) *Cabbage.*
- Spell cabbage. Get ready. (Tap for each letter.) C-A-B-B-A-G-E.

d. Word 3 is **maggot.** What word? (Signal.) *Maggot.*
- Spell maggot. Get ready. (Tap for each letter.) M-A-G-G-O-T.

e. Word 4 is **space.** What word? (Signal.) *Space.*
- Spell space. Get ready. (Tap for each letter.) S-P-A-C-E.

f. Word 5 is the name **Herman.** What name? (Signal.) *Herman.*
- Spell Herman. Get ready. (Tap for each letter.) H-E-R-M-A-N.

g. Let's read those words again, the fast way.
- Number 1. What words? (Signal.) *A record.*
- Word 2. What word? (Signal.) *Cabbage.*
- (Repeat for words 3–5.)

h. (Repeat step g until firm.)

Column 2

i. Find column 2. ✓
- (Teacher reference:)

1. lifetime	4. crawled
2. thrown	5. continued
3. tenth	

j. Word 1. What word? (Signal.) *Lifetime.*
- (Repeat for words 2–5.)

k. (Repeat step j until firm.)

Column 3

l. Find column 3. ✓
- (Teacher reference:)

1. fastest	4. rotten
2. apart	5. several
3. worm	6. distance

m. Word 1. What word? (Signal.) *Fastest.*
- (Repeat for words 2–6.)

n. (Repeat step m until firm.)

Individual Turns
(For columns 1–3: Call on individual students, each to read one to three words per turn.)

EXERCISE 3
COMPREHENSION PASSAGE

a. Find part B in your textbook. ✓
- You're going to read a story about a fly. First you'll read the information passage. It gives some facts about miles per hour.

b. Everybody, touch the title. ✓
- (Call on a student to read the title.) [Miles Per Hour.]
- Everybody, what's the title? (Signal.) *Miles Per Hour.*

c. (Call on individual students to read the passage, each student reading two or three sentences at a time.)

Miles Per Hour

When we talk about <u>miles</u>, we tell how far apart things are.

- Everybody, what does **miles** tell? (Signal.) *How far apart things are.*

When we talk about <u>miles per hour</u>, we tell how fast things move.

- Everybody, what does **miles per hour** tell? (Signal.) *How fast things move.*
- Remember, **miles** tells how far; **miles per hour** tells how fast.

The boat was three miles away. Does that tell how far or how fast?

- Everybody, what's the answer? (Signal.) *How far.*

The boat was going three miles per hour. Does that tell how far or how fast?

- Everybody, what's the answer? (Signal.) *How fast.*

The faster something moves, the bigger the number of miles per hour. Ten is a bigger number than nine. So ten miles per hour is faster than nine miles per hour.

- Everybody, which is faster, three miles per hour or seven miles per hour? (Signal.) *Seven miles per hour.*
- Which is faster, 100 miles per hour or 88 miles per hour? (Signal.) *100 miles per hour.*

Look at pictures A, B, and C. The number below each dog shows how fast that dog is running.

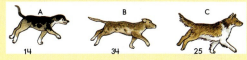

How fast is dog A running?

- Everybody, what's the number below dog A? (Signal.) *14.*
- So how fast is dog A running? (Signal.) *14 miles per hour.*

How fast is dog B running?

- Everybody, look at the number below dog B. How fast is dog B running? (Signal.) *34 miles per hour.*

How fast is dog C running?

- Everybody, what's the answer? (Signal.) *25 miles per hour.*

Which dog is running fastest?

- Everybody, what's the answer? (Signal.) *Dog B.*
- Which dog is running the slowest? (Signal.) *Dog A.*

Which dog is in front of the others?

- Everybody, what's the answer? (Signal.) *Dog C.*

Is that dog the fastest dog?

- Everybody, what's the answer? (Signal.) *No.*
- Dog B is the fastest. If they keep running, dog B will pass dog C.
- I'll say things that tell **how far** or **how fast.**
- Listen: 20 miles. Everybody, does that tell **how far** or **how fast**? (Signal.) *How far.*
- Listen: 20 miles per hour. Does that tell **how far** or **how fast**? (Signal.) *How fast.*
- Listen: 4 miles per hour. Does that tell **how far** or **how fast**? (Signal.) *How fast.*
- (Repeat until firm.)

EXERCISE 4
STORY READING

a. Find part C in your textbook. ✓
- We're going to read this story two times. First you'll read it out loud and make no more than 6 errors. Then I'll read it and ask questions.

b. Everybody, touch the title. ✓
- (Call on a student to read the title.) [A Push in the Opposite Direction.]
- Everybody, what's the title? (Signal.) A Push in the Opposite Direction.

c. (Call on individual students to read the story, each student reading two or three sentences at a time.)

- (Correct errors: Tell the word. Direct the student to reread the sentence.)
- (If the group makes more than 6 errors, direct the students to reread the story.)

d. (After the group has read the selection making no more than 6 errors:)
Now I'll read the story and ask questions.

A Push in the Opposite Direction

You've learned this rule: **The balloon moves in the opposite direction the air moves.**

You read about Goad. Here's the rule about Goad: **Goad moves in the opposite direction the air moves.**
If the air comes out of Goad's mouth in this direction ⟶, Goad moves in the opposite direction. She will move backwards, in this direction: ⟵.
If the air comes out of Goad's mouth in this direction ↗, in which direction will Goad move?

- Everybody, point and show which direction Goad will move. ✓

If the air coming out of Goad's mouth is blowing south, in which direction will Goad move?

- Everybody, what's the answer? (Signal.) *North.*

If the air coming out of Goad's mouth is blowing down, in which direction will Goad move?

- Everybody, what's the answer? (Signal.) *Up.*

There is a rule like this one for everything that moves. Look at picture 1. The boy is standing on a block of ice. The boy is going to move in this direction: ⟶.
When the boy starts to move in this direction ⟶, the block of ice will move in the opposite direction.
Look at picture 2. The arrow shows the boy moving in one direction and the ice moving in the opposite direction.

- Everybody, point to show the direction the boy is trying to move. ✓
- Point to show the direction the ice is moving. ✓
- Let's say the boy tries to jump to the east. In which direction will the block of ice move? (Signal.) *West.*

Look at picture 3. The girl wants to jump from the boat to the dock. Point to show which direction she will jump.

- Everybody, do it. ✓

If she jumps in that direction, the boat will move in the opposite direction.

- Everybody, show the direction the boat will move. ✓

When the boat moves in the opposite direction, the girl will fall in the water.
Picture 4 shows what happens when the girl tries to jump to the dock. In which direction did the girl start to move?

- Everybody, point to show me. ✓
- If the girl is trying to jump south, in which direction will the boat move? (Signal.) *North.*

In which direction did the boat move?

- Everybody, point to show me. ✓

Did the girl land on the dock?

- Everybody, tell me. (Signal.) *No.*

- Why not? (Call on a student. Idea: *Because the boat moved.*)

> **The rule about how things move works for everything. When something tries to move in one direction, something else tries to move in the opposite direction.**

- Everybody, what always happens when something tries to move in one direction? (Signal.) *Something else tries to move in the opposite direction.*

EXERCISE 5
PAIRED PRACTICE

You're going to read aloud to your partner. Today the **A** members will read first. Then the **B** members will read from the star to the end of the story.
(Observe students and give feedback.)

End-of-Lesson Activities

INDEPENDENT WORK

Now finish your independent work for lesson 36. Raise your hand when you're finished. (Observe students and give feedback.)

WORKCHECK

a. (Direct students to take out their marking pencils.)
- We're going to check your independent work. Remember, if you got an item wrong, make an **X** next to the item. Don't change any answers.
b. (For each item: Read the item. Call on a student to answer it. If the answer is wrong, say the correct answer. Refer to the Answer Key for the correct answers.)
c. Now use your marking pencil to fix up any items you got wrong. Remember, all mistakes must be fixed up before you hand in your independent work.

WRITING-SPELLING

(Present Writing-Spelling lesson 36 after completing Reading lesson 36. See Writing-Spelling Guide.)

ACTIVITY

(Present Activity 13 after completing Reading lesson 36. See Activities Across the Curriculum.)

Lesson 37

EXERCISE 1
VOCABULARY

a. **Find page 338 in your textbook.** ✓
- Touch sentence 9. ✓
- This is a new vocabulary sentence. It says: Several paths continued for a great distance. Everybody, read that sentence. Get ready. (Signal.) *Several paths continued for a great distance.*
- Close your eyes and say the sentence. Get ready. (Signal.) *Several paths continued for a great distance.*
- (Repeat until firm.)

b. The sentence says that **several** paths continued. That's more than two paths but less than many paths. Maybe there were four paths, maybe there were three or five. There were not fifty paths.

c. Several paths **continued.** If they continued, they kept on going. What's another word for **kept on going?** (Signal.) *Continued.*

d. A great distance is a very long way. The paths went for many miles. If the paths went for a **short** distance, they would not go very far. What's another way of saying **a very long way?** (Signal.) *A great distance.*

e. Listen: Several paths continued for a great distance.
- Everybody, say the sentence. Get ready. (Signal.) *Several paths continued for a great distance.*
- (Repeat until firm.)

f. What word refers to more than two but less than a lot? (Signal.) *Several.*
- What word means **kept on going?** (Signal.) *Continued.*
- What part means **a long way?** (Signal.) *A great distance.*
- (Repeat step f until firm.)

EXERCISE 2
READING WORDS

Column 1

a. Find lesson 37 in your textbook. ✓
Touch column 1. ✓

- (Teacher reference:)

  1. Kennedy Airport   4. busy
  2. speedometer   5. meant
  3. realized

b. Number 1 is **Kennedy Airport.** What words? (Signal.) *Kennedy Airport.*
- Kennedy Airport is a large airport in New York City. It is named after a famous president of the United States, John F. Kennedy.

c. Word 2 is **speedometer.** What word? (Signal.) *Speedometer.*
- A speedometer is the dial in a vehicle that shows how fast the vehicle is moving. Everybody, what's the name of the dial that shows how fast something is moving? (Signal.) *Speedometer.*

d. Word 3 is **realized.** What word? (Signal.) *Realized.*
- Spell **realized.** Get ready. (Tap for each letter.) *R-E-A-L-I-Z-E-D.*
- When you realize something, you suddenly understand it for the first time. When you realize that you were fooled, you suddenly understand that you were fooled. What's another way of saying **She suddenly understood that she was tired?** (Signal.) *She realized that she was tired.*
- What's another way of saying **She suddenly understood that she had no money?** (Signal.) *She realized that she had no money.*

e. Word 4 is **busy.** What word? (Signal.) *Busy.*
- Spell **busy.** Get ready. (Tap for each letter.) *B-U-S-Y.*

f. Word 5 is **meant.** What word? (Signal.) *Meant.*
- Spell **meant.** Get ready. (Tap for each letter.) *M-E-A-N-T.*

g. Let's read those words again, the fast way.
- Number 1. What words? (Signal.) *Kennedy Airport.*

h. Word 2. What word? (Signal.) *Speedometer.*
- (Repeat for words 3–5.)

i. (Repeat steps g through i until firm.)

Column 2

j. Find column 2. ✓
- These words all end with the letters **E-D**.
- (Teacher reference:)

1. crawled	4. buzzed
2. changed	5. rubbed
3. wiggled	6. rested

k. Word 1. What word? (Signal.) *Crawled.*
- (Repeat for words 2–6.)

l. (Repeat step k until firm.)

Column 3

m. Find column 3. ✓
- These words all have an ending.
- (Teacher reference:)

1. thrown	4. sleepy
2. Herman's	5. fly's
3. tenth	

n. Word 1. What word? (Signal.) *Thrown.*
- (Repeat for words 2–5.)

o. (Repeat step n until firm.)

Column 4

p. Find column 4. ✓
- (Teacher reference:)

1. a record	4. purse
2. per	5. lifetime
3. laid	

q. Number 1. What words? (Signal.) *A record.*

r. Word 2. What word? (Signal.) *Per.*
- What's another way of saying **The car moved 30 miles each hour?** (Signal.) *The car moved 30 miles per hour.*

s. Word 3. What word? (Signal.) *Laid.*
- (Repeat for words 4 and 5.)

t. Let's read those words again.
- Number 1. What words? (Signal.) *A record.*

u. Word 2. What word? (Signal.) *Per.*
- (Repeat for words 3–5.)

v. (Repeat steps t through v until firm.)

Column 5

w. Find column 5. ✓
- (Teacher reference:)

1. rotten	4. space
2. worm	5. crew
3. maggot	6. money

x. Word 1. What word? (Signal.) *Rotten.*
- (Repeat for words 2–6.)

y. Let's read those words again.
- Word 1. What word? (Signal.) *Rotten.*
- (Repeat for words 2–6.)

z. (Repeat steps y through z until firm.)

Individual Turns

(For columns 1–5: Call on individual students, each to read one to three words per turn.)

EXERCISE 3

VOCABULARY REVIEW

a. Here's the new vocabulary sentence: Several paths continued for a great distance.
- Everybody, say the sentence. Get ready. (Signal.) *Several paths continued for a great distance.*
- (Repeat until firm.)

b. What word means **kept on going?** (Signal.) *Continued.*
- What word refers to more than two but less than a lot? (Signal.) *Several.*
- What part means **a long way?** (Signal.) *A great distance.*

EXERCISE 4

COMPREHENSION PASSAGE

a. Find part B in your textbook. ✓
- You're going to start a story about a fly. First you'll read the information passage. It gives more information about pushes in the opposite direction.

b. Everybody, touch the title. ✓
- (Call on a student to read the title.) [More About Pushes in the Opposite Direction.]
- Everybody, what's the title? (Signal.) *More About Pushes in the Opposite Direction.*

c. (Call on individual students to read the passage, each student reading two or three sentences at a time. Ask the specified questions as the students read.)

More About Pushes in the Opposite Direction

You've learned that if something tries to move in one direction, something else tries to move in the opposite direction.

A paddle works that way. You move the paddle through the water. If the paddle moves through the water in this direction ⟶ , the boat moves in the opposite direction. It moves in this direction: ⟵ .

- Point and show me the direction the paddle is moving. ✓
- Point and show me the direction the boat will move. ✓

A jet engine works the same way. The jet engine pushes air toward the back of the plane. The plane moves in the opposite direction.

- Everybody, look at the picture. Point to show the direction the air is shooting from the jet engines. ✓
- Point to the show the direction the jet is moving. ✓

The faster the jet engines shoot air toward the back of the plane, the faster the plane moves forward.

- If the air shoots out of the engines very, very fast, what does the plane do? (Call on a student. Idea: *Moves very, very fast.*)
- Everybody, does the jet move in the **same direction** as the air shooting from the engines or the **opposite direction?** (Signal.) *Opposite direction.*

EXERCISE 5

STORY READING

a. Find part C in your textbook. ✓
- We're going to read this story two times. First you'll read it out loud and make no more than 8 errors. Then I'll read it and ask questions.
b. Everybody, touch the title. ✓
- (Call on a student to read the title.) *[Herman the Fly.]*
- Everybody, what's the title? (Signal.) *Herman the Fly.*
You'll be reading about Herman the fly for fourteen lessons.
c. (Call on individual students to read the story, each student reading two or three sentences at a time.)
- (Correct errors: Tell the word. Direct the student to reread the sentence.)
- (If the group makes more than 8 errors, direct the students to reread the story.)
d. (After the group has read the selection making no more than 8 errors:) Now I'll read the story and ask questions.

Herman the Fly

Herman was a fly. He was born on some old cabbage leaves that had been thrown out. Herman's mother laid eggs on the leaves, and two days after she laid them, Herman was born.

- Everybody, how long was Herman in an egg? (Signal.) *2 days.*

He had brothers and sisters. In fact, he had 80 brothers and 90 sisters. All Herman's brothers and sisters were born on those rotten cabbage leaves.
Right after Herman was born, he didn't look like he did when he was a full-grown fly. At first Herman looked like a worm because he was a worm. Here's the fact: When flies are born, they are worms called maggots.

- Everybody, listen to that fact again. When flies are born, they are worms called maggots.
- Say that fact. (Signal.) *When flies are born, they are worms called maggots.*
- (Repeat until firm.)
- First Herman was in an egg. Everybody, how long was he in that egg? (Signal.) *2 days.*
- What do we call the thing that came out of the egg? (Signal.) *A maggot.*

For nine days, Herman was a maggot that crawled around on the cabbage eating and eating and eating.

- Everybody, how long was Herman a maggot? (Signal.) *9 days.*

On the tenth day Herman felt sleepy. He stopped eating and went to sleep. When he woke up, he had changed. He was a fly. He wiggled out of his old maggot skin, and there he was, a fly. He was one centimeter long. Like all flies, he had six legs and two big eyes.

- Everybody, how many legs does a fly have? (Signal.) *6.*
- He was one centimeter long. Everybody, show me with your fingers how long he was. ✓

Here is something that you may not know about flies. Flies do not change size on the outside. But they change size on the inside.

- Everybody, do they grow on the outside? (Signal.) *No.*
- Do they grow on the inside? (Signal.) *Yes.*

When Herman first became a fly, he was just as big as he was when he was an old, old fly. A fly's outside body is like a shell. Inside that shell is the part of the fly that grows.

- Everybody, which part grows, the inside or the outside? (Signal.) *Inside.*
- What happens to the size of the outside shell when the fly gets older? (Call on a student. Ideas: *Nothing; it doesn't grow.*)

At first, the inside part is small. It looks like a little tiny foot in a great big shoe. There is lots of space between the part that grows and the shell. As the fly gets older and older, the inside part gets bigger and bigger until it fills up the shell.

- Everybody, touch picture A. ✓
- Is that fly the younger fly? (Signal.) *Yes.*
- How do you know? (Call on a student. Idea: *The inside is smaller.*)
- Everybody, touch picture B. ✓
- How do you know that fly is older? (Call on a student. Idea: *The inside is bigger.*)

Anyhow, it didn't take Herman long to grow up. Within nine days he was full-grown and doing those things that flies like to do.

- Everybody, how long did it take Herman to become a full-grown fly? (Signal.) *9 days.*
- How long was he in an egg? (Signal.) *2 days.*
- What did he become after he was an egg? (Signal.) *A maggot.*
- How long was he a maggot? (Signal.) *9 days.*
- Then what did he become? (Call on a student. Idea: *A young fly.*)

He buzzed around. He ate. He loved to find things that were rotten and warm. He rubbed his two front feet together as he rested.
Herman looked like any other fly. But he was different, very different. Herman has the record of flying farther and faster than any fly that has ever lived. Most flies fly a few hundred miles in their lifetimes. A few flies will fly over a thousand miles. Herman flew thousands and thousands of miles. In the next story, you'll find out how he did that.

MORE NEXT TIME

- What record does Herman have? (Call on a student. Idea: *Flying farther and faster than any other fly.*)
- The story says he flew thousands and thousands of miles, but I don't think a fly can fly that far. Can you think of any way a fly could fly thousands and thousands of miles? (Call on a student. Ideas: *Get on a plane; find a rocket;* etc.)

EXERCISE 6
PAIRED PRACTICE

You're going to read aloud to your partner. Today the **B** members will read first. Then the **A** members will read from the star to the end of the story.
(Observe students and give feedback.)

End-of-Lesson Activities

INDEPENDENT WORK

Now finish your independent work for lesson 37. Raise your hand when you're finished.
(Observe students and give feedback.)

WORKCHECK

a. (Direct students to take out their marking pencils.)
- We're going to check your independent work. Remember, if you got an item wrong, make an **X** next to the item.

b. (For each item: Read the item. Call on a student to answer it. If the answer is wrong, say the correct answer. Refer to the Answer Key for the correct answers.)

c. Now use your marking pencil to fix up any items you got wrong. Remember, all mistakes must be fixed up before you hand in your independent work.

WRITING-SPELLING

(Present Writing-Spelling lesson 37 after completing Reading lesson 37. See Writing-Spelling Guide.)

ACTIVITY

(Present Activity 14 after completing Reading lesson 37. See Activities Across the Curriculum.)

Lesson 38

EXERCISE 1
VOCABULARY REVIEW

a. Here's the new vocabulary sentence: Several paths continued for a great distance.
- Everybody, say the sentence. Get ready. (Signal.) *Several paths continued for a great distance.*
- (Repeat until firm.)

b. What part means **a long way?** (Signal.) *A great distance.*
- What word means **kept on going?** (Signal.) *Continued.*
- What word refers to more than two but less than a lot? (Signal.) *Several.*

EXERCISE 2
READING WORDS

Column 1
a. **Find lesson 38 in your textbook.** ✓
- Touch column 1. ✓
- (Teacher reference:)

1. San Francisco	4. pilot
2. passenger	5. idea
3. attendant	

b. Number 1 is **San Francisco.** What words? (Signal.) *San Francisco.*
- San Francisco is a city on the west coast of the United States.

c. Word 2 is **passenger.** What word? (Signal.) *Passenger.*
- A passenger is someone who rides in a vehicle. What do we call someone who rides in a vehicle? (Signal.) *Passenger.*

d. Word 3 is **attendant.** What word? (Signal.) *Attendant.*
- What does a flight attendant do? (Call on a student. Idea: *Takes care of passengers on a flight.*)

e. Word 4 is **pilot.** What word? (Signal.) *Pilot.*
- Spell **pilot.** Get ready. (Tap for each letter.) *P-I-L-O-T.*

f. Word 5 is **idea.** What word? (Signal.) *Idea.*
- Spell **idea.** Get ready. (Tap for each letter.) *I-D-E-A.*

g. Let's read those words again, the fast way.
- Number 1. What words? (Signal.) *San Francisco.*
- Word 2. What word? (Signal.) *Passenger.*
- (Repeat for words 3–5.)

h. (Repeat step g until firm.)

Column 2
i. Find column 2. ✓
- (Teacher reference:)

1. flew	3. blew
2. chew	4. crew

- These words all end with the letters **E-W.**

j. Word 1. What word? (Signal.) *Flew.*
- (Repeat for words 2–4.)

k. (Repeat step j until firm.)

Column 3
l. Find column 3. ✓
- (Teacher reference:)

1. <u>under</u>stand	4. <u>air</u>plane
2. <u>taxi</u>cab	5. <u>be</u>long
3. <u>sun</u>light	

- These words are all compound words. The first part of each word is underlined.

m. Word 1. What's the underlined part? (Signal.) *under.*
- What's the whole word? (Signal.) *Understand.*

n. Word 2. What's the underlined part? (Signal.) *taxi.*
- What's the whole word? (Signal.) *Taxicab.*

o. Word 3. What's the underlined part? (Signal.) *sun.*
- What's the whole word? (Signal.) *Sunlight.*

p. Word 4. What's the underlined part? (Signal.) *air.*
- What's the whole word? (Signal.) *Airplane.*

q. Word 5. What's the underlined part? (Signal.) *be.*

- What's the whole word? (Signal.) *Belong.*
r. Let's read those words again, the fast way.
- Word 1. What word? (Signal.) *Understand.*
- (Repeat for: **2. taxicab, 3. sunlight, 4. airplane, 5. belong.**)
s. (Repeat step r until firm.)

Column 4
t. Find column 4. ✓
- (Teacher reference:)

1. traffic	4. speedometer
2. realized	5. hung
3. busy	

u. Word 1. What word? (Signal.) *Traffic.*
- Everybody, what do we call all the vehicles that are driving on a street? (Signal.) *Traffic.*
v. Word 2. What word? (Signal.) *Realized.*
- What's another way of saying **He suddenly understood that he was hungry?** (Signal.) *He realized that he was hungry.*
- What's another way of saying **He suddenly understood that his pants were torn?** (Signal.) *He realized that his pants were torn.*
w. Word 3. What word? (Signal.) *Busy.*
- (Repeat for words 4 and 5.)
x. Let's read those words again.
- Word 1. What word? (Signal.) *Traffic.*
- (Repeat for words 2–5.)
y. (Repeat step x until firm.)

Column 5
z. Find column 5. ✓
- (Teacher reference:)

1. Kennedy Airport	4. meant
2. money	5. purse
3. driver	

a. Number 1. What words? (Signal.) *Kennedy Airport.*
- Word 2. What word? (Signal.) *Money.*
- (Repeat for words 3–5.)
b. Let's read those words again.
- Number 1. What words? (Signal.) *Kennedy Airport.*
c. Word 2. What word? (Signal.) *Money.*
- (Repeat for words 3–5.)
d. (Repeat steps b through d until firm.)

Column 6
e. Find column 6. ✓
- (Teacher reference:)

1. S-shaped	4. jumbo
2. bounce	5. travel
3. bouncing	

f. Word 1. What word? (Signal.) *S-shaped.*
- (Repeat for words 2–5.)
g. (Repeat step f until firm.)

Individual Turns
(For columns 1–6: Call on individual students, each to read one to three words per turn.)

EXERCISE 3
COMPREHENSION PASSAGE
a. Find part B in your textbook. ✓
- You're going to read the next story about Herman the fly. First you'll read the information passage. It gives some facts about speedometers.
b. Everybody, touch the title. ✓
- (Call on a student to read the title.) [*Speedometers.*]
- Everybody, what's the title? (Signal.) *Speedometers.*
c. (Call on individual students to read the passage, each student reading two or three sentences at a time.)

> **Speedometers**
> You know that miles per hour tells how fast something is moving. The faster something is moving, the bigger the numbers.
> Which is moving faster, something that goes five miles per hour or something that goes four miles per hour?

- Everybody, what's the answer? (Signal.) *Something that goes 5 miles per hour.*

> Picture 1 shows a speedometer inside a car that is moving. The arrow is pointing to a number. That number tells how fast the car is going.

PICTURE 1

PICTURE 2

- Everybody, touch the speedometer in picture 1. ✓
- Touch the number the arrow is pointing to. ✓
- What number is that? (Signal.) *35.*
- So how fast is the car going? (Signal.) *35 miles per hour.*

> **Picture 2 shows a speedometer inside a car that is not moving. That car is going zero miles per hour.**

- Everybody, touch the number the arrow is pointing to in picture 2. ✓
- What number is that? (Signal.) *Zero.*
- So how fast is that car moving? (Signal.) *Zero miles per hour.*
- Is that car moving at all? (Signal.) *No.*
- Right, it's standing still.

PICTURE 3

- Look at the speedometers in picture 3. Touch the number speedometer A is pointing to. ✓
- How fast is car A moving? (Signal.) *45 miles per hour.*
- Car B. How fast is car B moving? (Signal.) *20 miles per hour.*
- Which car is not moving? (Signal.) *C.*

EXERCISE 4

Note: Ask questions marked **1** during the first reading. Ask questions marked **2** during the second reading.

STORY READING

a. Find part C in your textbook. ✓
- The error limit for this story is 9.
- Read carefully and don't make more than 9 errors. I'm going to ask some questions as you read the story. Then I'll read the story and ask more questions.
b. Everybody, touch the title. ✓
- (Call on a student to read the title.) *[Herman Goes to Kennedy Airport.]*
- Everybody, what's the title? (Signal.) *Herman Goes to Kennedy Airport.*
- I'll bet that title gives us a hint about how Herman flies so far. Who has an idea about how he does it? (Call on a student. Ideas: *He goes on an airplane, a jet,* etc.)
c. (Call on individual students to read the story, each student reading two or three sentences at a time. Ask questions marked **1**.)

> - (Correct errors: Tell the word. Direct the student to reread the sentence.)
> - (If the group makes more than 9 errors, direct the students to reread the story.)

d. (After the group has read the selection making no more than 9 errors, read the story to the students and ask questions marked **2**.)

> **Herman Goes to Kennedy Airport**
>
> Herman became the fly that flew farther than any other fly. If you want to understand how this happened, you have to know where Herman lived.
>
> Herman was born in New York City.

2. The map shows the United States. The map shows where New York City is in the United States. Everybody, touch New York City. ✓
2. Is that on the east side of the United States or the west side? (Signal.) *East side.*

> He was born on a cabbage leaf that was about five miles from a large airport called Kennedy Airport. Kennedy Airport is very busy. You can go to Kennedy Airport at any time of the day or night and see planes. Some are in the sky, getting ready to land. Others are on the ground, getting ready to take off.

2. Everybody, what's the name of the airport? (Signal.) *Kennedy Airport.*

Lesson 38 205

2. What happens at airports? (Call on a student. Ideas: *Planes take off and land; people get on planes and fly to other places.*)
2. If you went to that airport in the middle of the night, would you see planes landing and taking off? (Signal.) *Yes.*

Herman went to Kennedy Airport. Five miles is pretty far for a fly to travel, but Herman didn't fly all the way. He was buzzing around, looking for food, when he saw a nice, warm yellow.

1. The story doesn't tell what Herman saw. To Herman, it was yellow, nice, and warm. Everybody, did he like it? (Signal.) *Yes.*

He didn't know what it was, but it was warm and yellow. So he landed on it.
It was a shiny new taxicab that was on its way to the airport. It was stopped at a traffic light when Herman landed on the roof. When the cab began to move, Herman thought he would fly away, but then he realized that the wind was blowing too fast. Here's the rule: The faster the cab moves, the faster the wind blows on Herman.

2. Everybody, what happens when the cab moves faster? (Signal.) *The wind blows faster.*
2. Did you ever stick your hand out the window of a car that was moving fast? (Call on a student.)
2. Did you feel a big wind? (Call on the same student.)

Flies don't take off when the wind is blowing very fast. Flies use their six legs to hang on as hard as they can. So Herman hung on as hard as he could, and the wind blew and blew.

2. The wind blew and blew, because the cab was moving fast. When the cab stops, the wind stops.
2. Why didn't Herman just fly away? (Call on a student. Ideas: *Because the cab was moving fast; flies don't take off when the wind is blowing fast.*)

But soon the wind blew slower and slower. And then the wind stopped.

2. What was the cab doing when the wind was slowing down? (Call on a student. Idea: *Slowing down.*)
2. What was the cab doing when the wind stopped? (Call on a student. Idea: *Stopping.*)

The cab had stopped at the airport. For Herman, this stop meant that he could fly away from the cab. For the two women inside the cab, this stop meant that they would have to start working. The women were part of the crew of a jumbo jet.

2. Who was riding inside the cab? (Call on a student. Idea: *Two women.*)
2. Why were they going to the airport? (Call on a student. Idea: *To go to work.*)
2. What is a jumbo jet? (Call on a student. Idea: *A very big airplane.*)
2. What is the crew? (Call on a student. Idea: *People who work on the airplane.*)

One of the women opened her purse. She took out some money to pay the cab driver. The sun was shining on the things in her opened purse. There was a pack of chewing gum. And there was some candy. CANDY. If there is one thing that flies love more than cabbage leaves and rotten meat, it is candy. And in the warm sunlight, what could be better than a piece of candy that is four times bigger than you are?

2. Everybody, show me with your fingers how big Herman is. ✓
2. Show me a piece of candy that is four times bigger than Herman. ✓

Herman saw that piece of candy. He made two circles in the air and one S-shaped move.

2. Everybody, use your finger to make two circles in the air and an S-shaped move. ✓

> **And he landed right on the candy. But just as he was ready to start eating, everything got dark.**

1. Go back to the beginning of the story. Follow along while I read.
2. Why did that happen? (Call on a student. Idea: *Because the purse closed.*)

EXERCISE 5
PAIRED PRACTICE

You're going to read aloud to your partner. Today the **A** members will read first. Then the **B** members will read from the star to the end of the story.
(Observe students and give feedback.)

End-of-Lesson Activities

INDEPENDENT WORK

Now finish your independent work for lesson 38. Raise your hand when you're finished. (Observe student and give feedback.)

WORKCHECK

a. (Direct students to take out their marking pencils.)
- We're going to check your independent work. Remember, if you got an item wrong, make an **X** next to the item.
b. (For each item: Read the item. Call on a student to answer it. If the answer is wrong, say the correct answer. Refer to the Answer Key for the correct answers.)
c. Now use your marking pencil to fix up any items you got wrong. Remember, all mistakes must be fixed up before you hand in your independent work.

Note: You will need a globe for lesson 39.

WRITING-SPELLING

(Present Writing-Spelling lesson 38 after completing Reading lesson 38. See Writing-Spelling Guide.)

Lesson 39

EXERCISE 1

Materials: You will need a globe for Exercise 5.

VOCABULARY REVIEW

a. You learned a sentence that tells how fast the traffic was moving.
- Everybody, say that sentence. Get ready. (Signal.) *The traffic was moving forty miles per hour.*
- (Repeat until firm.)

b. You learned a sentence that tells what he is supposed to do.
- Everybody, say that sentence. Get ready. (Signal.) *He is supposed to make a decision in a couple of days.*
- (Repeat until firm.)

c. Here's the last sentence you learned: Several paths continued for a great distance.
- Everybody, say that sentence. Get ready. (Signal.) *Several paths continued for a great distance.*
- (Repeat until firm.)

d. What word means **kept on going?** (Signal.) *Continued.*
- What word refers to more than two but less than a lot? (Signal.) *Several.*
- What part means **a long way?** (Signal.) *A great distance.*
- (Repeat step d until firm.)

e. Once more. Say the sentence that tells how far several paths continued. Get ready. (Signal.) *Several paths continued for a great distance.*

EXERCISE 2

READING WORDS

Column 1

a. Find lesson 39 in your textbook. ✓
- Touch column 1. ✓
- (Teacher reference:)

1. insect	4. peaceful
2. engine	5. thermometer
3. fastened	

b. Word 1 is **insect.** What word? (Signal.) *Insect.*
- Spell **insect.** Get ready. (Tap for each letter.) *I-N-S-E-C-T.*
- An insect is a bug that has six legs. How many legs does an insect have? (Signal.) *Six.*
- A spider is not an insect because it doesn't have six legs. It has eight legs. Name some insects. (Call on individual students. Ideas: *Fly, beetle, wasp, ant, bee,* etc.)

c. Word 2 is **engine.** What word? (Signal.) *Engine.*
- Spell **engine.** Get ready. (Tap for each letter.) *E-N-G-I-N-E.*
- The engine of a car is the part that makes the car run. What do we call the part of the car that makes it run? (Signal.) *Engine.*

d. Word 3 is **fastened.** What word? (Signal.) *Fastened.*
- Spell **fastened.** Get ready. (Tap for each letter.) *F-A-S-T-E-N-E-D.*

e. Word 4 is **peaceful.** What word? (Signal.) *Peaceful.*

f. Word 5 is **thermometer.** What word? (Signal.) *Thermometer.*

g. Let's read those words again, the fast way.
- Word 1. What word? (Signal.) *Insect.*
- (Repeat for words 2–5.)

h. (Repeat step g until firm.)

Column 2

i. Find column 2. ✓
- (Teacher reference:)

1. passengers	4. rules
2. brewed	5. cities
3. tossed	6. bouncing

- These words all have endings.

j. Word 1. What word? (Signal.) *Passengers.*
- What do we call people who ride in a vehicle? (Signal.) *Passengers.*

k. Word 2. What word? (Signal.) *Brewed.*
- Yes, they brewed coffee.

208 Lesson 39

l. Word 3. What word? (Signal.) *Tossed.*
- (Repeat for: **4. rules, 5. cities, 6. bouncing.**)
m. Let's read those words again.
- Word 1. What word? (Signal.) *Passengers.*
- (Repeat for: **2. brewed, 3. tossed, 4. rules, 5. cities, 6. bouncing.**)
n. (Repeat step m until firm.)

Column 3
o. Find column 3. ✓
- (Teacher reference:)

1. a record	4. attendant
2. San Francisco	5. pilot
3. per	6. boiling

p. Number 1. What words? (Signal.) *A record.*
- Herman set a record. What record? (Call on a student. Idea: *He flew farther and faster than any other fly.*)
- Number 2. What words? (Signal.) *San Francisco.*
q. Word 3. What word? (Signal.) *Per.*
- What's another way of saying **The car went 50 miles each hour?** (Signal.) *The car went 50 miles per hour.*
r. Word 4. What word? (Signal.) *Attendant.*
- What does a flight attendant do? (Call on a student. Idea: *Takes care of passengers on a flight.*)
- What does a hospital attendant do? (Call on a student. Idea: *Takes care of patients in a hospital.*)
s. Word 5. What word? (Signal.) *Pilot.*
- Word 6. What word? (Signal.) *Boiling.*
t. Let's read those words again.
- Number 1. What words? (Signal.) *A record.*
- Number 2. What words? (Signal.) *San Francisco.*
u. Word 3. What word? (Signal.) *Per.*
- (Repeat for words 4–6.)
v. (Repeat steps t through v until firm.)

Column 4
w. Find column 4. ✓
- (Teacher reference:)

1. flight	4. member
2. idea	5. chewing
3. crack	6. thaw

x. Word 1. What word? (Signal.) *Flight.*
- (Repeat for words 2–6.)
y. Let's read those words again.
- Word 1. What word? (Signal.) *Flight.*
- (Repeat for words 2–6.)
z. (Repeat step y until firm.)

Individual Turns
(For columns 1–4: Call on individual students, each to read one to three words per turn.)

EXERCISE 3
COMPREHENSION PASSAGE
a. Find part B in your textbook. ✓
- You're going to read the next story about Herman. First you'll read the information passage. It gives some facts about the people who work on airplanes.
b. Everybody, touch the title. ✓
- (Call on a student to read the title.) [Airplane Crew Members.]
- Everybody, what's the title? (Signal.) *Airplane Crew Members.*
c. (Call on individual students to read the passage, each student reading two or three sentences at a time.)

> **Airplane Crew Members**
>
> Here's a picture of some airplane crew members.
>
>
>
> <u>A</u> is the pilot. The others are flight attendants.

- Everybody, what's C? (Signal.) *A flight attendant.*
- What's D? (Signal.) *Flight attendant.*

> On a large jumbo jet, there may be fifteen flight attendants.
> Here are some facts:
> The pilot and some other crew members work in the front of the plane. They fly the plane.

Lesson 39 **209**

- Who works in front? (Call on a student. Idea: *The pilot and some other crew members.*)

The flight attendants work in the back of the plane. They take care of the passengers.

- Everybody, who works in the back of the plane? (Signal.) *Flight attendants.*
- Name some ways they take care of the passengers. (Call on a student. Ideas: *Serve meals to them; get pillows and blankets for them; make sure they have their seatbelts on.*)
- Everybody, touch the front of the plane. ✓
- You can see the pilot.
- Touch the part of the plane behind the pilot. ✓
- That's where the passengers sit and the flight attendants work.

EXERCISE 4

Note: Ask questions marked **1** during the first reading. Ask questions marked **2** during the second reading.

STORY READING

a. Find part C in your textbook. ✓
- The error limit for this story is 8.
- Read carefully and don't make more than 8 errors. I'm going to ask some questions as you read the story. Then I'll read the story and ask more questions.

b. Everybody, touch the title. ✓
- (Call on a student to read the title.) [*Herman Ends Up on a Jumbo Jet.*]
- Everybody, what's the title? (Signal.) *Herman Ends Up on a Jumbo Jet.*

c. (Call on individual students to read the story, each student reading two or three sentences at a time. Ask questions marked **1**.)

- (Correct errors: Tell the word. Direct the student to reread the sentence.)
- (If the group makes more than 8 errors, direct the students to reread the story.)

d. (After the group has read the selection making no more than 8 errors, read the story to the students and ask questions marked **2**.)

Herman Ends Up on a Jumbo Jet

For the next part of Herman's story, you have to know something about the United States.

2. Everybody, which country? (Signal.) *The United States.*

Kennedy Airport is in New York City. And New York City is on the east side of the United States.

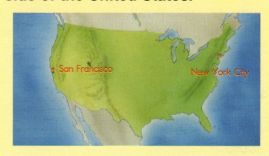

2. Everybody, where is New York City? (Signal.) *On the east side of the United States.*
2. Everybody, touch New York City on the map. ✓

There are cities on the west side of the United States. One of them is San Francisco.

2. Everybody, touch San Francisco on the map. ✓
2. Is San Francisco on the **east side** or the **west side** of the United States? (Signal.) *The west side.*

Herman was in a purse. That purse belonged to a member of a jumbo jet crew. The woman had closed the purse, and Herman couldn't get out.
At first, Herman didn't like the idea of being inside a dark place, but then he thought he would try to have a good time anyhow. So he started to eat the candy. Eating it was a little hard because things kept bouncing up and down and up and down. The crew members were walking through the airport on their way to their jumbo jet.

2. What was happening to make things bounce up and down? (Call on a student. Idea: *The woman was walking.*)

> That jumbo jet was going to fly from New York City all the way to San Francisco. Touch the map on page 246. Show where the jet starts out and where it will land.

1. Everybody, touch New York City. ✓
1. You're on the east side of the United States. Which side of the United States are you going to move to? (Signal.) *The west side.*
1. Do it. Move your finger all the way to the west side. ✓
1. What city do you end up in? (Signal.) *San Francisco.*

> The trip from New York City to San Francisco is about 25 hundred miles.

2. Everybody, how far? (Signal.) *25 hundred miles.*

> Herman kept trying to eat as the purse bounced up and down. Then suddenly everything went this way and that way. The crew member had tossed her purse on a shelf inside the jumbo jet. Herman didn't like to be tossed around like that. "Let me out of this dark," he thought to himself and tried to fly out of the purse.

2. Why didn't he like the purse anymore? (Call on a student. Ideas: *Because it was dark; because he got tossed around.*)

> He bounced around for a while, and then his eyes saw a crack where light was coming in. Herman ran up the inside of the purse and went through the crack. There were smells in the air, but most of them did not smell very good to Herman. They were the clean smells of clean seats and clean floors and clean windows.

2. What parts of the plane were clean? (Call on a student. Ideas: *The floors, the windows, the seats.*)
2. Everybody, did Herman like clean smells? (Signal.) *No.*

> Herman took off to find some better smells or some better light. He found a nice, warm red. It was fuzzy and very warm. Herman took a nap. He was on the back of a seat, right next to the window. The sun was shining through the window. That felt great.

1. Go back to the beginning of the story. Follow along while I read.
2. Everybody, what was the nice, warm red? (Signal.) *A seat.*
2. In what city was the plane? (Signal.) *New York City.*
2. Where was the plane going? (Signal.) *San Francisco.*
2. About how far is the trip from New York City to San Francisco? (Signal.) *25 hundred miles.*

EXERCISE 5

Note: You will need a globe for this exercise.

GLOBE

a. (Present a globe.) You have maps in your book. But the world is really round, like this globe.
b. (Touch New York City.) Here's where the plane is. Everybody, what city? (Signal.) *New York City.*
- (Trace the route to San Francisco.) Here's where the plane will go. What city will it go to? (Signal.) *San Francisco.*
- How many miles is that trip? (Signal.) *25 hundred.*
c. My turn. I'm going to spin the globe around and around and then see if I can find New York City. (Spin the globe.) (Touch New York City.)
- Here's New York City.
d. (Spin the globe.)
- See if you can find New York City. (Call on a student.) (Check and correct.)
- (Repeat with other students.)

EXERCISE 6
PAIRED PRACTICE

You're going to read aloud to your partner. Today the **B** members will read first. Then the **A** members will read from the star to the end of the story.
(Observe students and give feedback.)

End-of-Lesson Activities

INDEPENDENT WORK

Now finish your independent work for lesson 39. Raise your hand when you're finished.
(Observe students and give feedback.)

WORKCHECK

a. (Direct students to take out their marking pencils.)
- We're going to check your independent work. Remember, if you got an item wrong, make an **X** next to the item.

b. (For each item: Read the item. Call on a student to answer it. If the answer is wrong, say the correct answer. Refer to the Answer Key for the correct answers.)

c. Now use your marking pencil to fix up any items you got wrong. Remember, all mistakes must be fixed up before you hand in your independent work.

Note: Before presenting lesson 40, you will need to:
- Reproduce blackline masters for the Fact Game;
- Preview literature lesson 5, secure materials, and reproduce blackline masters. (See the Literature Guide.)

WRITING-SPELLING

(Present Writing-Spelling lesson 39 after completing Reading lesson 39. See Writing-Spelling Guide.)

Test 4

Lesson 40

Materials for Lesson 40

Fact Game

For each team (4 or 5 students):
- pair of number cubes (or dice)
- copy of Fact Game 40

For each student:
- their copy of the scorecard sheet

For each monitor:
- a pencil
- Fact Game 40 answer key (at end of textbook A)

Reading Checkout

Each student needs their thermometer chart.

Literature Lesson 4

See Literature Guide for the materials you will need.

EXERCISE 1
FACT GAME

a. You're going to play the game that uses the facts you have learned. Remember the rules. The player rolls the number cubes, figures out the number of the question, reads that question out loud, and answers it. The monitor tells the player if the answer is right or wrong. If it's wrong, the monitor tells the right answer. If it's right, the monitor gives the player one point. Don't argue with the monitor. The number cubes go to the left and the next player has a turn. You'll play the game for 10 minutes.
b. (Divide students into groups of four or five. Assign monitors. Circulate as students play the game. Comment on groups that are playing well.)
c. (At the end of 10 minutes, have all students who earned more than 10 points stand up.)
- (Tell the monitor of each game that ran smoothly:) Your group did a good job.

EXERCISE 2
READING CHECKOUTS

a. Today is a test day and a reading-checkout day. While you're writing answers, I'm going to call on you one at a time to read part of the story we read in lesson 39. When I call you to come and do your checkout, bring your thermometer chart.
- Remember, you pass the checkout by reading the passage in less than a minute without making more than 2 mistakes. And when you pass the checkout, you color the space for lesson 40 on your thermometer chart.
b. (Call on individual students to read the portion of story 39 marked with ✿.)
- (Time the student. Note words that are missed and number of words read.)
- (Teacher reference:)

> ✿ He bounced around for a while, and then his eyes saw a crack where light was coming in. Herman ran up the inside of the purse and went through the crack. There were smells in the air, but most of them did not smell very good to Herman. They were [50] the clean smells of clean seats and clean floors and clean windows.
>
> Herman took off to find some better smells or some better light. He [75] found a nice, warm red. It was fuzzy and very warm. Herman took a nap. He was on the back of a seat, right next ✿ [100] to the window.

- (If the student reads the passage in one minute or less and makes no more than 2 errors, direct the student to color in the space for lesson 40 on the thermometer chart.)
- (If the student makes any mistakes, point to each word that was misread and identify it.)

- (If the student does not meet the rate-error criterion for the passage, direct the student to practice reading the story with the assigned partner.)

EXERCISE 3
TEST

a. **Find page 253 in your textbook.** ✔
- **The rest of this lesson is a test. You'll work items you've done before.**
b. **Work carefully. Raise your hand when you've completed all the items.**
(Observe students but do not give feedback on errors.)

EXERCISE 4
MARKING THE TEST

a. (Check students' work before beginning lesson 41. Refer to the Answer Key for the correct answers.)
b. (Record all test 4 results on the Test Summary Sheet and the Group Summary Sheet. Reproducible Summary Sheets are at the back of the Teacher's Guide.)

EXERCISE 5
TEST REMEDIES

- (Provide any necessary remedies for test 4 before presenting lesson 41. Test remedies are discussed in the Teacher's Guide.)

Test 4 Firming Table

Test Item	Introduced in lesson	Test Item	Introduced in lesson	Test Item	Introduced in lesson
1	31	10	36	19	39
2	31	11	36	20	31
3	32	12	36	21	31
4	32	13	36	22	33
5	32	14	36	23	29
6	35	15	36	24	33
7	35	16	38	25	29
8	35	17	38	26	33
9	35	18	38		

LITERATURE

(Present Literature lesson 4 after completing Reading lesson 40. See Literature Guide.)

Lessons 41–45 • Planning Page

Looking Ahead

	Lesson 41	Lesson 42	Lesson 43	Lesson 44	Lesson 45
Lesson Events	Vocabulary Sentence Reading Words Vocabulary Review Comprehension Passages Story Reading Paired Practice Independent Work Workcheck Writing-Spelling Activity Optional Activity	Vocabulary Review Reading Words Comprehension Passage Story Reading Paired Practice Independent Work Workcheck Writing-Spelling	Vocabulary Review Reading Words Comprehension Passage Story Reading Paired Practice Independent Work Workcheck Writing-Spelling Activity	Vocabulary Review Reading Words Comprehension Passage Story Reading Paired Practice Independent Work Workcheck Writing-Spelling	Vocabulary Sentence Reading Words Vocabulary Review Comprehension Passage Story Reading Reading Checkouts Independent Work Workcheck Writing-Spelling
Vocabulary Sentence	#10: Boiling water will thaw ice in a few moments.	#10: Boiling water will thaw ice in a few moments.	sentence #8 sentence #9 sentence #10	#8: He is supposed to make a decision in a couple of days.	#11: They were eager to hear the announcement.
Reading Words: Word Types	modeled words multi-syllable words words with endings compound words mixed words	modeled words 2-syllable words words with endings compound words mixed words	words with endings mixed words multi-syllable words	modeled words multi-syllable words words with endings mixed words	modeled words words with endings multi-syllable words mixed words
New Vocabulary	Lake Michigan Chicago temperature takeoff	Denver degrees service captain weather runway	coast galley perfect panel	although copilot ocean figure weren't	Pacific Ocean Japan attention although
Comprehension Passages	1) *Insects* 2) *Facts About Speed*	*Temperature*	*Degrees*	*Finding the Direction of a Wind*	*Airplanes and Wind*
Story	*Getting Ready for Takeoff*	*Herman Takes Off for San Francisco*	*Herman Lands in San Francisco*	*Fly Spray Fills the Air*	*A Rough Trip*
Skill Items	Deductions Vocabulary sentences	Titles Vocabulary	Deductions Vocabulary sentence	Deductions Same and Different Vocabulary sentences	Titles
Special Materials					Thermometer charts
Special Projects/Activities	Activity after lesson 41		Activity after lesson 43		

Lesson 41

EXERCISE 1
VOCABULARY

a. **Find page 338 in your textbook.** ✓
  - Touch sentence 10. ✓
  - This is a new vocabulary sentence. It says: Boiling water will thaw ice in a few moments. Everybody, read that sentence. Get ready. (Signal.) *Boiling water will thaw ice in a few moments.*
  - Close your eyes and say that sentence. Get ready. (Signal.) *Boiling water will thaw ice in a few moments.*
  - (Repeat until firm.)

b. When water **boils,** it makes lots of bubbles and steam. Water boils when it is heated to 212 degrees. What's the boiling point of water? (Signal.) *212 degrees.*

c. When ice **thaws,** it melts. What word means **melt?** (Signal.) *Thaw.*

d. A few moments is a very few seconds. That's not a lot of time. A few moments might be seven or eight seconds. It would be way less than a minute. Remember, another way of saying **not very many seconds** is **a few moments.** What's another way of saying **not very many seconds?** (Signal.) *A few moments.*

e. Listen: Boiling water will thaw ice in a few moments.
  - Everybody, say the sentence. Get ready. (Signal.) *Boiling water will thaw ice in a few moments.*
  - (Repeat until firm.)

f. What word tells you that the water is 212 degrees? (Signal.) *Boiling.*
  - What's another word for **melt?** (Signal.) *Thaw.*
  - Which part of the sentence means **not very many seconds?** (Signal.) *A few moments.*
  - What's the boiling point of water? (Signal.) *212 degrees.*
  - (Repeat step f until firm.)

EXERCISE 2
READING WORDS

Column 1

a. **Find lesson 41 in your textbook.** ✓
  - Touch column 1. ✓
  - (Teacher reference:)

1. Lake Michigan	4. building
2. Chicago	5. super
3. temperature	6. frightened

b. Number 1 is **Lake Michigan.** What words? (Signal.) *Lake Michigan.*
  - Lake Michigan is one of the five great lakes. It is the second-largest great lake.

c. Word 2 is **Chicago.** What word? (Signal.) *Chicago.*
  - Spell **Chicago.** Get ready. (Tap for each letter.) *C-H-I-C-A-G-O.*
  - Chicago is a large city near the middle of the United States. It touches Lake Michigan.

d. Word 3 is **temperature.** What word? (Signal.) *Temperature.*
  - When you measure the temperature of something, you find out how hot it is. The higher the temperature is, the hotter the thing is. Everybody, when you measure how hot something is, what are you finding out? (Signal.) *Temperature.*
  - When is the temperature higher, on a hot day or on a cold day? (Signal.) *On a hot day.*

e. Word 4 is **building.** What word? (Signal.) *Building.*
  - Spell **building.** Get ready. (Tap for each letter.) *B-U-I-L-D-I-N-G.*

f. Word 5 is **super.** What word? (Signal.) *Super.*
  - Spell **super.** Get ready. (Tap for each letter.) *S-U-P-E-R.*

g. Word 6 is **frightened.** What word? (Signal.) *Frightened.*

h. Let's read those words again, the fast way.
  - Number 1. What words? (Signal.) *Lake Michigan.*
  - Word 2. What word? (Signal.) *Chicago.*
  - (Repeat for words 3–6.)

i. (Repeat step h until firm.)

Column 2
j. Find column 2. ✓
- (Teacher reference:)

> 1. supposed   4. livings
> 2. insects   5. peaceful
> 3. fastened

- All these words have endings.
k. Word 1. What word? (Signal.) *Supposed.*
- What's another way of saying **You should walk on the sidewalk?** (Signal.) *You are supposed to walk on the sidewalk.*
l. Word 2. What word? (Signal.) *Insects.*
- How is an insect different from some other bugs? (Call on a student. Idea: *An insect has six legs.*)
m. Word 3. What word? (Signal.) *Fastened.*
- (Repeat for words 4–5.)
n. (Repeat step m until firm.)

Column 3
o. Find column 3. ✓
- (Teacher reference:)

> 1. brushed   4. belts
> 2. engines   5. boiling
> 3. seated

- All these words have endings.
p. Word 1. What word? (Signal.) *Brushed.*
- (Repeat for words 2–5.)
q. (Repeat step p until firm.)

Column 4
r. Find column 4. ✓
- (Teacher reference:)

> 1. <u>take</u>off   3. <u>grass</u>hopper
> 2. <u>butter</u>fly   4. <u>W</u>-shaped

- These words are all compound words. The first part of each word is underlined.
s. Word 1. What's the underlined part? (Signal.) *take.*
- What's the whole word? (Signal.) *Takeoff.*
- When an airplane first leaves the ground, it's called the takeoff. What do we call it when an airplane first leaves the ground? (Signal.) *Takeoff.*
t. Word 2. What's the underlined part? (Signal.) *butter.*
- What's the whole word? (Signal.) *Butterfly.*
u. Word 3. What's the underlined part? (Signal.) *grass.*
- What's the whole word? (Signal.) *Grasshopper.*
v. Word 4. What's the underlined part? (Signal.) *w.*
- What's the whole word? (Signal.) *W-shaped.*
w. Let's read those words again, the fast way.
- Word 1. What word? (Signal.) *Takeoff.*
- (Repeat for words 2–4.)
x. (Repeat step w until firm.)

Column 5
y. Find column 5. ✓
- (Teacher reference:)

> 1. couple   4. speed
> 2. beetle   5. thermometer
> 3. spider

z. Word 1. What word? (Signal.) *Couple.*
- What does **couple** mean? (Signal.) *Two.*
- How long is a **couple** of days? (Signal.) *Two days.*
a. Word 2. What word? (Signal.) *Beetle.*
- (Repeat for words 3–5.)
b. Let's read those words again.
- Word 1. What word? (Signal.) *Couple.*
- (Repeat for words 2–5.)
c. (Repeat step b until firm.)

Column 6
d. Find column 6. ✓
- (Teacher reference:)

> 1. begun   3. thaw
> 2. flown   4. ice

e. Word 1. What word? (Signal.) *Begun.*
- (Repeat for words 2–4.)
f. (Repeat step e until firm.)

Individual Turns
(For columns 1–6: Call on individual students, each to read one to three words per turn.)

Lesson 41

EXERCISE 3
VOCABULARY REVIEW

a. Here's the new vocabulary sentence: **Boiling water will thaw ice in a few moments.**
- Everybody, say the sentence. Get ready. (Signal.) *Boiling water will thaw ice in a few moments.*
- (Repeat until firm.)

b. Which part of the sentence means **not very many seconds?** (Signal.) *A few moments.*
- What word tells you that the water is 212 degrees? (Signal.) *Boiling.*
- What's another word for **melt?** (Signal.) *Thaw.*
- What's the boiling temperature of water? (Signal.) *212 degrees.*
- (Repeat step b until firm.)

EXERCISE 4
COMPREHENSION PASSAGES

Passage B

a. Find part B in your textbook. ✓
- You're going to read the next story about Herman. First you'll read two information passages. The first one gives facts about insects.

b. Everybody, touch the title. ✓
- (Call on a student to read the title.) [Insects.]
- Everybody, what's the title? (Signal.) *Insects.*

c. (Call on individual students to read the passage, each student reading two or three sentences at a time.)

> **Insects**
>
> Most bugs are insects. Some bugs are not insects.
> An ant is an insect. A fly is an insect. A butterfly is an insect. A beetle, a bee, and a grasshopper are insects.

- Who can name all the insects we just read about? (Call on a student.) [*Ant, fly, butterfly, beetle, bee, grasshopper.*]
- Who can name some other insects? (Call on a student. Ideas: *Crickets, moths, mosquitoes, termites, wasps,* etc.)

> **Spiders are not insects.**
> Here are the rules about all insects:
> **An insect has six legs.**

- Listen to that rule again: An insect has six legs. Everybody, say that rule. (Signal.) *An insect has six legs.*
- How many legs does an insect have? (Signal.) *6.*
- If an animal does not have six legs, could it be an insect? (Signal.) *No.*

> **The body of an insect has three parts.**

- Listen to that rule again: The body of an insect has three parts. Everybody, say that rule. (Signal.) *The body of an insect has three parts.*
- How many parts does the body of an insect have? (Signal.) *3.*
- If an animal does not have a body with three parts, could it be an insect? (Signal.) *No.*

> **An ant has six legs. Its body has three parts. So an ant is an insect.**
> **A fly has six legs. Its body has three parts. So a fly is an insect.**

- Listen. A bee is an insect. Everybody, how many legs does it have? (Signal.) *6.*
- How many body parts does it have? (Signal.) *3.*

> **A spider has eight legs. Its body has two parts. So a spider is not an insect.**

- Everybody, how many legs does a spider have? (Signal.) *8.*
- How many body parts does a spider have? (Signal.) *2.*
- Who can name two reasons that a spider could not be an insect? (Call on a student. Idea: *It has 8 legs, and it has 2 body parts.*)

- Look at the picture. One of these animals is an insect. The body parts are marked. Count the body parts. Look at the legs. Figure out which of the animals is an insect. (Pause.)
- Everybody, is animal A an insect? (Signal.) *Yes.*
- How do you know? (Call on a student. Idea: *It has 6 legs and 3 body parts.*)
- Everybody, is animal B an insect? (Signal.) *No.*
- Why not? (Call on a student. Idea: *It has 8 legs and 2 body parts.*)
- Everybody, is animal C an insect? (Signal.) *No.*
- How do you know? (Call on a student. Idea: *It has too many legs and 2 body parts.*)

Passage C

d. Find part C in your textbook. ✓
e. Everybody, touch the title. ✓
(Call on a student to read the title.) [*Facts About Speed.*]
- Everybody, what's the title? (Signal.) *Facts About Speed.*
f. (Call on individual students to read the passage, each student reading one or two sentences at a time.)

Facts About Speed

When you tell how fast something is moving, you tell about the speed of that thing. Here are facts about speed:

A fast man can run 20 miles per hour.

- Everybody, tell me the speed of a fast man. (Signal.) *20 miles per hour.*

A fast dog can run 35 miles per hour.

- Everybody, tell me the speed of a fast dog. (Signal.) *35 miles per hour.*

A racing car can go 200 miles per hour.

- Everybody, tell me the speed of a racing car. (Signal.) *200 miles per hour.*

A jumbo jet flies 500 miles per hour.

- Everybody, tell me the speed of a jumbo jet. (Signal.) *500 miles per hour.*
- I'll name some speeds. You tell me what goes that fast.
- 500 miles per hour. Everybody, what goes that fast? (Signal.) *A jumbo jet.*
- 20 miles per hour. What goes that fast? (Signal.) *A fast man.*
- 200 miles per hour. What goes that fast? (Signal.) *A racing car.*
- 35 miles per hour. What goes that fast? (Signal.) *A fast dog.*
- (Repeat until firm.)

EXERCISE 5

STORY READING

a. Find part D in your textbook. ✓
- The error limit for this story is 7. Read carefully and don't make more than 7 errors. I'm going to ask some questions as you read the story. Then I'll read the story and ask more questions.
b. Everybody, touch the title. ✓
- (Call on a student to read the title.) [*Getting Ready for Takeoff.*]
- Everybody, what's the title? (Signal.) *Getting Ready for Takeoff.*
c. (Call on individual students to read the story, each student reading two or three sentences at a time. Ask questions marked **1.**)

- (Correct errors: Tell the word. Direct the student to reread the sentence.)
- (If the group makes more than 7 errors, direct the students to reread the story.)

d. (After the group has read the selection making no more than 7 errors, read the story to the students and ask questions marked **2.**)

Getting Ready for Takeoff

Herman was on a plane that was on the east side of the United States. That plane was going to a city on the west side of the United States.

1. Everybody, what city was Herman in? (Signal.) *New York City.*
1. What was the name of the airport he was in? (Signal.) *Kennedy Airport.*
1. What city is the plane going to? (Signal.) *San Francisco.*
1. How far is it from New York City to San Francisco? (Signal.) *25 hundred miles.*

Lesson 41 219

> Herman was taking a nap on a warm red. Suddenly something told him that he was in danger. A big dark was dropping on him. "You're not going to get me," Herman thought and took off just as the big dark dropped next to him.
>
> Then he ran into a living. That was bad. Herman liked to land on livings, but he didn't like to run into them. Then there was more danger. The living came after him. Herman did a W-shaped move and he got away from the living.

2. Everybody, show me the W-shaped move that Herman used to get away from the living. ✓
2. What are livings? (Call on a student. Ideas: *People; living things.*)
2. Look at the picture. ✓
2. You can see Herman running away from a living. Who is that living? (Call on a student. Idea: *A woman.*)

> Here's what had happened. The passengers had begun to get on the plane. One of them dropped a coat on the seat back where Herman was. If Herman hadn't flown away, the coat would have landed on him.
>
> Then as Herman was trying to get away from the coat, he flew right into the face of another passenger. That passenger tried to brush Herman away with her hand.

2. I'm going to read a part to you again and ask some questions.
   > Herman was taking a nap on a warm red. Suddenly something told him that he was in danger. A big dark was dropping on him. "You're not going to get me," Herman thought and took off just as the big dark dropped next to him.
2. Everybody, what was the big dark? (Signal.) *A coat.*
2. Then he ran into a living. That was bad. Herman liked to land on livings, but he didn't like to run into them.
2. Everybody, what part of the living did Herman fly into? (Signal.) *Face.*
2. Then there was more danger. The living came after him. Herman did a W-shaped move and got away from the living.
2. Everybody, what part of the living did Herman get away from with his W-shaped move? (Signal.) *Her hand.*

> Now Herman was flying around, trying to find a peaceful place in the sun, but he couldn't seem to find one. In every place he went there were lots of livings. He tried to land on a couple of livings, but they brushed him away. He didn't know it, but there were three hundred people on this jumbo jet, and the plane was getting ready to take off.

2. Everybody, how many people were on the plane? (Signal.) *300.*
2. What was the plane getting ready to do? (Signal.) *Take off.*

> The flight attendants were making sure that all the passengers were seated and they were wearing their seat belts. One flight attendant was telling passengers what they were supposed to do if the plane was in danger.

2. What were the flight attendants doing before take off? (Call on a student. Ideas: *Making sure that passengers were seated with seat belts fastened; making announcements.*)
2. What kind of danger could a plane have? (Call on a student. Ideas: *Run out of gas; lose power; crash; land in the water; lose oxygen;* etc.)

> Now the great jet engines of the plane were starting up. Outside, the sound was so loud that you would have to hold your hands over your ears. But to the passengers inside the plane the sound of the engines was no louder than a noisy car engine.
>
> **MORE NEXT TIME**

1. Go back to the beginning of the story. Follow along while I read.

EXERCISE 6
PAIRED PRACTICE

You're going to read aloud to your partner. Today the **A** members will read first. Then the **B** members will read from the star to the end of the story.
(Observe students and give feedback.)

End-of-Lesson Activities

INDEPENDENT WORK

Now finish your independent work for lesson 41. Raise your hand when you're finished.
(Observe students and give feedback.)

WORKCHECK

a. (Direct students to take out their marking pencils.)
- We're going to check your independent work. Remember, if you got an item wrong, make an **X** next to the item.

b. (For each item: Read the item. Call on a student to answer it. If the answer is wrong, say the correct answer. Refer to the Answer Key for the correct answers.)

c. Now use your marking pencil to fix up any items you got wrong. Remember, all mistakes must be fixed up before you hand in your independent work.

WRITING-SPELLING

(Present Writing-Spelling lesson 41 after completing Reading lesson 41. See Writing-Spelling Guide.)

ACTIVITY

(Present Activity 15 after completing Reading lesson 41. See Activities Across the Curiculum.)

OPTIONAL

(Sing the song "Shoo Fly Don't Bother Me" with the students.)

Lesson 42

EXERCISE 1
VOCABULARY REVIEW

a. Here's the new vocabulary sentence: **Boiling water will thaw ice in a few moments.**
- Everybody, say the sentence. Get ready. (Signal.) *Boiling water will thaw ice in a few moments.*
- (Repeat until firm.)

b. Which part of the sentence means **not very many seconds?** (Signal.) *A few moments.*
- What's another word for **melt?** (Signal.) *Thaw.*
- What word tells you that the water is 212 degrees? (Signal.) *Boiling.*
- What's the boiling temperature of water? (Signal.) *212 degrees.*
- (Repeat step b until firm.)

EXERCISE 2
READING WORDS

Column 1

a. **Find lesson 42 in your textbook.** ✓
- Touch column 1. ✓
- (Teacher reference:)

1. degrees	4. weather
2. service	5. oven
3. captain	

b. Word 1 is **degrees.** What word? (Signal.) *Degrees.*
- Spell **degrees.** Get ready. (Tap for each letter.) *D-E-G-R-E-E-S.*
- You measure temperature in degrees. The hotter something is, the more degrees it is. Which is hotter, something that is 55 degrees or something that is 45 degrees? (Signal.) *55 degrees.*

c. Word 2 is **service.** What word? (Signal.) *Service.*
- Spell **service.** Get ready. (Tap for each letter.) *S-E-R-V-I-C-E.*
- People who offer a service do a special job. What special job would a laundry service do? (Call on a student. Idea: *Wash and dry clothes.*)
- What special job would a lawn-mowing service do? (Call on a student. Idea: *Mow lawns.*)

d. Word 3 is **captain.** What word? (Signal.) *Captain.*
- Spell **captain.** Get ready. (Tap for each letter.) *C-A-P-T-A-I-N.*
- The captain of a ship or plane is the person in charge of the vehicle. If the captain gives an order, it must be followed.

e. Word 4 is **weather.** What word? (Signal.) *Weather.*
- When you tell about the weather, what do you tell? (Call on a student. Ideas: *How hot it is; if it is raining or snowing; what kind of wind there is; about the clouds.*)

f. Word 5 is **oven.** What word? (Signal.) *Oven.*

g. Let's read those words again, the fast way.
- Word 1. What word? (Signal.) *Degrees.*
- (Repeat for words 2–5.)

h. (Repeat step g until firm.)

Column 2

i. Find column 2. ✓
- (Teacher reference:)

1. buildings	4. pounding
2. boiling	5. trays
3. hearts	

- All these words have endings.

j. Word 1. What word? (Signal.) *Buildings.*
- (Repeat for words 2–5.)

k. (Repeat step j until firm.)

l. Let's read those words again.
- Word 1. What word? (Signal.) *Buildings.*
- (Repeat for words 2–5.)

m. (Repeat step l until firm.)

Column 3

n. Find column 3. ✓
- (Teacher reference:)

> 1. <u>for</u>ward
> 2. <u>run</u>way
> 3. <u>down</u>town
> 4. <u>them</u>selves
> 5. <u>next</u>-hottest
> 6. <u>loud</u>speaker

- These words are compound words. The first part of each word is underlined.

o. Word 1. What's the underlined part? (Signal.) *for.*
- What's the whole word? (Signal.) *Forward.*

p. Word 2. What's the underlined part? (Signal.) *run.*
- What's the whole word? (Signal.) *Runway.*
- A runway is like a large road that airplanes use when they take off. The plane goes faster and faster down the runway until it takes off.

q. Word 3. What's the underlined part? (Signal.) *down.*
- What's the whole word? (Signal.) *Downtown.*

r. Word 4. What's the underlined part? (Signal.) *them.*
- What's the whole word? (Signal.) *Themselves.*

s. Word 5. What's the underlined part? (Signal.) *next.*
- What's the whole word? (Signal.) *Next-hottest.*

t. Word 6. What's the underlined part? (Signal.) *loud.*
- What's the whole word? (Signal.) *Loudspeaker.*

u. Let's read those words again, the fast way.
- Word 1. What word? (Signal.) *Forward.*
- (Repeat for words 2–6.)

v. (Repeat step u until firm.)

Column 4

w. Find column 4. ✓
- (Teacher reference:)

> 1. Denver
> 2. temperature
> 3. wing
> 4. frightened
> 5. super
> 6. salad

x. Word 1. What word? (Signal.) *Denver.*
- Denver is a large city about halfway between Chicago and San Francisco. Which two cities is Denver halfway between? (Signal.) *Chicago and San Francisco.*

y. Word 2. What word? (Signal.) *Temperature.*
- (Repeat for words 3–6.)

z. Let's read those words again.
- Word 1. What word? (Signal.) *Denver.*
- (Repeat for words 2–6.)

a. (Repeat step z until firm.)

Individual Turns

(For columns 1–4: Call on individual students, each to read one to three words per turn.)

EXERCISE 3

COMPREHENSION PASSAGE

a. Find part B in your textbook. ✓
- You're going to read the next story about Herman. First you'll read the information passage. It gives some facts about temperature.

b. Everybody, touch the title. ✓
- (Call on a student to read the title.) [*Temperature.*]
- Everybody, what's the title? (Signal.) *Temperature.*

c. (Call on individual students to read the passage, each student reading two or three sentences at a time.)

> **Temperature**
>
> When we talk about how hot or cold something is, we tell about the temperature of the thing.

- Everybody, what word tells about how hot or cold the thing is? (Signal.) *Temperature.*

> Something that is very hot has a high temperature. Something that is very cold has a low temperature.

- Everybody, what kind of temperature does something have when it's very hot? (Signal.) *High.*
- What kind of temperature does something have when it's very cold? (Signal.) *Low.*

> Is the temperature of ice high or low?

Lesson 42

- Everybody, what's the answer? (Signal.) *Low.*

Is the temperature of boiling water high or low?

- Everybody, what's the answer? (Signal.) *High.*

Here's the rule: When an object gets hotter, the temperature goes up.

- Everybody, listen to that rule again: When an object gets hotter, the temperature goes up.
- Say that rule. (Signal.) *When an object gets hotter, the temperature goes up.*
- (Repeat until firm.)

Object A gets hotter. So what do you know about the temperature of object A?

- Tell me. (Call on a student. Idea: *It goes up.*)

When a floor gets cold, which way does the temperature go?

- Everybody, tell me. Get ready. (Signal.) *Down.*

A glass of water gets hotter. Tell about the temperature.

- Everybody, tell me if the temperature goes **up** or **down**. Get ready. (Signal.) *Up.*

EXERCISE 4
STORY READING

a. Find part C in your textbook. ✓
- The error limit for this story is 8. Read carefully and don't make more than 8 errors. I'm going to ask some questions as you read the story. Then I'll read the story and ask more questions.

b. Everybody, touch the title. ✓
- (Call on a student to read the title.) [*Herman Takes Off for San Francisco.*]
- What's going to happen in this story? (Call on a student. Idea: *Herman will take off for San Francisco.*)
- Everybody, in what city is Herman now? (Signal.) *New York City.*
- Where is he going? (Signal.) *San Francisco.*
- About how far is it from New York City to San Francisco? (Signal.) *25 hundred miles.*

c. (Call on individual students to read the story, each student reading two or three sentences at a time. Ask questions marked **1**.)

- (Correct errors: Tell the word. Direct the student to reread the sentence.)
- (If the group makes more than 8 errors, direct the students to reread the story.)

d. (After the group has read the selection making no more than 8 errors, read the story to the students and ask questions marked **2**.)

Herman Takes Off for San Francisco

The jet engines on a jumbo jet work the same way that Goad works when she wants to move very fast. When Goad got away from the Brown family, she let the air rush out. The air rushed out one way, and Goad went flying the other way. That's just how jet engines work. The air rushes out of the back of the engine. The engine moves in the opposite direction—forward. The engine is on the wing, so the wing moves forward. The wing is on the plane, so the plane moves forward.

1. Listen to that part again: The air rushes out of the back of the engine. The engine moves in the opposite direction—forward. The engine is on the wing, so the wing moves forward. The wing is on the plane, so the plane moves forward.
1. Everybody, does the air rush out of the **back** of the engine or the **front** of the engine? (Signal.) *Back.*
1. So the engine moves in the opposite direction. In which direction does the engine move? (Signal.) *Forward.*
1. The engine is on the wing. So how does the wing move? (Signal.) *Forward.*
1. The wing is on the plane. So how does the plane move? (Signal.) *Forward.*

1. Everybody, look at the picture on the next page. ✓
• Touch the jet engine in the picture. ✓
1. Now move your finger in the direction the air shoots out of the engine. ✓
1. Everybody, touch the **P** on the plane. ✓
1. Now move your finger in the direction the plane moves. ✓

> When jet engines work, they make a great, loud sound. The plane goes down the runway, faster and faster. The people inside try to act as if they are not frightened, but their hearts start pounding faster.

2. Why are their hearts pounding faster? (Call on a student. Ideas: *Because they're excited; scared; etc.*)

> The people begin to wonder how a plane that is almost as big as a school can take off and fly like a bird. Racing cars go two hundred miles per hour. The jet plane goes faster than most racing cars while the plane is still on the runway.

2. How fast is the plane going before it takes off? (Call on a student. Idea: *Over 200 miles per hour.*)

> Then the passengers look out the windows and have trouble believing what they see. They see their city, but it looks like a toy city—with tiny cars and buildings that look so small you could pick them up.

2. Everybody, touch the picture to the right. It shows what New York City looks like from a plane. ✓

> The plane circles around, and the passengers look at the buildings in downtown New York. "Wow," they say to themselves.

2. Why do they say "Wow"? (Call on a student. Ideas: *Because it looks so different; because the city looks so small,* etc.)

> Then the plane goes up and up until it is six miles above the ground. Think of it. Six miles high.

2. Everybody, how high does a jumbo jet go? (Signal.) *6 miles.*
2. Remember that.

> Now, a flight attendant talks to the passengers. "You may remove your seat belts and move around the plane now." The passengers start to talk to each other now. They feel safe. The plane doesn't seem to be moving at all. Walking around inside the plane is just like walking around inside a building. But the passengers inside the plane are moving along at the speed of five hundred miles per hour.

2. Everybody, how fast is the plane going? (Signal.) *500 miles per hour.*
2. Remember that fact. The plane was flying 500 miles per hour.
2. If the passengers can walk around inside the plane, does it feel like the plane is moving fast? (Signal.) *No.*

> Herman was moving at five hundred miles per hour. But he wasn't thinking much about it. He didn't feel like a super fly. In fact, he wasn't the only fly in that jumbo jet. Like most jumbo jets that fly in the summer, it had flies in it. There were six flies and one beetle.
> More next time

1. Go back to the beginning of the story. Follow along while I read.
2. Everybody, how many flies were on the plane? (Signal.) *6.*

2. Would the plane have that many flies in the wintertime? (Signal.) *No.*
2. Why not? (Call on a student. Idea: *Because there aren't any flies in the wintertime.*)

EXERCISE 5
PAIRED PRACTICE

You're going to read aloud to your partner. Today the **B** members will read first. Then the **A** members will read from the star to the end of the story.
(Observe students and give feedback.)

End-of-Lesson Activities

INDEPENDENT WORK

Now finish your independent work for lesson 42. Raise your hand when you're finished. (Observe students and give feedback.)

WORKCHECK

a. (Direct students to take out their marking pencils.)
 • We're going to check your independent work. Remember, if you got an item wrong, make an **X** next to the item.
b. (For each item: Read the item. Call on a student to answer it. If the answer is wrong, say the correct answer. Refer to the Answer Key for the correct answers.)
c. Now use your marking pencil to fix up any items you got wrong. Remember, all mistakes must be fixed up before you hand in your independent work.

WRITING-SPELLING

(Present Writing-Spelling lesson 42 after completing Reading lesson 42. See Writing-Spelling Guide.)

Lesson 43

EXERCISE 1
VOCABULARY REVIEW

a. You learned a sentence that tells what he is supposed to do.
- Everybody, say that sentence. Get ready. (Signal.) *He is supposed to make a decision in a couple of days.*
- (Repeat until firm.)

b. You learned a sentence that tells how far several paths continued.
- Everybody, say that sentence. Get ready. (Signal.) *Several paths continued for a great distance.*
- (Repeat until firm.)

c. Here's the last sentence you learned: Boiling water will thaw ice in a few moments.
- Everybody, say that sentence. Get ready. (Signal.) *Boiling water will thaw ice in a few moments.*
- (Repeat until firm.)

d. What word means **melt**? (Signal.) *Thaw.*
- What part means **not very many seconds**? (Signal.) *In a few moments.*
- What word tells you that the water is 212 degrees? (Signal.) *Boiling.*
- (Repeat step d until firm.)

e. Once more. Say the sentence that tells what boiling water will do. Get ready. (Signal.) *Boiling water will thaw ice in a few moments.*

EXERCISE 2
READING WORDS

Column 1

a. Find lesson 43 in your textbook. ✓
- Touch column 1. ✓
- (Teacher reference:)

1. coldest	4. trays
2. degrees	5. passed
3. cooking	6. kills

- All these words have an ending.

b. Word 1. What word? (Signal.) *Coldest.*
- Spell **coldest.** Get ready. (Tap for each letter.) *C-O-L-D-E-S-T.*

c. Word 2. What word? (Signal.) *Degrees.*
- Spell **degrees.** Get ready. (Tap for each letter.) *D-E-G-R-E-E-S.*

d. Word 3. What word? (Signal.) *Cooking.*
- Spell **cooking.** Get ready. (Tap for each letter.) *C-O-O-K-I-N-G.*

e. Word 4. What word? (Signal.) *Trays.*
- Spell **trays.** Get ready. (Tap for each letter.) *T-R-A-Y-S.*

f. Word 5. What word? (Signal.) *Passed.*

g. Word 6. What word? (Signal.) *Kills.*

g. Let's read those words again.
- Word 1. What word? (Signal.) *Coldest.*
- (Repeat for words 2–6.)

h. (Repeat step g until firm.)

Column 2

i. Find column 2. ✓
- (Teacher reference:)

1. coast	4. service
2. galley	5. perfect
3. Denver	6. panel

j. Word 1. What word? (Signal.) *Coast.*
- The coast is where the land meets the ocean. Everybody, what word tells where land and ocean meet? (Signal.) *Coast.*

k. Word 2. What word? (Signal.) *Galley.*
- The galley is the kitchen on a plane or ship.

l. Word 3. What word? (Signal.) *Denver.*
- Denver is about halfway between two cities in the United States. Which two cities are those? (Call on a student.) [*Chicago and San Francisco.*]

m. Word 4. What word? (Signal.) *Service.*
- What would a meal service do? (Call on a student. Idea: *Give meals.*)

n. Word 5. What word? (Signal.) *Perfect.*
- Something that is perfect has everything just the way it should be. If a plan has everything the way it should be, it's a perfect plan. What would you call a day that has everything the way it should be? (Signal.) *A perfect day.*

Lesson 43   227

o. **Word 6. What word?** (Signal.) *Panel.*
- A panel is a flat part that's shaped like a rectangle. What do we call a flat part that's shaped like a rectangle? (Signal.) *Panel.*

p. Let's read those words again.
- **Word 1. What word?** (Signal.) *Coast.*
- (Repeat for: **2. galley, 3. Denver, 4. service, 5. perfect, 6. panel.**)

q. (Repeat step p until firm.)

Column 3

r. **Find column 3.** ✓
- (Teacher reference:)

1. Lake Michigan	4. salad
2. captain	5. coffee
3. Chicago	

s. **Number 1. What words?** (Signal.) *Lake Michigan.*
- **Word 2. What word?** (Signal.) *Captain.*
- (Repeat for words 3–5.)

t. Let's read those words again.
- **Number 1. What words?** (Signal.) *Lake Michigan.*
- **Word 2. What word?** (Signal.) *Captain.*
- (Repeat for words 3–5.)

u. (Repeat step t until firm.)

Column 4

v. **Find column 4.** ✓
- (Teacher reference:)

1. oven	4. shrimp
2. spray	5. metal
3. stuff	

w. **Word 1. What word?** (Signal.) *Oven.*
- (Repeat for words 2–5.)

x. Let's read those words again.
- **Word 1. What word?** (Signal.) *Oven.*
- (Repeat for words 2–5.)

y. (Repeat step x until firm.)

Column 5

z. **Find column 5.** ✓
- (Teacher reference:)

1. figure	3. stack
2. quite	4. return

a. **Word 1. What word?** (Signal.) *Figure.*
- (Repeat for words 2–4.)

b. (Repeat step a until firm.)

Individual Turns
(For columns 1–5: Call on individual students, each to read one to three words per turn.)

EXERCISE 3
COMPREHENSION PASSAGE

a. **Find part B in your textbook.** ✓
- You're going to read the next story about Herman. First you'll read the information passage. It gives some more facts about temperature.

b. Everybody, touch the title. ✓
- (Call on a student to read the title.) [*Degrees.*]
- Everybody, what's the title? (Signal.) *Degrees.*
- This passage will tell you what we measure in degrees.

c. (Call on individual students to read the passage, each student reading two or three sentences at a time.)

> **Degrees**
>
> When an object gets hotter, does the temperature of the object go up or down?

- Everybody, what happens to the temperature? (Signal.) *It goes up.*

> We measure temperature in degrees. Here's the rule: When the temperature goes up, the number of degrees gets bigger.

- Listen to the rule again. When the temperature goes up, the number of degrees gets bigger. Everybody say the rule. Get ready. (Signal.) *When the temperature goes up, the number of degrees gets bigger.*
- Everybody, what do we measure temperature in? (Signal.) *Degrees.*
- When the temperature goes up, does the number of degrees get **bigger** or **smaller?** (Signal.) *Bigger.*

> Look at the picture. It tells how many degrees each object is.

A
40 degrees

B
10 degrees

C
70 degrees

- Everybody, touch glass A. ✓
- What's the temperature of that glass? (Signal.) *40 degrees.*
- Touch glass B. ✓
- What's the temperature of that glass? (Signal.) *10 degrees.*
- Touch glass C. ✓
- What's the temperature of that glass? (Signal.) *70 degrees.*

The hottest object has the biggest number of degrees.

- Everybody, which glass has the biggest number of degrees? (Signal.) *C.*
- Which glass is the hottest? (Signal.) *C.*
- How do you know it's the hottest? (Call on a student. Idea: *Because it has the biggest number of degrees.*)
- Which glass is the coldest? (Signal.) *B.*
- How do you know it's the coldest? (Call on a student. Idea: *It has the smallest number of degrees.*)

On a hot summer day, the temperature may reach 100 degrees. On a cold winter day when cars won't start, the temperature may get down to zero degrees.
The temperature inside your school is about 70 degrees.

- Everybody, about how high is the temperature in this room? (Signal.) *70 degrees.*

EXERCISE 4
STORY READING

a. Find part C in your textbook. ✓
- The error limit for this story is 8. Read carefully.
b. Everybody, touch the title. ✓
- (Call on a student to read the title.) [*Herman Lands in San Francisco.*]
- What's going to happen in this story? (Call on a student. Idea: *Herman will land in San Francisco.*)
- Everybody, in which city did Herman start his trip? (Signal.) *New York City.*
- Where was the jet going? (Signal.) *To San Francisco.*
- About how far is that trip? (Signal.) *25 hundred miles.*

c. (Call on individual students to read the story, each student reading two or three sentences at a time. Ask questions marked **1.**)

- (Correct errors: Tell the word. Direct the student to reread the sentence.)
- (If the group makes more than 8 errors, direct the students to reread the story.)

d. (After the group has read the selection making no more than 8 errors, read the story to the students and ask questions marked **2.**)

Herman Lands in San Francisco

Sometimes flies get inside jumbo jets. And sometimes these flies will go all the way across the United States. That's what happened to Herman. He went from a city on the east coast to a city on the west coast. And he wasn't the only fly on that trip.

1. The east coast is the same as the east side. Everybody, name the city on the east coast. Get ready. (Signal.) *New York City.*
1. The west coast is the same as the west side. Name the city on the west coast. Get ready. (Signal.) *San Francisco.*
1. How many flies were on that trip? (Signal.) *6.*

When the plane was over Chicago, the captain talked over the loudspeaker to the passengers. "Look below and you can see the city of Chicago. That lake you see next to Chicago is Lake Michigan."

2. Everybody, touch Chicago on the map. ✓
- That bright blue lake is Lake Michigan.
2. Touch Lake Michigan. ✓

Lesson 43   229

2. The arrow shows how far it is from New York City to Chicago. Everybody, how far? (Signal.) *700 miles.*

> Herman wasn't looking at any lakes. He was trying to find something to eat. He could smell some really good stuff.
> The crew was brewing coffee and cooking dinner for the passengers. It didn't take Herman very long to find the place where the food was. On a plane, that place is not called a kitchen. It is called a galley. The galley was warm, and it smelled great to Herman.

2. Everybody, what is the kitchen on a plane called? (Signal.) *A galley.*

> "We're going to begin our meal service now," a crew member said. "So please return to your seats."

2. What do flight attendants do during the meal service? (Call on a student. Idea: *Serve food to the passengers.*)

> Herman had already started his meal service. He started with a salad that had some shrimp in it. "Good," he thought to himself. Then he went to a piece of cheese. "Good, good," he thought to himself. Did that fly ever eat!

2. Herman had already started his meal service. What does that mean? (Call on a student. Idea: *Herman had already started to eat.*)
2. Everybody, in what part of the plane did Herman find such good things? (Signal.) *The galley.*
2. What did he eat first? (Signal.) *Salad.*
2. What did he eat next? (Signal.) *Cheese.*

> When the meal service was over, it was time for a nap. Herman found the perfect place. It was a metal panel next to the oven. It was very warm—just right.

2. Everybody, touch the metal panel in the picture. ✓
2. Why would that be a perfect place for Herman? (Call on a student. Idea: *Because it was warm.*)

> Herman napped for the rest of the trip. The crew members put away the food trays. They cleaned up the galley, and Herman had to get out of their way a couple of times. But he flew back to his nice warm metal panel and had a good rest. The trip from New York City to San Francisco took six hours. After the plane passed over Chicago, it went west over Denver, and then over Salt Lake City. And then it landed in San Francisco.

2. Everybody, how long did the trip from New York City to San Francisco take? (Signal.) *Six hours.*
2. About how many miles was that trip? (Signal.) *25 hundred.*
2. How fast did the plane fly? (Signal.) *500 miles per hour.*
2. Look at the map. I'll name the cities the plane went over. You touch each city I name. First it went over Chicago. Touch it. ✓
2. Then Denver. Touch it. ✓
2. Then Salt Lake City. Touch it. ✓
2. Then it landed in San Francisco.

230 Lesson 43

> When the plane landed in San Francisco, the passengers got off and said thank you to the crew members. Then the crew members got off and said, "Am I glad to be home." Then three flies got off.

2. Everybody, where did the crew members live, New York City or San Francisco? (Signal.) *San Francisco.*
2. How many flies got on the plane in New York? (Signal.) *6.*
2. How many flies got off in San Francisco? (Signal.) *3.*
2. How many were left on the plane? (Signal.) *3.*

> After the crew left the plane four men and three women came into the plane and cleaned up. They also filled the air with a spray that kills flies.
> **MORE NEXT TIME**

1. Go back to the beginning of the story. Follow along while I read.
2. If Herman is still on the plane, he's going to be in trouble.

EXERCISE 5
PAIRED PRACTICE

You're going to read aloud to your partner. Today the **A** members will read first. Then the **B** members will read from the star to the end of the story.
(Observe students and give feedback.)

End-of-Lesson Activities

INDEPENDENT WORK

Now finish your independent work for lesson 43. Raise your hand when you're finished. (Observe students and give feedback.)

WORKCHECK

a. (Direct students to take out their marking pencils.)
 • We're going to check your independent work. Remember, if you got an item wrong, make an **X** next to the item.
b. (For each item: Read the item. Call on a student to answer it. If the answer is wrong, say the correct answer. Refer to the Answer Key for the correct answers.)
c. Now use your marking pencil to fix up any items you got wrong. Remember, all mistakes must be fixed up before you hand in your independent work.

WRITING-SPELLING

(Present Writing-Spelling lesson 43 after completing Reading lesson 43. See Writing-Spelling Guide.)

ACTIVITY

(Present Activity 16 after completing Reading lesson 43. See Activities Across the Curriculum.)

Lesson 44

EXERCISE 1
VOCABULARY REVIEW

a. You learned a sentence that tells what he is supposed to do.
- Everybody, say that sentence. Get ready. (Signal.) *He is supposed to make a decision in a couple of days.*
- (Repeat until firm.)

b. I'll say part of a sentence. When I stop, you say the next word. Listen: He is supposed to make a decision in a . . . Everybody, what's the next word? (Signal.) *Couple.*

c. Listen: He is . . . Everybody, what's the next word? (Signal.) *Supposed.*
- Say the whole sentence. Get ready. (Signal.) *He is supposed to make a decision in a couple of days.*

d. Listen: He is supposed to make a . . . Everybody, what's the next word? (Signal.) *Decision.*

EXERCISE 2
READING WORDS

Column 1

a. Find lesson 44 in your textbook. ✓
- Touch column 1. ✓
- (Teacher reference:)

1. although	4. figure
2. copilot	5. gentlemen
3. ocean	

b. Word 1 is **although**. What word? (Signal.) *Although.*
- Spell **although**. Get ready. (Tap for each letter.) *A-L-T-H-O-U-G-H.*
- **Although** is another word for **but** in some sentences. Here's another way of saying **They went to school but they didn't feel well: They went to school although they didn't feel well.**
- What's another way of saying **She frowned but she was happy?** (Signal.) *She frowned although she was happy.*

c. Word 2 is **copilot**. What word? (Signal.) *Copilot.*
- Spell **copilot**. Get ready. (Tap for each letter.) *C-O-P-I-L-O-T.*
- A copilot is the person who works with the pilot in flying the plane. The pilot is in charge. The pilot tells the copilot what to do.

d. Word 3 is **ocean**. What word? (Signal.) *Ocean.*
- Spell **ocean**. Get ready. (Tap for each letter.) *O-C-E-A-N.*
- An ocean is a very large body of salt water. There are oceans on both sides of the United States.

e. Word 4 is **figure**. What word? (Signal.) *Figure.*
- Spell **figure**. Get ready. (Tap for each letter.) *F-I-G-U-R-E.*
- When you figure out something, you learn it. What's another way of saying **He learned how to work the puzzle?** (Signal.) *He figured out how to work the puzzle.*
- What's another way of saying **They learned how the machine worked?** (Signal.) *They figured out how the machine worked.*

f. Word 5 is **gentlemen**. What word? (Signal.) *Gentlemen.*

g. Let's read those words again, the fast way.
- Word 1. What word? (Signal.) *Although.*
- (Repeat for words 2–5.)

h. (Repeat step g until firm.)

Column 2

i. Find column 2. ✓
- (Teacher reference:)

1. finding	4. workers
2. cleared	5. stacked
3. facing	

- All these words have an ending.
j. Word 1. What word? (Signal.) *Finding.*
- (Repeat for words 2–5.)

k. Let's read those words again.
- Word 1. What word? (Signal.) *Finding.*
- (Repeat for words 2–5.)

l. (Repeat step k until firm.)

Column 3

m. Find column 3. ✓
- (Teacher reference:)

1. weren't	4. galley
2. decision	5. coast
3. weather	

n. Word 1. What word? (Signal.) *Weren't.*
- **Weren't is a contraction for the words were not.**
o. Word 2. What word? (Signal.) *Decision.*
- What's another way of saying **She made up her mind about going swimming?** (Signal.) *She made a decision about going swimming.*
p. Word 3. What word? (Signal.) *Weather.*
- Name some of the things you would mention when you tell about the weather. (Call on individual students. Ideas: *How hot it is; whether it's raining or snowing; what kind of wind there is; about the clouds.*)
- Who can tell about the weather today? (Call on individual students. Accept reasonable responses.)
q. Word 4. What word? (Signal.) *Galley.*
- What is the galley on a plane or ship? (Signal.) *Kitchen.*
r. Word 5. What word? (Signal.) *Coast.*
- What two things meet at the coast? (Call on a student. Idea: *Ocean and land.*)
s. Let's read those words again.
- Word 1. What word? (Signal.) *Weren't.*
- (Repeat for words 2–5.)
t. (Repeat step s until firm.)

Column 4

u. Find column 4. ✓
- (Teacher reference:)

1. perfect	4. quite
2. panel	5. frozen
3. dead	

v. Word 1. What word? (Signal.) *Perfect.*
- What would you call a place that has everything the way it should be? (Signal.) *A perfect place.*
w. Word 2. What word? (Signal.) *Panel.*
- (Repeat for words 3–5.)
x. Let's read those words again.
- Word 1. What word? (Signal.) *Perfect.*
- (Repeat for words 2–5.)
y. (Repeat step x until firm.)

Column 5

z. Find column 5. ✓
- (Teacher reference:)

1. dodge	3. huge
2. flown	4. June

a. Word 1. What word? (Signal.) *Dodge.*
- (Repeat for words 2–4.)
b. (Repeat step a until firm.)

Individual Turns

(For columns 1–5: Call on individual students, each to read one to three words per turn.)

EXERCISE 3

COMPREHENSION PASSAGE

a. Find part B in your textbook. ✓
- You're going to read the next story about Herman. First you'll read the information passage. It gives some facts about wind.
b. Everybody, touch the title. ✓
- (Call on a student to read the title.) *[Finding the Direction of a Wind.]*
- Everybody, what's the title? (Signal.) *Finding the Direction of a Wind.*
c. (Call on individual students to read the passage, each student reading two or three sentences at a time.)

> **Finding the Direction of a Wind**
>
> To find the direction of a wind, you face the wind so the wind blows in your face.

- Listen again: To find the direction of a wind, you face the wind so the wind blows in your face. What do you do to find the direction of a wind? (Call on a student. Idea: *You face the wind so the wind blows in your face.*)

> The direction you're facing tells the name of the wind. If you face east, the wind is an <u>east wind</u>. If you face north, the wind is a <u>north wind</u>.

- Everybody, name the wind if you're facing south. Get ready. (Signal.) *South wind.*
- Name the wind if you're facing west. Get ready. (Signal.) *West wind.*

- Listen: You face north. The wind is blowing against your back. You have to face the opposite direction for the wind to blow in your face.
- Everybody, what's the opposite direction of north? (Signal.) *South.*
- So which way do you have to face so you're facing into the wind? (Signal.) *South.*
- When you face south, how do you know you're facing into the wind? (Call on a student. Idea: *The wind is blowing in your face.*)
- Listen: You're facing south and the wind is blowing into your face. Everybody, so what's the name of that wind? (Signal.) *South wind.*

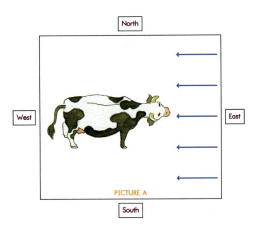

Look at picture A. The arrows show the direction the wind is blowing. The cow is facing into the wind.
Which direction is the cow facing?

- Everybody, what's the answer? (Signal.) *East.*

So what's the name of the wind?

- Everybody, what's the answer? (Signal.) *East wind.*

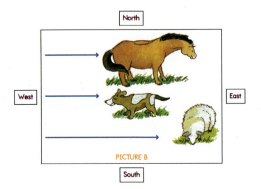

Look at picture B. The arrows show the wind. Which animal is facing into the wind?

- Everybody, what's the answer? (Signal.) *Dog.*

Which direction is that animal facing?

- Everybody, what's the answer? (Signal.) *West.*

So what's the name of the wind?

- Everybody, what's the answer? (Signal.) *West wind.*

EXERCISE 4

STORY READING

a. Find part C in your textbook. ✓
- We're going to do this story two times. First you'll read it out loud and make no more than 8 errors. Then I'll read it and ask questions.
b. Everybody, touch the title. ✓
- (Call on a student to read the title.) [*Fly Spray Fills the Air.*]
- Everybody, what's the title? (Signal.) *Fly Spray Fills the Air.*
c. (Call on individual students to read the story, each student reading two or three sentences at a time. Ask questions marked **1**.)

- (Correct errors: Tell the word. Direct the student to reread the sentence.)
- (If the group makes more than 8 errors, direct the students to reread the story.)

d. (After the group has read the selection making no more than 8 errors, read the story to the students and ask questions marked **2**.)

Fly Spray Fills the Air

Herman and five other flies were on the jumbo jet when it landed in San Francisco. Some of the flies got off the plane in San Francisco.

1. Everybody, how many flies got off? (Signal.) *3.*
1. How many were left on the plane? (Signal.) *3.*

Shortly after the plane pulled up to the gate, some men and women came into the plane and cleaned it. They filled the air with fly spray.

1. What does fly spray do? (Call on a student. Idea: *Kills flies.*)

When the air cleared and the workers left the plane, there were two dead flies. One fly felt quite well. This fly had been sitting on a warm metal panel in the galley. That panel was close to an outside door. Two workers had opened that door and then started to load the dinners for the next flight. Fresh air blew in through the open door. This air kept the fly spray from reaching Herman. Herman didn't know that the air saved his life.

2. Everybody, how many flies were killed by fly spray? (Signal.) *Two.*
2. Are there any **living** flies left on the plane? (Signal.) *Yes.*
2. How many? (Signal.) *One.*
2. Who is that? (Signal.) *Herman.*
2. If Herman was close to an open door, was he in **fresh air** or **air filled with fly spray**? (Signal.) *Fresh air.*
2. What would happen to Herman if he flew to a place where the outside air couldn't reach him? (Call on a student. Idea: *He'd die.*)

The workers stacked the dinners next to Herman. The dinners didn't smell very good because they were frozen, and flies do not like things that are too cold. The air was too cold for Herman. While it was blowing on him, he kept thinking, "This air is too cold. I should fly to a warmer place." Every time he got ready to take off, the air stopped blowing so hard and he could feel the nice warm panel. So he made a decision to stay on the metal panel.

2. Everybody, did Herman fly away from the open door? (Signal.) *No.*
2. Why not? (Call on a student. Idea: *Because every time he got ready to take off, the wind stopped blowing so hard.*)

If Herman had felt a nice warm breeze and sunlight outside, he would have flown out the open door. But on that day, the weather in San Francisco was as cool as it usually is. Here's why the weather is usually cool in San Francisco. San Francisco is next to the ocean. The air over the ocean is cool. The air blows from the ocean to San Francisco. So, San Francisco is cool.

2. Everybody, touch the **X** on the map. That's where the wind starts. ✓
2. Touch San Francisco. ✓
2. If you were in San Francisco and you wanted the wind to blow in your face, you'd have to face the **X**. Listen: Which **direction** would you face if you wanted the wind to blow in your face? (Signal.) *West.*
2. Listen to that part again: San Francisco is next to the ocean. The air over the ocean is cool. **The air blows from the ocean to San Francisco.** So, San Francisco is cool.
2. Everybody, which way does the air blow? (Signal.) *From the ocean to San Francisco.*

**The jet that Herman was on was going back to New York City. That jet would go faster on the trip to New York City. Here's why. The jet was going to fly in the same direction the wind was blowing.
MORE NEXT TIME**

1. Go back to the beginning of the story. Follow along while I read.
2. Everybody, would the plane go **faster** or **slower** when it goes in the same direction as the wind? (Signal.) *Faster.*
2. Would the plane go **faster** or **slower** when it goes in the opposite direction as the wind? (Signal.) *Slower.*

Lesson 44   235

2. When the plane went from New York City to San Francisco, was it going in the **same direction** or the **opposite direction** as the wind? (Signal.) *Opposite direction.*
2. How long did that trip take? (Signal.) *6 hours.*
2. Would the trip back to New York take **more than six hours** or **less than six hours?** (Signal.) *Less than 6 hours.*

EXERCISE 5
PAIRED PRACTICE

You're going to read aloud to your partner. Today the **B** members will read first. Then the **A** members will read from the star to the end of the story.
(Observe students and give feedback.)

End-of-Lesson Activities

INDEPENDENT WORK

Now finish your independent work for lesson 44. Raise your hand when you're finished. (Observe students and give feedback.)

WORKCHECK

a. (Direct students to take out their marking pencils.)
  - We're going to check your independent work. Remember, if you got an item wrong, make an **X** next to the item.
b. (For each item: Read the item. Call on a student to answer it. If the answer is wrong, say the correct answer. Refer to the Answer Key for the correct answers.)
c. Now use your marking pencil to fix up any items you got wrong. Remember, all mistakes must be fixed up before you hand in your independent work.

WRITING-SPELLING

(Present Writing-Spelling lesson 44 after completing Reading lesson 44. See Writing-Spelling Guide.)

Lesson 45

Materials: Each student will need their thermometer chart for exercise 6.

EXERCISE 1

VOCABULARY

a. **Find page 338 in your textbook.** ✓
- Touch sentence 11. ✓
- This is a new vocabulary sentence. It says: They were eager to hear the announcement. Everybody, read that sentence. Get ready. (Signal.) *They were eager to hear the announcement.*
- Close your eyes and say the sentence. Get ready. (Signal.) *They were eager to hear the announcement.*
- (Repeat until firm.)

b. When you're eager to hear something, you are really looking forward to hearing it. How would you feel if you were eager to play a game? (Call on a student. Idea: *Really looking forward to it.*)

c. An announcement is a message. Everybody, what's another word that means **message**? (Signal.) *Announcement.*
- What's another way of saying **They heard a message about the lifeboats?** (Signal.) *They heard an announcement about the lifeboats.*

d. Listen to the sentence again: They were eager to hear the announcement.
- Everybody, say that sentence. Get ready. (Signal.) *They were eager to hear the announcement.*
- (Repeat until firm.)

e. What word means **message**? (Signal.) *Announcement.*
- What word tells how they felt about hearing the announcement? (Signal.) *Eager.*

EXERCISE 2

READING WORDS

Column 1

a. **Find lesson 45 in your textbook.** ✓
- Touch column 1. ✓
- (Teacher reference:)

> 1. Pacific Ocean   4. attention
> 2. Japan   5. announcement
> 3. enemy

b. Number 1 is **Pacific Ocean.** What words? (Signal.) *Pacific Ocean.*
- The Pacific Ocean is the ocean that borders the west coast of the United States.

c. Word 2 is **Japan.** What word? (Signal.) *Japan.*
- Spell **Japan.** Get ready. (Tap for each letter.) *J-A-P-A-N.*
- Japan is a country that is 5 thousand miles from the United States.

d. Word 3 is **enemy.** What word? (Signal.) *Enemy.*
- Spell **enemy.** Get ready. (Tap for each letter.) *E-N-E-M-Y.*

e. Word 4 is **attention.** What word? (Signal.) *Attention.*
- When something catches your attention, you know it's there. If a smell catches your attention, you know the smell is there.

f. Word 5 is **announcement.** What word? (Signal.) *Announcement.*

g. Let's read those words again, the fast way.
- Number 1. What words? (Signal.) *Pacific Ocean.*
- Word 2. What word? (Signal.) *Japan.*
- (Repeat for words 3–5.)

h. (Repeat step g until firm.)

Column 2

i. Find column 2. ✓
- (Teacher reference:)

> 1. fastest   3. circled
> 2. pushing   4. warmer

- All these words have endings.

j. Word 1. What word? (Signal.) *Fastest.*
- (Repeat for words 2–4.)

k. Let's read those words again.
- Word 1. What word? (Signal.) *Fastest.*
- (Repeat for words 2–4.)

l. (Repeat step k until firm.)

Column 3

m. Find column 3. ✓
- (Teacher reference:)

| 1. headed | 3. ladies |
| 2. higher | 4. wrapper |

- All these words have endings.
n. Word 1. What word? (Signal.) *Headed.*
- (Repeat for words 2–4.)
o. Let's read those words again.
- Word 1. What word? (Signal.) *Headed.*
- (Repeat for words 2–4.)
p. (Repeat step o until firm.)

Column 4

q. Find column 4. ✓
- (Teacher reference:)

| 1. <u>al</u>though | 3. <u>co</u>pilot |
| 2. <u>fig</u>ure | 4. <u>tak</u>en |

- These words have more than one syllable. The first syllable is underlined.
r. Word 1 is **although.** What's the first syllable? (Signal.) *al.*
- What's the whole word? (Signal.) *Although.*
- What's another way of saying **He smiled but he was scared?** (Signal.) *He smiled although he was scared.*
s. Word 2. What's the first syllable? (Signal.) *fig.*
- What's the whole word? (Signal.) *Figure.*
- What's another way of saying **They learned where the secret panel was?** (Signal.) *They figured out where the secret panel was.*
t. Word 3. What's the first syllable? (Signal.) *co.*
- What's the whole word? (Signal.) *Copilot.*
u. Word 4. What's the first syllable? (Signal.) *take.*
- What's the whole word? (Signal.) *Taken.*
v. Let's read those words again.
- Word 1. What word? (Signal.) *Although.*
- (Repeat for words 2–4.)
w. (Repeat step v until firm.)

Column 5

x. Find column 5. ✓
- (Teacher reference:)

1. weren't	4. huge
2. dodge	5. eager
3. climb	

y. Word 1. What word? (Signal.) *Weren't.*
- What's another way of saying **The stones were not cold?** (Signal.) *The stones weren't cold.*
z. Word 2. What word? (Signal.) *Dodge.*
- (Repeat for words 3–5.)
a. Let's read those words again.
- Word 1. What word? (Signal.) *Weren't.*
- (Repeat for words 2–5.)
b. (Repeat step a until firm.)

Column 6

c. Find column 6. ✓
- (Teacher reference:)

| 1. blown | 3. June |
| 2. brave | 4. gentlemen |

d. Word 1. What word? (Signal.) *Blown.*
- (Repeat for words 2–4.)
e. Let's read those words again.
- Word 1. What word? (Signal.) *Blown.*
- (Repeat for words 2–4.)
f. (Repeat step e until firm.)

Individual Turns

(For columns 1–6: Call on individual students, each to read one to three words per turn.)

EXERCISE 3

VOCABULARY REVIEW

a. Here's the new vocabulary sentence: They were eager to hear the announcement.
- Everybody, say that sentence. Get ready. (Signal.) *They were eager to hear the announcement.*
- (Repeat until firm.)
b. What word tells how they felt about hearing the announcement? (Signal.) *Eager.*
- What word means **message?** (Signal.) *Announcement.*
- (Repeat step b until firm.)

EXERCISE 4

COMPREHENSION PASSAGE

a. Find part B in your textbook. ✓
- You're going to read the next story about Herman. First you'll read the information passage. It gives some more facts about wind.
b. Everybody, touch the title. ✓
- (Call on a student to read the title.) [Airplanes and Wind.]
- Everybody, what's the title? (Signal.) *Airplanes and Wind.*
c. (Call on individual students to read the passage, each student reading two or three sentences at a time.)

> **Airplanes and Wind**
>
> Look at the pictures on the next page.
> All the planes in the picture can go 500 miles per hour if there is no wind. But there is a wind in each picture.

 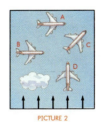

PICTURE 1   PICTURE 2

- Look at the pictures. The arrows in each picture show which way the wind is blowing. Point with your finger to show which way the wind moves in picture 1. ✓
- There's a cloud in picture 1. That cloud goes the same direction as the wind. Point to show the direction the cloud will move. ✓
- Point with your finger to show which way the wind moves in picture 2. ✓
- Touch the cloud in picture 2. ✓
- Point to show the direction that cloud will move. ✓

> **Here's the rule:** The planes go the fastest when they go in the same direction the wind is blowing.

- Everybody, when do they go the fastest? (Signal.) *When they go in the same direction the wind is blowing.*
- (Repeat until firm.)

- Touch the plane in picture 1 that is going the same direction the wind is blowing. ✓
- What's the letter of the plane you're touching? (Signal.) *A.*
- Plane A is going in the same direction the wind is blowing, so what else do you know about that plane? (Signal.) *It goes the fastest.*
- Touch the plane in picture 2 that is going the same direction the wind is blowing. ✓
- What's the letter of the plane you're touching? (Signal.) *D.*
- Plane D is going the same direction the wind is blowing, so what else do you know about that plane? (Signal.) *It goes the fastest.*

EXERCISE 5

STORY READING

a. Find part C in your textbook. ✓
- The error limit for this story is 8. Read carefully. I'm going to ask some questions as you read the story. Then I'll read the story and ask more questions.
b. Everybody, touch the title. ✓
- (Call on a student to read the title.) [Rough Air.]
- Everybody, what's the title? (Signal.) *Rough Air.*
When a plane goes through rough air, it feels like a car going over a rough road. The plane bounces up and down.
c. (Call on individual students to read the story, each student reading one or two sentences at a time. Ask questions marked **1**.)

- (Correct errors: Tell the word. Direct the student to reread the sentence.)
- (If the group makes more than 8 errors, direct the students to reread the story.)

d. (After the group has read the selection making no more than 8 errors, read the story to the students and ask questions marked **2**.)

> **Rough Air**
>
> Although Herman reached San Francisco in the middle of June, the air was cool because it was coming from a cool place.

Lesson 45   239

2. Everybody, what cool place was it coming from? (Signal.) *The ocean.*

> **When Herman's jet landed, the temperature was only 63 degrees.**

2. Everybody, what was the temperature when the jet landed? (Signal.) *63 degrees.*

> **An hour later, the temperature was 58 degrees, and the jet was ready to fly back to New York City.**

2. Everybody, had the temperature gone **up** or **down**? (Signal.) *Down.*
2. Was it **warmer** or **colder** outside when the plane was ready to leave? (Signal.) *Colder.*

> **A strong wind was blowing from the west. That wind was pushing big storm clouds over the United States. The captain of the jet plane knew about these clouds. He also knew that the jet would not be able to dodge them. The passengers were in for some rough air.**
>
> **The captain said to his copilot, who sat next to him, "We're going to have some frightened passengers before this trip is over."**

2. Why were the passengers going to be frightened? (Call on a student. Idea: *Because the plane was going to bounce a lot.*)

> **The captain was right. The jet took off and circled over the ocean. Then it turned and headed toward New York City.**

2. Everybody, when it headed toward New York City, which direction was it going? (Signal.) *East.*

> **The jet began to climb higher and higher. Then it reached the huge clouds that had been blown in by the strong west wind. "Ladies and gentlemen," the captain said over the loudspeaker. "Please stay in your seat and keep your seat belt fastened. We are going to run into some rough . . ."**

1. I'll read that part the way the captain said it:

   "Ladies and gentlemen, please stay in your seat and keep your seat belt fastened. We are going to run into some rough . . ."

1. Why do you think the captain stopped talking right in the middle of what he was saying? (Call on a student. Idea: *The plane started to bounce.*)

> **The plane suddenly bounced. Then it dropped. "Oh," some of the people said. They began to hang onto their seats. The plane bounced again and again.**
>
> **It seemed as if the plane was going over a very, very rough road. Some of the passengers looked at the wings. The wings were bouncing up and down. A lot of the passengers were thinking the same thing.**

1. What do you think they were thinking? (Call on a student. Idea: *That they might crash.*)

> **They thought, "We're going to crash," but they didn't say that. They tried to look brave. "This air is rough," they said with a smile. But they were not smiling inside.**

2. Everybody, did they really feel like smiling? (Signal.) *No.*
2. Why were they smiling? (Call on a student. Idea: *They were trying to look brave.*)
2. How did they really feel? (Call on a student. Idea: *Scared.*)

2. Some things in the picture show that the plane is bouncing pretty badly. What are they? (Call on a student. Ideas: *Drinks spilling; a necktie, hair, glasses, and necklace flying up.*)

The crew on the plane didn't mind the rough air very much. They knew that they would be out of the rough air as soon as they got above the clouds. They weren't the only ones who were not afraid.

1. Who else do you think wasn't bothered by the plane's bouncing around? (Call on a student. Idea: *Herman*.)

Herman had found a candy wrapper. And it was good, good, GOOD. The plane was much warmer now. And the food in the ovens was starting to thaw out. The smells of food filled the plane.

1. If you were a passenger being bounced around in that plane, would the smell of food be a **good smell** or a **bad smell** to you? (Signal.) *Bad smell.*
1. Why? (Call on a student. Idea: *Because my stomach would be upset*.)
1. Everybody, if you were Herman, would the smell of food be a **good smell** or a **bad smell** to you? (Signal.) *Good smell.*

While the passengers were thinking, "I'm going to be sick," Herman was thinking, "This place is good, good, GOOD."
The trip going to San Francisco had taken six hours.

1. Everybody, will the trip to New York take **more time** or **less time**? (Signal.) *Less time.*

The trip back to New York took only five hours.
  Can you figure out why?
       MORE NEXT TIME

1. Go back to the beginning of the story. Follow along while I read.
2. The wind is blowing from the west to the east. Everybody, in which direction is the plane going? (Signal.) *From the west to the east.*
2. So will the plane go **faster** or **slower** than it would if it went in another direction? (Signal.) *Faster.*
2. So the plane will get to New York City in less time.

EXERCISE 6

Note: There is a reading checkout in this lesson; therefore, there is no paired practice.

READING CHECKOUTS

a. Today is a reading-checkout day. While you're doing your independent work, I'm going to call on you one at a time to read part of the story from lesson 44. When I call on you to come and do your checkout, bring your thermometer chart.
- Remember, you pass the checkout by reading the passage in less than a minute without making more than 2 mistakes. And when you pass the checkout, you'll color the space for lesson 45 on your thermometer chart.
b. (Call on individual students to read the portion of story 44 marked with ✱.)
- (Time the student. Note words that are missed and total number of words read.)
- (Teacher reference:)

✱**The workers stacked the dinners next to Herman. The dinners didn't smell very good because they were frozen, and flies do not like things that are too cold. The air was too cold for Herman. While it was blowing on him, he kept thinking, "This air is too cold. I [50] should fly to a warmer place." Every time he got ready to take off, the air stopped blowing so hard and he could feel the [75] nice warm panel. So he made a decision to stay on the metal panel. If Herman had felt a nice warm breeze and sunlight outside, ✱ [100] he would have flown out the open door.**

- (If the student reads the passage in one minute or less and makes no more than 2 errors, direct the student to color in the space for lesson 45 on the thermometer chart.)
- (If the student makes any mistakes, point to each word that was misread and identify it.)

- (If the student does not meet the time-error criterion for the passage, direct the student to practice reading the story with the assigned partner.)

End-of-Lesson Activities

INDEPENDENT WORK

Now finish your independent work for lesson 45. Raise your hand when you're finished. (Observe students and give feedback.)

WORKCHECK

a. (Direct students to take out their marking pencils.)
- We're going to check your independent work. Remember, if you got an item wrong, make an **X** next to the item.

b. (For each item: Read the item. Call on a student to answer it. If the answer is wrong, say the correct answer. Refer to the Answer Key for the correct answers.)

c. Now use your marking pencil to fix up any items you got wrong. Remember, all mistakes must be fixed up before you hand in your independent work.

Note: You will need a globe for lessons 46, 47, and 48.

WRITING-SPELLING

(Present Writing-Spelling lesson 45 after completing Reading lesson 45. See Writing-Spelling Guide.)

Lessons 46–50 • Planning Page

Looking Ahead

	Lesson 46	Lesson 47	Lesson 48	Lesson 49	Lesson 50
Lesson Events	Vocabulary Review Reading Words Comprehension Passage Globe Story Reading Paired Practice Independent Work Workcheck Writing-Spelling	Vocabulary Review Reading Words Comprehension Passage Expanded Activity Story Reading Globe Review Paired Practice Independent Work Workcheck Writing-Spelling	**Vocabulary Sentence** Reading Words Vocabulary Review Comprehension Passages Story Reading Globe Review Paired Practice Independent Work Workcheck Writing-Spelling	Vocabulary Review Reading Words Story Reading Paired Practice Independent Work Workcheck Writing-Spelling Optional Activity	Fact Game Reading Checkouts Test Marking the Test Test Remedies Literature Lesson
Vocabulary Sentence	#11: They were <u>eager</u> to hear the <u>announcement</u>.	sentence #9 sentence #10 sentence #11	#12: The <u>lifeboat</u> <u>disappeared</u> in the <u>whirlpool</u>.	#12: The <u>lifeboat</u> <u>disappeared</u> in the <u>whirlpool</u>.	
Reading Words: Word Types	modeled words –ed words multi-syllable words mixed words	modeled words words with endings –s words 2-syllable words mixed words	words with endings modeled words mixed words multi-syllable words	modeled words –s words multi-syllable words mixed words	
New Vocabulary	strength human excitement several globe	Texas Ohio exit sweat mummy	whole	Italy Turkey China million eager	
Comprehension Passages	*More About the World*	*The Eye of a Fly*	1) *Facts About Spiders* 2) *The Size of Some States*		
Story	*Herman Heads to Japan*	*Herman Tries to Escape*	*The Jumbo Jet Lands in Japan*	*Herman is Cold-Blooded*	
Skill Items	Deductions	Vocabulary Vocabulary sentence	Vocabulary sentences Same and Different	Deductions	Test: Deductions; Vocabulary sentences #9-11
Special Materials	Globe	Globe	Globe		Thermometer charts, dice, Fact Game 50, Fact Game Answer Key, scorecard sheets, *materials for literature project
Special Projects/ Activities			Activity after lesson 48		

* Literature anthology; blackline masters 5A, 5B; lined paper; cotton balls; blindfold (scarf, towel, etc.).

Lesson 46

Materials: You will need a globe and material for marking trips on the globe for exercise 4.

EXERCISE 1
VOCABULARY REVIEW

a. Here's the new vocabulary sentence: **They were eager to hear the announcement.**
- Everybody, say that sentence. Get ready. (Signal.) *They were eager to hear the announcement.*
- (Repeat until firm.)

b. What word means **message?** (Signal.) *Announcement.*
- What word tells how they felt about hearing the announcement? (Signal.) *Eager.*
- (Repeat step b until firm.)

EXERCISE 2
READING WORDS

Column 1

a. Find lesson 46 in your textbook. ✓
- Touch column 1. ✓
- (Teacher reference:)

1. strength	4. excitement
2. human	5. California
3. mountain	

b. Word 1 is **strength.** What word? (Signal.) *Strength.*
- Spell **strength.** Get ready. (Tap for each letter.) *S-T-R-E-N-G-T-H.*
- Your strength is how strong you are. A person who is stronger has more strength. Who has more strength, a child or a grown-up? (Signal.) *A grown-up.*

c. Word 2 is **human.** What word? (Signal.) *Human.*
- Spell **human.** Get ready. (Tap for each letter.) *H-U-M-A-N.*

- Humans are people. Here's another way of saying **There were many people in the woods: There were many humans in the woods.**

d. Word 3 is **mountain.** What word? (Signal.) *Mountain.*
- Spell **mountain.** Get ready. (Tap for each letter.) *M-O-U-N-T-A-I-N.*

e. Word 4 is **excitement.** What word? (Signal.) *Excitement.*
- When you are worked up and have trouble sitting still, you feel excitement.

f. Word 5 is **California.** What word? (Signal.) *California.*

g. Let's read those words again, the fast way.
- Word 1. What word? (Signal.) *Strength.*
- (Repeat for words 2–5.)

h. (Repeat step g until firm.)

Column 2

i. Find column 2. ✓
- (Teacher reference:)

1. sprayed	3. cooled
2. cleared	4. napped

- All these words end with the letters **E-D.**

j. Word 1. What word? (Signal.) *Sprayed.*
- (Repeat for words 2–4.)

k. Let's read those words again.
- Word 1. What word? (Signal.) *Sprayed.*
- (Repeat for words 2–4.)

l. (Repeat step k until firm.)

Column 3

m. Find column 3. ✓
- (Teacher reference:)

1. <u>sev</u>eral	4. <u>hair</u>y
2. <u>con</u>tinue	5. <u>en</u>emy
3. <u>cor</u>ners	

- These words have more than one syllable. The first syllable is underlined.

n. Word 1. What's the first syllable? (Signal.) *sev.*
- What's the whole word? (Signal.) *Several.*
- If several people are meeting, could there be three people? (Signal.) *Yes.*

- Could there be four people? (Signal.) *Yes.*
- Could there be two people? (Signal.) *No.*
- Could there be a lot of people? (Signal.) *No.*

o. Word 2. What's the first syllable? (Signal.) *con.*
- What's the whole word? (Signal.) *Continue.*
- What do you do when you keep on working? (Signal.) *Continue working.*

p. Word 3. What's the first syllable? (Signal.) *corn.*
- What's the whole word? (Signal.) *Corners.*

q. Word 4. What's the first syllable? (Signal.) *hair.*
- What's the whole word? (Signal.) *Hairy.*

r. Word 5. What's the first syllable? (Signal.) *en.*
- What's the whole word? (Signal.) *Enemy.*

s. Let's read those words again.
- Word 1. What word? (Signal.) *Several.*
- (Repeat for: **2. continue, 3. corners, 4. hairy, 5. enemy.**)

t. (Repeat step s until firm.)

Column 4

u. Find column 4. ✓
- (Teacher reference:)

1. Pacific Ocean	4. free
2. globe	5. web
3. jet's	6. strip

v. Number 1. What words? (Signal.) *Pacific Ocean.*
- Is the Pacific Ocean on the **east** coast or the **west** coast of the United States? (Signal.) *West.*

w. Word 2. What word? (Signal.) *Globe.*
- A small model of Earth is called a globe. A globe is shaped like a ball.

x. Word 3. What word? (Signal.) *Jet's.*
- (Repeat for words 4–6.)

y. Let's read those words again.
- Number 1. What words? (Signal.) *Pacific Ocean.*
- Word 2. What word? (Signal.) *Globe.*
- (Repeat for words 3–6.)

z. (Repeat step y until firm.)

Column 5

a. Find column 5. ✓
- (Teacher reference:)

1. cross	4. closets
2. Japan	5. mean-looking
3. attention	6. moments

b. Word 1. What word? (Signal.) *Cross.*
- (Repeat for words 2–6.)

c. Let's read those words again.
- Word 1. What word? (Signal.) *Cross.*
- (Repeat for words 2–6.)

d. (Repeat step c until firm.)

Individual Turns

(For columns 1–5: Call on individual students, each to read one to three words per turn.)

EXERCISE 3

COMPREHENSION PASSAGE

a. Find part B in your textbook. ✓
- You're going to read the next story about Herman. First you'll read the information passage. It gives some facts about the world.

b. Everybody, touch the title. ✓
- (Call on a student to read the title.) *[More About the World.]*
- Everybody, what's the title? (Signal.) *More About the World.*

c. (Call on individual students to read the passage, each student reading two or three sentences at a time.)

> **More About the World**
>
> In today's story you will read about a trip from New York City to San Francisco and then to Japan.

- Everybody, where does the trip start? (Signal.) *New York City.*
- Where does it go next? (Signal.) *San Francisco.*
- Where does it go next? (Signal.) *Japan.*
- (Repeat until firm.)

> **The map shows that trip.**

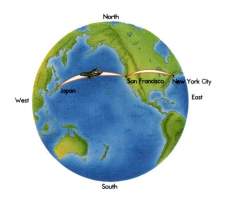

Touch New York City and go to San Francisco.

- Everybody, do it. ✓

In which direction did you go?

- Everybody, what's the answer? (Signal.) *West.*

Now go from San Francisco to Japan.

- Everybody, do it. ✓

In which direction did you go?

- Everybody, what's the answer? (Signal.) *West.*

Is it farther from New York City to San Francisco or from San Francisco to Japan?

- Everybody, what's the answer? (Signal.) *From San Francisco to Japan.*

Your teacher will show you a globe of the world. Find New York City on that globe. Then go west from New York City to San Francisco. Then go west from San Francisco to Japan.

EXERCISE 4

GLOBE

(Show a globe. Mark the trip from New York City to San Francisco and from San Francisco to Japan on the globe with yarn or with strips of tape. Have the students trace the trip and tell where they are going and in which direction they are going.)

EXERCISE 5

STORY READING

a. Find part C in your textbook. ✓
- The error limit for this story is 11. Read carefully.
b. Everybody, touch the title. ✓
- (Call on a student to read the title.) *[Herman Heads to Japan.]*
- Everybody, what's the title? (Signal.) *Herman Heads to Japan.*
c. (Call on individual students to read the story, each student reading one or two sentences at a time. Ask questions marked **1**.)

- (Correct errors: Tell the word. Direct the student to reread the sentence.)
- (If the group makes more than 11 errors, direct the students to reread the story.)

d. (After the group has read the selection making no more than 11 errors, read the story to the students and ask questions marked **2**.)

Herman Heads to Japan

The jumbo jet landed at Kennedy Airport five hours after it took off from San Francisco.

2. Everybody, in what city did the plane land? (Signal.) *New York City.*
2. How long did the trip take? (Signal.) *5 hours.*

The passengers got off the plane, and the crew got off the plane. Workers came and sprayed the inside of the plane with insect spray.

2. What does insect spray do? (Call on a student. Idea: *Kills insects.*)

After the air cleared, there were six dead flies and one dead ant in the plane.

1. Do you think Herman is dead now? (Call on a student. Student preference.)

But there was still one living fly. That fly had crawled inside one of the ovens.

1. Wouldn't he get burned up inside the oven? (Call on a student. Idea: *Only if the oven was on.*)

The oven had cooled some, but it was nice and warm.

Several hours later the oven was cool. Somebody opened it and Herman crawled out.

Passengers were coming into the plane. Some of the passengers were going to San Francisco. But some of them were going a lot farther. The jumbo jet was going to fly to San Francisco, and then it was going to continue to Japan.

1. Everybody, where was it going to stop first? (Signal.) *San Francisco.*
1. Then where was it going to go? (Signal.) *Japan.*
1. Were **all** the passengers going to go to Japan? (Signal.) *No.*
- Some of the passengers are getting off in San Francisco.
1. About how far is it from New York City to San Francisco? (Signal.) *25 hundred miles.*
- It's a lot farther to Japan.

After leaving San Francisco, the jet was going to cross a great ocean, called the Pacific Ocean.

2. Everybody, what's the name of the ocean? (Signal.) *Pacific Ocean.*

The trip from New York City to San Francisco is 25 hundred miles. After leaving San Francisco, a plane must fly west for another 5 thousand miles to get to Japan.

2. Everybody, how far is it from San Francisco to Japan? (Signal.) *5 thousand miles.*

Look at the map. It shows the world.

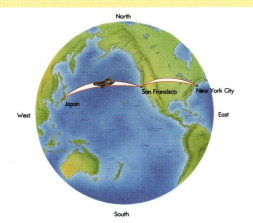

Touch New York City on the map, and follow the jet's trip to San Francisco and then on to Japan.

2. Everybody, first go from New York to San Francisco and then stop. ✓
2. Now go from San Francisco to Japan. ✓
2. What's the name of the ocean you go over after leaving San Francisco? (Signal.) *Pacific Ocean.*
2. In which direction do you go? (Signal.) *West.*

The trip to San Francisco took six hours. After the plane left San Francisco, the passengers napped and talked and ate. While they did that, Herman met an enemy. Herman was buzzing around near one of the coat closets in the jumbo jet. It was dark inside the coat closets, but some smells caught Herman's attention, so he buzzed inside one of the closets.

2. What does it mean: Some smells caught Herman's attention? (Call on a student. Idea: *Herman noticed some smells.*)

He buzzed up into one of the corners. And then he kept trying to fly, but his legs were stuck to something.

1. What do you think that something was? (Call on a student. Idea: *Anything that could be sticky, for example, bubble gum.*)

He buzzed his wings harder and harder. But he couldn't pull himself free. Once more, he buzzed. Time to rest.

2. Why does he have to rest? (Call on a student. Idea: *Because he was tired from trying to pull himself free.*)

Herman, like other flies, had big strange eyes that could see in all directions at the same time. Suddenly, Herman's eyes saw something moving toward him very fast. It was a large hairy thing with eight legs and a mean-looking mouth.

Lesson 46 **247**

1. What could it be? (Call on a student. Ideas: *A spider, a bug,* etc.)

> **Herman was stuck in a spider web, and the spider was ready to eat dinner.**
> **MORE NEXT TIME**

1. Go back to the beginning of the story. Follow along while I read.
2. Everybody, what did the spider plan to have for dinner? (Signal.) *Herman.*
2. What was holding Herman and keeping him from flying away? (Signal.) *The spider's web.*

EXERCISE 6
PAIRED PRACTICE

You're going to read aloud to your partner. Today the **A** members will read first. Then the **B** members will read from the star to the end of the story.

(Observe students and give feedback.)

End-of-Lesson Activities

INDEPENDENT WORK

Now finish your independent work for lesson 46. Raise your hand when you're finished.

(Observe students and give feedback.)

WORKCHECK

a. (Direct students to take out their marking pencils.)
- We're going to check your independent work. Remember, if you got an item wrong, make an **X** next to the item.
b. (For each item: Read the item. Call on a student to answer it. If the answer is wrong, say the correct answer. Refer to the Answer Key for the correct answers.)
c. Now use your marking pencil to fix up any items you got wrong. Remember, all mistakes must be fixed up before you hand in your independent work.

WRITING-SPELLING

(Present Writing-Spelling lesson 46 after completing Reading lesson 46. See Writing-Spelling Guide.)

Lesson 47

Materials: You will need a globe for exercise 6.

EXERCISE 1
VOCABULARY REVIEW

a. You learned a sentence that tells how far several paths continued.
- Everybody, say that sentence. Get ready. (Signal.) *Several paths continued for a great distance.*
- (Repeat until firm.)

b. You learned a sentence that tells what boiling water will do.
- Everybody, say that sentence. Get ready. (Signal.) *Boiling water will thaw ice in a few moments.*
- (Repeat until firm.)

c. Here's the last sentence you learned: They were eager to hear the announcement.
- Everybody, say that sentence. Get ready. (Signal.) *They were eager to hear the announcement.*
- (Repeat until firm.)

d. What word tells how they felt about hearing the announcement? (Signal.) *Eager.*
- What word means **message**? (Signal.) *Announcement.*

e. Once more. Say the sentence that tells what they were eager to hear. Get ready. (Signal.) *They were eager to hear the announcement.*

EXERCISE 2
READING WORDS

Column 1

a. Find lesson 47 in your textbook. ✓
- Touch column 1. ✓
- (Teacher reference:)

1. Texas	4. sweat
2. Ohio	5. poisonous
3. exit	6. warm-blooded

b. Word 1 is **Texas**. What word? (Signal.) *Texas.*
- Spell **Texas**. Get ready. (Tap for each letter.) *T-E-X-A-S.*
- Texas is a state. It is the second-largest state. The only state that is larger is Alaska.

c. Word 2 is **Ohio**. What word? (Signal.) *Ohio.*
- Spell **Ohio**. Get ready. (Tap for each letter.) *O-H-I-O.*
- Ohio is a state. It is between Chicago and New York.

d. Word 3 is **exit**. What word? (Signal.) *Exit.*
- Spell **exit**. Get ready. (Tap for each letter.) *E-X-I-T.*
- When you exit a place, you leave the place. Exit signs show where you can leave. What word means **leave**? (Signal.) *Exit.*

e. Word 4 is **sweat**. What word? (Signal.) *Sweat.*
- Spell **sweat**. Get ready. (Tap for each letter.) *S-W-E-A-T.*
- What is sweat? (Call on a student. Idea: *Salty moisture that appears when you're hot.*)

f. Word 5 is **poisonous**. What word? (Signal.) *Poisonous.*

g. Word 6 is **warm-blooded**. What word? (Signal.) *Warm-blooded.*

h. Let's read those words again, the fast way.
- Word 1. What word? (Signal.) *Texas.*
- (Repeat for words 2–6.)

i. (Repeat step h until firm.)

Column 2

j. Find column 2. ✓
- All these words have endings.
- (Teacher reference:)

1. tugged	4. crowded
2. biting	5. landing
3. leaning	

k. Word 1. What word? (Signal.) *Tugged.*
- (Repeat for words 2–5.)

l. Let's read those words again.
- Word 1. What word? (Signal.) *Tugged.*
- (Repeat for: **2. biting, 3. leaning, 4. crowded, 5. landing.**)

m. (Repeat step l until firm.)

Column 3

n. Find column 3. ✓
- All these words end with the letter **S**.
- (Teacher reference:)

1. moments	4. strips
2. works	5. pens
3. tries	6. papers

o. Word 1. What word? (Signal.) *Moments.*
- (Repeat for words 2–6.)

p. Let's read those words again.
- Word 1. What word? (Signal.) *Moments.*
- (Repeat for words 2–6.)

q. (Repeat step p until firm.)

Column 4

r. Find column 4. ✓
- These words have more than one syllable. The first syllable is underlined.
- (Teacher reference:)

1. <u>dis</u>tance	4. <u>a</u>gainst
2. <u>mum</u>my	5. <u>ea</u>ger
3. <u>luck</u>y	

s. Word 1. What's the first syllable? (Signal.) *dis.*
- What's the whole word? (Signal.) *Distance.*
- Is the distance larger between New York and Chicago or between New York and San Francisco? (Signal.) *Between New York and San Francisco.*

t. Word 2. What's the first syllable? (Signal.) *mumm.*
- What's the whole word? (Signal.) *Mummy.*
- One kind of mummy is a dead person all wrapped up in strips of cloth.

u. Word 3. What's the first syllable? (Signal.) *luck.*
- What's the whole word? (Signal.) *Lucky.*

v. Word 4. What's the first syllable? (Signal.) *a.*
- What's the whole word? (Signal.) *Against.*

w. Word 5. What's the first syllable? (Signal.) *ea.*
- What's the whole word? (Signal.) *Eager.*

x. Let's read those words again.
- Word 1. What word? (Signal.) *Distance.*
- (Repeat for words 2–5.)

y. (Repeat step x until firm.)

Column 5

z. Find column 5. ✓
- (Teacher reference:)

1. strength	4. human
2. slept	5. closet
3. stuff	

a. Word 1. What word? (Signal.) *Strength.*
- Which animal has more strength, a human or a lion? (Signal.) *A lion.*

b. Word 2. What word? (Signal.) *Slept.*
- (Repeat for words 3–5.)

c. Let's read those words again.
- Word 1. What word? (Signal.) *Strength.*
- (Repeat for words 2–5.)

d. (Repeat step c until firm.)

Column 6

e. Find column 6. ✓
- (Teacher reference:)

1. announcement	4. freed
2. California	5. label
3. excitement	

f. Word 1. What word? (Signal.) *Announcement.*
- (Repeat for words 2–5.)

g. (Repeat step f until firm.)

Individual Turns

(For columns 1–6: Call on individual students, each to read one to three words per turn.)

EXERCISE 3

COMPREHENSION PASSAGE

a. Find part B in your textbook. ✓
- You're going to read the next story about Herman. First you'll read the information passage. It gives some more facts about flies.

b. Everybody, touch the title. ✓
- (Call on a student to read the title.) *[The Eye of a Fly.]*

- Everybody, what's the title? (Signal.) *The Eye of a Fly.*
c. (Call on individual students to read the passage, each student reading two or three sentences at a time.)

The Eye of a Fly

If you look at a drop of water, you will see little pictures of things in the drop.

Look at the drop in the picture. You can see a window and a lamp in the drop.

- Everybody, touch the window in the drop. ✓
- Touch the lamp in the drop. ✓

Your eye works like a drop. It is round and it catches pictures the same way the water drop catches pictures.

Look at the eye. You can see the picture the eye is catching.

- Everybody, what two pictures do you see in the eye? (Signal.) *A window and a lamp.*

The eye of a fly is different from a human eye. Look at the fly in the picture. Below the fly is a large picture of the fly's eye.

- The large ball in the middle is the fly's eye. Everybody, touch the fly's eye. ✓
- You can see that the fly is looking at a blue dot and a yellow dot.

The eye of a fly is made up of many, many drops. Each drop catches a picture.

The fly's eye is catching pictures of a yellow dot and a blue dot.

Some drops on the eye catch a picture of the blue dot but not the yellow dot.

Some drops catch a picture of the yellow dot.

Some drops catch a picture of both dots.

- Everybody, touch the drop for arrow A. ✓
- Does that drop have a yellow dot, a blue dot, or both dots? (Signal.) *A yellow dot.*
- Touch the drop for arrow B. ✓
- Does that drop have a yellow dot, a blue dot, or both dots? (Signal.) *Both dots.*
- Touch the drop for arrow C. ✓
- Does that drop have a yellow dot, a blue dot, or both dots? (Signal.) *A blue dot.*

EXERCISE 4

EXPANDED ACTIVITY

a. If you look at a light, the picture of the light is on your eye.
b. (Call on a student.) Look at a light.
- Everybody, you can see the light in ___'s eye. (Permit the other students to look at ___'s eye.)

EXERCISE 5

STORY READING

a. Find part C in your textbook. ✓
- The error limit for this story is 7. Read carefully.
b. Everybody, touch the title. ✓
- (Call on a student to read the title.) [*Herman Tries to Escape.*]
- Everybody, what's the title? (Signal.) *Herman Tries to Escape.*
- Where did we leave Herman in the last story? (Call on a student. Idea: *In a spider's web.*)

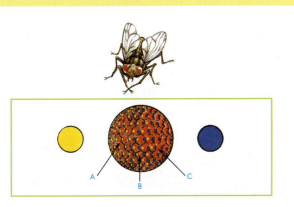

c. (Call on individual students to read the story, each student reading two or three sentences at a time. Ask questions marked **1**.)

- (Correct errors: Tell the word. Direct the student to reread the sentence.)
- (If the group makes more than 7 errors, direct the students to reread the story.)

d. (After the group has read the selection making no more than 7 errors, read the story to the students and ask questions marked **2**.)

Herman Tries to Escape

Herman was tired from trying to escape from the spider web, but when his eyes saw a big hairy spider moving toward him, Herman found a lot of strength.

1. What kinds of things would he do if he found a lot of strength? (Call on a student. Ideas: *Buzz his wings; move his legs;* etc.)

He buzzed harder than he had ever buzzed before. He tugged and pulled against the web. The web was sticky and it didn't let go of Herman's legs. But Herman kept trying.

Now the spider was trying to bite Herman and trying to wrap him up in a web.

2. What was the spider trying to do? (Call on a student. Idea: *Bite Herman and wrap him in a web.*)

The spider was much bigger than Herman—three times bigger.

2. Everybody, use your fingers to show me how big a fly is. ✓
2. Now show me how big something would be if it was three times bigger. ✓

The spider could walk on the web without getting stuck. But Herman was really stuck.

2. Everybody, who could walk on the web without getting stuck? (Signal.) *The spider.*
2. Could Herman do that? (Signal.) *No.*

Most spiders kill insects by biting them. Then they wrap the insect in a web. The insect looks like a mummy. Later, the spider comes back and eats the best parts of the dead insect. The spider leaves the rest of the insect hanging in the web.

2. Everybody, how do spiders kill insects? (Signal.) *By biting them.*
2. What do the spiders do after they bite the insect? (Call on a student. Idea: *Wrap the insect in a web.*)
2. What does the spider do when it comes back later? (Call on a student. Idea: *Eats the best parts of the dead insect.*)

The passengers in the jumbo jet were talking to each other or leaning back in their seats thinking about what they would do when they reached Japan.

1. Everybody, were the passengers thinking about the same things Herman was thinking about? (Signal.) *No.*
1. What were the passengers thinking about? (Call on a student. Idea: *What they would do when they reached Japan.*)
1. What was Herman thinking about? (Call on a student. Idea: *Getting away from the spider.*)

Once in a while, passengers would look below at the ocean. They would think, "Ocean, ocean, ocean. All you can see is ocean."

While the passengers sat and talked and thought, Herman was fighting for his life.

2. Everybody, did the passengers know that this fight was going on? (Signal.) *No.*
2. What is the name of the ocean the passengers were looking at? (Signal.) *The Pacific Ocean.*

Herman was lucky. The spider tried to turn Herman around and wrap him up. But when the spider turned Herman, the spider freed Herman's legs from the web. Herman gave a great buzz with his wings. Suddenly, he was in the air, with some sticky stuff still on his legs.

2. Everybody, was Herman still in the web? (Signal.) *No.*
2. What was the spider trying to do when Herman got free? (Call on a student. Idea: *Turn Herman around and wrap him up.*)
2. What did Herman have on his legs? (Call on a student. Ideas: *Sticky stuff; some of the spider web.*)
2. Everybody, where did that sticky stuff come from? (Signal.) *The spider web.*

> **"Get out of that dark,"** Herman thought.

1. Everybody, what dark was Herman thinking about? (Signal.) *The closet.*

> He flew from the closet to the bright part of the jet. A moment later, Herman landed on a warm red and rubbed his front legs together.

1. What do you think that warm red is? (Call on a student. Idea: *A seat.*)

> As Herman sat on the seat back, he did not remember what had just happened. For Herman, things were warm and red. And he was tired. Time to nap.
> **MORE NEXT TIME**

1. Go back to the beginning of the story. Follow along while I read.
2. Everybody, did Herman remember the fight with the spider? (Signal.) *No.*

EXERCISE 6
GLOBE REVIEW

a. I'll point to different places on the globe. You tell me the name of each place.
- b. (Touch Japan.) Everybody, what country is this? (Signal.) *Japan.*
  - (Touch the United States.) What country is this? (Signal.) *United States.*
  - (Touch San Francisco.) What city is this? (Signal.) *San Francisco.*
  - (Repeat step b until firm.)
- c. (Touch New York City.) What city is this? (Signal.) *New York City.*
  - (Touch Chicago.) What city is this? (Signal.) *Chicago.*

EXERCISE 7
PAIRED PRACTICE

You're going to read aloud to your partner. Today the **B** members will read first. Then the **A** members will read from the star to the end of the story.
(Observe students and give feedback.)

End-of-Lesson Activities

INDEPENDENT WORK

Now finish your independent work for lesson 47. Raise your hand when you're finished. (Observe students and give feedback.)

WORKCHECK

a. (Direct students to take out their marking pencils.)
- We're going to check your independent work. Remember, if you got an item wrong, make an **X** next to the item.
b. (For each item: Read the item. Call on a student to answer it. If the answer is wrong, say the correct answer. Refer to the Answer Key for the correct answers.)
c. Now use your marking pencil to fix up any items you got wrong. Remember, all mistakes must be fixed up before you hand in your independent work.

WRITING-SPELLING

(Present Writing-Spelling lesson 47 after completing Reading lesson 47. See Writing-Spelling Guide.)

Lesson 48

Materials: You will need a globe for exercise 6.

EXERCISE 1
VOCABULARY

a. **Find page 338 in your textbook.** ✓
- Touch sentence 12. ✓
- This is a new vocabulary sentence. It says: The lifeboat disappeared in the whirlpool. Everybody, read that sentence. Get ready. (Signal.) *The lifeboat disappeared in the whirlpool.*
- Close your eyes and say the sentence. Get ready. (Signal.) *The lifeboat disappeared in the whirlpool.*
- (Repeat until firm.)

b. **Lifeboats** are emergency boats that are on large ships.

c. If the lifeboat **disappeared,** you couldn't see it anymore. Everybody, what word means you couldn't see it? (Signal.) *Disappeared.*

d. The sentence says the lifeboats disappeared in the **whirlpool.** Whirlpools are the kind of currents you see when water goes down a drain. The water goes around and around as it goes down.

e. Listen to the sentence again: The lifeboat disappeared in the whirlpool.
- Everybody, say that sentence. Get ready. (Signal.) *The lifeboat disappeared in the whirlpool.*
- (Repeat until firm.)

f. What word names an emergency boat that's on a large ship? (Signal.) *Lifeboat.*
- What word tells what happened to the lifeboat when you couldn't see it anymore? (Signal.) *Disappeared.*
- What word refers to water that goes around and around as it goes down? (Signal.) *Whirlpool.*
- (Repeat step f until firm.)

EXERCISE 2
READING WORDS

Column 1

a. Find lesson 48 in your textbook. ✓
- Touch column 1. ✓
- (Teacher reference:)

1. labeled	4. placed
2. webs	5. disappeared
3. marked	

- All these words have endings.
b. Word 1. What word? (Signal.) *Labeled.*
- (Repeat for words 2–5.)
c. Let's read those words again.
- Word 1. What word? (Signal.) *Labeled.*
- (Repeat for words 2–5.)
d. (Repeat step c until firm.)

Column 2

e. Find column 2. ✓
- (Teacher reference:)

1. aisle	4. fist
2. whole	5. Ohio
3. eager	

f. Word 1 is **aisle.** What word? (Signal.) *Aisle.*
- Spell **aisle.** Get ready. (Tap for each letter.) *A-I-S-L-E.*
- Yes, they walked down the aisle.
g. Word 2. What word? (Signal.) *Whole.*
- This word means the whole thing and not just a part.
h. Word 3. What word? (Signal.) *Eager.*
- (Repeat for words 4 and 5.)
i. Let's read those words again.
- Word 1. What word? (Signal.) *Aisle.*
- (Repeat for words 2–5.)
j. (Repeat step i until firm.)

Column 3

k. Find column 3. ✓
- (Teacher reference:)

> 1. sweat
> 2. fifty
> 3. Texas
> 4. exit
> 5. country

l. Word 1. What word? (Signal.) *Sweat.*
- (Repeat for words 2–5.)

m. Let's read those words again.
- Word 1. What word? (Signal.) *Sweat.*
- (Repeat for words 2–5.)

n. (Repeat step m until firm.)

Column 4

o. Find column 4. ✓
- (Teacher reference:)

> 1. poisonous
> 2. lifeboat
> 3. California
> 4. whirlpool

p. Word 1. What word? (Signal.) *Poisonous.*
- (Repeat for words 2–4.)

q. (Repeat step p until firm.)

Individual Turns

(For columns 1–4: Call on individual students, each to read one to three words per turn.)

EXERCISE 3
VOCABULARY REVIEW

a. Here's the new vocabulary sentence: The lifeboat disappeared in the whirlpool.
- Everybody, say that sentence. Get ready. (Signal.) *The lifeboat disappeared in the whirlpool.*
- (Repeat until firm.)

b. What word refers to water that goes around and around as it goes down? (Signal.) *Whirlpool.*
- What word names an emergency boat that's on large ships? (Signal.) *Lifeboat.*
- What word tells what happened to the lifeboat when you couldn't see it anymore? (Signal.) *Disappeared.*

EXERCISE 4
COMPREHENSION PASSAGES

Passage B

a. Find part B in your textbook. ✓
- You're going to read the next story about Herman. First you'll read two information passages. The first one gives some facts about spiders.

b. Everybody, touch the title. ✓
- (Call on a student to read the title.) *[Facts About Spiders.]*
- Everybody, what's the title? (Signal.) *Facts About Spiders.*

c. (Call on individual students to read the passage, each student reading two or three sentences at a time.)

> **Facts About Spiders**
>
> In the last Herman story, Herman met an enemy. What kind of animal was that enemy?

- Everybody, what's the answer? (Signal.) *A spider.*

> Here are facts you already know about spiders:
>   Spiders are not insects.

- Everybody, say that fact. Get ready. (Signal.) *Spiders are not insects.*

> Spiders have eight legs, not six legs.

- Everybody, say that fact. Get ready. (Signal.) *Spiders have eight legs, not six legs.*
- How many legs do spiders have? (Signal.) *8.*
- How many legs do all insects have? (Signal.) *6.*
- So a spider can't be an insect.

> The body of a spider has two parts, not three.

- Everybody, say that fact. Get ready. (Signal.) *The body of a spider has two parts, not three.*

> Here are some new facts about spiders:
>   Many spiders make webs to catch insects.

- Everybody, say that fact. Get ready. (Signal.) *Many spiders make webs to catch insects.*
- Touch the spider web in the picture. ✓

Lesson 48   255

Some spiders are bigger than your fist.

- Everybody, listen to that fact again: Some spiders are bigger than your fist.
- Say that fact. Get ready. (Signal.) *Some spiders are bigger than your fist.*
- (Repeat until firm.)
- Show me how big one of those spiders would be. ✓

Most spiders are not poisonous to people.

- Everybody, listen to that fact again: Most spiders are not poisonous to people.
- Say that fact. Get ready. (Signal.) *Most spiders are not poisonous to people.*
- (Repeat until firm.)

Passage C
a. Find part C in your textbook. ✓
- This information passage gives some facts about states.
b. Everybody, touch the title. ✓
- (Call on a student to read the title.) *[The Size of Some States.]*
- Everybody, what's the title? (Signal.) *The Size of Some States.*
c. (Call on individual students to read the passage, each student reading two or three sentences at a time.)

The Size of Some States

The United States is a <u>country</u>.

- Everybody, what is the United States? (Signal.) *A country.*

It is called the United States because it is made up of many <u>states</u>. There are fifty states in the United States.

- Everybody, how many states are in the United States? (Signal.) *Fifty.*

The map shows the states that are in the United States. Four states are labeled.

- Not all the states in the United States are labeled. Everybody, how many states are there in the United States? (Signal.) *Fifty.*
- How many are labeled? (Signal.) *Four.*

The state that is marked <u>1</u> is Alaska. It is the biggest state in the United States.

- Everybody, what's the name of the biggest state in the United States? (Signal.) *Alaska.*
- Touch Alaska on the map. ✓
- It is north of the other states.

State <u>2</u> is Texas. It is the second biggest state.

- Everybody, what's the second biggest state? (Signal.) *Texas.*
- Touch Texas on the map. ✓
- It is in the south part of the United States.

State <u>3</u> is the third biggest state. What is the name of that state?

- Everybody, touch state 3 on the map. ✓
- What name? (Signal.) *California.*
- The city of San Francisco is in the state of California.

State <u>4</u> is one of the smaller states. Its name is Ohio.

- Everybody, touch Ohio. ✓

Do you know the name of the state that you live in?

- Everybody, what's the name of the state we live in? (Signal.)

The United States is much bigger than the country of Japan.

- Everybody, which country is bigger, the United States or Japan? (Signal.) *The United States.*

> **The whole country of Japan is smaller than the state of Alaska. The picture shows what the whole country of Japan would look like if it were placed next to Alaska.**

- Everybody, touch Japan in the picture. ✓
- It looks as long as Alaska, but it's much thinner. Remember, Japan is a country. The United States is a country. But the United States is much, much bigger than Japan.
- Everybody, what **state** is bigger than Japan? (Signal.) *Alaska.*

EXERCISE 5
STORY READING

a. Find part D in your textbook. ✓
- The error limit for this story is 5. Read carefully.
b. Everybody, touch the title. ✓
- (Call on a student to read the title.) [*The Jumbo Jet Lands in Japan.*]
- Everybody, where's the jumbo jet going to land? (Signal.) *Japan.*
c. (Call on individual students to read the story, each student reading two or three sentences at a time. Ask questions marked **1**.)

- (Correct errors: Tell the word. Direct the student to reread the sentence.)
- (If the group makes more than 5 errors, direct the students to reread the story.)

d. (After the group has read the selection making no more than 5 errors, read the story to the students and ask questions marked **2**.)

> **The Jumbo Jet Lands in Japan**
>
> Herman had just escaped from a spider web and he was on a warm red seat back. For Herman it was a time to nap. But for the passengers, it was a time for excitement. Off in the distance were green strips of land and a great mountain with a white top. "It's Japan," the passengers said to themselves.

2. Everybody, who was excited? (Signal.) *Passengers.*
2. Why? (Call on a student. Idea: *Because they were almost in Japan.*)
2. Everybody, who was not excited? (Signal.) *Herman.*
2. What was Herman doing? (Call on a student. Idea: *Sleeping.*)
2. Who remembers how far it is from San Francisco to Japan? (Call on a student.) [*5 thousand miles.*]
2. What was the only thing the passengers had seen during that trip? (Call on a student. Ideas: *The ocean; water.*)
2. The picture shows what the passengers saw when they looked out of the window. Everybody, what country are they looking at? (Signal.) *Japan.*
2. Touch the mountain. ✓

> **The plane was no longer six miles above the earth. It was less than a mile above the earth and it continued to get lower as it approached the land. "Look at those tiny lines down there," one of the passengers said and pointed. "That's the airport."**

2. Everybody, how high did the plane fly during most of the trip? (Signal.) *6 miles.*
2. How high was it now? (Signal.) *Less than a mile.*
2. Now what could the passengers see down below? (Call on a student. Ideas: *Tiny lines; airport.*)

> **Now the passengers began to get ready for the plane's landing.**

1. What kinds of things would they do to get ready? (Call on a student. Ideas: *Put on their seat belts; put their shoes back on; put things away;* etc.)

> **Some people fixed their hair. Others put away their pens and papers. Every few moments, they looked out the windows again. "It's beautiful," they said. It was. As the passengers felt this excitement, Herman slept.**

1. Everybody, who was feeling excitement about landing? (Signal.) *The passengers.*
1. What was Herman feeling? (Call on a student. Ideas: *Nothing; sleepy.*)

> **Japan is a small country compared to the United States. But many people live in Japan. Japan is smaller than the state of Alaska. But there are more people in Japan than there are in these three states put together: Texas, Alaska, and Ohio.**

2. Everybody, which is bigger, Japan or the United States? (Signal.) *The United States.*
2. Name a state in the United States that is bigger than Japan. Get ready. (Signal.) *Alaska.*
2. Which has more people, Japan or Alaska? (Signal.) *Japan.*

> **The passengers on the plane were eager to leave. After the plane was on the ground, the passengers lined up and slowly moved toward the exit door.**

1. What is an exit door? (Call on a student. Idea: *The door used to leave a place.*)
1. How would you feel if you had been sitting on that plane for over ten hours? (Call on a student. Ideas: *Bored; ready to move around;* etc.)

> **Herman slept through this excitement. He slept until the plane became cool.**
> **MORE NEXT TIME**

1. Go back to the beginning of the story. Follow along while I read.
2. Everybody, when did he stop sleeping? (Signal.) *When the plane became cool.*

EXERCISE 6
GLOBE REVIEW

a. I'll point to different places on the globe. You tell me the name of each place.
b. (Touch Japan.) Everybody, what country is this? (Signal.) *Japan.*
- (Touch Chicago.) What city is this? (Signal.) *Chicago.*
- (Touch the United States.) What country is this? (Signal.) *United States.*
- (Touch San Francisco.) What city is this? (Signal.) *San Francisco.*
- (Repeat step b until firm.)

c. (Touch New York City.) What city is this? (Signal.) *New York City.*
- (Touch California.) What state is this? (Signal.) *California.*
- (Touch Texas.) What state is this? (Signal.) *Texas.*
- (Touch Alaska.) What state is this? (Signal.) *Alaska.*
- (Repeat step c until firm.)

EXERCISE 7
PAIRED PRACTICE

You're going to read aloud to your partner. Today the **A** members will read first. Then the **B** members will read.

End-of-Lesson Activities

INDEPENDENT WORK

Now finish your independent work for lesson 48. Raise your hand when you're finished. (Observe students and give feedback.)

WORKCHECK

a. (Direct students to take out their marking pencils.)
- We're going to check your independent work. Remember, if you got an item wrong, make an **X** next to the item.
b. (For each item: Read the item. Call on a student to answer it. If the answer is wrong, say the correct answer. Refer to the Answer Key for the correct answers.)

c. Now use your marking pencil to fix up any items you got wrong. Remember, all mistakes must be fixed up before you hand in your independent work.

WRITING-SPELLING

(Present Writing-Spelling lesson 48 after completing Reading lesson 48. See Writing-Spelling Guide.)

ACTIVITY

(Present Activity 17 after completing Reading lesson 48. See Activities Across the Curriculum.)

Lesson 49

EXERCISE 1
VOCABULARY REVIEW

a. Here's the new vocabulary sentence: The lifeboat disappeared in the whirlpool.
- Everybody, say that sentence. Get ready. (Signal.) *The lifeboat disappeared in the whirlpool.*
- (Repeat until firm.)

b. What word names an emergency boat that's on large ships? (Signal.) *Lifeboat.*
- What word tells what happened to the lifeboat when you couldn't see it anymore? (Signal.) *Disappeared.*
- What word refers to water that goes around and around as it goes down? (Signal.) *Whirlpool.*

EXERCISE 2
READING WORDS

Column 1

a. **Find lesson 49 in your textbook.** ✔
- Touch column 1. ✔
- (Teacher reference:)

> 1. Italy   4. million
> 2. Turkey   5. earth
> 3. China

b. The first three names are countries. The countries are **Italy, Turkey,** and **China.**
- Touch word 1. What word? (Signal.) *Italy.*
- Spell **Italy.** Get ready. (Tap for each letter.) *I-T-A-L-Y.*

c. Touch word 2. What word? (Signal.) *Turkey.*
- Spell **Turkey.** Get ready. (Tap for each letter.) *T-U-R-K-E-Y.*

d. Touch word 3. What word? (Signal.) *China.*
- Spell **China.** Get ready. (Tap for each letter.) *C-H-I-N-A.*

e. Word 4 is **million.** What word? (Signal.) *Million.*
- Spell **million.** Get ready. (Tap for each letter.) *M-I-L-L-I-O-N.*

- A million is a very large number. It is one thousand thousand. If you had piles of money with a thousand dollars in each pile, you'd need a thousand piles to have a million dollars.

f. Word 5 is **earth.** What word? (Signal.) *Earth.*

g. Let's read those words again, the fast way.
- Word 1. What word? (Signal.) *Italy.*
- (Repeat for words 2–5.)

h. (Repeat step g until firm.)

Column 2

i. Find column 2. ✔
- All these words end with the letter **S.**
- (Teacher reference:)

> 1. butterflies   4. rabbits
> 2. changes   5. robins
> 3. fleas

j. Word 1. What word? (Signal.) *Butterflies.*
- (Repeat for words 2–5.)

k. Let's read those words again.
- Word 1. What word? (Signal.) *Butterflies.*
- (Repeat for words 2–5.)

l. (Repeat step k until firm.)

Column 3

m. Find column 3. ✔
- (Teacher reference:)

> 1. eager   4. exit
> 2. warm-blooded 5. lined
> 3. cold-blooded

n. Word 1. What word? (Signal.) *Eager.*
- How would you feel if you were eager to see a movie? (Call on a student. Idea: *Excited about seeing the movie.*)

o. Word 2. What word? (Signal.) *Warm-blooded.*
- (Repeat for words 3–5.)

p. Let's read those words again.
- Word 1. What word? (Signal.) *Eager.*
- (Repeat for words 2–5.)

q. (Repeat step p until firm.)

Column 4

r. Find column 4. ✔
- (Teacher reference:)

1. slowing	4. visiting
2. sweat	5. aisle
3. unless	

s. Word 1. What word? (Signal.) *Slowing.*
- (Repeat for words 2–5.)

t. Let's read those words again.
- Word 1. What word? (Signal.) *Slowing.*
- (Repeat for words 2–5.)

u. (Repeat step t until firm.)

Individual Turns

(For columns 1–4: Call on individual students, each to read one to three words per turn.)

EXERCISE 3
STORY READING

a. Find part B in your textbook. ✔
- The error limit for this story is 9. Read carefully.

b. Everybody, touch the title. ✔
- (Call on a student to read the title.) [*Herman Is Cold-Blooded.*]
- Everybody, what's the title? (Signal.) *Herman Is Cold-Blooded.*

c. (Call on individual students to read the story, each student reading two or three sentences at a time. Ask questions marked **1.**)

- (Correct errors: Tell the word. Direct the student to reread the sentence.)
- (If the group makes more than 9 errors, direct the students to reread the story.)

d. (After the group has read the selection making no more than 9 errors, read the story to the students and ask questions marked **2.**)

Herman Is Cold-Blooded

Herman hated cold things. You can understand why flies don't like cold things or cool weather if you understand how flies are different from humans or dogs.

1. What are we going to find out about flies? (Call on a student. Ideas: *How they are different from humans or dogs; why flies don't like cold things or cool weather.*)

All insects are cold-blooded. Flies are insects. So flies are cold-blooded.

2. I'll say that one more time. Then you'll say all three sentences. Listen: All insects are cold-blooded. Flies are insects. So flies are cold-blooded. Your turn to say those three sentences. Get ready. (Signal.) *All insects are cold-blooded. Flies are insects. So flies are cold-blooded.*

Here are some other animals that are cold-blooded: ants, fleas, spiders, frogs, and butterflies.

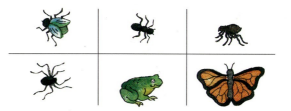

1. You can see them in the picture.
2. Name another cold-blooded animal. (Call on a student. Ideas: *Bees, worms, mosquitoes, snakes, turtles,* etc.)

Cold-blooded animals are different from warm-blooded animals.

2. Everybody, what are the two different types of animals? (Signal.) *Cold-blooded and warm-blooded.*
2. Which type is a fly? (Signal.) *Cold-blooded.*

Here are some animals that are warm-blooded: robins, dogs, rabbits, cows, humans, horses, and deer.

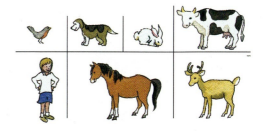

1. You can see them in the picture.

Lesson 49 261

2. Name some other warm-blooded animals. (Call on a student. Ideas: *Cats, squirrels, mice,* etc.)

> **If an animal is warm-blooded, the temperature inside that animal's body always stays the same.**

2. Everybody, does the temperature inside the body change? (Signal.) *No.*

> **If the outside temperature goes up, the inside temperature does not change. If the outside temperature goes down, the inside temperature does not change.**

2. Everybody, if it gets hotter outside, does the temperature inside a warm-blooded animal change? (Signal.) *No.*
2. If it cools off outside, what happens to the inside temperature of a warm-blooded animal? (Call on a student. Ideas: *Nothing; it stays the same.*)

> **If an animal is cold-blooded, the inside temperature of that animal changes when the outside temperature changes. If the outside temperature goes up, what happens to the inside temperature?**

1. Everybody, what's the answer? (Signal.) *It goes up.*

> **If the outside temperature goes down, what happens to the inside temperature?**

1. Everybody, what's the answer? (Signal.) *It goes down.*

> **Humans are warm-blooded. Your body temperature is always around 98 degrees. When the air outside is 15 degrees below zero, your fingers may get cold. Your feet may feel very cold. But the inside of your body is 98 degrees. When the temperature outside is 90 degrees, you may feel very warm and sticky. You may sweat. But the inside of your body is still 98 degrees.**

2. Everybody, are you **warm-blooded** or **cold-blooded**? (Signal.) *Warm-blooded.*

2. So does your inside temperature change? (Signal.) *No.*
2. What is your inside temperature when it's 90 degrees outside? (Signal.) *98 degrees.*
2. What is your inside temperature when it's 53 degrees outside? (Signal.) *98 degrees.*

> **Flies are different. Their inside temperature changes as the temperature outside their body changes. When the air is 90 degrees outside, the inside of the fly is 90 degrees. When the air is 45 degrees outside, you know the temperature inside the fly.**

1. Everybody, what temperature is inside the fly? (Signal.) *45 degrees.*
1. Does the inside of a fly stay the same temperature all the time? (Signal.) *No.*
1. If the temperature outside is 53 degrees, what's the temperature inside the fly? (Signal.) *53 degrees.*

> **Because flies work this way, they have a problem: Their body slows down when it gets cold.**

2. Everybody, on a cold day, what happens to their body? (Signal.) *It slows down.*
2. Does the inside of your body slow down on a cold day? (Signal.) *No.*

> **Try catching a fly on a warm day. It is hard to do because the fly is fast. The fly is fast because everything inside the fly's body is hot and is working fast.**

2. Why is the fly fast? (Call on a student. Idea: *Because everything inside the fly's body is hot and is working fast.*)

> **Try catching a fly when the weather is very cool.**

1. Everybody, will it be **easier** or **harder**? (Signal.) *Easier.*
1. Why? (Call on a student. Idea: *Because the fly will be slow.*)

> The fly is slow and easy to catch. The fly is slow because everything inside the fly's body is cool and is working very slowly. Remember: A fly's body slows down when it gets cold.

2. Everybody, listen to the rule again: A fly's body slows down when it gets cold. What's the rule? (Signal.) *A fly's body slows down when it gets cold.*
• Remember the rule.

> Herman didn't know this rule. He did know that he didn't like cool places and he didn't like dark places unless they were warm. He was in Japan. He wanted to leave the jet because it was getting too cool for him. The air temperature was down to 45 degrees.

1. Everybody, what's the temperature inside Herman's body now? (Signal.) *45 degrees.*
1. So is the inside of his body working **fast** or **slow**? (Signal.) *Slow.*

> He was slowing down. And his eyes could see that something was coming toward him.
> **MORE TO COME**

1. Go back to the beginning of the story. Follow along while I read.
2. What do you think that might be? (Call on a student. Ideas: *Flight attendants; people to service the plane;* etc.)

EXERCISE 4

PAIRED PRACTICE

You're going to read aloud to your partner. Today the **B** members will read first. Then the **A** members will read from the star to the end of the story.
(Observe students and give feedback.)

End-of-Lesson Activities

INDEPENDENT WORK

Now finish your independent work for lesson 49. Raise your hand when you're finished. (Observe students and give feedback.)

WORKCHECK

a. (Direct students to take out their marking pencils.)
• We're going to check your independent work. Remember, if you got an item wrong, make an **X** next to the item.
b. (For each item: Read the item. Call on a student to answer it. If the answer is wrong, say the correct answer. Refer to the Answer Key for the correct answers.)
c. Now use your pencil to fix up any items you got wrong. Remember, all mistakes must be fixed up before you hand in your work.

WRITING-SPELLING

(Present Writing-Spelling lesson 49 after completing Reading lesson 49. See Writing-Spelling Guide.)

> *Note:* Before presenting lesson 50, you will need to:
> • Reproduce blackline masters for the Fact Game;
> • Preview Literature lesson 6, secure materials, and reproduce blackline masters. (See the Literature Guide.)

OPTIONAL ACTIVITY

(Sing the song "I Know an Old Woman Who Swallowed a Fly" with the students.)

Lesson 50

Test 5

Materials for Lesson 50

Fact Game

For each team (4 or 5 students):
- pair of number cubes (or dice)
- copy of Fact Game 50

For each student:
- their copy of the scorecard sheet

For each monitor:
- a pencil
- Fact Game 50 answer key (at end of textbook A)

Reading Checkout

Each student will need their thermometer chart.

Literature Lesson 5

See Literature Guide for the materials you will need.

EXERCISE 1
FACT GAME

a. You're going to play the game that uses the facts you have learned. Remember the rules. The player rolls the number cubes, figures out the number of the question, reads that question out loud, and answers it. The monitor tells the player if the answer is right or wrong. If it's wrong, the monitor tells the right answer. If it's right, the monitor gives the player one point. Don't argue with the monitor. The number cubes go to the left and the next player has a turn. You'll play the game for 10 minutes.

b. (Divide students into groups of four or five. Assign monitors. Circulate as students play the game. Comment on groups that are playing well.)

c. (At the end of 10 minutes, have all students who earned more than 10 points stand up.)
- (Tell the monitor of each game that ran smoothly:) Your group did a good job.

EXERCISE 2
READING CHECKOUTS

a. Today is a test day and a reading-checkout day. While you're writing answers, I'm going to call on you one at a time to read part of the story we read in lesson 49. When I call on you to come and do your checkout, bring your thermometer chart.
- Remember, you pass the checkout by reading the passage in less than a minute without making more than 2 mistakes. And when you pass the checkout, you color the space for lesson 50 on your thermometer chart.

b. (Call on individual students to read the portion of story 49 marked with ❋.)
- (Time the student. Note words that are missed and number of words read.)
- (Teacher reference:)

❋ Because flies work this way, they have a problem: Their body slows down when it gets cold. Try catching a fly on a warm day. It is hard to do because the fly is fast. The fly is fast because everything inside the fly's body is hot and is working [50] fast.

Try catching a fly when the weather is very cool. The fly is slow and easy to catch. The fly is slow because everything [75] inside the fly's body is cool and is working very slowly. Remember: A fly's body slows down when it gets cold.

Herman didn't know this ❋ [100] rule.

- (If the student reads the passage in one minute or less and makes no more than 2 errors, direct the student to color in the space for lesson 50 on the thermometer chart.)

- (If the student makes any mistakes, point to each word that was misread and identify it.)
- (If the student does not meet the rate-error criterion for the passage, direct the student to practice reading the story with the assigned partner.)

EXERCISE 3

TEST

a. **Find page 331 in your textbook.** ✔
- **The rest of this lesson is a test. You'll work items you've done before.**
b. **Work carefully. Raise your hand when you've completed all the items.**
(Observe students but do not give feedback on errors.)

EXERCISE 4

MARKING THE TEST

a. (Check students' work before beginning lesson 51. Refer to the Answer Key for the correct answers.)
b. (Record all test 5 results on the Test Summary Sheet and the Group Summary Sheet. Reproducible Summary Sheets are at the back of the Teacher's Guide.)

EXERCISE 5

TEST REMEDIES

- (Provide any necessary remedies for test 5 before presenting lesson 51. Test remedies are discussed in the Teacher's Guide.)

Test 5 Firming Table

Test Item	Introduced in lesson	Test Item	Introduced in lesson	Test Item	Introduced in lesson
1	41	12	46	23	48
2	41	13	46	24	48
3	41	14	49	25	48
4	42	15	49	26	46
5	42	16	49	27	41
6	42	17	49	28	45
7	44	18	49	29	37
8	44	19	41	30	37
9	44	20	44	31	45
10	46	21	44	32	41
11	46	22	44	33	41

LITERATURE

(Present Literature lesson 5 after completing Reading lesson 50. See Literature Guide.)

Lesson 50 265